Sonderpublikation der GTZ, No. 238

Rural Development Series
Agricultural Extension
Volume 2

Deutsche Bibliothek Cataloguing-in-Publication Data

Rural development series / Dt. Ges. für Techn. Zusammenarbeit (GTZ) GmbH, Technical Cooperation – Federal Republic of Germany. [Publ. by Bundesministerium für Wirtschaftl. Zusammenarbeit ...]. – Rossdorf: TZ-Verl.-Ges.

Dt. Ausg. u.d.T.: Handbuchreihe ländliche Entwicklung. – Franz. Ausg. u.d.T.: Manuels développement rural. – Teilw. publ. by Bundesministerium für Wirtschaftliche Zusammenarbeit

NE: Deutsche Gesellschaft für Technische Zusammenarbeit <Eschborn>; Deutschland <Bundesrepublik> / Bundesminister für Wirtschaftliche Zusammenarbeit

Agricultural extension.
Vol.2 Examples and background material. – 1990

Agricultural extension / Dt. Ges. für Techn. Zusammenarbeit (GTZ) GmbH. [Publ.: Bundesministerium für Wirtschaftl. Zusammenarbeit (BMZ) ... Comp. and prepared by: Volker Hoffmann; Waltraud Hoffmann. Transl.: Peter C. Brown]. – Rossdorf: TZ-Verl.-Ges.

(Rural development series)
Dt. Ausg. u.d.T.: Landwirtschaftliche Beratung. – Franz. Ausg. u.d.T.: Vulgarisation agricole

NE: Hoffmann, Volker [Hrsg.]

Vol. 2. Examples and background material / Hartmut Albrecht ... – 1990
(Sonderpublikation der GTZ; No. 238)
ISBN 3-88085-405-X (GTZ)

NE: Albrecht, Hartmut [Mitverf.]; Deutsche Gesellschaft für Technische Zusammenarbeit <Eschborn>: Sonderpublikation der GTZ

Rural Development Series

Agricultural Extension

Volume 2
Examples and
Background Material

Hartmut Albrecht, Herbert Bergmann, Georg Diederich,
Eberhard Großer, Volker Hoffmann, Peter Keller,
Gerhard Payr, Rolf Sülzer

Deutsche Gesellschaft für
Technische Zusammenarbeit
(GTZ) GmbH

Technical Cooperation –
Federal Republic of Germany

Eschborn 1990

This English translation is based on the second fully revised German edition (1987)

Publishers: Bundesministerium für wirtschaftliche Zuammenarbeit (BMZ),
D-5300 Bonn

Deutsche Gesellschaft für Technische Zusammenarbeit (GTZ)
GmbH, D-6236 Eschborn

Technical Centre for Agricultural and Rural Cooperation (CTA),
NL-6700 AJ Wageningen

Compiled and
prepared by: Volker Hoffmann, Waltraud Hoffmann

Translation: Peter C. Brown; Check-reading: Terence Oliver, Volker Hoffmann

Cover layout: Manfred Sehring

Graphics: Volker Hoffmann

Printed and
distributed by: TZ-Verlagsgesellschaft mbH, Postfach 1164, D-6101 Rossdorf,
Federal Republic of Germany

ISBN: 3-88085-405-X
ISSN 0930-1070

I/0390/2,5
All rights reserved.

Contents

Volume 1: Basic Concepts and Methods

		Page
I	Importance and role of agricultural extension in developing countries	21
II	Approaches to extension	41
III	Basic concepts for extension	55
IV	Experience of extension projects	101
V	Extension methods	107
VI	Situation analysis	157
VII	Planning extension work	177
VIII	Organisation and management in extension	201
IX	Basic and advanced training of advisers	223
X	Evaluation of agricultural extension	233

Volume 2: Examples and Background Material

A	Case studies of approaches to extension	15
B	Selected project descriptions	75
C	Description of recurring problems	131
D	Cases and examples of method	195
E	Practical guidelines	265
F	Checklists	341
G	Presentation and structure: examples and suggestions	383

Table of contents: Volume 2
Examples and Background Material

	Page
Summary and table of contents	5

A Case studies of approaches to extension

- A 1 Production technology approach: "Operation Riz" in Madagascar ... 15
- A 2 Improvement of farming systems: The "Ladder of Progress" Approach in Salima, Lakeside Region, Malawi ... 19
- A 3 Socio-economic development approach: "Community Development" in India ... 25
- A 4 Socio-economic development approach: "Animation Rurale" in Francophone Africa ... 31
- A 5 Action research and education: "Comilla Approach" in Bangladesh ... 37
- A 6 Promoting basic training: "Farmer Training Centres" in Kenya and Senegal ... 43
- A 7 Decentralised, and participatory development work: "DESEC" in Bolivia ... 47
- A 8 The "CFSME' Extension System ... 51
- A 9 The "Training and Visit System" of the World Bank ... 61
- A 10 Research and development: improving agricultural land-use systems by means of "Farming Systems Research" ... 67

B Selected project descriptions

- B 1 Agricultural extension in the Central Region of Togo – strategy, content, methods, means ... 75
- B 2 Extension and credit in farm systems in the project: Kericho District, Kenya ... 85
- B 3 Extension services with the aim of improving the food situation in the project: Paktia Province in Afghanistan ... 87
- B 4 Self-help groups and associations among the TIV in Nigeria ... 89
- B 5 The reorganisation of agricultural extension in the Atlantic Province of the People's Republic of Benin ... 91
- B 6 Minka – the evolution of a peasants' newspaper in Peru ... 109

C Description of recurring problems

- C 1 "The cow": an example of failure in intercultural communication ... 131
- C 2 Traditional level of knowledge in target groups and communicating new agricultural information ... 139
- C 3 Effectiveness and design of pictorial representation ... 143
- C 4 Illusions of communication between projects and their target groups: a cautionary example in Nigeria ... 161
- C 5 Experience of technical demonstrations in agricultural development projects ... 177

			Page
C	6	Problems of working with contact farmers	181
C	7	Problems of leadership style in organisations	185
C	8	"Extension", an international terminology problem	191

D Cases and examples of method

D	1	Problem-solving method of RIP in Botswana	195
D	2	Problem-solving approach in the "Tetu Extension Project" in Kenya	197
D	3	Deciding on extension methods in the "Kawinga RDP" in Malawi	199
D	4	Committees as intermediaries between target groups and development organisations in Malawi	205
D	5	The role of stimulation in the CFSME extension system in Kibuye, Rwanda	209
D	6	Awareness creation and training in the CFSME extension system in Kibuye, Rwanda	221
D	7	"Majeutics" – GRAAP's pedagogic approach to self-development	241
D	8	A table of contents of an extension programme: the "Goat Project" in Ngozi, Burundi	251
D	9	"Extension Centre Day": festivities and agricultural exhibition by CARDER Atlantique, Benin	255

E Practical Guidelines

E	1	Identifying target groups and differentiating sub-groups	265
E	2	Participation of target groups	269
E	3	Deciding on target groups and development measures	273
E	4	How to select contact farmers	275
E	5	The methodology of extension talks	281
E	6	Laying out and using plots to demonstrate crop rotations	291
E	7	Demonstrating the use of portable sprays for pest control	295
E	8	Programming field days	299
E	9	Example of extension work at markets	303
E	10	Preparing and running local agricultural exhibitions	305
E	11	Establishing a school garden	309
E	12	Evaluating training events	311
E	13	Pre-testing pictorial material	319
E	14	Circulars for advisers	323
E	15	How to prepare and deliver a speech in the context of mass extension	325
E	16	Structuring group sessions to identify problems	327
E	17	Using visualisation to improve group communication	329
E	18	Suggestions for setting up participatory external evaluation missions	335
E	19	The use of vehicles in extension organisations	339

F Checklists
F	1	Checklist of constraints on participation of target groups	341
F	2	Checklist of weaknesses in extension work	343
F	3	Checklist of features of successful development work and extension	345
F	4	Checklist for information gathering in the situation analysis	349
F	5	Checklist of assumptions about the extent and speed of the diffusion of innovations	355
F	6	Checklist for evaluating innovations	357
F	7	Checklist for selecting contact farmers	359
F	8	Points for the field adviser to bear in mind when forming village committees	363
F	9	Points to bear in mind when preparing and conducting individual extension talks	367
F	10	The advisory process: questions for guidance	371
F	11	Checklist for preparing and running a meeting during a campaign	373
F	12	Checklist for using media	377

G Presentation and structure: examples and suggestions
G	1	Data plan for the situation analysis – sub-section extension	383
G	2	Suggested structure of feasibility studies for extension	385
G	3	Excerpt from a card index of terms	387
G	4	Example of a routine report form for a target group organisation	389
G	5	Example of a circular on the introduction of improved weeding	391
G	6	Example of calculating the time needed for demonstrating a portable spray	395
G	7	Example of the personnel requirements of a regional agricultural administration in Malawi	397
G	8	Three examples of structuring work programmes for field advisers	399
G	9	Instructional material for creating awareness and for training in the central region of Togo	403
G	10	Instructional material for creating awareness and for training from the agricultural extension project Nyabisindu, Rwanda	415
G	11	Instructional material for creating awareness and for training from GRAAP, Burkina Faso	433

Table of contents: Volume 1
Basic Concepts and Methods

	Page
Preface	5
List of diagrams	17
List of tables	17
Introduction	19

I. Importance and role of agricultural extension in developing countries ... 21
   1. Assistance for small farmers: background and basic approaches ... 22
      1.1 Typical features of the situation of small farmers ... 22
      1.2 Rural poverty and its main causes ... 24
      1.3 Basic approach to aid for small farmers ... 29
   2. Functions, aims and tasks of agricultural extension ... 33
      2.1 General characteristics of extension ... 33
      2.2 Special characteristics of agricultural extension work ... 36

II. Approaches to extension ... 41
   1. The production technology approach ... 41
   2. The problem-solving approach and its consequences ... 42
      2.1 Target-group orientation ... 46
      2.2 Participation ... 49
      2.3 Phased project planning and implementation ... 52

III. Basic concepts for extension ... 55
   1. Explanation of the selection and use of concepts ... 55
   2. Framework model of extension ... 57
   3. Four examples from extension practice ... 59
   4. Behaviour and behaviour modification ... 62
   5. Perception ... 66
   6. Defence mechanisms ... 68
   7. Problem solving and decision making ... 69
   8. Groups and group processes ... 73
   9. Social structure and the institutions of society ... 76
   10. Culture ... 76
   11. Communication ... 78
   12. Structuring of learning processes ... 84
   13. Organisation and management ... 86
   14. The diffusion of innovations ... 90
      14.1 The innovator as disruptive element ... 93
      14.2 The critical phase ... 93

		Page
	14.3 Transition to the self-sustaining process	94
	14.4 Final phase of the wave	95
	14.5 The situation-specific approach	95
	14.6 Conclusions for the methodology of extension work	98

IV. Experience of extension projects ... 101
1. The role of extension in different development approaches ... 101
2. The situation of target groups ... 103
3. The situation of the advisers ... 103
4. Conditions for successful extension ... 105

V. Extension methods ... 107
1. Individual extension ... 107
   - 1.1 Individual extension on the farm ... 108
   - 1.2 Individual extension in the office or home of the field adviser ... 109
2. Group extension ... 110
   - 2.1 Group discussion ... 112
   - 2.2 Demonstrations ... 114
   - 2.3 Field days ... 118
   - 2.4 Extension work in training centres ... 121
3. Mass extension ... 123
   - 3.1 Campaigns ... 124
   - 3.2 Agricultural shows ... 127
4. Extension in rural schools ... 130
5. Use of extension aids ... 134
   - 5.1 Types of extension aids ... 135
     - 5.1.1 The spoken and written word ... 137
     - 5.1.2 Pictorial illustration ... 139
     - 5.1.3 Slides and films ... 142
     - 5.1.4 Video recordings ... 143
     - 5.1.5 Television ... 144
     - 5.1.6 Three dimensional presentation ... 145
     - 5.1.7 Methods of live presentation ... 145
   - 5.2 The potential of media ... 146
   - 5.3 Conditions for the use of extension aids ... 151

VI. Situation analysis ... 157
1. Situation analysis as an instrument of planning ... 158
   - 1.1 Use of the situation analysis ... 159
   - 1.2 Planning the investigation ... 161
   - 1.3 Importance of the analysis of the social system ... 164
2. Methods of collecting information ... 165
   - 2.1 Acquisition and evaluation of existing data ... 166

			Page
	2.2	Surveys in the project country	168
		2.2.1 Observation and description	169
		2.2.2 Methods of enquiry	170
		2.2.3 Direct measurement	174
		2.2.4 Trials	175

VII. Planning extension work ... 177
1. Defining the extension concept ... 177
2. Deciding on the composition of extension ... 182
   - 2.1 Participation by target groups ... 182
   - 2.2 Participation by field advisers ... 184
   - 2.3 Role of higher levels of management ... 184
3. Links with complementary services ... 184
   - 3.1 Research ... 185
   - 3.2 Infrastructure ... 187
   - 3.3 Provision of production means ... 187
   - 3.4 Credit ... 188
   - 3.5 Marketing ... 190
4. Division of territory and density of advisers ... 191
5. Resource base of extension services ... 193
   - 5.1 Living quarters and offices ... 193
   - 5.2 Transport ... 194
   - 5.3 Extension aids ... 195
   - 5.4 Budgeting ... 198
6. Programming extension work ... 199

VIII. Organisation and management in extension ... 201
1. Fundamentals of organisation and management ... 201
2. Types of organisation in extension ... 203
   - 2.1 State extension services ... 205
   - 2.2 Commercial extension services ... 206
   - 2.3 Extension services run by projects ... 208
   - 2.4 Self-help organisations ... 208
3. Personnel in extension work ... 209
   - 3.1 Functions of extension personnel ... 210
   - 3.2 Technical qualifications ... 214
   - 3.3 Personal aptitude ... 216
   - 3.4 Living and working conditions ... 218
   - 3.5 Appraisal of advisers ... 219
4. Proposals for improving reports ... 221

IX. Basic and advanced training of advisers ... 223
1. Training and advanced training of senior advisers ... 223
2. Basic and advanced training of field advisers ... 228

			Page
	3.	Selection and use of teaching staff for the basic and advanced training of advisers	230
	4.	Use of teaching aids	231

X. Evaluation of agricultural extension ... 233
    1. Criteria and indicators for evaluating extension ... 235
    2. Methods of evaluation ... 237
        2.1 Monitoring evaluation ... 240
        2.2 Ex-post evaluation ... 243
    3. Evaluation procedure ... 243
        3.1 Selecting assessors ... 244
        3.2 Presentation of results ... 245
    4. Cost of the evaluation ... 248

Bibliography ... 251
Keyword index ... 267

Case studies of approaches to extension

Production technology approach: "Opération Riz" in Madagascar

"Opération Riz", a rice cropping programme, was started in Madagascar in 1966. The agricultural potential of the highlands of Madagascar meant that it was possible to **raise rice production** above current levels, but it would require the introduction of **new production techniques** like plant raising, row cultivation, weeding and irrigation.

Since it was beyond the powers of the state extension service, the supervision of 158 000 farms with 111 100 ha cropped with rice (an average of 0.71 ha/farm) was transferred to an **autonomous body** – the "Groupement Opération Productivité Rizicole" (GOPR). The management personnel were supplied by three European firms (1966 = 34 people). At province level the staff consisted of a director and specialists with responsibility for cultivation, irrigation, the provision of the means of production, credit and training advisers. At district level the staff consisted of an agronomist and experts in extension, credit and production inputs. Finally, at the community level there was a "head of sector", who was responsible for supplies, working together with 5 – 7 advisers (encadreurs). Each adviser supervised a "cell" (a pre-cooperative) of approximately 250 farms. There was a staff of 601 when the campaign began in 1966, and by 1969/70 as many as 1 027 people were employed.

GOPR was financed via the government of Madagascar by the European Community.

The running and control of the project were in the hands of the French SATEC (Société d'Aide Technique et de Coopération) which is roughly equivalent to GTZ.

GOPR laid down **explicit outline conditions**:

(1) independence of financial regulations of the administration

(2) commercial transactions at its own discretion

(3) autonomy in staffing matters

When the mass campaigns were carried out, they were specifically restricted to a limited package of innovations.

The functions of the management were carefully organised to integrate the advisers fully into the work of the project. The main objectives were that:

A 1

- the farmers should be shown the direction to follow, but **not compelled** – they had to be convinced of the advantages of an innovation;
- every project worker should be **personally responsible** for his area of operations;
- every field adviser has **operational targets** for the year and should be involved in drawing them up;
- the work of the field advisers should be closely **supervised**;
- the field advisers should be given **continuing further training**.

To put these objectives into practice in extension work, a plan of operations was worked out with alternating training and practical work:

(1) The field advisers were given a **short induction course**.

(2) Every fortnight the field advisers were brought together by the "chef de secteur" for a **two-day training course**.

(3) "Chefs de secteur" were themselves given training at somewhat longer intervals by the "chefs de zone".

(4) During this in-service training the field advisers learned how to set themselves operational targets, e. g. working out the number of farmers to be supervised, the number of improved seed beds needed and precise **work schedules**.

(5) After these **schedules** had been discussed with their superiors, they became mandatory for field advisers.

(6) The work of field advisers and the "chefs de secteur" was **checked regularly**, because senior staff were able to establish with the help of the work schedules **where** an adviser was supposed to be working **and what** he was supposed to be doing.

The clear advantage of this type of organisation was that field advisers were set realistic objectives. There are many obvious parallels with the "Training and Visit System" (→ A 9).

GOPR's endeavour to find solutions was based on a management philosophy that believed efficiency would be increased by **clearly defining targets**, by **continuous supervision and involving project workers** in the allocation of duties.

From the viewpoint of extension, the work of GOPR's advisers at village level is given coherence by the following factors:

- GOPR began its extension work by building up "cells" or cooperatives and concentrating on a limited range of crops. The cooperatives were then used to introduce innovations, to distribute production inputs to the members and to allocate credit (checking creditworthiness is thereby made easier).

- The network of extension services was grouped round the local adviser who was responsible for any measures that had to be taken – from working in the fields to recruiting cooperatives after the harvest.

- In his work the local adviser concentrated on the members of the cooperatives.

- The objectives were clearly defined: increasing production, extending the land under cultivation and raising the yield per unit of area.

- The local advisers were well paid and were provided with adequate technical know-how and materials.

- SATEC produced brochures, detailed visual materials, etc., specifically for field advisers, giving for example practical instructions and illustrations: "How do you demonstrate sowing along a line?"

- Each adviser was responsible for several villages (up to 20) and was therefore less likely to be drawn into conflict situations in any one village.

- They focussed their activities on individual farmers and they did not therefore interfere in existing power structures.

The **extension method** itself was devised by a psychologist (C. MAGUEREZ) and was successfully tested by SATEC. It was based on detailed material for training advisers (manuel de moniteur) and instruction sheets for the advisers themselves (fiche de vulgarisation) that contained all the necessary information for different stages of the cropping calendar.

The rapid success of the project is summarised in → Table 1. But in the early 1970s the price of rice fell and the package was no longer attractive. Moreover, yields declined as a result of poor weather conditions. Despite the fact that women play an important role in society in Madagascar, the extension programme did not specifically address them until 1970. They take charge of money and are responsible for food production in rainfed farming and husbandry in irrigated rice cultivation. But as long as the project's financial attraction was guaranteed, they did nevertheless become involved in the programme, particularly as it incidentally

A 1

Table 1:

Performance of GOPR 1966 – 1971			
	1966 – 67	1968 – 69	1970 – 71
Farms reached	28 000	130 000	169 000
Improved cropping land in ha	4 500	45 000	86 000[1]
Average land per farm in ha	0.16	0.35	0.50
Increased yields in t	7 000[2]	83 000	121 000[3]
Average yields in t/ha	1.55	1.85	1.41
1) approx. 9.1 % of the total land cropped with rice 2) approx. 0.4 % of total production 3) approx. 6.5 % of total production			

relieved their burden: for example, by involving men in transporting mineral fertiliser to the fields and working with rotary hoes.

"Opération Riz" can be regarded as a typical example of an extension-oriented aid initiative that concentrated on production technology.

Bibliography:

E. M. KULP: Designing and managing basic agricultural programs. Bloomington, Indiana University, Intern. Development Institute, 1977, pp. 40 – 42.

J. O. MÜLLER: Die Förderung der Reisproduktion in Madagaskar. In: Intern. Africa-Forum, Munich, 4, 1968, pp. 620 – 627.

R. OLDENBURG: Das Konzept der Massenberatung bei der Steigerung der Reisproduktion im Hochland von Madagaskar. Unpublished thesis, Göttingen, 1977.

H. RUTHENBERG: Landwirtschaftliche Entwicklungspolitik. Frankfurt: DLG-Verlag, 1972, especially pp. 125 – 136.

Compiled by:

Rolf SÜLZER, Gerhard PAYR

A 2

Improvement of farming systems: The "Ladder of Progress" Approach in Salima, Lakeside Region, Malawi

Since 1966 an integrated project combining agricultural extension and training, credit, marketing, infrastructure, land development, experimentation and village centres to train craftsmen has been carried out in the region bordering Lake Malawi (approximately 3 600 km^2, with about 32 000 farms and an average of 5 persons per farm). While the project was being established, it concentrated exclusively on promoting cotton cropping and began to build up information on crop rotation systems.

Because of the limited success of these measures, a new approach was introduced that encompassed extension work in food cropping, animal production and rice cultivation. **Six categories of farm** (→ Figure 1) were created using a combination of area, crops, degree of market integration and the existence of farm planning, so that extension could be programmed and appropriate packages of innovations devised.

The extension approach was based on a step-by-step mobilisation effect, called the **"ladder of progress"**. Farmers were to be advised in such a way that they would develop, with the help of the project's package of innovations, from subsistence farming to being fully integrated in the market. The organisational core of the project was therefore extension. Tightly organised extension work would create the mobilisation effect, and the concept of selective aid and extension was formulated in the hope that innovations would spread autonomously:

- The adviser density was too low to provide the approximately 30 000 families with individual extension. Moreover, the poor level of training of the advisers restricted the use of group and mass extension work.

- The population was first divided into six categories according to willingness to adopt the innovations offered. The lowest was category I, comprising the subsistence farms, while the most progressive farms with farm planning, rotations and integrated livestock keeping were in category VI. The higher the category, the greater the number and complexity of innovations on offer, and the intensity of extension was correspondingly increased. While categories V und VI were given intensive individual extension, the other groups were supposed to be reached principally by group and mass extension (→ Figure 1).

A 2

Figure 1:

Farm categories and the Development Measures available						
Category	I	II	III	IV	V	VI
Type of farm	Subsistence and part-time farmers	Cash-crop farmer at low level	Improved cash-crop farmer	Progressive cash-crop farmer	Farmer with farm planning	Farmer with farm planning and cattle keeping
Farm system	Local maize, groundnuts, rice, some cotton with – out pest control	Local maize + Mani Pintar or local maize + cotton or improved rice cropping.	Fertilised maize + cotton, or fertilised rice	Fertilised maize + cotton + Mani Pintar or fertilised rice + water control in groups	Rotation of maize + cotton + groundnuts	As category V + pasturing
Extension	Group and mass extension (field days, demonstrations, meetings, film shows, campaigns, etc.)	Individual advice on tilling, recognition and control of pests, otherwise group extension	As category II + advice on fertilising + advice on storage	As category III + preparation for farm planning in farm institute	Continuing individual advice on management questions, special seminars	As category V + special advice on animal keeping
Credit	No right to credit	Insecticides, back sprays, Mani Pintar seed	As category II + maize seed and fertiliser for 1 acre	As category III but for 1.5 acres of maize on request	All production inputs according to area, after 2 successful years also draught oxen and equipment	As category V + livestock breeding

- After one year all farmers who showed improvement were given the opportunity of going up into the next category, which would automatically give them the right to more aid (ladder of progress). The aim of the development endeavours was to get the majority of farmers into category VI.

- This development concept aimed deliberately to create inequalities. It was hoped that the more backward farmers would be stimulated to greater efforts by the example of the more progressive farmers. Thus envy was to be converted into the desire for progress. Equality of opportunity was therefore guaranteed, since all farmers had, as a matter of principle, the chance to rise to a higher category.

This unbalanced spread of extension work led automatically to concentration on the small group of farmers in the highest category. Farm planning was carried out in only about 260 holdings, but in the lowest category there were some 16 000 subsistence farms. However, the anticipated demonstration effect of the small number of very advanced farms did not materialise because of:

A 2

- the high difference between the cash resources of the farms;
- the fact that almost a third of the farms in the lowest category were run by women;
- incomes derived from the non-agricultural sector (migrant labour, fishing, basket weaving, etc.);
- being completely integrated in the traditional social structure.

Contrary to expectation, there was no transfer from one category to another in the first three years of the project. The proportion of farmers in category II only rose from 2.5% to 18.5% and the combined share of categories III, IV and VI amounted to only 2.2%. An analysis of the reasons why selective development measures had failed revealed that the intensity of extension was extremely unbalanced:

Table 1:

Intensity of extension in each category of farm		
Category	Number of farmers	Hours of extension per farmer per year (1973)
I	22 082	0.48
II	5 858	1.39
III/IV	2 158	2.26
V/VI	182	28.30

- The six categories were shown to be a **purely arbitrary division** of the target population. The socio-economic analysis showed the existence of only three homogeneous target groups: subsistence and part-time farmers, cash-crop farmers with hoe cultivation and a small number of larger-scale farmers with draught oxen and livestock husbandry.

- There was a tendency for the advisers to **counsel the most progressive farmers more intensively**, because they were the first to adopt innovations or request advice spontaneously.

- Most progressive farmers live and work without reference to other people, and in practice therefore they can **only be reached by individual extension**. Advising privileged farmers on an individual basis can be to the personal advantage of the adviser (status, connections, presents).

- These farmers could **not** possibly be effective **as a model** for the poorer farmers because the factor provision of traditional hoe farmers prevented

A 2

them adopting innovations in the same way. Moreover, sanctions imposed by neighbours curtailed the efforts of particularly ambitious hoe farmers (demands made by relatives, arson, the threat of witchcraft, etc.).

- It proved impossible to explain the neatly devised but complicated system of categories to both farmers and advisers and therefore to convince them of its usefulness. **Recording and keeping** a check on which farmers belonged to particular **categories** also created high administrative costs.

- The **inadequate training** of advisers was a basic reason why group and mass extension methods were not used often enough.

- Another reason was the **poor programming** of extension work. The measures and the target groups were indeed defined in great detail, but the method of implementation was left largely to the advisers themselves.

Success was not forthcoming until, as a result of continuous evaluation, the aid and extension measures were directed at the three target groups that actually existed, the ladder of progress was reduced to two steps, group and mass extension were given priority, the target groups were involved much more in the planning and implementation of measures by creating village committees, and the focus of development aid was shifted from progressive farmers to the mass of hoe cultivation holdings.

In the second phase of the project, concentration on individual extension was abandoned in favour of **participatory group extension work**. This method involved the creation of about 500 **village committees** (→ D 4) onto which up to 14 people were voted by the villagers (heads of extended families, representatives of the women's league, business people). These village committees acted as a platform for extension, but were also intended to be a channel of communication for the population in turn to voice its aims (flow of information upwards and downwards). The village committee met once a month. Proposals and criticisms were then passed on to the project's committees by the advisers – for example at weekly meetings of advisers to programme work for the week ahead or at monthly meetings at project or regional level.

Consistent application of this two-way flow of information was accompanied by frequent contact between advisers and farmer (2 400 single visits per adviser annually plus demonstrations).

The adaptation of the ladder of progress to the level of ability of the subgroups and the provision of specific innovations relevant to subsistence and cash crops improved the efficiency of the advisers and the response of the population as well.

By 1977, when the project was handed over, more than 80 % of the farms had been brought into the development programme.

Bibliography:

W. KOCK: Beratung in Regionalprojekten – Erfahrungen aus dem Regionalprojekt Salima in Malawi. In: Zeitschrift f. Ausl. Landw., 10, Heft 2, 1971.

G. PAYR: Förderung und Beratung tradioneller Kleinbauern in Salima/Malawi. Munich: Weltforum Verl. 1977.

M. RÜCKER: Vergleich des Beratungsansatzes in ausgewählten ostafrikanischen Entwicklungsprojekten. Unpublishes thesis, Hohenheim 1976.

Complied by:

Gerhard PAYR, Rolf SÜLZER

Socio-economic development approach: "Community Development" in India

The hypothesis underlying the integrated Community Development approach is that the development of society as whole benefits from the development of its many small constituent parts and that the economic and social conditions in a nation can only be improved by the concerted efforts of individuals and all public institutions (including communities).

The basic assumptions are that:

- the **activities** must be **voluntary** – they must give expression to the will and needs of the communtiy;

- the activities must be " **concerted campaigns**" embracing all sectors of society;

- the members of the community should be given the opportunity to **participate in** and eventually to administer **planning and implementation;**

- the local "leaders" and people of influence should be **trained** during the course of the programme.

Two successful projects related to the work of GHANDI and TAGORE led to the rapid development of CD in India and to the state becoming the official sponsor.

The "Firka Development Scheme" (FDS) was established in Madras in 1946. A "Firka" is a unit of area for taxation purposes (about half the size of the present-day "Blocks", with approximately 150 000 inhabitants). The 34 FDSs practised the principles of GHANDI: they operated on the basis of cooperation and self-sufficiency, in other words independently of external relations. At village level Gram Savaks or Gram Savikas (male or female servants of the village) were responsible for the programme. They gave priority to measures to promote cropping and self-administration, receiving the necessary support from the Firka Development Officer who had a staff of specialists at his disposal. Thus evolved the basic formula but also the inherent dilemma of CD: a multipurpose village level worker, relying on back-up by specialists, was intended to coordinate a rural development programme.

The American town planner, Albert MAYER, developed and organised the parallel pilot project "Etawah" District (Uttar Pradesh). When this project was mounted in 1946 the Gram Savak (later to be called village level worker, VLW) again played the key role, because MAYER had observed that the existing services provided by the ministries had no contact with the village population and failed to work together where cooperation was vitally necessary. Thus fragmentation in specialist departments triumphed over the problem-oriented approach.

From the very beginning it was clear to all concerned that the technical efficiency of the VLWs would be low. The intention was, however, to raise the level of their expertise and self-confidence by means of coordination and assistance. The work of the advisers was to be made easier by bringing them together for regular discussions, personal supervision by subject matter specialists and concentration on a limited number of important tasks.

The formal organisation of CD in the Etawah Project was as follows:

Figure 1:

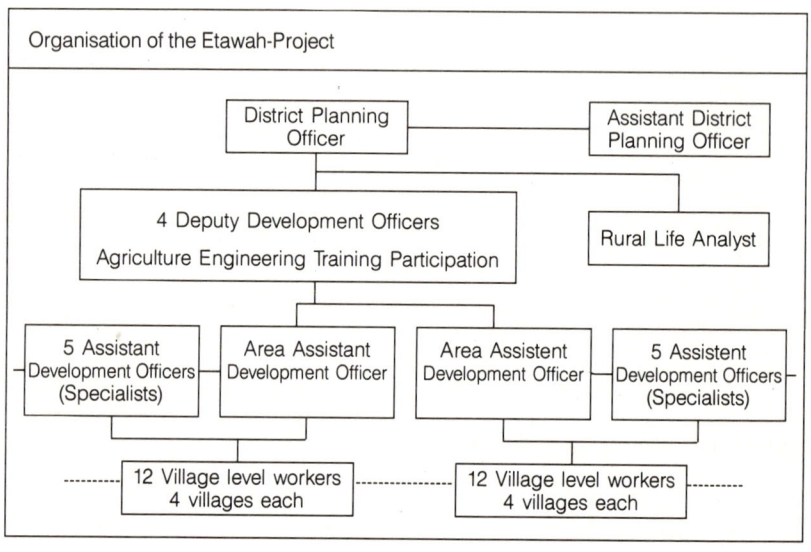

The basic ideas in the two projects were taken up by the commission thät drew up the first 5-year plan:

"Community Development is the method and the National Extension Service the institution by means of which the 5-year plan seeks to set in motion a process of reform of the social and economic life of people in villages." (KANTOWSKI, 1970, p. 9).

The programme began in 1952. It was welcomed with enthusiasm and achieved rapid success. In October 1953 there were 220 Blocks and in 1965 the number had risen to 5 238. (Each federal state in India is divided into a total of 320 Districts, each of which consists of about 10 – 20 Blocks. These are the basic geographical units and each has approximately 100 villages with an average of 60 – 70 000 inhabitants, although this figure can be as high as 150 000.

It soon became apparent that in practice the village advisers could not have the same enthusiasm as their superiors. Precisely because the programme spread so quickly, the VLWs received inadequate preparation for their duties, whereas today they are given a thorough two-year training. They soon saw themselves pulled in opposite directions: on the one side there were the demands of the national plans and supervision by BDOs (Block Development Officers), with inadequate back-up by the subject matter specialists (about 1 SMS for 100 villages) – and on the other side the people in the villages made very specific demands of the Gram Savak or Gram Savika.

Because the setting up phase was so rapid and involved so many activities, agricultural production showed scarcely any increase at the end of the first 5-year period. Moreover, the VLWs were not in a position to encourage cooperation in the villages, since they tended to respond more to the wishes of land-owning farmers.

It was not until 1954/55 that specific steps were taken to involve women and children in the CD programme. But since CD was a rural project, the women's programme was geared mainly towards the family, the household, hygiene and health. Little effort was made to assist women in their agricultural and economic activities. The project aimed to employ female personnel for the social and health aspects of the programme in the CD Blocks in addition to the two VLWs per Block. Special emphasis was placed on training personnel to carry out the social side of the project. The already relatively unimportant female VLWs became even less important after the practice of training men and women together ceased.

The **first evaluation** (METHA Report, 1957) **led to** the following **modifications**:

(1) concentration on agricultural development (75% of the time of a VLW to be spent on this sector);

(2) the introduction of autonomous administrative bodies at all levels (village, Block, District = Panchajati Raj).

The evaluation of the METHA Report resulted in the improved training of personnel and better programme planning, although even improved training could not prevent the failure of the two fundamental ideas inherent in CD. A cooperative approach was alien to the traditions of the hierarchic administrative structure, and the VLWs preferred working with land-owning farmers.

A 3

The CD programme in India has been sharply criticised for two reasons: first, the neat formal divisions between the various training facilities — 100 VLW training centres, 20 VLW training centres for women, 3 extension training institutes, 45 departments in colleges, 15 graduate departments for SMSs and BDOs and a National Institute of Community Development for senior functionaries. Secondly, only landowners were represented in the village, Block and District councils.

The Indian village had never simply been a unit, a harmonious and classless community. This is presumably where the basic mistake was made: instead of taking account of actual interests and conflicts of interest in different groupings, the village was treated as a unit. However, this illusion of a coherent whole only endured as long as the various groups were dependent on one another socially and on each other's labour.

The **duties of the personnel in CD** were as follows:

The **Village Level Worker** was responsible for:

- carrying out all technical operations in the fields;
- giving instruction and spreading the ideas of CD in groups and with individuals (seed, cropping methods, etc.);
- links with all other service institutions (marketing, credit, means of production, etc.);
- supporting non-agricultural activities (construction of wells, biogas, etc.);
- developing the work of Panchajati Raj at village level.

In theory the female VLWs were also supposed to carry out the same duties, but they were only marginally involved in the last three activities. The attitude of senior staff to gender roles meant that female VLWs were largely excluded from this work.

The **Subject Matter Specialist** (SMS) was stationed at the headquarters of the Block and worked as an extension officer (EO or BEO) mainly with the VLWs, the traditional village leaders and the chairmen of cooperatives and village committees. The group of village advisers and specialist advisers was directed by the **Block Development Officer** (BDO) and the **District Planning Officer** (DPO).

The programme aimed to create unity but in fact gave rise to even more inequality: "The inequitable rural economy has allowed prosperous farmers to monopolise the institutions and to turn them into the preserve of the politically and socially influential groups in the higher castes" (from a report in the newspaper "Northern India Patrika", 04.08.65; quoted in KANTOWSKI, 1970, p. 11). The Untouchables (Harijans) were not reached by the programme.

A 3

When the programme is assessed as a whole, the following **advantages** of the integrated approach can be seen:

- The creation of new village institutions produced development stimuli.

- People saw signs of change, and hopes were aroused that the old order could be radically changed.

- The whole innovation process was accelerated by a uniform development administration.

As a result of the **METHA Report**, changes were made in the supply of production means which were conducive to a considerable increase in agricultural output.

But there were also clear **disadvantages**:

- Economic development has given rise to a pronounced discrepancy between the prosperous section of the population and small farmers.

- The programme was expanded far too quickly. Before it was possible to check its effects, the model had acquired its own momentum and the most business-like farmers had seized the advantage.

- There was no real participation in the programme by the population.

- The poorer people were far too often expected to carry out manual work (road building, etc.).

- There was no clear, practical target, so that the VLWs were often left to themselves and they worked together with village committees rather than with the ordinary people.

- Because of their low status in the village hierarchy, the VLWs failed to assert themselves, and as a consequence they were not treated with the respect necessary for them to carry out their work.

- The hierarchic structure of the administration made planning into a bureaucratic exercise and produced only paperwork.

- Personnel of low status were entrusted with a key development activity; extension was delegated to people who had neither standing nor influence in the village. Jobs were allocated that defied precise definition, with the result that personnel who should have acted as intermediaries were overburdened.

A 3

Moreover, **conflict situations** always arose where **extension work** and the **extension approach** were implemented via the village adviser:

(1) conflict between subject-oriented training and giving jobs to colleagues (cooperation, etc.) in a hierarchic structure;

(2) conflict between the norms of the plan and the wishes of the villagers or influential groups;

(3) conflict created by the multiplicity of tasks: agricultural extension, road construction, procuring production inputs, building up cooperatives, statistics and credit accounting.

Bibliography:

H. ALBRECHT: Community Development − Kritik des Förderungsansatzes auf der Basis der Erfahrungen in Indien. In: Zeitschrift für Ausl. Landwirtschaft. Frankfurt/Main 1969, pp. 20−38.

D.C. DUBEY, W. SUTTON: A Rural "Man in the Middle", Community Development. In: Human Organization 24, 1965, pp. 148−151.

A.M. HANSON: The process of planning. A study of India's five-year-plans. 1950 − 1964. London: Oxford University Press, 1966.

D. KANTOWSKY: Dorfentwicklung und Dorfdemokratie in Indien. Formen und Wirkungen von Community Development und Panchayati Raj detailliert dargestellt am Beispiel eines Entwicklungsblocks und dreier Dörfer im östlichen Uttar Pradesh. Bielefeld 1970.

F. KUHNEN: Community Development. Folgerungen aus den Aktivitäten in Indien, Pakistan und Südkorea. In: Strukturwandel und Strukturpolitik im ländlichen Raum. Festschrift on the 65th birthday of HELMUT RÖHM (Ed.) by J. STARK and M. DOLL, Stuttgart 1978, pp. 104−122.

A. MAYER et al: Etawah, pilot project, India: The story of rural development at Etawah, Uttar Pradesh. Berkeley: University of California Press, 1959.

Compiled by:

Rolf SÜLZER, Gerhard PAYR

A 4

Socio-economic development approach: "Animation Rurale" in Francophone Africa

The method used in "Animation Rurale" was developed by IRAM, a private French development aid institute (Institut de Recherches et d'Application des Méthodes de Développement). IRAM's philosophy is founded on the analysis of post colonial societies in Africa whose former unity has been economically, socially and culturally fragmented. The mass of the rural population exists side by side with an urban class of functionaries but without any real contact. Thus the main objective of AR is the integration of rural areas in the national economic and social system. Instead of rural communities being regarded as harmonious units, as in the case of Community Development, they are seen as units composed of groupings with diverse, even conflicting interests and power struggles.

The aim of AR was to turn rural communities into confident, development-oriented partners capable of challenging the local development administration and to force them to abandon their colonial role of passive receivers of instructions. The communities were supposed to articulate their own needs and present them as projects in the national discussion of the development plan (see the parallel to the "Majeutics" of GRAAP, → D 7). On this basis, contracts to provide services were to be drawn up with the development administration.

Animation Rurale started by **tackling two basic weaknesses**:

- Colonial adminstration had created a rural population that was not accustomed to articulating needs. Nor had it the confidence to **take responsibility and act politically**. Thus it was necessary to create or activate the right attitudes and abilities.

- The rural population did not have the **technical know-how** to go beyond the expression of basic needs or to define development projects and to carry them out by means of self-help.

These deficiencies were to be remedied by training "Animateurs". Every community was to have at least one Animateur. He was to be delegated by the community to represent them. By virtue of his training, he was supposed to be able to initiate discussion and stimulate the community's own development efforts. He was expected to maintain the momentum and also to establish links with the various development administrations. The Animateur was to take on a leadership role without competing with the traditional leaders in the village. The Animateur remained part of his community and was not paid. The community had therefore to motivate him to carry on with his work.

This concept was first applied successfully in Morocco and then transferred in 1959 to Senegal. The following procedure was adopted:

A 4

1st stage: Creation of an "Animation Rurale" service in the Ministry of Rural Development

- creation of a central authority
- selection of regions for programmes
- creation of a "Centre d'Animation" at regional and "department" level
- preparation of course programmes

2nd stage: Preparation of selected farmers for their role as "Animateurs Ruraux" (AR)

- recruitment of future Animateurs
- running courses at first level

3rd stage: Mobilising communities

- supervision, control, further training of Animateurs on the job
- running courses; 2nd level = technical and organisational know-how
- restructuring the rural communities in the larger projects to create "Cellules de Développement".

4th stage: Creation of new administrative and social structures and integration in the national political system.

The crucial stage in the programme was selecting Animateurs, training them and encouraging them in their work situation. The aim was of necessity to recruit personnel who were basically selfless individuals, and the villages chose the AR according to the following criteria:

- 25 – 45 years old; or in societies where the age structure was important, they were to be mature adults;
- recognised achievements as farmers;
- good social position in the village (not a "leader");
- accepted unreservedly by the village as the AR and representative of the village.

A 4

The three-week course at the first level comprises general political orientation, economic and technical topics and practical preparation for the first project activities in the village.

This programme can only be implemented with the full and open support of governments. If they do not share the basic philosophy, IRAM cannot even begin its work. Thus we see the direct link between politics and development work most clearly demonstrated in this programme, even though it plays basically the same role in other programmes as well.

The government of **Senegal** was the first to provide the resources to carry out this programme (1959) and in 1967 seven thousand Animateurs were employed. The Ministry for Rural Development was formally responsible for implementing Animation Rurale. Shortly after the establishment of Animation Rurale, so-called "Centres d'Expansion Rurale" (CER) were set up in the lowest administrative units with the aim of bringing together and coordinating the various development administrations to produce common programmes. In the CER the communities, made receptive by Animation Rurale, could have found ideal discussion partners who possessed the above-mentioned technical expertise. But, with the exception of a few isolated cases, the CER were prevented by internal administrative factors from playing this ideal role.

A parallel and largely independent enterprise was the work of the agricultural advisers of the private French company SATEC (Société d'Aide Technique et de Coopération), which is comparable with GTZ. They had a clear extension brief and the necessary technical and financial support. These advisers were recruited from the rural population in the same way as Animateurs. The majority of the staff in the rural services that were brought together in CER rejected the basic idea of Animation, namely limited self-determination in rural communities. Since the Animateurs were of peasant origin and despised by the better educated functionaries, negative attitudes determined the level of cooperation. Thus Animateurs were regarded as unpaid helpers who were there to carry out the orders of the administration at village level.

Little credit was given for the political work of AR, not only later in Senegal but also in other countries. The Animateurs themselves were in an ambivalent position. The advisers belonging to the specialised intervention companies were superior as far as technical know-how was concerned. Because they worked with the farmers, the Animateurs could identify projects – but when it was a question of actually implementing them, AR and its personnel were no longer mentioned. And finally it was maintained and accepted that farmers needed specialist services. This situation was created by internal political power struggles and the restructuring of rural services, but the general economic difficulties of Senegal were an additional contributory factor. These difficulties resulted from the years of decline in the price of groundnuts, the country's main export crop.

A 4

There is an "Animation Rurale Feminine" (ARF) in all francophone African countries. ARF has often adopted the European image of women. Thus when women were the subject of development aid, issues important to African women were rarely addressed and specifically European objectives were pursued instead, like child-care, hygiene, domestic science and nutrition. This approach was destined to failure, since the sometimes very independent position of women was not taken into account.

Summary

(1) The Animateurs were intended to occupy a social position in the village. But it was impossible to create a firm foundation for a new role of this kind in a relatively short time. No one, not even the Animateur himself, knew where he really belonged in the traditional social structure.

(2) This uncertainty regarding status was exacerbated by ill-defined responsibilities, in direct contrast with the agricultural adviser, and by the lack of political support from the low-level officials.

(3) People were frequently chosen as Animateurs who fulfilled the urban "standard" but were not representative of the villages.

(4) Thus as innovators they were marginalised, whereas their "colleagues" from SATEC were welcomed as innovators.

(5) Female advisers were trained according to the European image of women. Since their function was also only marginal, female advisers did not achieve the influential and independent position of African women in agriculture.

Like other approaches described in this book, Animation Rurale did not fail as a philosophy of extension. Its lack of success was due to having to wrestle with different problems in each of the different locations where it was introduced. Thus it did not achieve a large-scale breakthrough on a national level. There were too many opposing forces for this to happen, and in addition the general economic conditions were not in its favour. Nevertheless, in the regional context and in specific locations, AR did achieve many encouraging successes. Some of the important basic ideas and methodological principles of AR are still applied and successfully emulated today. This also applies to countries outside francophone Africa.

Although most of the early IRAM members have now become French university teachers, the institute as such still exists — its work has not become superfluous even today. Further information can be obtained from: IRAM, 49 Rue de la Glacière F 75013 Paris, France.

Bibliography:

Y. GOUSSAULT: Rural "Animation" and Popular Participation in French-Speaking Black Africa. In: Intern. Labour Review, 1968, pp. 525 – 550.

Y. GOUSSAULT: Interventions éducatives et animation dans les développements agraires (Afrique et Amérique Latine). Paris: Presses Universitaires de France, 1970, p. 257.

L. B. ILLY, H. F. ILLY: Mobilisierung der ländlichen Bevölkerung im frankophonen Afrika. Eine Kritik der "Animation Rurale" als Partizipationsmodell. Bonn: Deutsche Vereinigung für Polit. Wiss. 1977.

B. JOERGES: Animation Rurale in Afrika. Die Methoden der IRAM. In: Zeitschrift für Ausl. Landwirtschaft, Frankfurt/Main, 6, 1967, pp. 293 – 309.

A. MOLLET: L'animation rurale à Madagascar. In: Développement et Civilisation (21) 1965.

Compiled by:

Rolf SÜLZER, Gerhard PAYR

Action research and education: "Comilla Approach" in Bangladesh

The Academy for Rural Development was founded in East Pakistan (now Bangladesh) in 1959. (It was originally the Pakistan Academy for Rural Development – PARD and is now referred to as BARD). It is a successor to the Village Aid Academy that played a leading role in Pakistan in the Community Development programme that was financed by the Americans. It was and still is an educational establishment that also carries out research for rural social scientists, psychologists, administration specialists, agricultural economists, agricultural producers and educationalists.

The basic concept underlying its programme is **action research**, i.e. applying the results of observation (observational research) and systematic surveys (survey research) in practical projects. The scientist's duty is therefore to take responsibility for converting the results of research into practice.

BARD is situated in the Comilla District, which covers an area of 260 km^2 and has approximately 200 000 inhabitants. Its main objective was to familiarise administration specialists with rural development. BARD approached this task in an unusual way: first, after initial socio-economic surveys, pilot projects were started and tested in the vicinity of the Academy. They included new production methods, local self-administration and also infrastructure programmes.

Initial reactions to this programme and experience gained in India gave rise to two major projects:

(1) The "Thana Training and Development Centre" (TTDC). The ideas of the first director of BARD, A.H. KHAN, were influenced by experience of Danish adult education, that had encouraged the setting up of new facilities and meeting places in rural areas. Thus the TTDC rather than the police station became the central public building. Public administration was concentrated in one building: agriculture, animal breeding, fishing, health, education. These were specialist departments of the National Extension Service. A local government council was also created and housed in the TTDC.

(2) The new administrative unit TTDC was supplemented by cooperatives at village level (KSS = Krishi Sambaya Samit) that took over extension work for both members and non-members. The "Kotawali Thana Central Cooperative Association" (KTCCA) had several functions: purchasing produce and marketing, savings and credit, hiring out equipment, water supply, training in agriculture and coordinating development efforts with the services already available in the villages.

A 5

A new extension approach was finally established with the help of the "Thana Training Centre" and the village cooperatives, each of which selected a model farmer (in the non-agricultural sector a "local leader") who came to the TTDC for one day every week. Thus he was given regular training, and when he returned to his village he took with him simple instruction sheets and drawings.

These model farmers had to commit themselves contractually to pass on their knowledge, to test new methods and to establish contact with the specialist advisers of the National Extension Service at village gatherings.

In place of a "discouraged army of poorly paid and inadequately trained and motivated village advisers, local leaders (receptive farmers) were now trained by specialist advisers. These leaders were selected for training in the "Thana Training Centre" by groups in the villages" (KHAN/HUSSAIN 1963, p. 14).

The pursuit of individual aims in isolation was prevented by the fusion of general extension services, representatives of village cooperatives, the government and BARD in the Local Government Council of the "Thana Training Centre".

To raise efficiency in the agricultural production sector, two more projects were created:

(3) One was the "Rural Works Programme" (RWP) to carry out road construction, drainage, canal and dam building and to create out-of-season employment for landless workers. This programme was supported in technical matters by the engineers of the Road Construction Department and the Water and Power Development Authority (WAPDA) so that there was no need to call in outside construction firms.

(4) The other project was the "Thana Irrigation Programme" (TIP). In this case too a subsidiary effect was employment for landless workers plus training in technical skills.

The principles underlying the Comilla approach to rural development make it quite different from the Indian Community Development Programme (→ A 4):

- The village cooperatives (KSS) were at the heart of the development programme. They were not formed as a condition for receiving credit and means of production (a practice seen, for example, in the IRD Pprogramme in Bangladesh) but were active working groups of farmers and non-farmers who exchanged ideas and information.

- The programme did not set out to address the whole population of a village. Only farmers with several acres of land were considered for the cooperatives, since they required contributions and investment of savings on the part of the farmers. At that time a "small farmer" was interpreted as someone who owned about 5 – 15 acres divided into several plots. This was the group to be targeted and activated, not primarily the farmer with 0.8 acres. This meant in effect that more than two thirds of the population were excluded. The aim was to build up the optimum unit size of the cooperative as quickly as possible, so that wells could be constructed, tractors used and credit given – comparable to large holdings with 50 acres.

- The cooperatives were to be democratically managed and to accumulate so much capital over time that they could run their own central processing facilities.

- The concept was based on **village development plans** that indicated where enterprises could not be run by a village or cooperative alone. Thus eventually plans were extended to cover a number of villages, giving rise finally to a Thana development plan. This plan evolved therefore from the ideas and discussions that had started at the lowest level.

- The continuous training programme was an integral element. Whereas CD operated with the Village Level Worker who was responsible for everything, in the Comilla approach there was no professional adviser to implement a programme on behalf of the government. Training and extension were carried out by the members of the cooperative itself and not by outsiders. Outside help was made available as often as possible – either through BARD or by foreign experts, members of the Peace Corps, etc. – but it was help that was requested and not imposed.

It has to be emphasised that the aim of the overall programme using the Comilla approach was to mobilise local resources (material and non-material). No development objective was prescribed (number of cooperatives, increase in production), but people were shown the route to follow. Put in simpler terms, we can say that **the route itself was the objective**.

Since 1961/2 women from the strictly Moslem Bengali villages have been included in the Academy's programme. The same principle applies to both men and women. For a small remuneration, women volunteers act as a link between the training institute and the wives of neighbours. As in the CD programme, they are involved in a wide variety of activities, but agricultural work outside the home is out of the question.

Cooperation between the sexes was and still is impossible because of strict segregation of men and women. However, a women's group was tolerated, but only where a male cooperative already existed. This meant that the women were not only restricted in terms of location but were also dependent on the men. Without consulting the women, the male groups took decisions affecting the cooperative as a whole. (When financial problems arose, the savings of the women were sometimes used but not returned.)

The success of women's groups depended much more than men's groups on the female advisers and the teaching staff at the training centre. Because of the limited resources and the social restrictions, the chances of female advisers working in the villages were slight.

Newly founded or disintegrating groups fluctuated greatly because of inadequate extension work and poor supervision. A further obstacle was the fact that women in the villages had no experience of group work, and communication with them was therefore extremely difficult.

The IRDP programme for women (Integrated Rural Development Programme) that has been implemented since 1976 in some parts of Bangladesh has built on the experience gained in the Comilla project. In this case it has proved possible to create women's groups that are independent of the men's groups, and efforts are being made to encourage not only a higher level of self-reliance but also involvement in economic activities.

The initial indications are that there is a surprisingly high level of participation in the programme, although really effective work is hampered by a shortage of credit for women. Experience certainly shows that women are more reliable than men when it comes to repayment of loans, but nevertheless women are not regarded as creditworthy under the usual loan conditions, since they have no security.

It was mainly for political reasons that the endeavour to propagate the Comilla approach on a national scale was short-lived.

With the help of foreign donors, the Comilla model was instituted on a national level in 1978 under the title "Intensive Multi-sectoral Area Development Projects of IRDP". What was intended as a development programme over 30 years – spreading gradually from village to village and Thana to Thana – is now in the hands of the state. The "International Agency for Development", which is financed by Danish, Swedish and other development organisations, carries out comprehensive regional projects and a programme of "supervised credit" and marketing. The cooperatives at village level (KSS) are still the corner-stone of the system, but today this is not due so much to their own initiative. The formation of cooperatives has become a precondition for sharing the financial resources at the disposal of the management of "Integrated Rural Development" and for sharing the benefits of cooperative societies.

The name has been retained, but the functions have changed. As in the case of Community Development in India (→ A 4), the result of creating hierarchies and national planning has been that the capacity for self-help has been weakened rather than encouraged.

Bibliography:

M. N. HAQ: Entwicklungsprojekte in Ost-Pakistan. In: Offene Welt, Nr. 91, 1966, pp. 70 – 81.

A. H. KHAN, M. Z. HUSSAIN: A new rural cooperative system for Comilla Thana, Pakistan Academy for Rural Development. Comilla, East-Pakistan, Third Annual Report 1963.

M. A. RAHMAN: The Comilla Program in East Pakistan. In: WHARTON, (Ed.): Subsistence Agriculture and Economic Development. Chicago, Aldine Publishing Co. 1966, pp. 415 – 424.

E. A. SCHULER: The origin and nature of the Pakistan Academies for Village Development. In: Rural Sociology, 29, 1964, pp. 304 – 312.

H. SCHUMAN: Economic Development and Individual Change: A Social-Psychological Study of the Comilla Experiment in Pakistan. Harvard Univ., Center for Intern. Affairs, Unpubl. Paper, 1967.

Compiled by:

Rolf SÜLZER, Gerhard PAYR

A 6

Promoting basic training: "Farmer Training Centres" in Kenya and Senegal

It is not only in Europe that training farmers was recognised long ago as an essential ingredient in rural development. The underlying hypothesis is that basic training enables the farmer to adapt at a later stage and of his own volition to changed circumstances, to absorb new information and to modify his farming techniques accordingly.

In Kenya, this kind of training began outside Nairobi in 1934. The aim was and still is today to train male and female subsistence farmers to be market-oriented, commercial farmers by means of first a two-year and then a one-year basic course. Women are especially important, because 45% of households in Kenya are run by women.

This objective was initially supported in Kenya by the British Colonial Government and then by the Ministry of Agriculture that provided back-up measures.

With the sponsorship of the ministry (Farmer Training Section) the FTCs are the responsibility of each District Agricultural Officer (DAO). This nominally ensures close links with the state extension service. This arrangement also applies to the six of the total of 27 FTCs that are sponsored by the National Christian Council of Kenya.

The FTCs have always catered for women in training courses – partly because of their obligation to foreign donors. But from the outset these courses were always shorter then those for men and had little relevance to the concerns of rural women. Training for leading roles in extension is open to women in theory only, since participation is mostly frustrated by "minor obstacles". Boarding facilities, for example, exist only for men.

From the beginning, the FTCs in Kenya were concentrated (as in other countries like Senegal, Tanzania, Uganda, Lesotho, Korea) in the vicinity of research and training institutes and in particularly fertile regions with existing links with the market and where production could be raised quickly.

The **objectives** influenced the training programmes in a characteristic way. The basic training was reduced from two years to one year, and by today it lasts only **one week,** which means that **short courses** in very specific techniques to produce marketable crops have replaced integrated programmes.

Thus the people reached by the one and two-year training phase and later by short courses were mainly progressive male and female farmers. The short training pro-

A 6

grammes (with about 40% of the participants being women) comprise courses in general agriculture, livestock, breeding, tea and coffee cultivation, cotton and pyrethrum cropping and domestic science. With this concentration on the requirements of the market there is little scope for problem-oriented courses from the viewpoint of the farmers. The clear shift of interest in recent years is revealed by a number of indicators:

(1) Even though costs were relatively low (US$ 2 = 15 Kshs per week), in 1971 40% of the total 1 500 places were not taken up and 30% of the courses were cancelled.

(2) This interruption was not compensated by the fact that more and more other courses had been shifted to the FTCs before 1971:
    - courses for local "leaders";
    - basic and further training programmes for advisers;
    - further education for employees of the ministry;
    - special programmes for women and young people.

(3) Attendance by male and female farmers dropped by 45% between 1966 and 1971.

(4) Constantly changing teaching staff at the FTCs and little interest in the problems of the farmers is causing the situation to deteriorate even more.

There are **more** cases of **failure than success** in the FTCs. Many factors combine to cause the constant decline in courses and participants:

(1) The heads of the FTCs and the representatives of the ministries have tacitly **assumed** that these institutions are **well known**; but in actual fact surveys show that even farmers in close proximity to FTCs have only a vague notion of what they are.

(2) Both male and female farmers are reluctant to **leave their familiar surroundings** for a week or more; thus, once again, the people who are attracted are already relatively mobile.

(3) For years the FTCs concentrated on **work in the classroom**, and practical activities were only introduced at a much later stage.

(4) Course programmes were regularly **planned without consulting representatives of the farmers**, women or the advisers. In practice, the arrangement of courses consisted in the DAO or a member of the FTC giving an order to the front line extension worker: "You are to recruit a course on such a date, on such a subject" (BARWELL, 1975).

A 6

(5) Classes were often composed of people of different age, sex, education, agricultural know-how and with different farming systems, etc. Course **material**, that was often **delivered parrot-fashion** by the junior extension staff, rarely made a positive impression on the participants.

(6) In summary, two sets of factors can be said to have significantly affected the work of the FTCs:

Factors partly under the control of the heads of FTCs:

- poor teaching;
- low prestige of teachers;
- inadequate programme planning;
- lack of participation by people attending courses;
- little publicity;
- inadequate job description for the staff;
- little coordination between practical extension in the fields and the FTCs;
- slackness in recruiting participants;
- poor transport facilities;
- insufficient follow-up or none at all.

Factors partly beyond the control of the heads of FTCs:

- low level of finance for annual programmes;
- poor provision of teaching and learning materials, especially practical equipment;
- no funds to replace old or unusable materials;
- poor transport facilities (the public system and FTCs' own)
- organisational deficiencies (schedules, programme planning, uncoordinated use of personnel, etc.);
- non-evaluation of success and failure (listing mistakes, etc.);
- no account taken of major occurrences like droughts, animal epidemics or plant diseases;
- insufficient accommodation in FTCs;
- no telephone links with the DAO, local authorities or the ministry.

This training/extension approach that is operated in **Senegal** in Rural Training Centres (RTCs) initially achieved marked success in larger farms and with market-oriented farmers. In Senegal, only married farmers with more than 2 ha of land were chosen as the target group in the expectation that, as in Kenya, they would have a **demonstration or pilot effect** after returning from their training session. But, in Senegal too, marginal social and technical conditions have prevented this process.

At first the number of participants was lower than expected. In the first phase there were 382 instead of the planned 700 participants, which is attributable to poor publicity. An evaluation of those who did take part showed a short-term yield increase of about 50% per ha, but a demonstration effect did not materialise. The

A 6

trainees were supposed to constitute a new "elite", but they tended to be rejected by their neighbours. The same was true of the innovations that they introduced. The initial positive effects were eventually lost because of inadequate follow-up by the FTCs and the lack of technical services, marketing and credit.

In conclusion, the lesson to be learned from the work of FTCs: if only a few trained extension staff are available, concentration on one crop and systematic training in specific cropping techniques can represent a successful programme for individual farmers. But an FTC programme can only be sustained in the long run if all influencing factors can be controlled. A programme can only have a demonstration effect on the small-farmer population if it is really relevant to their work and problem situations.

The FTCs in East and West Africa have largely ignored women in their programmes, although it is precisely in these locations that women are almost exclusively responsible for food crops. The female advisers working in the countryside can only operate in the domestic sphere. They are not responsible for cultivation or livestock husbandry, marketing or credit, all of which are, however, necessary for meaningful extension work in household matters, since it is women who take charge of feeding the family, from the production to the processing of food crops. If, moreover, the whole supply system in the primary and tertiary sectors cannot be coordinated (ranging from production inputs to marketing), we anticipate the collapse of the FTC initiative for small farmers in the long term.

Bibliography:

C. BARWELL: Farmer Training in East-Central and Southern Africa. Rome: FAO, 1975, p. 115.

Compiled by:

Gerhard PAYR, Rolf SÜLZER

Decentralised and participatory development work: "DESEC" in Bolivia

We now illustrate a decentralised and participatory aid and project policy by taking as an example an extension and development programme that started with a relatively low input of resources and then progressed in phases.

The title "DESEC" (Centre for Social and Economic Development – Centro para el Desarollo Social y Economico) stands for a private development programme for Bolivian small farmers. Since 1963 DESEC has organised 200 groups that have involved some 3 000 families. This work was started by a Bolivian adviser (DEMEURE) who investigated the feasibility of rural projects on behalf of the Latin-American Institute for Socio-Economic Development. He commenced his practical work with existing Catholic action groups in the highlands of Bolivia.

According to his **development hypothesis,** sufficient financial resources and institutions already exist, but the small farmers, who find it difficult to articulate their needs, have no access to them. The only way to break down the peasant families' mistrust of development aid is by open and frank discussion. Matters are discussed with women in particular. The men (the traditional targets of extension) in any case discuss with them any measures to be taken. Moreover, women have to be encouraged as a matter of urgency to take part in social and agricultural programmes and concerted campaigns.

Women and small farmers whose farms were smaller than the national average of approximately 2.5 ha were defined as the **first target groups** to be addressed. The aims of the programme were not specified in advance, but the approach was prescribed: each development group should formulate its own interests and work out a development plan for the group.

The **organisation** of the programme took the form of meetings in schools, at market places and festivals where staff of DESEC spread the idea of farmers' groups working out their own aid programme, a set of rules and a development plan. This led to the following course of action:

- Local groupings formulate their interests; committees representing regions or aspects of the programme see that the work of the programme is actually carried out (for example, rice, sugar, cooperatives, house building).

- Using existing facilities, finance is raised with the help of DESEC.

- The groups, working independently, receive technical support from the four linked institutions belonging to the umbrella organisation DESEC. After

A 7

some time it proved necessary to strengthen these, since they lacked the required level of technical backing. The four **"centres"** concentrated on the following:

ASAR   agriculture, animal husbandry, crafts and rural services;
VIPO   house building;
SEPSA   health measures;
ICE   training small farmers.

- With a staff of three the centre runs basic courses in the local language on all aspects of the rural economy.

- Participation in any programme is definitely voluntary. Working in a local group involves individuals just as much as in the umbrella organisation. There is no collective membership and therefore no automatic representation of a local group at a higher level in the organisation.

It is incumbent on the local groups to formulate the **content of extension and measures** in a development plan. The centres act only as a lobby for the farmers and their families. They try to find out where resources exist and what measures families can carry out for themselves. Extension work consists mainly of:

- helping groups to discuss their problems and to work out ways of solving them;

- subsequently helping groups to achieve their aims by training measures, drafting applications for credit and raising the necessary finance.

Table 1:

Financing and costs of the DESEC Programme 1973/74 in US $	
Gross national product (GNP) per capita	190 $
Growth rate of GNP per capita	2.2%
Returns/costs ratio	1.75
Long-term returns	2 392 000 $
Long-term costs	1 363 000 $
Average farm size in acres	5.0
Percentage of farms in the programme with farm size below the national average	100.0%
Growth of annual farm income	11.1%
Level of repayment for short-term credit	96.0%
Project costs	70.0%
Annual interest rate (adjusted to take account of inflation)	6.9%
Average family income	300 $
Number of farms in the programme	3 000

A 7

The setting-up phase of the programme lasted from 1963 – 66. There was political opposition from the clergy in particular. The Bolivian government did not involve itself until the charity Misereor had taken over the financing of the programme (→ Table 1).

Source:

E.R. MORSS et al: Strategies for small farmer development. Vols. 1 and 2, Boulder/-Col. 1976. Vol. 1, pp. 15, 109, 175, 249 and Vol. 2, pp. 250 and 254.

Compiled by:

Rolf SÜLZER, Gerhard PAYR

A 8

The "CFSME" Extension System

A systematic extension approach was developed in the late 1970s in the Swiss agricultural project in the "Préfecture Kibuye" in Rwanda. In 1979 this approach was officially introduced in Rwanda's monthly agricultural magazine and then elevated by the Rwandan government to the "National Extension System" (SNV).

A free translation of what appeared in the publication in 1979 is as follows:

CFSME = C – Conscientisation = awareness creation
F – Formation = training
S – Stimulation = stimulation, motivation
M – Moyens = resources
E – Evaluation = evaluation

Introduction

Effective agricultural extension is achieved by an optimum combination of the above elements. They complement each other and are only fully effective if they form a coherent whole.

The system has to be adapted to particular circumstances so that it has an integrating function, i.e. so that the methods of creating awareness, training and motivating and the proposed resources ensure that these activities form an integral part of the socio-economic and cultural context. Thus the methods can be adjusted and applied elsewhere. But to achieve this kind of adaptation, it is essential to be thoroughly acquainted with local circumstances, so that the system is perceived as genuine help in the process of development and emancipation of a particular population and not as something imposed from above by the authorities.

The best extension method is the method that is appreciated by the people and not necessarily the one that is technically perfect. The CFSME type of extension is not necessarily confined to agriculture. It is quite possible to use the same system to carry out health counselling (preventive medicine and nutrition), skills development or multisectoral extension, i.e. a combination of, for example, agriculture, nutrition and manual skills, so that interconnected problem areas are tackled.

Extension in the CFSME system is organised in geographically defined regions that also coincide with social communities. If the people targeted in this kind of system know each other, they are more likely to want to work together to solve shared problems. The administrative division of Rwanda into communities and community sectors is ideal for this approach.

A 8

The central body in extension using the CFSME system is the **extension commission,** consisting of:

- the member of the community in charge of the sector;
- the representatives of the cells;
- the agricultural field advisers, the veterinary assistant and the social worker for the sector.

The extension commission is trained, advised, supervised and supported by the **multidisciplinary group of** staff employed by **the Community**. This group combines the skills of:

- an agronomist;
- a vet;
- a medical assistant;
- a social assistant;
- the mayor, etc.

This varied group at Community level should be trained by a central service in the Prefecture. Such a service could be provided, for example, by the Training and Development Centre in the Prefecture (CPFDP) that has the job of developing and producing teaching materials for use in advisory sessions. This teaching material should serve equally to train extension staff and the population. It should enable farmers to recognise their own problems and their situation and show them ways of overcoming them. It should be attractive enough to stimulate the interest of the people.

The course of extension in the CFSME system:

→ Figure 1 gives an overview of all the phases of extension in one year. It also explains the most frequently used abbreviations.

First phase:

The staff of the Community and the Prefecture make contact with the local people in their specific environment, so that they can study the population's perceived and unperceived problems, familiarise themselves with the socio-economic and cultural context in which the problems occur and analyse the problems to identify causes, to find out how the problems are structured, etc. The content and topics of extension are then selected and the teaching material is developed on the basis of this information. After making contact for the first time, more opportunities arise to discuss and examine possible solutions and their chances of success with the representatives of the population.

Figure 1:

	The complete CFSME extension system in a sector over one year.		
	C = conscientisation (Awareness creation) F = Formation (Training) S = Stimulation (Stimulation) M = Moyens (Resources) E = Evaluation (Evaluation)		
Sequence	What?	How?	Who?
1st Phase C	1. Getting to know the locality 2. Analysing the acute and latent needs of the population 3. Working out priorities for intervention	1. Field visits 2. Discussions with farmers and 3. Synthesis of needs analysis and technical factors	Population, technical personnel of the Prefecture and the enquiries communities, SAF Technical personnel of the Prefecture, SAF
2nd Phase C,M	1. Deciding 3–5 extension topics 2. Devising teaching aids to increase the problem awareness of advisers and the population and to train them 3. Setting up the required infrastructure	1. Meeting of all technical personnel and representatives of the population 2. Teaching materials workshop of SAF 3. Fields for seed propagation, tree nurseries, organisation of seed distribution	Representatives of cells and farmers in an advisory capacity, technical personnel of the Prefecture and the communities, SAF SAF Personnel of the Prefecture and the communities
3rd Phase C,F	1. Forming an extension commission (CV) 2. Training the extension commission (CV) 3. Deciding the rules of the agricultural competition (CA)	1. Nomination and election of commission members 2. Training on 5–10 days on the selected extension topics 3. Taking as a model the rules worked out by the extension commission of the Prefecture	Mayor, technical personnel of the community, SAF SAF, CCDFP, technical personnel of the communities CV, SAF, technical personnel of the communities
4th Phase F,S,M	1. Measures to increase sensitivity to problems and to train the population 2. Visits to farmers who adopt extension topics	1. Regular meetings with the population (Umuganda, CSD, CN) training on the extension topics 2. Visits every 2–3 months, each visit concentrates on one topic	CCDFP, technical personnel of the communities, SAF CV, technical personnel, SAF
5th Phase S,M,E	1. Last visit by the extension commission 2. Evaluation of how farmers have put measures into practice 3. Awarding prizes, final celebration by the people in the sector	1. Visit to all farmers who have put extension topics into practice 2. Comparison of results in different communities using standardised evaluation for the whole Prefecture 3. Prizes in the form of materials and other incentives (publication of the names of prize winners, etc.)	CV, technical personnel of the communities, SAF CV, technical personnel of the communities, SAF Mayor, CV, technical personnel of the Prefecture and the community
6th Phase E,C	1. Reformulation of extension topics in the light of evaluation results 2. Adapting problem sensitivity programmes and training programmes to the new topics 3. Further training for the extension commission (CV) 4. Information from the people on organising the agricultural competition (CA) in the following year	1. Replacing topics with the next most important topics when the aims have been achieved 2. Linking the problem sensitivity programmes and training programmes to the new extension topics 3. Preparing the extension commission for the new topics 4. Information-gathering meeting at cell level	CV, technical personnel of communities, SAF CV, technical personnel of the communities, SAF Technical personnel of the community, SAF CV, technical personnel of the community, SAF
Explanation of abbreviations	CA = Concours Agricole; CCDFP = Centre Communal de Développement et de Formation Permanente; C,F,S,M,E see top line of table; CN = Centres Nutritionnels; CSD = Centres Sociaux de Développement; CV = Commission de Vulgarisation SAF = Service Animation / Formation Umuganda = "voluntary" community work, organised by the communities, in which everyone has to take part for half a day every week.		

A 8

It is not advisable to confront the farmers with too many different problems at once, since they are more likely to be discouraged and confused, and they then become indifferent to development efforts and give up altogether. For this reason it is important to define the short, medium and long-term priorities clearly and systematically.

Second phase:

Teaching materials are developed that will create awareness and increase responsiveness. These materials have to be adapted to the local circumstances and take account of field surveys, so that they act as a kind of mirror in which the people see some of their problems, their causes and how they interrelate with other problems. The objective of this second phase is to get the people to ask themselves: "How can we solve this problem?"

The process of creating awareness and increasing responsiveness must take place in the countryside, i.e. we have to go to the people, because they see no point in trekking to some distant meeting place if they are not aware that problems exist. It is of the utmost importance to create attractive materials to make people sensitive to problems and to heighten their awareness. Awareness creation is then carried out selectively in cells or sectors by a team (awareness creation campaign). The "Umuganda" of men, women and children (voluntary community work on one half day each week) provides an interesting context in which to create problem awareness. Instead of the usual physical labour, everyone works together on awareness creation and training. Thus the members of a cell come together regularly over several weeks for training and development of problem awareness instead of working in the area.

By the end of this second phase, between two and five extension topics should have been decided on. The content of the topics should be as balanced as possible and the following criteria should be borne in mind:

- topics that are attractive, i.e. promise the people rapid results;
- topics that are less attractive, i.e. promise results but only in the longer term;
- topics that are selected according to the labour requirement in different seasons, e.g. two topics in the dry season and three in the rainy season.

Some methods of creating awareness:

- theatre;
- picture sequences on felt boards;
- visits to farms and discussion of farmers' problems;
- demonstration plots;
- songs and poems;

- observations in the fields; inspecting an eroded field, visiting a progressive farmer, inspecting well fertilised fields, etc.

Third phase:

Formation of the extension commission:

The Community's group of various specialists organises technical training sessions on the selected topics for the extension commission. These sessions last for a week to ten days and they aim to prepare the extension commission for the work it is to undertake. Thus they provide basic training to equip the commission to take advantage of the solutions that may emerge (establishing erosion control, building stalls, etc.).

In the course of these training sessions the **conditions and rules of an agricultural competition** are worked out in conjunction **with the extension commission**. The agricultural competition is an incentive and a means of motivating in the CFSME system. During the meetings to raise the level of sensitivity and problem awareness, the people are then told about the rules of the competition and how it will function.

Fourth phase:

Every two to three months, the extension commission makes visits to those farmers who have accomplished something as part of the competition. On these occasions the commission discusses progress with the farmers, advises them and encourages them to even greater achievement or to start new initiatives. At the same time these visits are a way of increasing farmers' insight into problems, training them, giving them encouragement and evaluating achievements so far. The extension commission should not see its role as criticising what has been done badly but should above all acknowledge, admire and praise what has been done well, in order to motivate the farmers.

At the same time the multidisciplinary team of community staff, using carefully adapted, appropriate teaching materials, systematically trains the people in the extension topics.

This training can take place in the context of "Umuganda" (one to two cells over several weeks). It is an advantage if the topics dealt with in the training period fit the seasons (for example, stall building in the dry season, reforestation in November, erosion control in March, etc.). Training of this kind can be carried out in any centre, e. g. a social and development centre or nutrition centre or anywhere in the countryside depending on the facilities available.

A 8

Methods and materials suitable for training are:

- picture sequences on felt boards;
- posters, calendars, etc.;
- discussions, talks, exchange of ideas (visits by the extension commission);
- visits to model farms;
- visits to demonstration fields, etc.;

The training and evaluation work of the extension commission is spread over the whole year, during which it is vital that the Community's employees maintain the **infrastructure necessary** to satisfy the farmers' need for erosion control grass, fruit trees, forest trees, fodder plants and vegetable seed — always in keeping with the topics dealt with in extension (plant propagation fields, sale of seed, tree nurseries, etc.).

Farm notebooks can be introduced to help carry out evaluation. Improvements are noted down, a plan of the farm is drawn showing the different plots and their location, and yields are entered on each plot, etc. If possible, this **farm record** is filled in by the farmer himself with the help of the adviser. The advisers can extract important information from these records to help them to encourage and counsel other farmers.

The extension commission also keeps a record of the names of farmers visited, achievements recognised and also a keyword account of discussions with farmers. In this way, it is possible to trace the development of performance over a whole year. The information in the record is then the source of data necessary to evaluate the performance of a farm at the end of the year for the agricultural competition.

It is axiomatic that an extension commission has greater credibility if its own members set a good example and demonstrate improvements on their own farms. To ensure that this happens, one or two mutual help groups should be formed from the members of the extension commission who visit each other on a weekly rotating basis to put improvements into practice (erosion control, stall building, reforestation, etc.). This is at the same time an excellent opportunity for the multidisciplinary group of community staff to extend and deepen the training already given to the extension commission.

Fifth phase:

A year after the start of the agricultural competition the extension commission comes together again for a final round of visits to all the farmers who have undertaken improvements that qualify to be considered for a prize. During these visits the

A 8

extension commission judges the achievements and how they have been maintained over the whole year. Their verdict is then expressed in points and the farmers with the highest scores are awarded prizes in the form of tools (artificial stimulation → D 5).

Prize giving is accompanied by a celebration in which all the local people take part and the progressive farmers are introduced to all those present. During this celebration, theatre, songs, poems and dances can be introduced to draw attention to further problems to be addressed (for example, a song and poetry competition could refer to one of the topics planned for the second year of the agricultural competition).

Some suggestions for prizes are:

- hoes, machetes, picks, shovels, rakes, forks, empty petrol canisters, roof gutters, building materials for a stall;
- roof tiles for a house, a sack of cement, spraying equipment for a cell, wheelbarrows for a cell;
- tools for the Umuganda in a cell;
- lime fertiliser for soil improvement;
- improved seed;
- vegetable seed and mineral fertiliser.

The CFSME system deliberately aims to raise the prestige of progressive farmers, so that aspiring to prestige becomes a generally worthwhile target for the rest of the population. Incentives, awareness creation and training play a major role in this endeavour.

Some ways of motivating farmers are:

- authorities visiting progressive farmers;
- a certificate being issued to progressive farmers by the Community;
- publication of the names and photographs in the newspaper;
- naming them on the radio;
- presenting medals to progressive farmers;
- signboards at model farms;
- visits by the extension commission to progressive farmers.

The end of a year-long competition is also an opportunity to give the people some results in detail, e. g.:

- the increase in yield on a plot since the farmer started using fertiliser;
- the increase in value of a reforestation initiative over one year;
- the value of the dung of five goats of this or that farmer over one year, etc.

A 8

All the evaluation results of the previous year can be summarised in the report drawn up by the extension commission.

Possible instruments of evaluation:

- record book (to be kept up-to-date by the farmer or a functionary);
- report book of the extension commission;
- survey with prepared questionnaire;
- record of individual farms kept by the advisers;
- record of plants issued by nurseries and plant multiplication fields kept by the person in charge;
- animal servicing record kept by the person in charge of the stud station;
- diary entries by the farmer and the Community vet;
- list of modern techniques adopted in the region after one year of the agricultural competition.

Sixth phase:

The agricultural competition is modified for the coming year in keeping with the results of evaluation. The topics can thus be amended in the light of experience. Prizes should match the importance placed on material incentives in the next extension topics to be dealt with. Similarly the awareness creation and training programme has to be thought through again in the light of experience and new priorities. This work is carried out by the extension commission in conjunction with the multidisciplinary group of Community staff and the Centre for Development and Training in the Prefecture. Once the programme has been determined, the people are informed and the whole process starts afresh.

Concluding remarks:

The CFSME extension system was developed in the Kibuye agricultural project, thoroughly tested over many years and put into operation in the whole Prefecture. A development and training service took responsibility for devising the teaching materials and training the Community functionaries in their use and the organisation and implementation of extension.

Over the next few years the Rwandan Ministry of Agriculture incorporated important elements of this extension approach in the "National Extension System". It appears, however, that the idea of participation and the philosophy of development based on emancipation, that are fundamental to this approach, have had little chance of survival as they were in conflict with the traditions and methods of the Rwandan state administration. At present, discussions are in progress on a new national extension system.

A 8

The CFSME extension system cannot simply be prescribed for the whole country. Like all extension systems it cannot possibly be applied elsewhere in toto. Transfer without modification to other locations is out of the question. If transfer is to have any chance of success, we must understand the principles of the system and the basic underlying connections and above all we must be convinced that the extension philosophy that shapes them is correct. → B 1 gives an example of applying CFSME in a completely different African context. More information about the CFSME system is given in → E 12, → D 5 and → D 6. GRAAP, → D 7, adopts a very similar pedagogic approach.

Source:

Ernst GABATHULER: Le système de vulgarisation CFSME/AE. In: Bulletin agricole du Rwanda, 12. 10. 1979, pp. 188 – 199.

Bibliography:

Ernst GABATHULER: Résumé du cours de formation sur le Système National de Vulgarisation (SNV) du Rwanda, donné aux Agronomes et Vétérinaires des Communes, appuyé par le Projet Agro-Pastoral de Nyabisindu. Projet Agro-Pastoral de Nyabisindu, 8, 1982, 26 p.

Compiled by:

Volker HOFFMANN

The "Training and Visit System" of the World Bank

With similar ideas to those in SATEC (→ A 1) – but without involving the project personnel – an extension programme for irrigated cotton cropping was launched in the lower Seyhan Plain in Turkey.

The **farmer education service** (CES = Ciftci Egitim Servisi) was financed by the World Bank (IBRD). The organisational structure was developed by an Israeli firm of consultants. The advisers' plan of operations comprised:

- working out weekly programmes;
- keeping in touch with farmers;
- passing problems on to "specialists" at the next level;
- collecting data on yields, leased land, etc., for the annual report of CES;
- giving the agricultural bank the names of farmers entitled to credit;
- attending further training courses lasting one and a half months in the winter.

Opinions are divided on the success of CES in cotton cropping. With the support of the World Bank, the organisational structure was revised for use in other countries, especially Asia, and introduced under the name "Training and Visit System" (T & V).

The originators of T & V regard a clear political willingness to reform the existing extension service as a **precondition** for introducing efficient extension. The **organisation**, the **content of extension** and the **selection of farmers** have to be completely restructured according to the principles of **unification**, **simplification** and the **creation of priorities**.

(1) The existence of rural services operating side by side is eliminated. A **unified extension service** is constructed from the ministry down to village level. Some existing services are incorporated in it.

(2) The extension service is responsible for **extension work only** and does not have other functions like exercising control, collecting statistics, issuing credit, etc.

(3) After the reform of the extension service, a **well structured plan of operations** is worked out, specifying:

   a) the number of contact-farmer holdings per adviser;
   b) the planned visits to contact-farmer holdings;
   c) weekly or fortnightly further training for advisers;
   d) weekly visits by the "supervisor" and the adviser to the farmers' fields.

(4) There is concentration on **rapid results** and appropriate technology and recommendations.

(5) **Contact farmers** are carefully selected and operations are concentrated on them in the first instance.

(6) Existing resources are exploited and recommendations are worked out that are **adapted to** the **abilities of** the **farmers**.

(7) **Direct links** are established **with agricultural research** that is appropriate to the circumstances of the farmers (applied research and specialists at the regional level of the extension service).

(8) **Direct links** are created **to the supply** of production means and credit.

(9) The programme is subject to continuous improvement and modification by internal and external evaluation (**monitoring and evaluation**).

The World Bank's approach to extension imposes certain political and administrative conditions which are not easily fulfilled, and calls for a tightly structured project management. In contrast to GOPR (→ A 1), the field advisers are not involved in setting targets. Even the farmers are selected by the extension organisation itself, although they are then supervised very closely.

Thus the T & V system is an amalgam of experience from the "package programmes", the programmes of Integrated Rural Development and the French intervention companies. Not included in this production-oriented programme are the social aspects of development aid that are so important in the Community Development and Group Farming approaches.

However, although a reformed extension service with political backing brings undeniable benefit and practical advantages, we also observe less desirable developments.

Difficulties arise in practice when the system that was originally developed for irrigation projects is transferred wholesale to rainfed agriculture. The **critical points** are:

- the selection of contact farmers. Experience has shown that the flow of information not infrequently stops here, only a small proportion of farming families profit, and inequalities are the result.

- the target group problem. Farmers' families live in a variety of situations. The centralised approach finds it difficult to take account of differing circumstances.

- the field advisers' training is usually confined to production techniques.

There is no appreciation of the relation between farm and family, and even the subject matter specialists rarely deal with this aspect satisfactorily.

- the field advisers sometimes feel that the prescribed system of visits is unjustified patronization by senior staff.

- the field advisers often do not have adequate transport to carry out the prescribed visits to the villages.

- increasing the number of staff and the running costs of the system place a burden on the country's finances. It is doubtful whether the recipient country could continue running the scheme if financing by the World Bank and other donors ceased. (In the Yemen Arab Republic, for example, because the aim was quick success, the World Bank's extension service has become a completely independent service, and it has not therefore led to a state service being built up).

Other authors adopt an even more critical attitude towards experience of the system so far. Taking a relatively narrow critical framework, they regard the above deficiencies as significant and not easily remedied or they criticise them more severely. Thus, it is argued, the system of fortnightly visits over long periods during the year has proved totally impractical and irrelevant, the organisation fails to take due account of the differing locational, transport and socio-economic conditions, the rural poor who are really in need of help are not being reached, and reorganising the state services is not worth the cost involved.

Some experts with knowledge of the problems argue in favour of T & V; others argue against the system. This phenomenon leads one to assume that:

- the authors base their views on different value judgements and concepts of development;

- T & V has different meanings for different people (when does a modified system cease to be a T & V system?);

- the cases they have observed are the product of widely differing circumstances.

If these assumptions are true, we are simply left with a compromise: the suitability of a particular approach can only be judged in relation to the prevailing conditions (the situation-specific approach → Chapter III.14.5).

The words "Extension System" in fact promise more than the actually recommended extension approach can deliver. To achieve success, perfectly satisfactory circumstances are interfered with indiscriminately; traditional, generally accepted working practices and detailed new instructions exist side by side. Nobody bothers to explain the interrelations that would draw the many elements together into a "system".

In our estimation this raises the question of whether and how the original T & V approach can be adapted to the prevailing conditions and combined with aspects and methods of the participatory approach to mobilising the farmer population. The answer is indicated among other things by the fact that both approaches depend on establishing the actual situation of the target groups, the interactions created by activities, observation and the evaluation of results. In other words, they have to adopt appropriate procedures to achieve the objectives. We can readily appreciate that, for example, questions of farming systems research, adaptive research (socio-economic as well as locational), monitoring and evaluation, training and advanced training of field advisers and senior personnel, cooperation with other institutions, taking account of inhibiting and constraining factors are all of general significance. But we also appreciate that all these factors can only be evaluated in terms of and with reference to a specific extension approach.

It is therefore regrettable that despite the rapid spread of the T & V approach and the different ways it can be evaluated, hardly any empirical studies have been carried out.

In the meantime, some of the projects of GTZ have shown that many elements from T & V's catalogue of recommendations can be applied successfully provided they have been checked for suitability and tried out under the prevailing conditions. The reader is referred in this handbook to, for example, → B 1 and → B 5.

Bibliography:

Y. AKTAS: Landwirtschaftliche Beratung in einem Bewässerungsprojekt der Südtürkei. Sozialökonom. Schriften zur Agrarentwicklung, Band 18, Saarbrücken: Breitenbach 1976, 243 p.

D. BENOR, J.Q. HARRISON: Agricultural extension. The Training and Visit System. Washington, D.C. World Bank 1977.

BENOR, D., HARRISON, J.Q., BAXTER, M., 1984: Agricultural Extension: the Training and Visit System. Washington, D.C. The World Bank.

VON BLANCKENBURG, P.: The Training and Visit System in Agricultural Extension. A Review of First Experiences. In: Quarterly Journ. of Agriculture, Vol. 21, No. 1, Jan. – March 1982, pp. 6 – 25.

CERNEA, M.M., J.K. COULTER, J.F.A. RUSSEL, 1984: Strengthening Extension for Development: Some Current Issues. Seminar Strategies for Agric. Extension in the Third World, IAC, Wageningen, The Netherlands.

CERNEA, M.M., B.J. TEPPING: A System for Monitoring and Evaluating Agricultural Extension Projects. World Bank Staff Working Paper. No. 272, December 1977. Washington, D.C. 20433.

A 9

COCHRANE, G.: Social Inputs for Project Appraisal. Intern. Dev. Review, 1977/2, Focus pp. 9 – 12.

GTZ (ed.): The Training and Visit Extension System in India. Report of the familiarization trip by a GTZ study group to India. Eschborn: GTZ 1980

HOWELL, J.: Issues, non-issues and lessons of the T and V Extension System. Seminar Strategies for Agric. Extension in the Third World, Jan. 18 – 20, 1984. Intern. Agric. Centre, Wageningen, The Netherlands.

NAGEL, U. J.: The modified training and visit system in the Philippines. A study on the Extension Delivery System in Region III. TU Berlin, FB Intern. Agrarentwicklung (FIA) Seminar f. Landw. Entwicklung (SLE), Reihe Studien Nr. IV/43, 1983.

Compiled by:

H. ALBRECHT, V. HOFFMANN, G. PAYR, R. SÜLZER

A 10

Research and development: Improving agricultural land-use systems by means of "Farming Systems Research"

Farming Systems Research (FSR), or in French "Recherche des Systèmes d'Exploitation Agricole" (RSEA), is today in the forefront in developing new agricultural technologies and further developing existing production systems. Because it employs an interdisciplinary approach and advocates close ties between research and practice, FSR is akin to the various forms of extension approaches.

1. Historical perspective

The new agricultural technologies that were introduced in the colonies were aimed primarily at the production of export crops. Large-scale land ownership with monocrop plantations predominated. After several decades, a considerable rise in population, an increasing flight from the land and urbanisation, the supply of basic food for the market no longer sufficed. For this reason more attention was then paid to the small farmers who had traditionally been the suppliers of food.

The green revolution made new technologies available, so that the production of basic foods could be intensified. The biggest increases in yield were seen in fertile regions and those where production inputs were intensively applied. This means that the green revolution was only of limited benefit to the small farmers, since they either had no access to the necessary operating funds or were apprehensive of the higher risks involved. Robust, more productive varieties suited to difficult production conditions were not developed until the following generation.

In many parts of the world, regional rural development projects were created in the early 1970s whose aim was a comprehensive development concept that went beyond simply raising production. Rethinking development policy in this way did not occur by chance or in isolation. At the same time there were signs of holistic thinking emerging in the industrialised countries. The Club of Rome published its models of limited growth, and everywhere the connections between the use of fertilisers and drinking water, effluent and marine pollution were perceived. We all became painfully aware that we exist as integral parts of a system and that we are all to some degree dependent on each other.

Recognition of this mutual dependence is now reflected in the fact that we regard every field, every plot, every farm and every village community as a system in its own right in which it is impossible to exchange or modify the parts without running the risk of destroying the balance of the whole.

A 10

2. What does FSR do within this multiplicity of systems?

It is not easy to answer this question because all systems are interlinked and sometimes overlap. This is why the schools of thought interpreting FSR in slightly different ways are on the increase. Figure 1 is more expressive than words.

A farming system is a living organism and, according to development, preference or other influences, it can adapt and change. Any change, however, has repercussions on the total system. The system can be dealt with at different levels, depending on the particular school of thought. Let us take a single field as an example. It is the aim of agriculture to keep this field productive and in the long term to optimise its yield potential. In this system analysis, an FSR programme would concentrate on the effect of mixed cropping and rotations, soil fertility and changes in soil structure, fertiliser fixation and the water balance.

Figure 1:

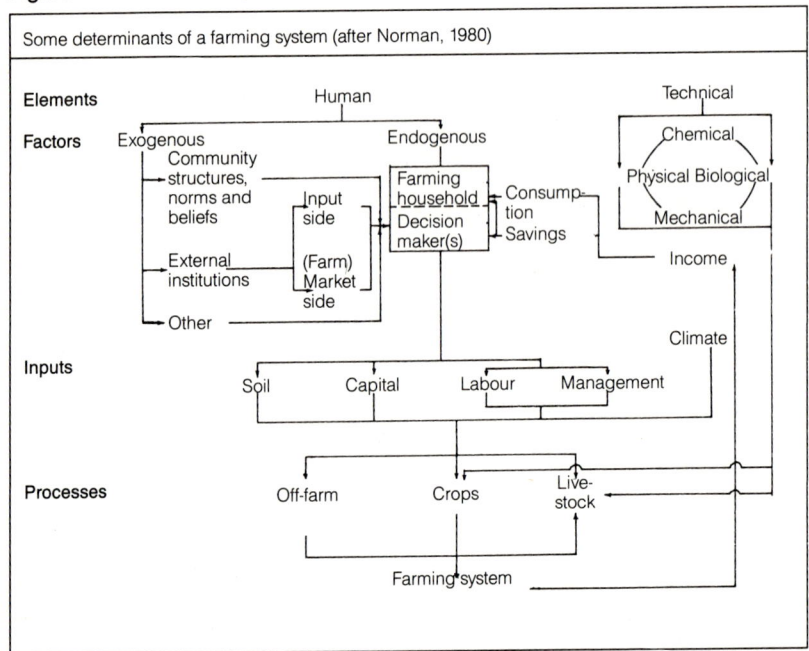

Some determinants of a farming system (after Norman, 1980)

Elements: Human, Technical

Factors:
- Exogenous: Community structures, norms and beliefs; External institutions; Other
- Endogenous: Farming household Decision maker(s), Input side, (Farm) Market side, Consumption, Savings
- Technical: Chemical, Physical, Biological, Mechanical
- Income, Climate

Inputs: Soil, Capital, Labour, Management

Processes: Off-farm, Crops, Livestock → Farming system

At another level, where the whole farm system is under investigation, research examines the effect of cropping and animal keeping, whether the fodder base is adequate or what would be the consequences of using organic fertiliser. Another important issue is the seasonal workload and whether outside help is required. We also have to examine the mutual effects of the various types of farming in a single holding.

The term FSR (in the way it is usually applied) also comprises social and market factors. Individual farmers' families prefer different types of holding or have different food preferences. In addition, there is the cultural and religious background of the various population groups to consider (cattle or pig keeping in the case of Hindus or Moslems respectively, etc.).

Norman and Collinson, two FSR researchers, specify the following aim (1986):

The primary aim of FSR is to improve the wellbeing of individual agricultural families by increasing the yield on the farms while bearing in mind their limited resources and the norms of their environment.

It is clear from what has been said so far that FSR does not concern itself with remedying injustices like land distribution and the world economic order, although much underdevelopment is directly attributable to these factors.

3. How is FSR applied in practice?

Norman and Collinson identify four phases:

- a) **A descriptive, investigative phase**
  An interdisciplinary team of experts (agronomist, sociologist, economist, ethnologist) tries to establish in as short a time as possible what the farming families see as their needs, what limits and constraints they are subject to and what scope for action the present system allows.

- b) **A planning phase**
  The experts work out possible solutions to problems. Their proposals may be the product of discoveries made by research stations, they may be the results of field trials or may be derived from the fund of know-how and experience of the farmers themselves.

- c) **A test phase**
  The most promising alternatives are selected and tested under the conditions prevailing among the interested farmers. The whole topic of on-farm research (OFR) belongs in this phase.

d) A dissemination phase
The dissemination phase still contains a research component, since the effects of the innovations that have been applied are observed and analysed. Of course, if different topics are being examined, the four phases could run in parallel but at different rates. Also, new issues might arise in, for example, the planning phase.

4. What has the FSR approach achieved?

It becomes clear from what has been said above that it is extremely difficult to recognise all the determinants in a system and to decide how to weight them appropriately.

The most important innovation is that the small farmer is regarded as the focal point, i.e. that research is target-group oriented. Thus research is no longer determined exclusively by the programmes of research stations but by the needs of the farmers and their specific type of land use. This presupposes that, before a research station is asked to investigate a topic, the farmers' operating conditions are defined very precisely (climate, soil, irrigation, labour, machines, fertilisers, use of pesticides, etc.) and their preferences are established. The existing farming system must be regarded as a total unit in which we cannot arbitrarily implant new technologies.

We can only conclude that technical staff must first learn from the farmer and must understand his farming system, before they can suggest alternatives. The crucial issue is whether they can suggest appropriate solutions to the most serious problems.

5. How do we distinguish FSR from on-farm research (OFR)?

It is frequently but incorrectly assumed that OFR and FSR are interchangeable concepts. Just because an expert carries out his experiments with a farmer on his farm, this is not synonymous with FSR. OFR is an important part of FSR, especially in the test phase. Thus OFR operates within FSR but concentrates on management of the land and techniques of agriculture. By means of OFR we can establish the yield and profitability of a crop and compare the various cropping techniques or rotations. This type of research can also be carried out with varying degrees of reference to the farmer himself. Thus a research worker can introduce a new crop or technique on a farmer's land and then supervise it himself or leave everything to the farmer. But it is always the farmer who ultimately accepts or rejects and who in the final analysis decides whether an innovation is compatible with his farming system. The point at which OFR begins to operate is when the key problem has been identified, solutions have been proposed and then have to be tested under the farmer's operating conditions. FSR goes beyond OFR because it takes into account the preferences of the farming families and their behaviour, includes the social environment, considers the availability of input sources and marketing channels and incorporates yield-maintaining and ecological measures.

6. What progress has already been made?

We have to appreciate that farmers do not act irrationally but always strive to maintain their farming system in a state of equilibrium under all circumstances. This explains why experts have become more modest, more willing to learn from the people they are dealing with. It is also important to remember that many of the decisions in a peasant agricultural system are made by women, so that it is incumbent upon us to listen to what women have to say and to draw them into our decision-making process.

Numerous land-use systems have been researched in great detail, for example, in semi-arid locations and in the humid tropics. This research has revealed the interrelations that exist and the delicate nature of the balance in these systems.

Whole new systems have been developed for specific conditions. In other locations mixed forms of land use have been closely observed and further developed, for example, tree and shrub growing has been included in research programmes. Thus, in general, research programmes have been drawn up and carried out making much greater use of the farmers' knowledge than in the past.

Ecological awareness and thinking in terms of interrelations have now spread far and wide.

7. Why has FSR often been criticised?

There are many areas of tension within the various fields of research, some of which are:

- Systems research is a long drawn-out process and is under pressure, therefore, from farmers to produce success and from financiers to fulfil their expectations. The farmers get tired of endless questioning; they want to see results.

- Because of our training, we tend to see components as interchangeable, and our technological training concentrates on individual items of technology. We are not trained in holistic thinking or working together in interdisciplinary groups.

- In their effort to produce even more precise documentation and analyses, many systems researchers spend all their time on describing systems without ever making concrete proposals. Despite a great deal of time and effort there are no tangible results.

- The right kind of institutional base for developing the interdisciplinary approach does not exist. Agriculturalists, ethnologists, ecologists, technical personnel for land and water management, animal and plant experts all operate in different institutes and may be dependent on various ministries.

- Cooperation between research and extension rarely functions well. For a long time advisers who felt abandoned by research have been carrying out their own limited research and experimentation programmes and today, now that research has discovered the farmer as an important source of information, they prefer to approach the farmer directly.

- Thus the advisers become communicators of solutions without having first examined the extension measures themselves. Their knowledge and good contact with farmers are not exploited by research.

- The short-term interests of farmers that arise from their personal preferences or their predicament are not compatible with long-term yield security (fire clearance – erosion; deforestation – climatic change). Their behaviour patterns are analogous to our own in industrialised countries (everyone wants his own car – air pollution – dying forests).

These examples are testimony to how little we have been trained to think in terms of systems and interconnections and how our behaviour is determined by very short-term benefits and convenience.

8. What conclusions can we draw for the future?

The systems approach is important and must not be ignored at any level – micro, macro or global. Even if the farmer is only willing or able to change his system little by little, we must not forget, when each new innovation is introduced, that we are dealing with a complex system of interrelations. Moreover, every single step in a new direction must be to the advantage of the farmer; otherwise he will refuse to comply. The most important factors are trust and cooperation between advisers, researchers and farmers. Above all, they call for understanding on the part of researchers and advisers of the existing farming systems and appreciation that they are the product of a long tradition and adaptation to the prevailing conditions. Only when they are fully cognizant of a system can they propose carefully considered changes.

A 10

Cooperation between research and extension is vital and could receive a long overdue boost from FSR.

Source:

Tonino ZELLWEGER: Verbesserung landwirtschaftlicher Nutzungssysteme. Eine Einführung in Farming-System-Research (FSR). In: Berater-News, LBL, Lindau, 2/86, pp. 6 – 13

Bibliography:

Derek BYERLEE, Larry HARRINGTON, Donald L. WINKELMANN: Farming Systems Research: Issues in Research Strategy and Technology Design. In: American Journal of Agricultural Economics, Vol 64, No 5, 1982, 5 p.

Robert CHAMBERS, B.P. GHILDYAL: Agricultural Research for Resource-Poor Farmers: the Farmer-First-and-Last Model. IDS Discussion Paper, April 1985, 30 p.

Michael COLLINSON: Farming Systems Research: Diagnosing the Problem. A Paper for the 1984 Annual Agricultural Symposium. The World Bank, Washington, Jan. 9 – 13 1983, 22 p.

Richard H. HARWOOD: An Overview of Farming Sytems Research Methodology. Presented at the Symposium on Farming Systems Research, Jefferson Auditorium, USDA South Building, Washington, DC, December 8 – 9, 1980. 12 p.

Peter E.HILDEBRAND, Sergio RUANO: El Sondeo. Una metodología multidisciplinaria de caracterización de sistemas de cultivo desarrollada por el ICTA. Instituto de Ciencia y Tecnología Agricolas, Guatemala. Folleto Tecnico 21, 1982, 15 p.

J.V. REMENYI,(Ed.): Agricultural Systems Research for Developing Countries. Proceedings of an international workshop held at Hawkesbury College Richmond, N.S.W., Australia, 5, 1985, pp. 12 – 15.

Robert E. RHOADES: Understanding small-scale farmers in developing countries: Sociocultural perspectives on agronomic farm trials. In: Journal of Agronomic Education, Vol 13, 1984, pp. 64 – 68

Norman W. SIMMONDS: The State of The Art of Farming Systems Research. World Bank Technical Paper Number 43. 100 p.

Compiled by:

Volker HOFFMANN, Tonino ZELLWEGER

Selected project descriptions

B 1

Agricultural extension in the Central Region of Togo
– Strategy, content, methods, means –

1. The basic problem

The traditional cropping system in the central region is characterised by shifting hoe cultivation and fire clearance. The fields are cultivated for four years and then left fallow. This system is only stable if the population density does not rise above 15 – 20 people/km^2.

The growth rate of the population is up to 13% per annum in some zones in the central region, where as well as the normal population increase there is a high level of immigration, especially of Kabyés from the north. In these zones the population density rises to 90 people/km^2. According to the calculations of the Ministry of Planning, all the arable land in the central region will be under cultivation by 1995. A model calculation has shown that, if we assume soil fertility declines at 1% a year (a very low estimate), farm income will fall by 25% by the year 2000.

The character of the infrastructure is determined by the north – south axis Lomé – Dapaong. On this axis lie the most important markets, transport routes, Red Cross stations and schools. This pattern of infrastructure is very attractive and makes the population less inclined to move, resulting in long distances between the fields and the village. A journey of 12 km is quite common.

The majority of the rural population can neither read nor write. Literacy programmes in local languages are just beginning. The written language is French, which is only understood, however, by a few young people. Communication with the mass of the population and traditional decision makers through the medium of French is not possible.

2. Possible solutions

We have tried to find long-term solutions in field studies with Professor Egger working on the development of ecologically based extension measures, E. Gabathuler on the extension system, Dr. Werth on the identification of target groups and target zones and Dr. Zeuner on the total project concept. This led to the long experimental programme Kazaboua, the creation of the CFSME extension system (→ A 8, → D 5, → D 6) and the media workshop and to the selection of four special zones in which to concentrate the initiative.

B 1

Extension content is determined by the following logical process:

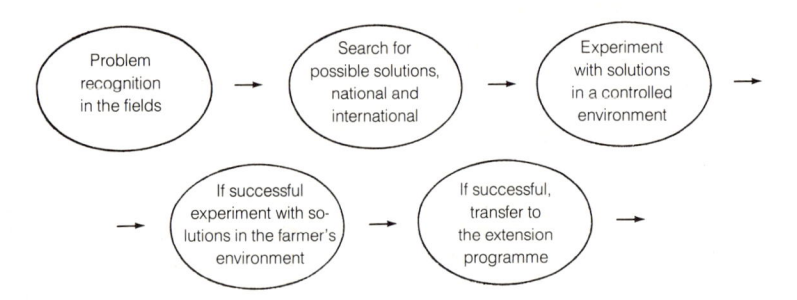

```
Problem              Search for            Experiment
recognition   →      possible solutions,  →  with solutions      →
in the fields        national and         in a controlled
                     international        environment

       If successful           If successful,
  →    experiment with so-  →  transfer to        →
       lutions in the farmer's  the extension
       environment           programme
```

3. Research

To work out the content of extension we have developed a small experimental programme that specifically addresses the most important agricultural problems. Taking the most serious problems of the central region as the starting point, the aim of the research endeavour is:

- developing measures to maintain soil fertility in both the short and long term (green manuring, improved fallow, rotations, cover plants, mixed cropping);

- devising a stable, permanent cropping system with trees integrated into fields (agro-forest system);

- introducing new leguminous crops (soya, cowpeas);

- improving the cultivation of yams and manioc.

The programme therefore comprises the following experiments:

- selecting the optimum amount of seed and deciding the best time to sow plants that will produce intensive fallow. Crotalaria r., Cajanus c., Mucuna and Canavalia e. have shown themselves to be suitable for this purpose;

- selecting trees that are suitable for an agro-forest system and meet the needs of the population – up to now 20 varieties have proved to be suitable. These include both fast and slow-growing trees for timber (e.g. Cassia, Albizzia, Khaya), traditional harvest trees whose fruit, leaves and bark are used in the kitchen and pharmacy (e.g. Parkia, Butyrospermum) and fruit trees (mango, orange);

- selecting varieties of soya and appropriate cropping systems;

- selecting varieties of yam and techniques for applying the miniset method developed by IITA. In this way production costs should be reduced;

- selecting productive varieties of manioc.

The most promising methods are then tested in the farm situation under semicontrolled conditions.

By using this approach the extension contents available in 1986 were:

1. agro-forest system;
2. mixed cropping with Cajanus – maize or sorgho;
3. soya cropping;
4. adapted land clearance;
5. improved storage.

4. Running a campaign

4.1. Training

Once the annual plan has been completed and the teaching materials have been produced, the extension personnel are given their training.

Every extension year begins with the topic "awareness creation", followed by "cycle of nutrients" and "soil fertility". Then the annual programme is presented – also in picture form – and registration lists for the technical subjects on offer are made available.

Extension personnel and farmers are then trained shortly before the actual time of implementation. There are never more than four weeks between training extension personnel and putting theory into practice.

Sequence of events in a training cycle

Extension personnel are taught in 2 – 3 day courses about the content of a particular extension topic and how to communicate it.

The first step consists of working out together why there is a need for the topic at all (with the help of cards and pinboards). When giving instruction on improved storage, the starting point was "Traditional storage methods and their problems", so that we could then define accurately the benefits of improved storage.

Then the teaching material, a sequence of pictures with a written commentary, is studied in detail and, using the role play technique (farmer – adviser), each adviser has to present the pictures himself. Whenever possible, aspects of the theoretical training are put into practice (for example, marking out contour lines for creating an agro-forest system). Finally the approach to be adopted in the village is discussed (target groups for particular topics, contacts, which people should be shown the topic presentation first).

The adviser then returns to his village and informs the village committee and the headman about what he has learned. He arranges with them the times and places for showing the series of pictures.

Presenting an extension topic with the aid of a series of pictures always begins with the question: "What can you see in this picture?" The adviser thus helps his audience to identify individual aspects of the picture and then to see the picture as an integrated whole. Interjections like: "Do you have this problem in your village?" raise the level of participation of the target group in working out the subject matter of the topic. At the end, the content of the pictures is summarised by one or more of the participants.

When an adviser presents a picture sequence for the first time, one of the training staff should be present and briefly interview participants afterwards to see whether the adviser succeeded in communicating his message.

When the topics of training are put into practice, close cooperation between farmers and advisers is essential; similarly, the supervision of advisers by senior staff is essential if mistakes are to be avoided.

4.2 Evaluation/final celebration

Evaluation is a joint endeavour by farmers and advisers. After the extension topics have been put into practice, the results are examined by the process of evaluation. Evaluation takes place twice a year: at the end of the rainy season in the case of arable farming topics and in the dry season in the case of storage.

The aims of evaluation are:

- the exchange of ideas about agricultural problems and extension topics by farmers among themselves and between farmers and advisers;

- developing further the improvements made by farmers to extension topics;

- telling farmers how to improve their fields, if this proves necessary;

- congratulating farmers on their achievements by inspecting their fields and thus encouraging them to carry on their good work;
- identifying deficiencies in the adviser's work (was the message put across in the right way and at the right time?).

The evaluation committee comprises farmers from the villages in question and extension personnel. The evaluation process takes the following form:

1. devising an evaluation checklist in keeping with the criteria of success that were laid down at the planning stage and incorporated in training;

2. theoretical and practical training of advisers;

3. training those farmers in the villages who are to take part in evaluation;

4. all participants agree on a date for evaluation;

5. on the agreed day the criteria are gone through again by all those involved in the evaluation process;

6. on arrival at the field to be appraised, the criteria are read out and checked by the committee members;

7. if the layout of the field differs from the proposals in the extension topic, the following points are discussed with the farmer:
   - has he found a better solution?
   - did the information fail to get through to him properly?
   - were there other reasons?

8. the committee calculates the results of the evaluation, and if it is positive the farmer is congratulated on his field and the awards to the farmer and the village are made public;

9. in the evening the results are commented on over a calabash of millet beer.

At the end of the campaign all the villages in a canton organise a final celebration. There is eating, drinking, music and dance and each village gives an account of its activities over the past year. Different soya recipes are demonstrated and tasted by everyone present.

All successful farmers are awarded a certificate. The Prefect and DRDR Director take part in the celebration and congratulate farmers on their success. In this way, not only individual farmers but whole villages are encouraged in their work (the celebration is held in the most successful village in the canton).

B 1

4.3 Target group participation/village committees

From the outset the farmers take part in discussing the possible ways of solving their problems. The village committee represents all the farmers in a village and consists of the different tribal and age groups, both men and women, representatives of the different sections of the village, and the village headman. Topics discussed with this committee are:

- how the problems in the village came about;
- how they can be avoided in future;
- solutions proposed by the farmers;
- what jobs are to be carried out by the farmers, the village committee and the advisers when the solutions are implemented.

4.4 Stimulation

Small articles or non-material incentives are given to the farmers to encourage them to take part in the extension programmes. These incentives may take the form of a hand grinder, a jute sack, improved mango or best of all a machete. The value per farmer never exceeds DM 6. The incentive scheme is made known at the beginning of the campaign and the people are told that awards depend on the results of evaluation.

There is a collective award for the village that is based on the number of trees planted. If 2 000 trees have been planted, the village receives the equivalent of DM 120. With this money the village can finance anything it wants, for example cement to repair the school, a football, its contribution towards the construction of a well, etc.

The non-material incentives also play an important role, for example, certificates for the most successful farmers, selecting the most successful village as the venue for the final celebration, congratulations from prominent politicians, etc.

4.5 Materials – trees – tree nurseries

If extension theory is to be successfully put into practice, making and collecting the necessary materials must be started at an early stage. In particular, it takes more than a year to establish tree growing for the agro-forest system or the orchard round the house.

B 1

The plant material is largely cultivated in local, private nurseries. It is easy to find someone in the villages that do not run short of water in the dry season who will grow trees for the village and possible for neighbouring villages too. The prospect of cheap fruit trees in particular makes a tree nursery a very attractive proposition for all the villagers.

The project gives these village tree nurseries grow-bags, watering cans, seed if required, and a small reimbursement of costs. The nurseries sell the trees themselves. The long-term aim is that the tree nurseries should also take over the planning of tree production for their own village and those in the vicinity.

The advantages for the project are the low production costs compared with tree production in state nurseries and the fact that there are no distribution costs (lorries, fuel, management). Expertise in tree cultivation, husbandry and grafting is engendered and the skills remain in the villages. This means that there is a far greater chance of this campaign being continued when support by the project is withdrawn.

4.6 Data surveys

The department of monitoring and evaluation is continuously engaged in collecting data about farmers, cropping systems, rotations, yields, crop varieties, etc. On the basis of these data, decisions are taken regarding the content of extension work and other activities in the rural development project.

4.7 Annual planning

Establishing precise data for the coming year has proved to be very helpful. On the one hand, work within a fairly large department can be coordinated:

- who does what and when?
- what material has to be prepared?
- when must tree cultivation be started for the next campaign?

On the other hand, precise planning is essential for coordination between departments:

- when are field advisers free?
- when is the training centre occupied?

Objectives-oriented project planning (ZOPP) in conjunction with operational planning has proved its worth as a planning instrument.

B 1

5. CFSME plus T & V

With the implementation of the "nouvelle stratégie" of the "Ministère du Développement Rural", the CFSME extension method has been linked since 1986 with the training and visit system (→ A 9).

Aspects of T & V were adopted:

1. tightly organised fortnightly visits by advisers to the farmers and the fixed training sessions and meetings for advisers;
2. the phased training of extension personnel (from the specialist department to advisers with responsibility for a region and down to the advisers at village level). Thus the subject matter of training sessions has to be structured to fit into the pattern of the advisers' visits.

The practical, participatory teaching approach of CFSME was retained (→ A 8):

Awareness creation → training by means of teaching materials → stimulation → joint evaluation → final celebration.

6. Teaching materials

Once the results of an experiment are available — or from other sources like the plant protection service in the case of improved storage — an aide mémoire is devised for the picture sequence. It contains all the statements that are to be made to the target group. At the same time the pictures are categorised, and for every picture notes are drawn up on the details that will be mentioned (for example perspective, which culture, how many people, their clothing).

Sketches are made to accompany the aide mémoire, reproducing the most significant details of the picture. At this stage the results of this work are discussed for the first time with representatives of the target group.

The first series of pictures is worked out in its final form and discussed again in the wider group. The series is then tested (→ E 13), modified and tested a second time.

The pictures are then duplicated either manually (outlines drawn by hand using a light table and then coloured in), or by photocopying, screen printing or offset printing.

B 1

If any drawbacks are revealed in training or when the pictures are being used by advisers, or if new information comes to light, they are taken into account when the series is revised at a later stage.

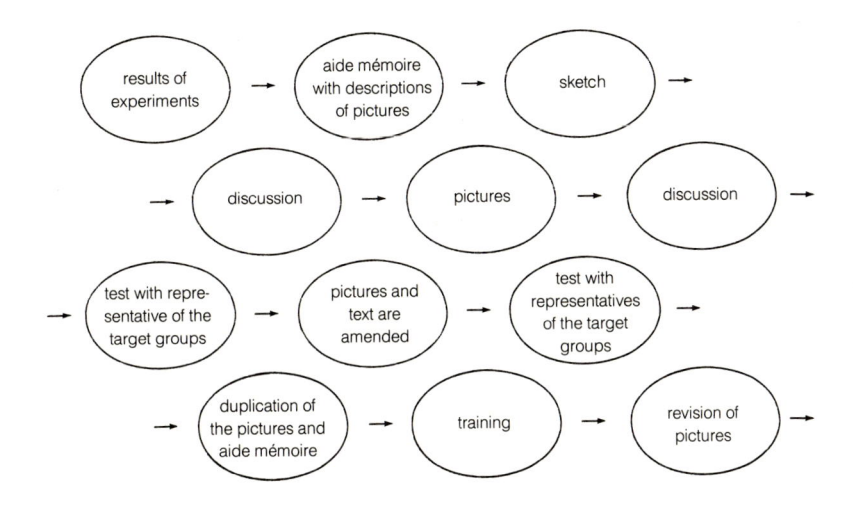

```
results of experiments → aide mémoire with descriptions of pictures → sketch →
→ discussion → pictures → discussion →
→ test with representative of the target groups → pictures and text are amended → test with representatives of the target groups →
→ duplication of the pictures and aide mémoire → training → revision of pictures →
```

The reader is referred to → G 9 for examples of picture sequences used in awareness creation and for training purposes.

Source:

Ingo BINNEWERG: Landwirtschaftliche Beratung, Strategie, Inhalt, Methode, Mittel. Zentralregion Togo, Sokodé, 1986

Compiled by:

Ingo BINNEWERG

B 2

Extension and credit in farm systems in the project: Kericho District, Kenya

In the small-farmer District of Kericho (approximately 5 000 km^2, 479 000 inhabitants, 31 % farms under 2 ha), extension and credit were begun in 1963 and carried out by a supervised credit programme.

The demand on the part of the previously nomadic population became intense as a result of the activities in the project: operational plans were carefully drawn up, there was supervision and follow-up, data were collected continuously, and individual and group extension work was carried out on model farms.

The systematic drawing up of **operational plans for seven types of farm** had an indirect effect on the advisers: in the project they learned to plan a farm stage by stage. With the use of figures, felt boards and scale models of farms, extension work was therefore improved in a planned way. Extension was programmed by a "Farm Management Bureau" with a staff of 25 advisers and 74 assistant advisers, i. e. approximately one adviser to 1 200 farms.

The advisers were responsible for all information and all decisions; the foreign personnel in the project and the senior Kenyan advisers restricted their activities to contacting farmers, training, bringing out farm-management handbooks and brochures, running short courses in the training centre and working out operational plans.

The advisers first made one or two initial-contact visits and then proceeded to giving group extension and arranging demonstrations. For demonstration fields ordinary farmers were preferred to the chiefs, since they had no significant social function and operated their farms for the most part on their own. 500 – 1 000 people often gathered to watch demonstrations.

The farmers' main access to extension was through the regular farm visits by the advisers. But African and foreign experts also drove through the project territory at least twice a week to hold discussions. At the end of the working week, there was always a joint discussion of problems and successes. On these occasions, any personal difficulties encountered by advisers were discussed as well.

The formal organisation of extension and credit was such that an entry in the land register served as security. The programme was restricted to about 50 % of the farms. Credit was granted in the form of goods (four parts productive, one part unproductive, e. g. fences) with a 5-year repayment period. The interest rate was 9 % and the inflation rate 20 %.

B 2

The farm systems were converted to include maize cropping with tea cultivation, pasturing/cattle keeping and pyrethrum cropping. Three basic constraints restricted the development of the programme:

- For small farms with up to 1.9 ha there were no entries in the land registry.

- Cash surpluses in the small farms (up to 1.7 ha) were sometimes unattractively low (without credit 111 shillings, with credit 176 shillings) compared with those in large-scale holdings (e. g. 500 shillings without and 1 800 shillings with credit).

- The density of advisers was too low to meet the demand at the required level of activity (one supervisory visit to each farm every week).

Bibliography:

Extension Services, Ministry of Agriculture, Kenya: Farm Management Information, Kericho District. Nairobi 1973

Ministry of Agriculture: Labour requirements, availability and economics of mechanization. Farm management handbook of Kenya, Vol. 1, Nairobi 1979

Herbert STRÖBEL, et al.: An economic analysis of smallholder agriculture in the Kericho District, Berlin 1973

Herbert STRÖBEL: Entwicklungsmöglichkeiten landw. Kleinbetriebe, Kericho District, Kenya, unter besonderer Berücksichtigung des Einsatzes von Kleinkrediten mit Beratung. Munich 1976.

Compiled by:

Gerhard PAYR, Rolf SÜLZER.

B 3

Extension services with the aim of improving the food situation in the project: Paktia Province in Afghanistan

From 1965 the focal point of extension work in this regional project became the creation of a network of village advisers. The region, consisting of about 18 000 km^2 with approximately 2 500 km^2 of agricultural land, produced some 0.25 million t of grain after deduction of storage losses, i.e. about 180 kg per head of population per annum. The group of advisers decided on direct extension work as a way of improving the food situation, and the region was divided into 8 extension territories, each with 2 500 large-scale holdings (with about 20–80 people in each). Each extension territory was subdivided into 12–15 village extension areas, each with 4 500 inhabitants and to be supervised by one village adviser. Four or five of these village extension areas constituted one extension district.

The village advisers were recruited in the extension territory. Applicants had to fulfil certain conditions: they had to be able to read, write and do arithmetic and they also had to have in writing the support of the majority of the village mayors in the planned village extension area. A monthly salary comparable to that of a primary school teacher plus payment in kind was offered as an incentive. The selected candidates were then given training for six weeks in the slack part of the year (winter courses). They were repeated every year as refresher courses.

Extension work was carried out on a 6-day cycle (for example, seed, fertilising, demonstrations, river damming, dealing with applications for the services of the project). After five days working in the villages, accounts were drawn up on the sixth day in the local extension centre, a written report and a work plan for the coming week were handed in and gone through with senior extension staff (a German agricultural expert and an Afghan colleague).

Both the systematic division of the region into smaller units and the staffing of the village adviser network with people who had grown up with the special characteristics of the area proved to be a viable concept. Difficulties in carrying out the concept arose mainly because:

- there was no verifiable information about yield ratios and other important quantitative indicators;

- due to the social structure, the village advisers were obliged to seek contact with prominent people. The specific development of small farmers therefore tended to be neglected;

- the project took over far-reaching executive powers that limited the authority of the Afghans;

- the adoption rate and introduction of high-yielding varieties of wheat slowed down and finally came to a halt for financial, social and presumably also cultural reasons;

- the supply of production means and credit was only guaranteed in the early days of the project; from 1970 the supply fell short of the total demand in terms of both quality and quantity. Without mineral fertiliser, the yields of the new varieties were lower than those of local varieties;

- extension work was finally taken over by the Afghan government, the network of village advisers was abolished and they were replaced by college graduates who had little practical experience and few technical qualifications.

In the meantime, the war that has been going on for years has interrupted all development efforts and has presumably wiped out the last vestiges of past project work.

Bibliography:

A. Ghafar LAKANWAL: Das Übernahmeverhalten paschtunischer Landwirte in bezug auf produktionstechnische Neuerungen (Saatgut und Düngemittel). Eine empirische Untersuchung in drei Dörfern des östlichen Beckens von Khost/Afghanistan. Unpublished thesis, Hohenheim, 1974

A. Ghafar LAKANWAL: Situationsanalyse landw. Beratungsprogramme in Entwicklungsländern. Sozialökonomische Schriften zur Agrarentwicklung, Band 30, Saarbrücken, 1978, especially pp. 106 – 194.

Compiled by:

Rolf SÜLZER, Volker HOFFMANN

B 4

Self-help groups and associations among the TIV in Nigeria

Since 1950, cooperatives and credit associations that are based on traditional self-help groups have been founded at tribe level in Nigeria (Benue Plateau State, the TIV tribe). There is a tradition of voluntary associations of this kind among young people and both men and women, an example being the "ton" in Mali (groups of young people who do work for the benefit of the whole community). Both men and women frequently organise themselves in savings clubs of 10 – 20 people.

In the case of the TIV, the savings and credit groups are called "Bams". The importance of women in the economic system is reflected in the structure of the "Bams", most of which are led by women. TIV women keep surpluses of yams so that they can sell them when there is a shortage and then act as money lenders. These "Bams" have a democratic structure, which is illustrated by, among other things, annual elections. Between 1950 and 1974, the subsistence economy in the Plateau region developed into a market economy in that it supplied the Nigerian market with yams and rice. This development was based on 5 000 "Bams" comprising about 300 000 people with their own extension service and cooperative.

As in the case of the cacao farmers in Ghana this development was initiated by the local leaders themselves. One of them had travelled, and he took the opportunity to collect information on banks and credit systems. He then transferred their basic features to the traditional social structure. Local leaders held several meetings and founded a "Bam" (credit group), bearing in mind the following points:

(1) The practice of women saving money by selling yams should be incorporated as the savings component of a "Bam".

(2) The tradition of electing local leaders should also apply to the "Bam".

(3) The high level of discipline and strict social structure was regarded as sufficient to guarantee repayment.

(4) The "Bam" should be created for one year only, so that families would not become dependent. At the end of a year they could decide on a new "Bam".

The group is reconstituted every year (with about 60 – 100 members). At the first meeting it decides on its internal structure. There is normally a chairman, secretary, treasurer, finance committee and a fixed place for arbitration in the case of disputes. All posts are filled by election. The members decide on the frequency of meetings (mostly fortnightly) and the level of deposits (between 0.60 and 60.— DM). At each meeting they collect the savings deposits that are eventually to be paid out at the end of the year. Then projects are thought out, loans granted and

B 4

payment difficulties discussed. The average amount of money that passes through a "Bam" in the course of a year is about 30 000 – 40 000 DM.

A TIV adviser then put forward the idea of making these "Bams" into permanent institutions that would help to raise production levels. The council of the TIV agreed with his proposal and founded a Farmers' Association that had 60 members in 1966 (1968: 1 000 members; 1974: 33 000 members; monthly contributions: 0.30 DM).

The main activity taken over by this Farmers' Association was extension work that the national extension service was not able to carry out itself (each state adviser had a work load of 1 650 farms).

The first recommendation was the introduction of fertiliser for rice and yams. The TIV adviser brought together the chairmen in the Farmers' Association for a demonstration and set up experiments on their farms.

The success of these experiments gave the chairmen the incentive to develop a distribution system for fertiliser and to decide with their members on distribution points and the farmers who were to be in charge.

After this initial campaign, they decided to transfer the Farmers' Association to the village level. The village cooperatives were in frequent contact with the advisers, with weekly meetings and discussions of new methods and evaluation of experiments with the specialists of the state extension service several times a year.

Important conditions for success are evidently:

- a functioning social structure that puts obligations on the individual;
- the confidence to achieve solutions independently without waiting to be told by the government what to do;
- a dense communications network ("Bams", village cooperatives, village councils, etc.) that can spread an innovation quickly;
- the ability to set up an effective infrastructure;
- direct control of work in the cooperative by farmers or their wives;
- actively seeking out the extension service, checking but also facilitating its work;
- joint discussion and evaluation of the programme at least once a year.

Compiled by:

Gerhard PAYR, Rolf SÜLZER

B 5

The reorganisation of agricultural extension in the Atlantic Province of the People's Republic of Benin

The People's Republic of Benin has created regional development authorities in each province (CARDER = Centre d'Action Régional pour le Développement Rural) to promote integrated rural development. The CARDER de L'Atlantique is supported by a GTZ project.

It was realised in 1983 that the problems in agricultural extension were so serious that a thorough reorganisation was imperative. In the meantime, this reorganisation has been successfully carried out, and elements of the "Training and Visit" scheme have been incorporated (→ A 9). In our opinion, the success of the undertaking shows how similar problems can be solved elsewhere.

1. Problems of the old extension organisation

A. Target groups

- Restricted by national policies to production cooperatives;

- Extension compromised by jobs unrelated to extension;

- The foundation of new cooperatives is on the decline; many were founded after the revolution for political reasons but were not economically viable.

B. Field advisers

- The staff of the CARDER was continually changing, with new personnel coming from:

  a) the university;

  b) disbanded state companies;

- In December 1983 there were 200 field advisers and 175 cooperatives.

- There were too many extension tasks and too many tasks not connected with extension (9 departments all wanting to make use of the selfsame adviser for their own purposes).

- Sometimes activities were incompatible.

- The programme of work was not structured and therefore not controllable.

B 5

C. Extension topics

- Too complicated and not specific enough for agricultural extension and often not understood by the field advisers.

D. Inequitable allocation of duties

- Numerous "sous-secteurs" without target groups (cooperatives);
- Concentration of most ad-hoc activities on a few "sous-secteurs".

E. Low motivation on the part of extension workers

- Poor salaries;
- Inadequate transport and operational aids;
- Unsatisfactory level of support, lack of supervision, control and acknowledgement of achievements.

F. Deplorable relation between expenditure and results

- 200 field advisers supervised 175 cooperatives = approximately 2 000 farms = approximately 1 000 ha.
- Compared with costs of 560 000 DM, a verifiable rise in maize production of about 1 000 t = approximately 420 000 DM.

2. Aims of the reorganisation

1. To relieve the burden of everyday work at all levels;
2. To encourage field advisers to work more efficiently;
3. To clearly define everyone's:
   - areas of responsibility
   - areas of activity
   - jobs
   - supervision structures
   - extension and contact partners.

The above as contributions to the overall goal of: "increasing production, especially in small and medium-scale farms".

B 5

3. Principles of the new extension organisation

A. Agricultural extension centres (CVA) established in the "sous-secteurs" and supplying or arranging all the services of the Carder; set up as near to the farmer as possible;
   → average distance of CVA from a farmer = 6.5 km.

B. Separation of agricultural extension from advisory work in cooperatives;
   → limiting the activities of field advisers to cropping issues and raising the number of advisers to cooperatives, responsibility for all other aspects of extension remaining with the specialist at sector level.

C. Reaching about 15% of the target population, → advising individual farmers organised in groups (extension contact groups).

D. Structuring the work-flow at all levels to make the execution and supervision of jobs easier;
   → fixed weekly plan of work.

E. To make it easier for the farmer to adopt extension topics;
   → breaking them down into steps that are attractive for the farmer and have a logical order.

F. To ensure the dissemination and communication of extension topics by the field advisers;
   → converting them into weekly tasks for the field advisers;
   → provision of weekly further and advanced training.

4. Organisation chart and job allocation in the new extension structure

→ Figure 1 shows the new organisational structure. Starting at the bottom of the chart with the extension contact groups, we describe the most important functions.

A. Extension contact groups

In the new structure of extension, there are 522 groups of which 174 were already existing cooperatives. After the CVA territory has been divided into three zones (1 per field adviser), the people are informed about the new extension approach, and at meetings in the villages and hamlets the selection criteria are explained. The field adviser establishes who is interested and the CVA team then decides, using the following criteria, who is to be in the group:

B 5

Figure 1:

```
Organisation of the new extension structure
```

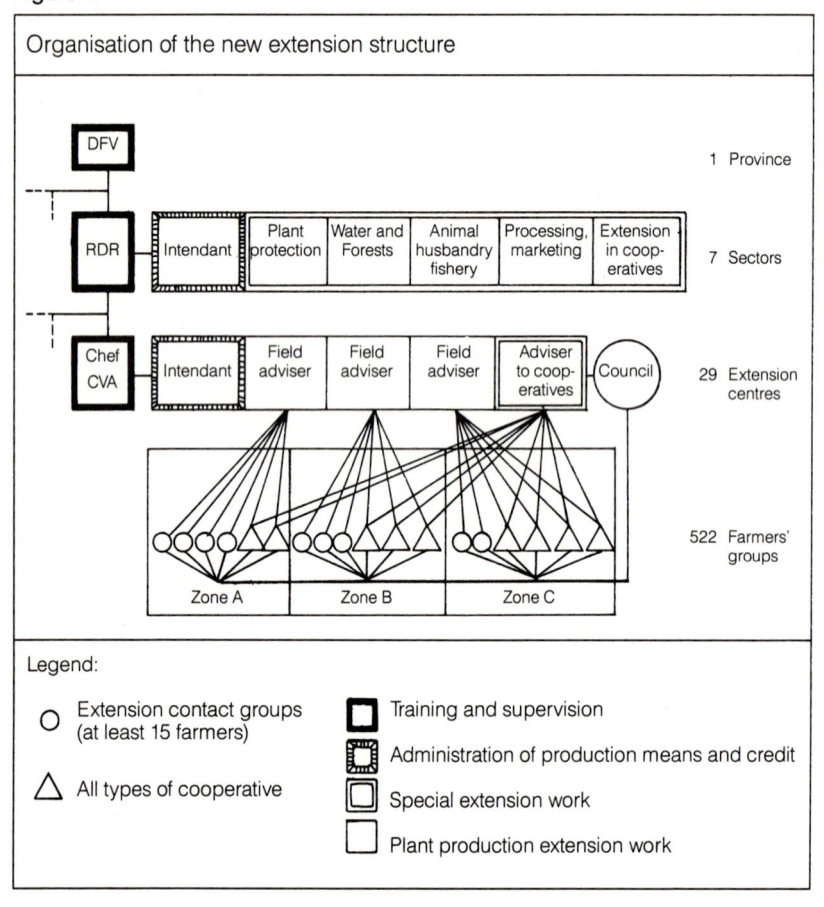

DFV							1 Province
RDR	Intendant	Plant protection	Water and Forests	Animal husbandry fishery	Processing, marketing	Extension in coop-eratives	7 Sectors
Chef CVA	Intendant	Field adviser	Field adviser	Field adviser	Adviser to coop-eratives	Council	29 Extension centres
		Zone A	Zone B	Zone C			522 Farmers' groups

Legend:
- ○ Extension contact groups (at least 15 farmers)
- △ All types of cooperative
- ▨ Training and supervision
- ▥ Administration of production means and credit
- ▢ Special extension work
- ▢ Plant production extension work

1. Obligatory criteria

   a) Occupation: the candidates must be farmers

   b) Land: the candidates must have land, either leased or in family ownership

   c) Motivation: the candidates must be interested enough in working with a field adviser to meet him once a week

B 5

2. Desirable criteria
    a) Organisation: when creating groups, preference may be given to existing associations, like "tontines" (savings clubs), "adjolu" (communal work), "tam-tam" (folk groups), "hameau" (hamlets, etc.)
    b) Homogeneity: the aim when selecting groups should be the maximum economic and social homogeneity

B. Conseil Consultatif = Consultative Council

This council consists of 1 elected representative from each of the 6 extension contact groups per field adviser and the functionaries of the CVA = 24 members. It convenes every three months and is concerned with:
- analysis and evaluation
- planning;
- preparations for the following season and important campaigns like marketing maize, inoculations, literacy, "journée CVA" = celebrations at the extension centre with exhibitions and competitions (→ D 9).

C. AVA = Agent de Vulgarisation Agricole = Agricultural Field Adviser

- passing on the technical recommendations in his weekly programme regarding plant production;

- calling in specialists in the sector for all other problems and introducing them to the extension contact groups (g. c. e.);

- communication between contact groups and the stores manager at CVA;

- participation in the weekly discussion in the CVA to evaluate and prepare work and to participate in further training;

- writing reports on his work.

D. CC = Conseiller Coopératif = Adviser to Cooperatives

- establishing the need for credit and subsidies from the village development fund and reporting this information to his superior;

- supervising all cooperatives in the catchment area of CVA regarding all activities except plant production, the emphasis being on management;
- advising the processing cooperatives on technical matters.

E. Intendant = Manager of Finance and Stores
- all work connected with subsidies and credit issued by the village development fund;
- administering the stores of production inputs in the CVA;
- establishing the exact requirement of production means in the CVA's territory, ordering them from the sector, distributing them and organising payment by the farmers;
- passing on information: he is always on hand and knows about visits by CVA members; he is a channel of communication.

F. Chef CVA = Manager of an Extension Centre
- supervises the work of his staff in the CVA;
- weekly further training of CVA personnel;
- participates in weekly staff meeting at sector level;
- writes reports on operations.

G. Spécialistes/Chefs Sections = Special Advisers
- carrying out official state tasks, special campaigns and specialist advisory work with contact groups;
- present at the weekly staff meeting with the managers of centres and support for the RDR;
- proposing and preparing special campaigns at extension centre level for the RDR.

H. Intendant = Manager of Finance and Stores in the Sector
   - ensures an adequate supply of production means in his sector;
   - administers the stores at sector level;
   - investigates and lists the requirement of production means;
   - administers finance;
   - assists with the marketing campaign;
   - produces reports on operations.

I. RDR = Responsable pour le Développement Rural = Head of Agriculture and Rural Development in a Sector
   - supervises the special advisers and managers of extension centres in the field;
   - ensures that managers receive further training;
   - decides with the managers what extension work is to be carried out in the following week;
   - takes charge of the supply of production means;
   - examines applications for credit and subsidies;
   - supervises the issue and repayment of credit;
   - writes reports on operations;
   - supports the Prefect and the political institutions;
   - takes part in the monthly discussions at the top level of management.

J. DFV = Division Formation et Vulgarisation du CARDER = Department of Training and Extension (at Province level)
   - training and further training of extension workers in the whole province;
   - supervision of extension work;
   - deciding on extension measures and the methods of delivering them;

B 5

- providing extension aids (technical brochures, teaching materials, demonstration aids);

- supervising central demonstrations;

- coordinating activities with the other departments of CARDER.

5. Regular weekly plan of operations

The outline programme in → Figure 2 applies to the whole year. Deviating from this programme should only be allowed when absolutely necessary and with the

Figure 2:

Model outline programme for planning operations over one week					
	Monday	Tuesday	Wednesday	Thursday	Friday
RDR	Office	Office	Office	Office	Office
	Committees Policies	Supervision of Chefs CVA	Committees Meetings	Supervision of Chefs CVA	Sector discussion
Special Advisers	Office or discussions	Field visits by request or according to their own monthly programme			Sector discussion
Chef CVA	CVA discussion Further training of advisers	Supervision of advisers in the field			Sector discussion
	Office			Office	
Advisers to co-operatives	CVA discussion Further training Discussion in the Sector	Cooperative 1,2	Cooperative 3,4	Cooperative 5	Cooperative 6
				Office	Held in reserve
Field Advisers	CVA discussion Further training	Visits to groups 1,2	Visits to groups 3,4	Visits to group 5	Visits to group 6
	Office			Office	Held in reserve

full knowledge of the Intendants. Thus every single member of the organisation knows what he has to do and where he has to do it. Random checks can easily be carried out on all personnel. In their capacity as supervisors, senior staff have regular on-the-job contact with workers in the field.

6. Continuous flow of information in both directions (oral and written)

In no case should it take more than a week to deal with a problem, since a regular flow of information is guaranteed by the organisational structure shown in → Figure 3. Efficient top-level management is only possible if there is a system of feedback that functions without disruption.

Figure 3:

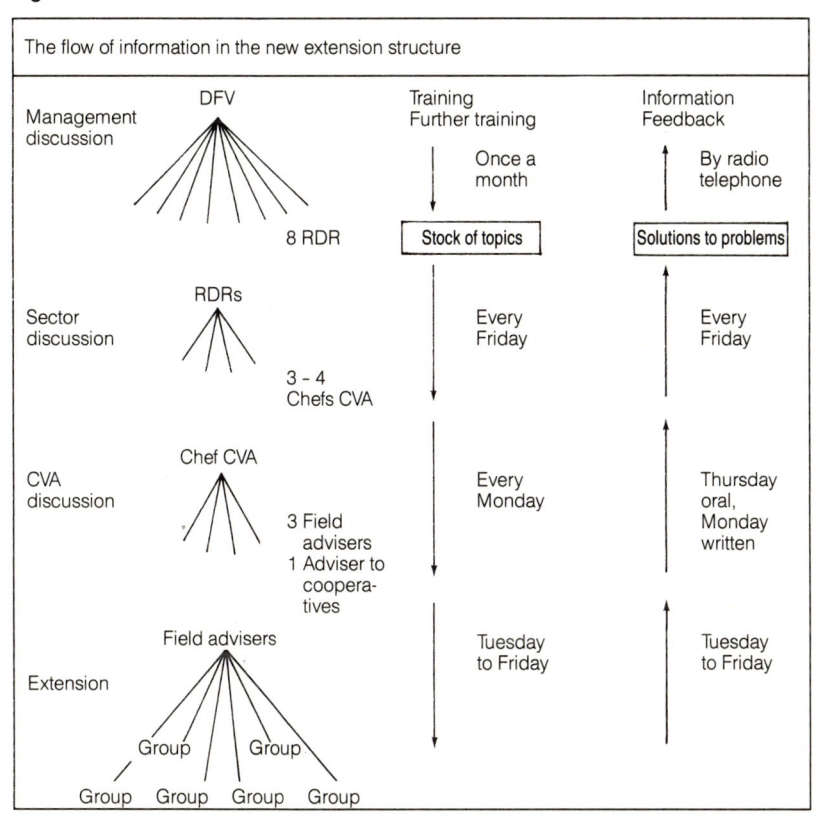

The flow of information in the new extension structure			
Management discussion	DFV (8 RDR)	Training / Further training	Information Feedback
		Once a month ↓	↑ By radio telephone
		Stock of topics	**Solutions to problems**
Sector discussion	RDRs (3-4 Chefs CVA)	Every Friday ↓	↑ Every Friday
CVA discussion	Chef CVA (3 Field advisers, 1 Adviser to cooperatives)	Every Monday ↓	↑ Thursday oral, Monday written
Extension	Field advisers (Group Group Group Group Group Group)	Tuesday to Friday ↓	↑ Tuesday to Friday

B 5

7. Planned order of topics for plant production

For plant production a sequence of topics is planned that builds up over 3 years and aims to achieve the maximum diffusion. This sequence is shown in → Table 1.

Table 2:

The scheduled order of topics for plant production		
Year	Topic	Aim
1	Mineral fertiliser, spray insecticide on beans, improved seed for maize and beans…	To gain the confidence of the farmers by addressing a few topics that lead to a definite increase in yield and whose effects are clearly visible. Adoption is also made easier by credit for production inputs to accelerate the diffusion process.
2	(Mineral fertiliser, seed) rotation, green manuring, improving the fallow, yam cropping…	To diversify the topics of extension and to introduce more complex topics.
3a	(Mineral fertiliser, seed) rotation, diversifying cropping, green manuring, improving the fallow, rows of trees and hedges…	Concentration on ecological topics that stress the maintenance of soil fertility and other essentials of production.
3b	Ox teams, grain hopper with fumigation facility	To introduce topics that call for high investment and therefore high levels of credit but also promise high profit from rationalisation as an additional incentive to adopt the ongoing innovations.

8. The development of new extension topics

Since it soon became apparent that the work could not be carried out by the national and international research centres, a whole range of methods and institutions was created in stages to devise new extension measures in CARDER de l'Atlantique. Ideas on farming systems research and on-farm research were the guiding principles as the research and development initiative was created (compare → A 10). In → Figure 4 we see the stage reached by 1986.

Figure 4:

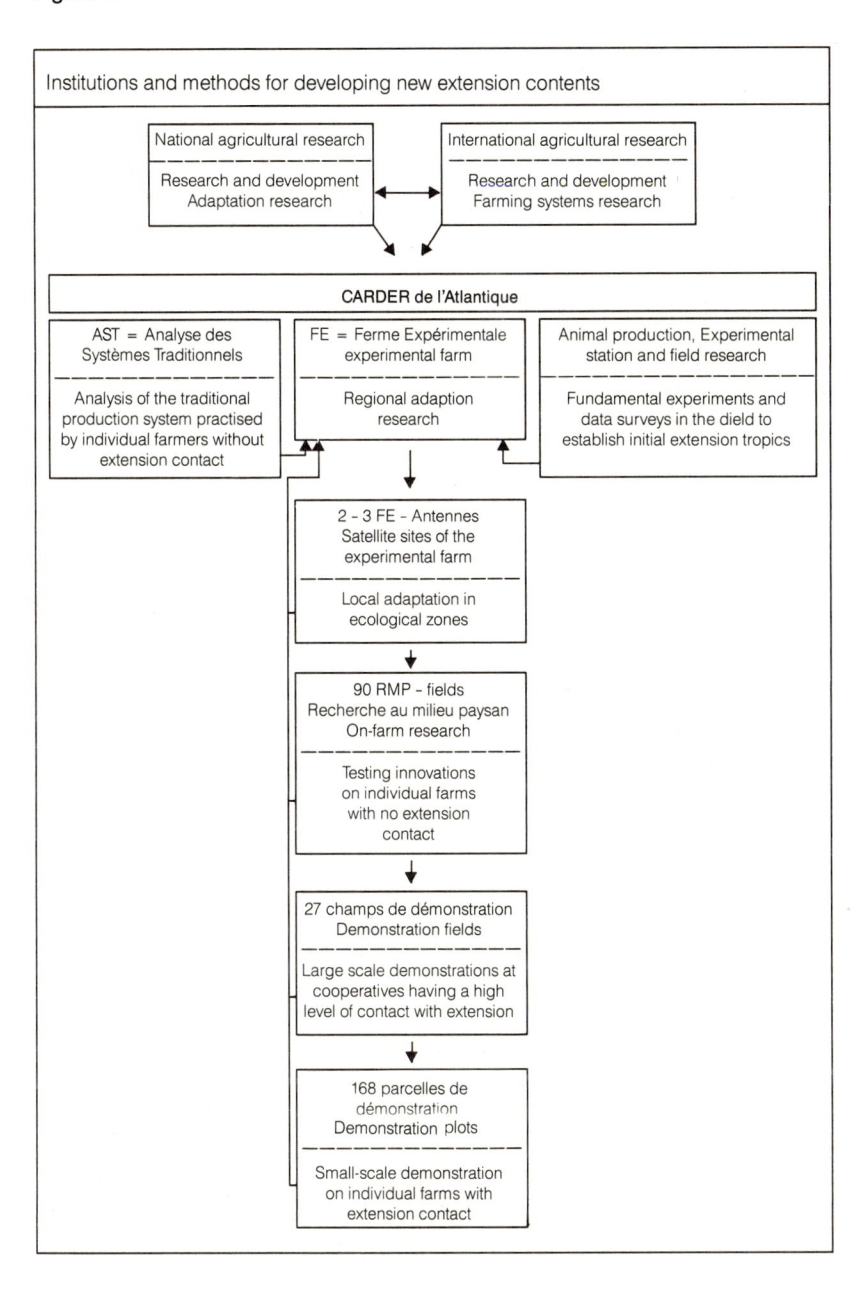

Institutions and methods for developing new extension contents

National agricultural research
Research and development
Adaptation research

International agricultural research
Research and development
Farming systems research

CARDER de l'Atlantique

AST = Analyse des Systèmes Traditionnels
Analysis of the traditional production system practised by individual farmers without extension contact

FE = Ferme Expérimentale experimental farm
Regional adaption research

Animal production, Experimental station and field research
Fundamental experiments and data surveys in the dield to establish initial extension tropics

2 – 3 FE – Antennes Satellite sites of the experimental farm
Local adaptation in ecological zones

90 RMP – fields Recherche au milieu paysan On-farm research
Testing innovations on individual farms with no extension contact

27 champs de démonstration Demonstration fields
Large scale demonstrations at cooperatives having a high level of contact with extension

168 parcelles de démonstration Demonstration plots
Small-scale demonstration on individual farms with extension contact

B 5

9. Further development of extension methods

Just as the topics for the farmers should develop from simple advice showing quick returns to complex questions, extension methods also undergo a change.

At the beginning, clear technical information and simple weekly instructions are enough. With this approach the aims of extension in the first year can be attained, and it is in keeping with the field advisers' level of training. But this method becomes less and less suitable as the target groups themselves change in the course of time. It then becomes essential to give intensive training and careful attention to approach if the communication of extension is to be improved. → Table 2 shows the main development of method.

Table 2:

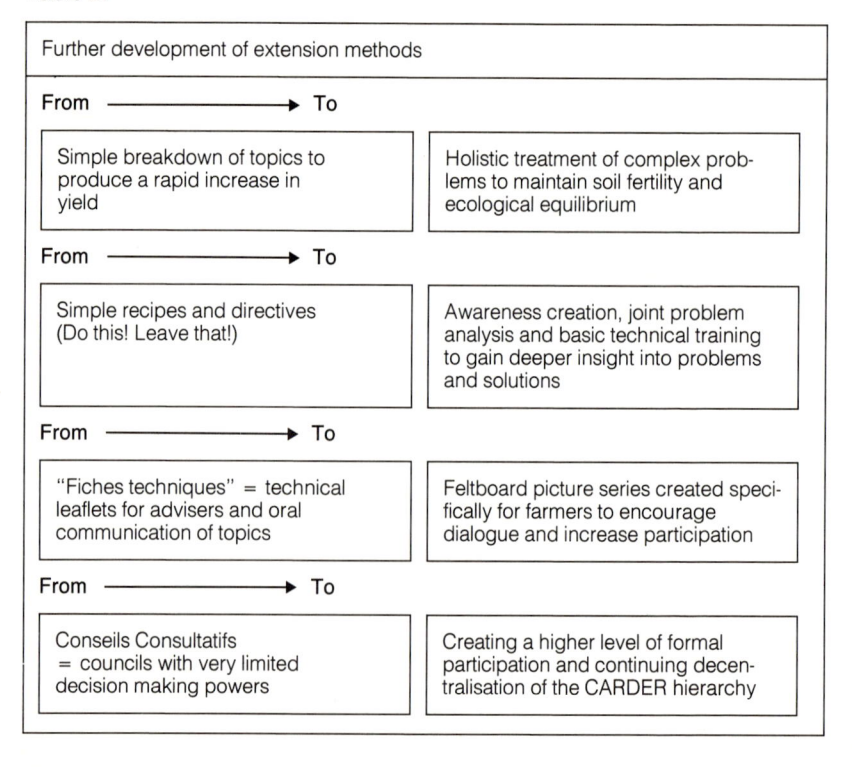

Further development of extension methods	
From ⟶	To
Simple breakdown of topics to produce a rapid increase in yield	Holistic treatment of complex problems to maintain soil fertility and ecological equilibrium
From ⟶	To
Simple recipes and directives (Do this! Leave that!)	Awareness creation, joint problem analysis and basic technical training to gain deeper insight into problems and solutions
From ⟶	To
"Fiches techniques" = technical leaflets for advisers and oral communication of topics	Feltboard picture series created specifically for farmers to encourage dialogue and increase participation
From ⟶	To
Conseils Consultatifs = councils with very limited decision making powers	Creating a higher level of formal participation and continuing decentralisation of the CARDER hierarchy

10. Requirements of materials and infrastructure

1. Buildings

    a) Required: 29 storerooms
                           29 CVA buildings with 2 offices, 1 room for meetings
    b) Already available: 16
    c) New buildings: 13
    d) Converted buildings: 6

2. Furniture

    a) Required: 5 tables, 10 chairs, 10 benches (per CVA)
    b) Purchased: 145 tables, 290 chairs, 190 benches

3. Materials:

    a) Required by CVA: 1 pair of scales (300 kg), 1 pair of scales (20 kg), 3 ULV sprays, 1 backspray, 1 board with felt reverse side, 1 seed-dusting drum
    b) Purchased: 29 large scales, 24 small scales, 77 ULV sprays, 29 backsprays, 29 boards, 29 seed-dusting drums

4. Vehicles

    a) Required: RDR: 7 cars, 7 mobylettes
                   Special advisers: 35 motorbikes
                   Intendants in the sectors and the CVAs: 36 mobylettes
                   Chefs CVA: 29 motorbikes
                   CC, CVA: 29 mobylettes
                   AVA, CVA: 87 mobylettes
    b) Purchased: 86 mobylettes (plus regular purchase of spare parts for all vehicles)

5. Introduction of primes/indemnités

   = a bonus system + reimbursement (especially subsistence and petrol costs)

B 5

11. Staff requirements

→ Figure 5 shows the staffing plan. The result is selection, transfer or dismissal of 50 staff by the ministry.

Figure 5:

Staffing plan for the new extension structure

1. Requirements
 	
 a) in the 7 sectors
 	
  51   7 RDRs, 7 Intendants, 35 special advisers
 	
 b) in the 29 centres
 	
  174   29 managers, 29 Intendants, 87 field advisers, 29 advisers to cooperatives
 ———
  225
  ===

2. Existing establishment
 	
 a) in the 7 sectors
 	
  7 RDRs
  7 Intendants
  24 Special advisers
 	
 b) in 35 sub-sectors
 	
  35 Chefs sous-secteur
  117 Chefs centre (including 30 female advisers)
 	
 c) Others
 	
  70 former workers from disbanded state companies (SOBEPALH, SONIAH)
  15 available at headquarters level
 ———
  275
  ===

3. Balance   Available 275 ▽ Needed 225   Surplus 50

12. Cost of the new extension system

In the first 26 months of operation the new extension system cost DM 625 000 per annum (→ Table 3). However, these figures have little meaning unless we put them into a comparative context.

Table 3:

Total cost of the new extension system over 26 months (from 10/1983 – 12//1985 in DM)			
Donors	Investment	Operating costs	Total
RPB		994 800	994 800
FRG	343 000	84 500	358 500
Total	343 000	1 010 500	1 353 500

What is perhaps more interesting is the "unit cost" per contact between a field adviser and a group member, which is shown in → Table 4. Organisations whose bookkeeping enables them to calculate such a figure can make their own comparisons. The fact that the cost per contact by an adviser fell by about a third between 1984 and 1985 can be explained by the number of extension contact groups rising from 4 to 6 after the system had been introduced and the teething troubles had been overcome.

Table 4:

Annual "unit costs"		
	1984	1985
Running an extension centre CVA	20 356	23 205
1 contact between field adviser and group member	2.70	1.84

13. Success of extension: major campaign – maize

One year after the new extension system had become fully operational, a follow-up evaluation study undertaken by management at Province level of 624 farms (of which 234 were members and 390 non-members of extension groups) showed

B 5

how attractive the innovations were as soon as improved seed had been adopted (→ Table 5). It also revealed how cost-effective the extension input was even in the first year in respect of maize, which as the main crop occupies some 90% of the arable land in the Atlantic Province (→ Table 6).

Table 5:

The yield potential of innovations (on-farm measurements)		
Method	Av. yield in kg/ha	Av. yield increase in kg/ha
1. Traditional cropping, broadcast sowing and untreated local seed	1 115	
2. Row seeding, weeded twice, untreated local seed	1 280	165 = 15%
3. Improved seed, treated + 2	1 629	514 = 46%
4. Improved seed, treated, mineral fertiliser + 2	2 916	1 287 = 115%

Table 6:

Production increase achieved by adopting innovations							
Innovation, Method	Direct effect on extension farmers			Indirect effect on non extension farmers			Total effect in t
	Area	Adoption rate	Production increase	Area rate	Adoption increase	Production	
2.	11 500 ha	13.5%	256 t	66 650 ha	–	–	256 t
3.	11 500 ha	19.0%	1 647 t	66 650 ha	7%	2 398 t	4 045 t
4.	11 500 ha	6.25%	925 t	66 650 ha	0.5%	429 t	1 354 t
Total	–	–	2 828 t	–	–	2 827 t	5 655 t

The extra return for the farmers thus works out at 5 655 t x 60 FCFA/kg = 339 300 000 FCFA. This equals 380% of the annual cost of the extension system (89 240 800 FCFA), ignoring the results of the short season! And this was achieved after just one year with the new organisational structure. By increasing the number of extension groups by 50% in the following year (from 4 to 6 groups per field adviser), a still better relation between costs and returns was created.

This balance improves only slightly as more extension recommendations are adopted. In the future we can expect the cost effectiveness of the extension input to increase steadily because innovations affecting maize may well be taken up more and more spontaneously, so that no extra extension costs are incurred. Only the services for the purchase and sale of seed and mineral fertiliser and the marketing of maize increase more or less proportionately to the adoption of innovations.

Sources:

CARDER Atlantique, DFV: L'organisation de la vulgarisation agricole dans la province de l'Atlantique. Cotonou, 1985

CARDER Atlantique, DSEI: Enquete rendement maïs, grande saison 1985. Enquête spécifique No. 3. Cotonou 1985

CORREZE,A., HOFFMANN,V., LAGEMANN, J., MACK,R.P., NEUMANN,I., YEBE, C.: Evaluation du Projet CARDER de l'Atlantique, République Populaire de Bénin. Unpublished appraisal for the GTZ, Eschborn, 1986

Compiled by:

Volker HOFFMANN

Minka – the evolution of a peasants' newspaper in Peru

We now show the lessons learned from producing a newspaper for farmers that was intended to back up improved agricultural extension in the Andes in Peru. Our intention is to draw attention to the methods that were found to be effective but also to the mistakes that were made, so that the reader can avoid the same pitfalls.

A. Evolution and aims

Since 1979 the group "Talpuy" has been publishing the newspaper "Minka" at three-monthly intervals for the farmers of the Mantaro Valley in the central highlands of Peru. "Talpuy", which in the Huanka language means "to sow", is one of the regional, non-governmental organisations that was founded in the 1970's to compensate for the lack of state development aid for farmers. A characteristic of the "Talpuy" group is their critical attitude to conventional development policy and their search for alternatives, which has to be seen in the following context:

- For 25 years the official Peruvian extension service had little success in disseminating and implementing development models and extension methods that had been applied worldwide.

- Between 1968 and 1975 the extension service was replaced by an ideological, state-run system with the aim of mobilising farmers and integrating them in a national modernisation process.

- Since the end of the 1970's foreign extension models have again been applied.

Despite three decades of intensive extension work, the rural population has hardly been touched by innovations. At the same time poverty and social disintegration have increased.

Because of this state of affairs, "Talpuy", a registered association of ethnologists and art teachers, resolved to support agricultural development by means of research and counselling and to encourage initiative and creativity in the peasant population. This aim was the product of the debate on the role of technology in rural development aid, which is summarised in the first issue of "Minka".

B 6

"The technology that is still being supplied in rural communities ignores the collective efforts of farmers and only serves to exacerbate the structural, economic and political crisis. We, on the other hand, show that alternative development can be achieved by mobilising the technological and social forces that have been shaped by experience in farming communities" (Minka, No. 1, 1979).

B. Why was Minka necessary?

The debate focussed attention on one of the obstacles preventing the development of small farmers, namely the lack of technical information or the spread of useless information. "Minka" (in Huanka: "work for the community") intended to remedy this deficiency. The newspaper takes account of the following features of the population in the Mantaro Valley:

- About half (200 000) live in the countryside.

- The livelihood of these highland farmers is based on a combination of commercial and subsistence agriculture, cattle rearing and trades. Farm incomes are supplemented by men leaving to work in the mines or in the capital, Lima.

- The social structure of the rural population of the Mantaro Valley comprises both village communities (312 in all) and extended families.

- 70% of the rural population have attended school and can read and write (according to the official statistics).

- The rural population are either bilingual (Huanka and Spanish) or have Spanish as their mother tongue.

- The majority of the population have a high regard for the written word, like the Bible or the laws. For example, a written record of the minutes of all village meetings is kept in the village register and signed by everyone in attendance.

- Cultural features like regional costume, skilled handicrafts and traditional celebrations are important aspects of life.

C. The first edition, a clear failure

The first "Minka" employed the following ideas and methods:

B 6

The title page → picture 1 has five messages:

1. dyeing with alder
2. sowing vegetables
3. more milk for my baby
4. layout of a house
5. the natural cycle

Picture 1:

The following reactions of farmers to the title page were recorded:

— "All very interesting, but which is the most important?"
— "Who is that working, where is it, what is he doing?"
— "What are those clocks at the end supposed to mean?"
— "Who is that on the photograph?"

The article: "Dyeing with alder", → picture 2, is a set of instructions, logically ordered:

A. proportions of dye and wool
B. production of the dye
C. preparation of the wool
D. dyeing
E. achieving the required depth

Farmers' reactions:

— "How does it work? How are we supposed to read that?"
— "Where does it begin?"

The article: "More milk for my baby", → picture 3, was in the form of a comic strip. It shows a peasant mother who is afraid that her newborn son could die like her first child. In the dialogue with her husband, they both state that her sister has very healthy children. The following day the sister comes and says: "You haven't got much milk because you are too weak. You must eat meat and eggs and drink milk". And the conversation continues like this. The sister, who is obviously to be emulated, first points out that everything the inexperienced mother is doing is wrong and she then informs her how she should feed her child properly and what food she should give it.

Farmers' reactions to this comic strip:

— "We are not so stupid that we would treat our children like that."
— "And we don't look funny like them, either."

B 6

Picture 2:

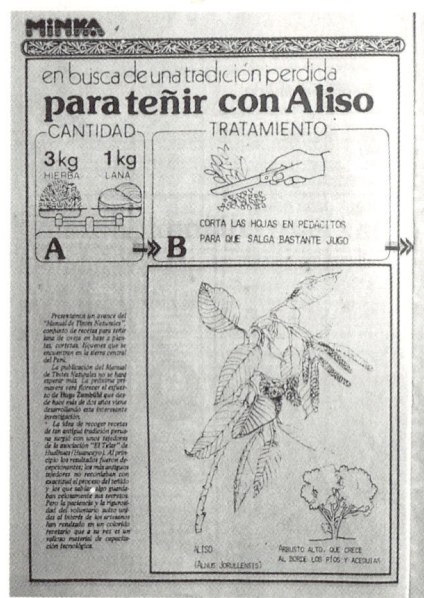

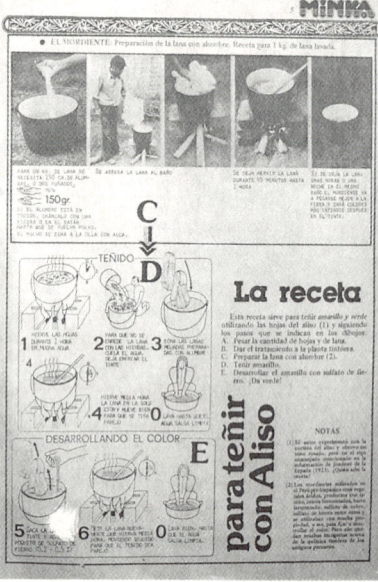

Picture 3:

Picture 4:

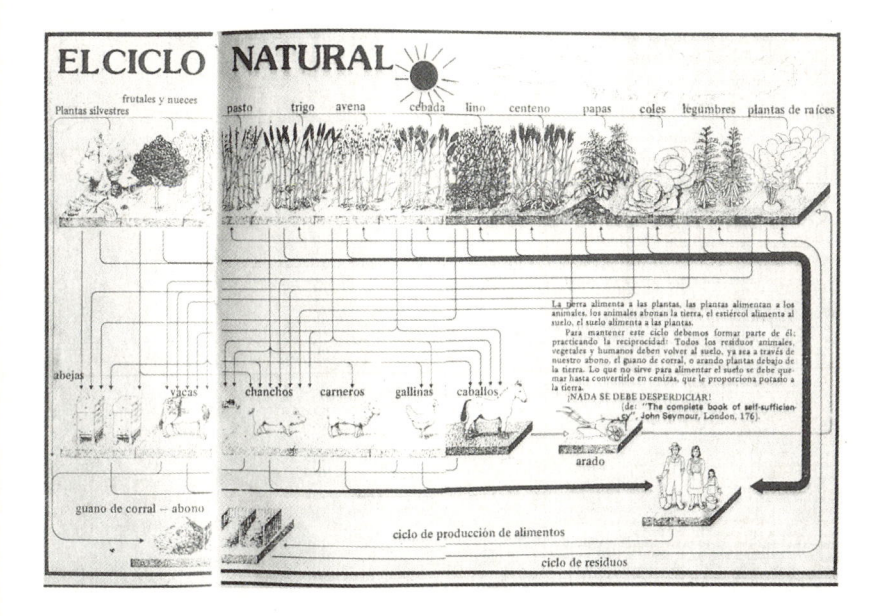

![El Ciclo Natural diagram]

The drawing of the "natural cycle", → picture 4, reproduces on a reduced scale an illustration by the English author John Seymour, and using thick and thin arrows it shows the interaction between plants, animals and human beings.

All the farmers interviewed found this drawing utterly confusing.

The article: "Layout of a house", → picture 5, suggests how farmers' houses can be improved by planning, the main considerations being how much space families need, the number of bedrooms, size of the kitchen, arrangement of the furniture, cupboards and doors. These features are illustrated in sketches drawn to scale.

The farmers made comments like:

- "Our houses don't look like that."

- "If we want to build our own houses, we don't need to draw pictures. We know what to do and where and how."

- "Where is the cattle shed?"

- "We only need one bedroom."

B 6

— "The thing that really matters is organising help by the rest of the family, not drawing pictures."

Analysis: the basic mistakes

By analysing the farmers' comments and thinking about the issues, the "Talpuy" group (editors, graphic artists) were able to identify basic errors of approach.

The first "Minka" paper was one-sided in its choice of topics and style of illustration.

Even though the subjects dealt with were of general relevance to farmers, the actual choice and treatment of topics were determined by the expertise and the criteria of urban professionals. This is why some articles read like lectures instructing the farmers how to grow vegetables, feed children, plan houses, dye wool and interpret nature.

The graphics were based on such conventional illustrative devices as arrows, a work process shown in separate stages, house plans, scale drawings, sketches and comic strips that were alien to the farmers and prevented them from understanding the messages. The frequently used comic strip called forth a hostile reaction; It was impossible for farmers to identify with the caricatures that were supposed to represent them.

Picture 5:

D. The second edition: the first enquiries

The composition and the line taken in the next "Minka" were determined by the farmers' reactions and other feedback from development workers. The leader expressed the opinion of a farmer:

– "Do we need help from outside or can we solve our own problems? It is difficult to decide. Sometimes we can't tell, but we do carry out experiments and take note of new techniques. Now we have got to increase our knowledge because there is still a lot to do. In our village community we have a great deal to learn and a great deal of work lies ahead of us." ("Minka", No. 2).

The point is made emphatically that the flow of information should no longer be in one direction only. The farmers' own experience should be taken into account as an ongoing experiment in the critical processing of information.

Picture 6:

For example, the second edition of "Minka" had a key issue on its title page: "Is mechanisation progress, and if so, for whom?" (→ picture 6). To illustrate the theme, there is a picture of two oxen pulling a tractor with several men standing behind it. This is an authentic photograph.

The title page was intended to be a critical introduction to the problem of mechanisation. The following articles appeared in this edition:

– "How much does a tractor cost?"
– "Useful life below the surface of the earth."
– "The apprentice plough-boy and the wild bull."
– "Description of a simple plough."
– "Mama Jashi and nutrition in farming families
– "El Rhuki, an old, traditional spade."
– "Growing potatoes."

Picture 7:

El aprendiz de gañan y el toro chúcaro

Por Jesús Lindo Revilla

Don Aquilino es el "trome" del arado en Huarisca; Roque, su hijo mayor tiene buenas cualidades y pretende ser gañán. Hoy, es la doble prueba: probarán al "Mulush" (toro chúcaro) en la punta derecha, al lado del "Yana", novillo experimentado en la punta zurda y por si acaso estará la vecina Lucía como guía, adelante.

Previa las recomendaciones de Don Aquilino, Roque santiguándose arranca con "fierro a fondo" y... empieza el "correteo" ... ¡Lucía, ataja!, grita Roque... ¡pisa el arado!, ordena Don Aquilino... no mires tanto a Lucía, concéntrate en el arado... Los surcos parecen culebras, pero ahí va...

Háblale al toro —replica Don Aquilino; "Chuta, chuta... parejo Ukju"... "Vuelta, vuelta... niño" y Roque va tomando seguridad: "Shoush... Soó... jala derecho negro"... "Chuta derecho mulush".

Por fin, la yunta obedece a Roque, y todo contento Don Aquilino le dice: "Ahora que has dominado el 'Mulush', y sabes hacer un surco derecho... puedes pensar en casamiento con Lucía..."

The farmers' reactions to this edition were:

- They asked what the terms 'mechanisation' and 'progress' meant on the front page. They thought the photographs were absurd, illogical and unrealistic. They missed the irony in the picture.

- They made few comments on the articles dealing with tools used by farmers.

- When groups of farmers tried to evaluate the comic strips, they could not understand them, even though the illustrations of people were more realistic in this edition.

- But people in the village communities can still recall "Minka" today on account of the illustrated story "The apprentice ploughboy and the wild bull" (→ picture 7).

Analysis

This edition of "Minka" was equally incomprehensible and failed to communicate, but this time on a different level. Whereas the content and form of the messages in the first edition were formulated from the standpoint of the sender and were simply presented for consumption by the uninitiated, in the second edition the receivers of the messages were involved in the communication process. All the articles were directed at a clearly defined readership of farmers. The messages are formulated not only **for** farmers, but also **about** farmers.

Analysis of the positive reception of the illustrated story underlines the components necessary to communicate an important message:

- The title used colloquial language and drew on the common experience of peasant farmers.

- The text was supplemented by exciting pictures.

- The topic was treated with the kind of humour that appealed to the farmers.

- The active involvement of the farmer is crucial. He tells his own story as a real person in his own natural and social environment. Above all, the article reflects the farmers' perception of a familiar occurrence.

The later editions of "Minka" followed these guidelines, but there were still problems again.

E. The third edition: symbolism, perception, cognition

Picture 8:

The subject of the third edition was drought (→ picture 8), introduced by the very direct title: "Is there a shortage of water?" The illustration shows the consequences of a lack of water. The rays of the sun on the horizon beat down on a wilting maize plant in the foreground and the skull of a dead cow.

On the inside pages the articles describe ways of solving the problem in different rural regions of Peru and also take an example from China. One of the articles concentrates on a successful technological solution – a reservoir dating from the pre-Inca era.

By providing exact and detailed information, the articles were trying to draw the attention of the farmers to archaeological remains to illustrate how problems were solved in the past (→ picture 9).

The comic strip "Mama Jashi" emphasised the technological potential of farmers (→ picture 10).

The readers reacted very sceptically to the title page. The article about reservoirs in pre-Inca times was comprehensively rejected. The third attempt at using comic strips was again unsuccessful.

Analysis

The reason for the sceptical reaction to the picture on the front page of the paper was the misuse of features of the natural world that have a clear symbolic meaning in peasant culture. The sun, plants, earth and skull are recognisable motifs in themselves, but for the peasant they have a very precise significance. All these motifs belong to the sphere of magic, where a different logic applies. The sun, which in both Spanish and Huanka is masculine, always shines from high in the sky, whereas in this picture it shines from low down. The female force of the moon (feminine in Spanish and Huanka) ought to be placed next to the male power of the

Picture 9:

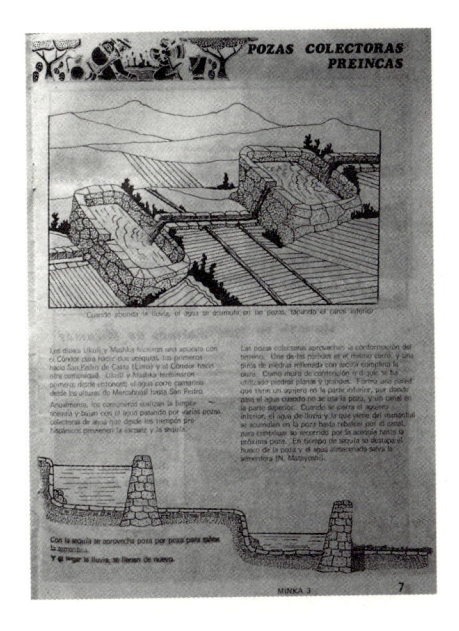

Picture 10:

sun, but the moon was not shown at all in the picture. In the symbolic thinking of the farmers, the realm of death is beneath the earth; the surface is the setting for human life, so that in the picture the representation of death is wrongly located in the sphere of the living on the earth.

We have here the wrong use of codes (units of meaning) in a message where the sender and receiver belong to different cultures.

Despite the unambiguous text and precise illustrations, the intended message was not communicated because it did not take account of the importance of symbolism in the peasants' perception of reality.

In the same way we can explain the rejection of the information about the pre-Inca water tanks, but in this case there is another factor as well. The symbolic level is not a complete explanation; it tells us more about social relations, living together in society. The article presents the pre-Inca water tanks as archaeological sites whose technical principles can be applied elsewhere, but for the farmers they are places occupied by the spirits of their forefathers whose presence is still felt today. This is the realm of the dead; this is where people communicate with the underworld. The spirits of the dead can both protect and punish, and for this reason these hallowed places are visited with respect, the visitor bringing his offering to placate his forefathers. This behaviour pattern is comparable with the esteem farmers have for their parents and grandparents. The social norm is founded on respect and mutual help, because peasant society is structured on blood-ties. Both these norms are ignored in this article, so that there is no communication with the peasant reader.

For the third time the comic format was not understood, and not simply because the illustration made people look ridiculous or because the subject matter was unfamiliar. By examining very carefully how the farmers read the comic strip, we came to the following conclusions:

- The comic form describes reality in glimpses: the illustrator starts with a wide-angle view and then zooms in for close-ups and detail.

- There are no transitions between one slice of reality and the next.

- The language is compressed so that statements will fit into the balloons; this reduces them to slogans.

These three aspects of presentation make the comic incomprehensible for the farmer, who, on the one hand, sees reality more globally and, on the other, in his use of language in a social context, spells out his meaning and creates humour by, for example, play on words. The rural population have not learned or absorbed fragmentation of reality and deduction, despite literacy campaigns and schooling.

The farmers have developed a holistic way of thinking, because they perceive nature as a series of cycles. Their mode of thought has its own ritualised forms of abstraction and cognitive structures that do not accommodate details torn from their context or shifts of focus without transition.

The way in which the language in comics is simplified conflicts with the use of language in peasant society. Despite the influence of school and mass media, oral communication remains the traditional way of passing on values and knowledge. Myths, stories, jokes and word-play shape communication in the social setting. The communicative ideal of the farmers is not brevity but using a rich fund of expressions that call forth an emotional response from the listener.

Since this richness is not used in the comic strip, it is neither comprehensible nor attractive for the peasant reader.

F. The fourth edition, Small farmers' aesthetic values

Minka No. 4 appeared one year after the first edition, during which time many readers' letters and comments and criticisms by farmers and technical personnel encouraged the continued publication of the paper.

The title page announced the "Techniques and advantages of mixed crops".

The drawing on the front page provoked various reactions:

- Technical personnel and experts criticised the exaggerated dimensions of the house, because they said it was impossible to build a house like that with "adobes" (clay bricks).

- They also stated that details like the sun, moon, doves, flowers and fruit had nothing to do with the subject matter of the paper and would therefore only make it more difficult to understand.

- The same title page was "read" by the farmers, who identified the sun (father) and the moon (mother) as the guardians of the house and plants. For them the entwined plants corresponded to maize intermixed with beans and pumpkins.

Analysis

The illustration makes use of the peasants' idea of art to convey the message in con-

B 6

Picture 11:

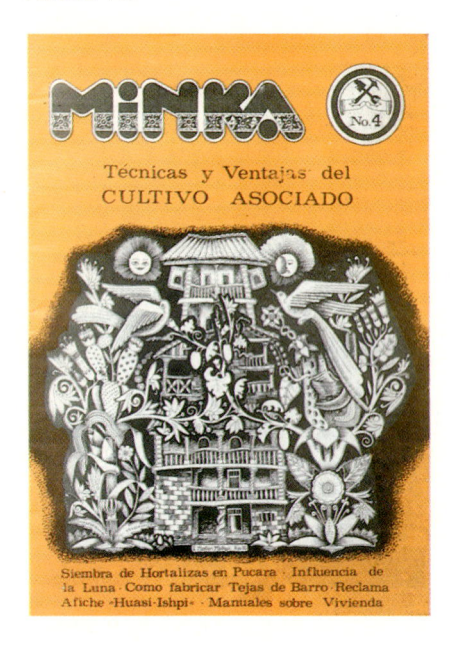

The main illustration is a drawing of a house with several storeys, round which several very large plants are entwined, crossing each other or joining in the middle. At the top left of the picture is the sun and at the top right the moon.

Underneath some of the contents are listed:

– Growing vegetables in Pucara

– Effects of the moon

– How are roof tiles made using clay?

– Send for the poster "Huasi Ishpi" (topping out ceremony in Huanka) (→ picture 12)

– Brochures on house building

crete terms. We can compare the composition of the picture on the title page with the embroidery on the skirts made by peasant women. The plant and house motifs occur in peasant art not only in embroidery but also in the work of silversmiths, pumpkin artists, weavers and potters in the villages of the Mantaro Valley. Crafts and farming go hand in hand and belong to the material and symbolic culture of the peasants in the highlands.

The same can be said of the poster "Huasi Ishpi Huanca", → picture 12, which also uses the peasants' aesthetic codes to make the illustration of the message as faithful to real life as possible. Also, the poster shows people in recognisable social interaction. The guardians of the new house are carrying the cross decorated with symbols, which is then placed on the roof. Friends and the whole family take part, symbolising the social origins of the family unit.

Building the house and then everyone involved celebrating with eating and music are the two sides of the same coin. The work on the house and the feast are two aspects of real life, and the poster would not be readily understood, or at least would be incomplete, if it failed to illustrate both aspects of peasant life.

Picture 12:

B 6

G. The fifth edition: Farmers' expertise

These methods of creating pictures and text were refined in the following editions of "Minka". We now look at the content of the text separately, although communication is in fact the combined effect of both text and pictures.

If we analyse the first edition of "Minka" from the point of view of content, we see that it attempts to deal with numerous, unrelated topics. This approach is then changed in the next few issues, resulting in fewer topics, but each is treated in several short articles. This change was made in response to the farmers' request for more information on the problems or subjects broached. The earlier treatment of topics like house building, mixed cropping, tools, vegetable cultivation and drought appealed directly to the farmers, but it was superficial and therefore unsatisfactory. Although the following "Minkas" contained more information supplied by the peasants themselves, the topics were still not dealt with in enough detail to satisfy the small farmers. By observing the reading habits of the farmers in the Mantaro Valley, it was established that:

The average farmer read the newspaper in the same way as other reading material, i.e. each article was read aloud in the family, after work in the fields had finished in the afternoon. The different generations (the old people, adults and children) all expressed their sometimes differing opinions on the articles.

On the other hand, they were in no hurry to finish reading "Minka", because there was not much reading material available on farming topics. Thus a family might spend two or three weeks reading and discussing one edition. But the farmers found that the content of "Minka" was not sufficiently detailed for reading and discussion with the older generation over this length of time. The farmers turned this initial weakness of the paper into a benefit in later editions: in their dissatisfaction, some peasant "specialists" approached the editors to be interviewed and to demonstrate their (very detailed) knowledge.

Peasant specialists

It has become abundantly clear that there exists in peasant society a fund of knowledge that, instead of being written down, is stored and implemented by "specialists". These experienced farmers enjoy social recognition and are confirmed in their authority by other farmers. Their standing and prestige cannot be replaced by a newspaper or any other institution introduced into their society. As contact with these peasant specialists became more frequent, the topics in "Minka" became more relevant and the editorial team devised a new approach. Starting with Minka No. 5, emphasis was now placed on one central topic that drew on the expertise of the peasant specialists and was therefore described in detail and examined in depth.

Picture 13:

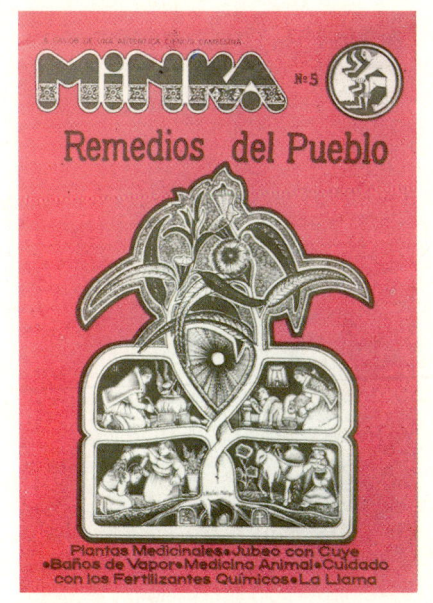

Minka No. 5 was produced with this new approach to subject matter, which in this case was "popular medicine", → picture 13. Various popular remedies are explained, from the use of selected curative plants to diagnosing diseases with the help of the "Jubeo con Cuy" (the guinea-pig diagnosis → picture 14).

This article deserves special attention because when it was published it had a dynamic effect, leading to a further clarification of the role of peasant knowledge.

The article shows in detail both the ritual and technical approach used by a healer to identify what disease her patient is suffering from.

She uses a live guinea pig that she rubs over the body of the patient to locate the disease. Then she kills the animal, cuts it open and "reads" the entrails to see what is wrong with her patient. The illness may be the result of a spell cast by a witch-doctor or of not paying his tribute (money) to the forces of nature, i.e. he has disrupted the balance between this world and the supernatural world. As soon as the healer has recognised the source of the illness, she announces how it should be treated.

The first edition of "Minka" had a circulation of 2 000 copies, but by the fifth edition it had risen to 9 000, proving how much the interest of the peasants in the paper had increased. Their explanation of the paper's success was that diagnosis and cure of sickness by using a guinea-pig had been suppressed by doctors and medical personnel, whereas the paper gave this traditional method as much attention as other remedies.

What is noteworthy about this reaction is that peasant knowledge in the Andes had traditionally been dismissed as superstition, ideological distortion, folklore or pseudo-science, and the fact that the peasants were fully aware of this denigration. The positive reaction to an upgrading of peasant knowledge in "Minka" was a clear lesson, because it had been quite wrong to try and separate it from the system of beliefs and the social structure, both of which are fundamental to cultural and historical awareness in that society. By drawing attention to a remedy frowned upon in the towns, "Minka" touched on the central idea in the cultural world of the

Picture 14:

El Jubeo con Cuye

Somos concientes que nuestra cultura tradicional reúne una serie de conocimientos que por efectos de la dominación y dependencia han quedado estancados en su desarrollo y perfeccionamiento.

Tratamos a la memoria, la sabiduría popular de los pueblos pretende ser defensora de lo humano, de lo que otros llaman "la Ciencia" se ve incapacitada a afrontarlos. Al recordar métodos de la sabiduría popular pretendemos un camino para las clases populares en términos económicos como culturales.

EL JUBEO O HUYHUACHICO

Se conoce como el procedimiento de empatar el cuerpo de una persona enferma con un pequeño animal como el cuye, el conejo, cachorrito de perro, periquitos recién nacidos. "Chihuaco Malihua", sapo, etc. También se conoce con los nombres de: "restregado" cuando son frescos de vacunos, etc. El empleado traslado la enfermedad de una persona hacia el animal u objeto.

EL JUBEO O HUYHUACHICOJ CON CUYE

Dentro de nuestra cultura tradicional, al parecer, es la técnica mejor conocida por sus características curativas y preferencia. Cura enfermedades conocidas como el "chucho" (susto en los niños), "hatun" (enfermedad del hígado), "gentil", "chupado" (traducido como apero o resto de energías por parte de otras muertas de los siglos pasados enterrados en árboles muy antiguos), "pugujo", "mal aire", "ayna" (enfermedad al moleste repentino del cuerpo por causa del choque con gases estancados en pozas purificadas), "pacha" (susto por contacto con la tierra seca o "ayac chay" (susto por ver a un muerto), "rasca" (órganos fuera de su lugar), "nauta", "dolor de cerebro, enfermedad de los nervios etc.

EL CUYE A UTILIZAR

Preferentemente debe ser cuye negro, de edad y sexo acorde al paciente. Así, por ejemplo, para un bebé o "wawa" se requiere cuye de pocos días de nacido. Los mayores para los jóvenes y los mejores para adultos y ancianos. (Por razones humanitarias se deben usar los cuyes preñados).

LA PERSONA QUE JUBEA

Generalmente es una mujer, amenazada de una serie de prejuicios. Corre peligro la integridad física y mental, ya sea por los contagios de la enfermedad o la posibilidad de cambiar el mal hacia su persona ("cambio de suerte"). Por ello generalmente existe una lista de la curandera ("cuandera") que exige un salario económico. Se cobra la mejoría del paciente como acompañados del "valor" o genio, para él la mejoría a su domicilio por determinado camino y no por otras mientras y limosnas y, por su puesto, buena remuneración económica a algo equivalente a ello.

NOCHES DE JUBEO

Preferentemente deben ser los días Martes y Viernes a partir de las 12 de la noche, esto es la enfermedad del paciente es estacionaria, pero en casos extremos se procede a cualquier hora y día.

DESCRIPCION

Lugar y acto solemne al lado del enfermo. Una mesa fue de vela o candil o kerosene alumbra el escenario. Junto con coca y aguardiente. Ven y vienen la "Llipta", la "toca", la

cal o el azúcar para endulzar el "coca jacho" (bola de coca), entre los "chacchadores" (masticadores de coca). Alguien dice "Mara miquereho", es decir, la ayuda con disimulo comienza a efectuarse, el jarro con dolencia comienza a circular.

"Mas azúcar o toco dulce ¿nerviosamente comienzan el licor a que la curandera la tiraja, el agua florida, el ajenjo contrato. El cigarro y su humareda espesa y cavernosa, "ya una doce de la noche, dice la estas", pide la jubeadora, sobre y luego sopla en la barriga del cuye, así que con la mano un poco de vinagre con alcohol sobre la barriga y cintura del paciente. "Que pase sus males", "mal aires", "pena", "mal aire", y oíles. Con el cuye a mano y sobre la persona y mira, lo toma de las patitas, por las extremidades traseras y procede a emplear, por la parte anterior de los brazos, el cuerpo del enfermo primero por el brazo izquierdo y continuo con vientre y su extremidad inferior, voltea el cuerpo. Avanza hacia el pecho, el corazón, partes inferiores de la mandíbula, boca, frente, luego hace por el lado derecho del cuerpo. Para procesos al otro lado del trazo, espalda, cintura. En cada movimiento (estribillo), orina al animal. Deja el animal y lo casa la muerte. A veces ocurre que el cuye demora mucho para morir o a veces no muere lo que indica que la enfermedad no es de gravedad.

ANALISIS EN EL DESPOJO DEL CUYE

Terminando el empleado, la curandera hace que el enfermo se acoque totalmente y le deja su sabidura a varios acompañantes, especialmente a uno como responsable. Mientras tanto se retira a otra habitación contigua, juntamente con el cuerpo muerto del cuye ejecutando el trabajo ligero. Con el filo de un cuchillo, comenzando por masticar y tomar un poco de aguardiente. Limpiado algunos familiares cercanos al enfermo. Así está el aura de toda feroz la emoción. Se limpian los utensilios las interiores del cuye bordeando la cabeza del aguardiente. Ya arrancado el pelaje y las carnes del cuye para dejar el esqueleto, se puede ver las partes del cual se determina las fallas de las partes que están dañadas del cuerpo del cuye. Esta la piel y estos partes de la sangre muerta las encias, y algunos fundamentales, orinados a pacíficos debajo de la mandíbula y axilas superiores, el

corazón tremendamente inflamado con gran cantidad de sangre muerto, manchas bastantes en los pulmones, intestinos en mala posición que afecta al funcionamiento del corazón o hígado.

Entonces la curandera se concentra los partes afectadas del organismo: "hatun cuyeri, está mal del hígado", "sara chachu", "gentil" etc.

Los comentarios entre los asistentes hacen conocer los síntomas del paciente divulgan la madre a la curandera.

Mientras tanto alguien de sexo masculino se encarga de ir al corral o chara para realizar el entierro de los restos del cuye o en todo caso dueño de éste con un pan grande y cubrir hasta que este devorado todo.

Luego colocan herramientas el fierro activado debajo de la cama el paciente jubeado, o fracción de los raíles al reposo de la enfermedad si es posible durante 2 a 3 horas.

Generalmente después de esto la curandera entra (previa dosis de aguardiente), "cura el cuenta" juntamente con sus acompañantes "hasta el camino". El enfermo con los fieles familiares están al cuidado del enfermo. Mientras la curandera no puede servir jutamente el medio día, en protección de no cobrar con otro rumor del animal sacrificado.

En la mayoría de los casos los pacientes están bastante mal o en todo caso pacientes estar totalmente curado, con lo que psicológico lo más normal y sin contratiempos, tratando de no recoter el mal que ha sufrido.

Caben muchas preguntas sobre la dimensión explícita y diagnóstico del cuye, pero los comentos subjetivos del paciente, así en el caso de los niños.

Creemos que conocer profundamente, revalorizar y difundir la sabiduría popular es una noticia a favor del pueblo.

Ojo: Lo casa de bronquios, o neumonía no se debe aplicar el jubeo con cuye, ya que este raíz caso puede empeorar la enfermedad.

Emilio Mentor, Mollipul

Andean peasants, who felt they had been recognised and their society enhanced. This broke the ice.

From the point of view of communication, Minka No. 5 introduced a third stage that differed in quality from the previous editions:

The one-way flow of information that characterised the early editions (like a monologue) was followed by emphasis on the peasants' reactions (feedback). But this emphasis nevertheless still contained various technical proposals that the receiver was intended to adopt after they had first been decided on and developed by the sender (Minka). When the information was not understood and difficulties of feedback occurred, new approaches were tried in order to adapt the information to the receivers. In this way, elements of peasant aesthetics were incorporated, together with everyday expressions, basic concepts, symbolism and the peasants' personal perception of reality. This was continued until the fifth edition, at which point the receivers became the subjects of the communication process. The role and value of peasant knowledge were now recognised and the way in which messages could be communicated changed for both the sender and the receiver. The result was a dialogue, a process of mutual understanding in which the subject matter and the form of the message were no longer derived from unrelated aspects of peasant life but arose naturally from the socio-cultural process.

H. Later editions as topic-based newspapers

Using this method, the later editions of "Minka" are restricted to a single topic, for example, house building (No. 8), crops in the Andes (No. 10), the village community (No. 11), education in peasant society (No. 12), farm implements in the Andes (No. 13), vegetable cultivation in Pucara (No. 14).

Three positive points should be stressed from the experience of "Minka":

a) The peasants initiated a constant process of discussion, criticism and thinking about the topics, without the staff of "Minka" being directly involved.

b) Ways of developing written extension aids were devised.

c) Information about peasant culture and technology was gathered and disseminated.

I. The approach that was finally adopted:

The concept of "Minka" that applied in the "guinea-pig diagnosis" was given greater depth in subsequent numbers. After the initial didactic approach, handing down instructions to the peasants, "Minka" progressed to a communications strategy based on the appreciation of peasant culture.

With this strategy the local "Minka" team operated as follows:

1. On the basis of answers and discussions with farmers from the village communities, they put forward topics that could feature in later issues of "Minka". They decided on the next topic after considering the various possibilities (depending on peasant specialists, their own expertise).

2. By talking to farmers, problems and possibilities were investigated from the farmers' point of view, and then many farmers were interviewed.

3. The interviews obtained were critically evaluated by the editorial team, for example, with the question: "In what way is their culture being enhanced?"

4. The statements were collected, ordered and used in the illustrations, language and thinking of the paper. Peasants were asked for drawings and articles and these were then included in "Minka".

5. Before final decisions on layout and printing, random checks were made to see how effectual and readable pictures and texts were.

6. The paper was then printed at one of the local offset-printers.

7. A network of peasant distributors sold the paper in the villages.

8. Finally discussions were held with farmers and then the editorial team discussed and criticised the current issue to get ideas and suggestions for the following editions.

Using this approach, the "Minka" team tried to harness the following aspects of peasant culture and to work them into the content of the paper:

1. the holistic and unifying experience of the perceived world in contrast to the fragmentation that is characteristic of specialists;

2. the way the peasants in the Andes see themselves as taking the initiative in their society, experimenting and changing their techniques;

3. the ritualisation of the historical interaction between the individual, family and society, and between man and nature;

4. the perspective of peasant technology in the Andes that:

- uses knowledge, abilities, forms of labour and implements in a rich natural environment;

- reacts flexibly to local conditions and is adapted to specific situations;

- is communicated by specialists and is socially accessible;

- is a part of a material and symbolic system.

Photographs:

Volker HOFFMANN

Compiled by:

Maria Angelica SALAS de TILLMANN

B 6

Picture 15:

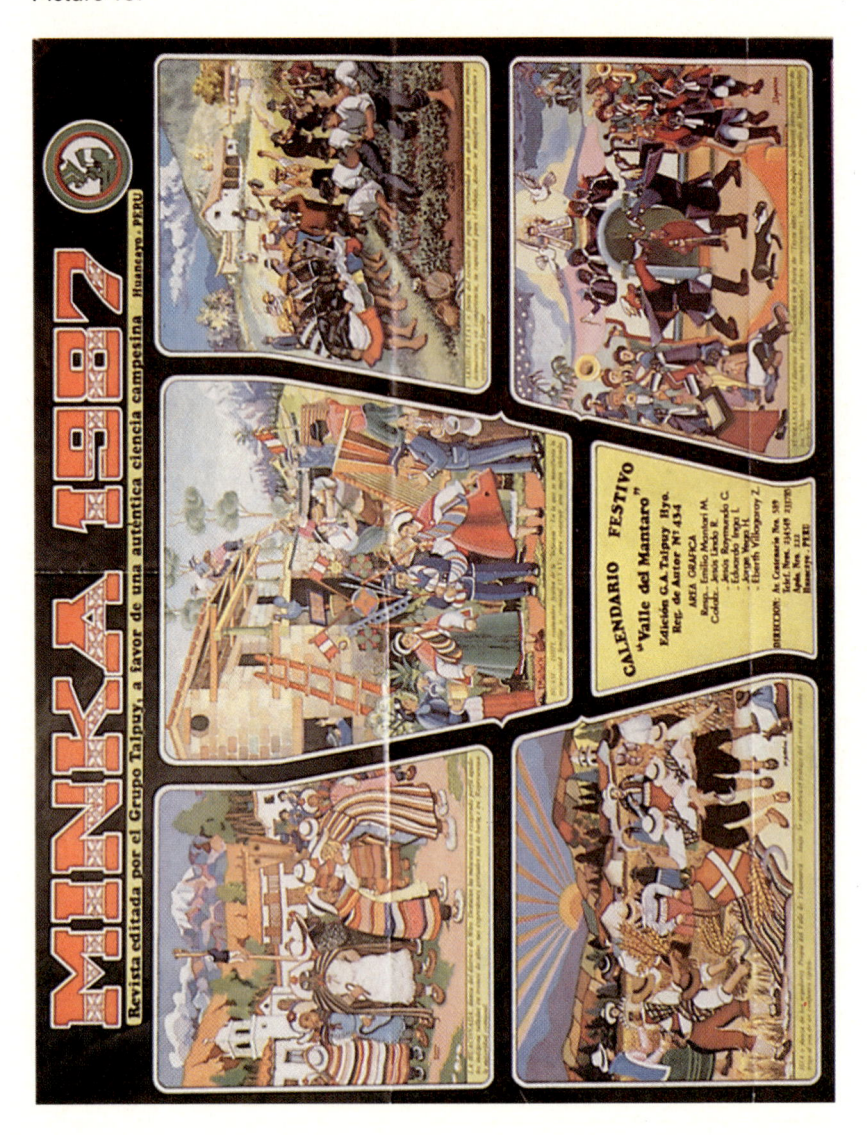

Description of recurring problems

"The Cow": an example of failure in intercultural communication

I am treating this working paper as if it was an oral presentation of the topic: "Extension and intercultural communication using a poster." An introduction and background information are felt to be unnecessary.

The poster reproduced on the next page was created and used in Egypt. Please take a careful look at it. Can you understand what it is trying to say? But of course it does not mean anything to you, because it is in Arabic. So it means as little to you as it does to most of the Egyptian peasants who it was produced for. They are illiterate. Maybe you can understand the two pictures without a text. Have a go!

If you were an Egyptian peasant, eager to know what the poster is saying, you could try to find someone to read it out for you. Perhaps one of your children could, if he has been to school. If he only went to the Koran school, he will have problems with some of the words. Maybe the village school teacher could read it for you, or the agricultural extension adviser, if you know him or come across him. If this were to happen, what you would find out is as follows (please look at the drawing on the next page but one). The small print on the lower edge of the poster, if you are sufficiently interested, tells you: (bottom right) Ministry of Agriculture, Headquarters of Agricultural Extension, Project for Agricultural Information; (bottom left) German – Egyptian Project El Nahda; Headquarters of Extension and Training; (bottom centre) Printed in the International Centre "Sirs Allian".

You may have understood the advice straightaway without having to read the text. But it is really only clear once you have sorted out the text. Egyptian peasants are in the habit of leading their cattle on a rope in a downright inconsiderate and inhumane way. They wind the rope round the horns and then again round one ear. This does not do the ears or the whole animal much good in the long run. It's all very obvious – a European halter ought to be used instead.

The whole topic may seem clear and basically very simple, and yet this wonderful poster is full of pitfalls if we care to look more closely. Perhaps we can spot some of them ourselves, but most of the difficulties only became apparent when the poster was held up in front of Egyptian farmers and they were asked to describe what they could see. We now list the critical points:

1. The "right" solution is in fact wrong

The graphic artist was an Egyptian, and he had obviously never tied a European halter. At the point where the loop round the animal's neck and the loop over the nose join at the side, they are knotted together so that the free end of the lead

كيفية ربط الماشية

| خطأ | صحيح |

العيوب

- تسبب آلام والتهابات وقطع بالأذن
- ضعف الشهية
- إنتاجية أقل

المميزات

- لا تسبب آلام ومريحة للحيوان
- شهية جيدة
- إنتاجية جيدة

should start here. In the picture the lead begins too high up, the knot near the mouth is wrong in the drawing and impossible to imitate. This is a fundamental error, but it pales into insignificance when we look further.

2. The red cross is particularly striking

Even if illiterate peasants merely glance at the picture, their attention is caught as if by magic by the red cross over the face of the cow on the right. They have never seen anything like it in their lives. The alienation principle, attracting attention by showing something familiar in a new light, and the eyecatching red do their duty. There is nothing strange like this about the cow on the left, and people pay it hardly any more attention. So the mistake in showing how the rope is tied is now relatively unimportant.

3. Wrong interpretation of the red cross

If we ask the farmers what the red cross means, they see two strange red ropes that mean nothing to them at all. Crossing out in red to show something is wrong is a typical symbol traditionally used in European schools where teachers correct in red. An illiterate cannot possibly be familiar with such conventions.

4. The tear misinterpreted

After the red rope, the farmers refer to the drop falling from the eye of the cow on the right. The cow is sick; it has a festering inflammation of the eye. This interpretation is absolutely correct, of course. Cattle cannot cry. Their tear mechanism does not convulse and empty when they feel pain. Logically, therefore, the connection between the tear, pain and a bleeding ear is absurd.

5. An appeal to pity is inappropriate

A central European, even though he knows about the anatomy of a cow's eye, will automatically see the discharge from the eye as a tear because he sees a connection with the bleeding ear. Blood and tears are such closely related concepts, linked by the idea of pain, that in the context of love of animals they immediately give rise to pity. But love of animals is for the most part alien to Egyptian culture. The peasant farmer regards his cow and his donkey as objects in the same way as his plough and his house. If his cow loses an ear, it only means that he has to tie the rope on the other side. This makes the cow just as useful as it was before.

C 1

HOW TO TIE A HALTER TO CATTLE

correct way	wrong way
ADVANTAGES	DISADVANTAGES
● does not hurt	● causes pain and inflammation
● is comfortable	● cuts the ear off
● normal appetite	● poor appetite
● good production	● low production
very small print	very small print

very small print

6. Misinterpretation of the breed of cattle

Although the artist definitely took the local breed of cattle as his model, the farmers said they saw two black and white cows on the poster. They remained convinced of this despite the fact that the basic yellow brown clearly pointeded to a local breed. The shaded areas were interpreted by the farmers as patches of black, which never occurred in the local breed. Local cattle were always of one colour only. Cattle with more than one colour had to be Friesians therefore. They had become familiar with them through the activities of the neighbouring "Cattle Breeding Project El Nahda" that had organised slide shows and film evenings on

Friesians. And who else but the Germans would think of printing and hanging up posters? The combination with yellow may be not quite right, perhaps you do see cows like that sometimes, but there is no doubt that the cows on the poster are Friesians from Germany.

7. No connection between halters, health and "production"

The farmers cannot follow the connection established by the text. The word "production" is a foreign word in Arabic, too. Even if it is spelled out in terms of milk and meat, that does not help much either. It is true that the farmer now knows what is meant, but it does not concern him because he does not use his cow for "production". He needs it for work, for cultivating his fields. Milk is used primarily for raising calves. The family will consume 2 – 3 litres a day if there is any left over. There is practically no local and certainly no wider market for milk. There is limited sale of home-made cheese. Fattening cattle is practically the preserve of larger landowners. The farmer will only sell his cow when it is no longer capable of working. Healthy or sick, what difference does it make? Selling an old cow cannot be termed meat production. The local breed is tough, placid and hardy, and a bleeding or festering ear is not a worse condition than tick infestation or extreme shortage of fodder in the summer drought. The cows carry on working, come what may.

8. "Wild animals" need strong handling and control

The farmers were inclined to overlook the European halter on the poster, but, if they were specifically asked about it during interviews, they had clear reasons for rejecting it. The halter might well be suitable for the placid Friesians but would be useless with the lively and often wild local animals. This is not an objectively valid statement, nor is it merely the product of an understandable local pride. When Friesians first appeared in the village, they were presumably well fed, had plenty of fodder and were about twice the weight of the local cattle. Perhaps they were weary because of the summer sun in Egypt (though they can tolerate it much better than expected), and finally they would have been led by a European halter in the strong hand of a German master dairyman. It is not surprising, then, that they looked especially mild-tempered.

How different the local breed! They are only well fed in the spring after a lush and rainy winter season which, according to rotation, produces fresh Alexandrine clover every day in the fields. But over the summer they are reduced to skin and bone, fed only on rice straw, water and any greenery growing by the tracks at the side of ditches and canals of the irrigation system, and on harvest residues and weeds that sprout between harvest and the next sowing. Moreover they have to compete with donkeys, sheep and camels. With an average of 2 ha of irrigated cropping land, the peasant family's own needs mean that fodder cropping in summer is out of the question.

The result of this is that the animals have to be taken out to graze every day in the summer. They are not led by men, however, but by little children who are under school age and are still too young to work in the fields. I myself have often seen 6 – 8 year old girls walking with up to three cows from the village to the fields. And if a cow played up, a quick jerk on the rope was enough to bring it to heel.

9. Confirmation of the "wrong" solution

All these various points combine to create an overall impression of the poster; they influence and endorse each other. It can be no surprise to learn then that the majority of farmers summed up their reactions with: "How are we supposed to tie a halter to cattle? As in the picture on the right, of course! Even the Germans think this method is best for their Friesians."

Their conclusions give the story a kind of happy ending and perhaps we should be grateful for this outcome. It saved the numerous, respectable institutions named in the small print from losing face, at least in the eyes of the less educated small farmers.

But if there is still any doubt about how to put a rope on a cow in Egypt, a visit to Sakkara, behind the pyramids of Gizeh near Cairo, is recommended. There you can see the tombs with their wonderful friezes in low relief showing among other things rural life in Egypt 4 000 years ago. They show, in such natural detail that we can imitate it today, how halters were put on cows long ago. And for good reason!

Postscript

Since there was no introduction, a postscript would appear appropriate.

1. Correction

For maximum impact I have deliberately ignored other views on the poster. I have also been somewhat satirical and humorous – a stylistic approach intended to contrast with the sad, almost hopeless core of the message. The reader of this serious handbook and the creators of the poster perhaps deserve an apology and certainly have a right to be treated more objectively.

Everything I have described was the product of empirical investigation, but it was far from representative of all the farmers interviewed. The overall level of comprehension of the intended message established by interview is shown in → Table 1.

C 1

Table 1:

	Illiterate		Literate without school leaving certificate		with school leaving certificate		Total	
Message fully understood	10	15.6%	19	52.8%	5	71.4%	34	31.8%
Message partly understood	13	20.3%	7	19.4%	2	26.8%	22	2.6%
Message not understood	41	64.1%	10	27.8%	–	–	51	47.7%
Total	64	100.0%	36	100.0%	7	100.0%	107	100.000

2. Source

I certainly had considerable doubts about the effectiveness of the poster, but I am grateful to ABDEL HAMID IBRAHIM AHMED, an agricultural engineer from the Agricultural Extension Research Center, Cairo, for providing me with detailed information and the above table.

While I was present in the project "Development Support Communication" in Mariut near Alexandria, Abdel Hamid carried out surveys to evaluate project activities with small farmers. One of the questions in his survey for his Master's thesis concerned the cow poster. When he happened to mention his results, I was immediately interested. When the poster evaluation was presented to the project workers for the first time, its impact was striking.

3. Origins of the poster

On the one hand there are some typical mistakes in the poster that will unfortunately be repeated again and again in development cooperation. On the other hand, this poster was a one-off item and is to be understood as such.

Both the El-Nahda project and the neighbouring Mariut media project were in the process of being built up or restructured. The personnel were new to the location. Both projects were under pressure to get things moving. Above all, project cooperation had to show immediate results. The idea of the expert on animal husbandry for this poster was welcomed and seemed perfectly reasonable. There was no time for tests. It was imperative to print something. But in the end they have learned their lesson from this failure.

C 1

I have not used this incident to gloat over the misfortunes of others or to ridicule the man who created the poster; I simply want others to learn from the mistakes that were made.

4. Some ideas on how to exploit this case

Presenting this poster has proved its worth as a component in training and further training. It is advisable to put the poster presentation at the beginning of general theoretical explanations and discussions. It is then possible, depending on the aims, the situation and the participants, to probe more deeply into the problems of intercultural communication (→ Chapter III.10, → III.11, → C 2), human perception (→ Chapter III.5), stages in systematic problem solving (→ Chapter III.7), basic questions of the function of agricultural extension (→ Chapter I.2) or the principles of creating illustrative material (→ C 3).

Sources:

ABDEL HAMID, J. Achmed: Agricultural Extension Services in the New Regions of Amria – An Evaluation. Diploma of the Institute of National Planning. Cairo, 1978/79.

Volker HOFFMANN: Bericht über die Durchführung eines Beratervertrags im Rahmen der technischen Zusammenarbeit mit Ägypten im Projekt: Development Support Communication Mariut. Eschborn: GTZ, unpublished, 1979, pp. 27 – 29.

Volker HOFFMANN: Intercultural Communication: The "Cow-Case" and its Use in Training and Teaching. In: H. Albrecht, V. Hoffmann, (Eds.): Proceedings of the Fifth European Seminar on Extension Education, 31.8. – 4.9. 1981 at Stuttgart Hohenheim, University of Hohenheim, 1982, pp. 64 – 68

Giuliano CESARINI: Assistenza e divulgazione agricola. Edagricole. Bologna 1984. pp. 96 – 100

MOHARAM, Ibrahim, S. E & ABDEL HAMID, I. Achmed: Communication with Posters. Why Posters fail to Convey Ideas and Information? Unpublished conference paper, Regional Seminar on Audiovisual Aids in Cooperative Education in the Arab World. 13. – 18.12. 1986, Amman, Jordan. 17p.

Compiled by:

Volker HOFFMANN

C 2

Traditional level of knowledge in target groups and communicating new agricultural information

People in extension organisations often have a crudely simplified or wrong idea or indeed no idea at all of the knowledge, abilities and general level of education of the target groups in a different culture. It is usually assumed that they will react to statements, information and illustrations in the same way as the originators of these methods of communication. As long as people are engaged in discussion, they can clear up uncertainties, but this kind of dialogue is impossible in larger-scale extension programmes where pre-prepared materials have to be used. Therefore, we must start analysing the possibilities for communication in the feasibility study.

The target groups' knowledge of production methods is born of long practice. In this respect they are far superior to advisers unfamiliar with the region and their foreign colleagues. Exceptions to this rule might be, for example, new settlers with no agricultural background. The target groups' frame of reference is practical experience; new information is measured by this and not by the frame of reference of the foreign experts or advisers. If we want to devise an effective communication strategy, we have to be familiar with the existing frame of reference for knowledge and skills into which new information is to be fitted.

Especially in the small farmer sector, we find ourselves dealing with people who have highly developed practical skills but usually no understanding of abstract concepts (reading, mathematical operations, use of symbols, etc.) simply because they have never learned them. Nevertheless extension works with a multitude of very abstract concepts and symbols that have never been used in the target group and its different culture. But people find it impossible to decipher unfamiliar symbols (for example, the fact that putting a cross through something means it is wrong and not that it is emphasising a particularly important message). In the same way, chemical formulas are meaningless to the non-chemist.

Foreign written or spoken language, foreign symbols, etc., obviously need to be interpreted and explained, even to people who have attended school for several years.

By way of illustration, a few examples in → Table 1 show first of all what hidden concepts are concealed in the content of current extension.

C 2

Table 1:

Content of agricultural extension, hidden abstract concepts and operations	
Content of extension	Planting out, ploughing, fertilising, spraying, irrigating, harvesting, storage, etc.
Hidden abstract concepts	Area, speed, depth, time, angle, money, relations, fractions, weight, volume, pressure, flow, yield per unit of area, percentages, prices, costs (monetary according to man-hours), optimisation models, etc.
Relations that must be established	Area = length x width Plant interval = length ÷ number Calculation of time spent on ploughing = distance ÷ speed Quantity of mineral fertiliser = area x quantity ÷ unit of area
Hidden mathematical operations and knowledge of mathematics	Enumeration (concept of numbers), reading scales, basic arithmetic, timing, weighing, establishing quantities and volumes, calculating percentages, etc.

The people in the target group have different concepts. Underlying their work is knowledge to which the advisers often have no access. The target group's know-how is usually organised along different lines. Production and marketing are organised according to their own rules that are not based on the same concepts – but they nevertheless function very well. In some regions there are, for example, no rectangular plots and no concept of area at all. Instead, people only have an idea of length, e. g. 20 paces wide by the path and as far back as you can work. And yet they have a rough idea of the size of plots (measured in yield, the seed required, etc.). This kind of knowledge expresses reality as perceived by these people. It may not be "exact" but it is applied in practice and determines the actions they take. With school education and social change, European concepts and measuring techniques will increasingly penetrate a society. But the old dimensions and concepts will endure for a long time, just as in Europe. For this reason they are the meeting point with extension. → Table 2 gives examples of how we can sometimes make use of them in extension.

In principle, every project develops its own operational methods and forms of communication appropriate to the culture and the problems it encounters. However, it is essential to develop methods before programming extension work, before the adviser sets out and tries, because he has no alternative, to communicate what he has learned from books – which his target group will certainly not be able to follow.

Table 2:

Suggested ways of overcoming difficulties of comprehension when recommending extension measures	
Plant intervals:	Use a planting stick with an appropriate forked branch for the distance between plants.
Spraying:	Give the proportions to be mixed in terms of familiar and available containers, e.g. put 1 Coke can full of powder in the water tank of the 101 backspray, or the original can of insecticide into the 1-litre container of the ULV spray, which is then filled with water, etc. Practise a walking pace and watch out for drifting in the wind. Test: what area was the spray intended to cover, what area was actually covered? Better to adjust by changing the walking speed than the proportions of the mixture. Practise protective measures: face mask, rubber boots, cleaning the equipment, removing empty containers and any liquid that is left over, washing to remove spray.
Damage threshold:	Use a counting board with holes and coloured bands, for example. Walk 100 paces down a row of plants. Check carefully for pests. For each pest a peg is put into a hole in the counting board. If the pegs do not reach the middle coloured band, do not spray; if the pegs reach the middle band, watch for a few days to see if pest infestation develops, or ask adviser; if the pegs reach the last coloured band, spray within 2 days at the latest.
Spraying date:	Instead of using a leaflet, poster, etc., the insecticide bag is nailed at the appropriate time to the shade tree, hung up in the coffee house, displayed in the cooperative or at other meeting points (and taken down again!)
Fertilising:	Instead of recommending fertiliser dosages per unit of area, we can calculate the amounts by the sack or by volume in relation to the amount of seed used or the average yield of each field, for example the heaps at the threshing point. We have to know the type of fertiliser and its nutrient content and take this into account in our recommendation.

Bibliography:

Andreas FUGLESANG: Applied Communication in Developing Countries. Ideas and Observations. Uppsala: Hammarskjöld Foundation, 1973.

Sandra WALLMANN: The Communication of Measurement in Basutoland. In: Human Organization, 24, 1965, pp. 236–243

Compiled by:

Rolf SÜLZER, Volker HOFFMANN

C 3

Effectiveness and design of pictorial representation

1. Introduction

"A picture says more than a thousand words" – therein lies the problem. A picture can give rise to many more misunderstandings than a discussion.

We can deduce from the rules of perception (→ Chapter III.5) that the act of deciphering a picture is accompanied by several processes that run parallel to each other. Thus a picture only really takes shape in the eye of the beholder.

- The observer selects, i.e. he only sees parts of the total picture.

- The observer projects, i.e. he supplements the picture, enlarges its scope and completes it, seeing what he is looking for, what his experience and usual way of looking at pictures tell him to see.

- The observer orders and differentiates, i.e. he links similar things and he regards familiar things as more important.

- The observer interprets, i.e. he gives meaning, shape and significance to what he sees in the picture.

People in a culture that "reads" pictures have developed an ability to decipher messages, but in other cultures "reading" pictures creates problems. People may be "visually illiterate".

Thus people have to learn to decipher pictures, to "read" them just as they learn to read the printed or written word. It is a problem that is often overlooked. People who are unable to read pictures are confronted not only by photographs and graphic illustrations of "real" things but also with such symbols as arrows, an illustration crossed out or the expectation that they will read a poster "logically" from top left to bottom right.

But unless people have had a good deal of training, they may well read pictures from quite different standpoints: their attention is attracted first by colours and anything that appears strange, and it might only occur to them later that the picture is trying to "say" something. Also they may assume that the pictures are there to be looked at for pleasure, not so that they can learn something or decipher "messages".

The message the communicator (e.g. the adviser) intends to send and the message actually received (e.g. by the farmer) may be worlds apart. We have to bridge this gap if communication by means of pictures is to be effective.

C 3

Is it really worth the effort? The answer is a categorical "yes". Pictures capture the attention, people do look at them, they stimulate discussion, they help to call to mind situations and to organise thoughts and ideas. People are definitely interested in pictures.

But this does not alter the fact that we must:

(1) **try out** a picture to see what effects it has;

(2) (perhaps) **help** the targeted individuals to **learn how to read** pictures.

When they do so, it is helpful to bear the following principle in mind: the actual meaning does not lie in what the artist tried to express but in how most people interpret the picture and in the messages they deduce from it.

We now explain and illustrate these general assertions in more detail. We describe how pictorial illustrations are perceived in various cultures and in each case conclusions can be drawn about how best to create pictures.

2. Analysis of actual pictures – important conclusions and recommendations

There have been many surveys of how pictures are interpreted in rural societies in developing countries and they are often compared with industrialised countries. These investigations have revealed some typical problems (even though the explanatory models may vary). Once the problems have been identified, we are in a position to create better picture materials for use in extension and adult education. In the following we illustrate and interpret some typical "hurdles" and come to some conclusions about how to create and utilise pictures.

2.1 Subject and background

As car drivers, we would not cope with modern traffic conditions if we were not able to select from a multitude of optical impressions the most important ones at any given moment. Because we concentrate our attention on the traffic lights, the distance between us and other vehicles in front or in the rear mirror, etc., we do not register the shop window displays, the clothes of passers-by or illuminated advertisements.

But if we are moving through the tropical rainforest, "we can't see the wood for the trees", whereas a local guide who knows the forest can select important sense impressions from the vast array that surrounds him: the monkeys in the treetops, the tracks on the forest floor that we can hardly even see, etc. This means that what we actually perceive as the subject or background depends on the geographical and socio-economic environment in which we have developed our skill of perception. We learn in childhood to reduce what we have observed to basic structural features that enable us to recognise things again.

Thus the way we perceive and differentiate subjects and background depends on how we were brought up and how we live. The way we look at pictures is affected by the same factors, plus our experience of "reading" pictures.

People who are not skilled in picture reading, i. e. the majority of people in the rural regions in Africa read pictures detail by detail and try to interpret every single element. The interpretation of the total picture is therefore largely dependent on the interpretation of the individual parts. In contrast, when the skilled reader of pictures first looks at a poster, for example, he takes in the main message and then looks at the details to check his interpretation of the overall picture.

Picture 1: Erosion control

The picture on the left showed fields with various crops and erosion control strips, but people saw just a few trees and fields full of birds and snakes. Fear of bird damage deterred farmers from laying out strips like these. The picture on the right was interpreted correctly.
(BIMENYIMANA/GÖRGEN).

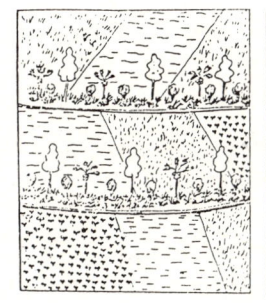

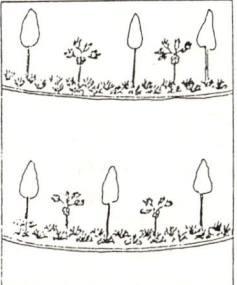

Striking details can easily make the unskilled reader overlook the main message. Several surveys have shown that a lot of detail causes confusion and hinders perception (e. g. FUGLESANG, GRAAP, BIMENYIMANA/GÖRGEN). Details are not only studied closely, but are also compared with the observer's own experience and judged by this standard. Someone wearing different clothes, with a different hairstyle from people in the locality, is not "one of us" and his problem or his solution to problems is therefore irrelevant. These are facts whose importance for educational and extension work cannot be overstated.

C 3

Picture 2: Family meal

This picture was used in a nutrition aid course as an example of a family eating a meal. The farmers easily recognised the situation, "family round the table for a meal", but they also concluded that this must be the family of a functionary, since they themselves did not have their meals sitting on chairs round a table (tested by the Service Animation et Formation, Kibuye, Rwanda).

This communication problem did not occur to the local artist, who was accustomed to sitting at table to have his meals.

In our culture we readily identify with people from other socio-cultural backgrounds and this is exploited by psychologists in advertising (e.g. smokers are promised "freedom and adventure" on horseback in the prairie). But in the rural regions of developing countries people seem to be less willing to identify with others (see the studies by A. GOSH of how rural women in India interpret films).

Conclusions:

Pictures should only contain the details necessary to ensure that the message will be understood. The background should, if possible, be left out altogether. The details must be accurate, i.e. the illustration must be a true reflection of life regarding clothes, hairstyles, the implements used, etc. This means that specific adaptation to regional, sometimes very local circumstances is vitally important.

2.2 Perspective

A basic problem in the way we perceive pictures is the loss of a spatial dimension when three-dimensional reality is transformed into a two-dimensional illustration.

C 3

This spatial dimension is expressed by means of perspective, based on the optical principle that parallel lines meet in the distance.

Perspective means, among other things, that the relative size of illustrated objects depends on their distance from the observer, and the fixed point of the observer results in objects or parts of objects in the background being concealed by those in the foreground (superimposed image). Illustrations that use perspective are by no means universal, and even in Europe it was only developed in the Italian Renaissance. Experience of using pictures in rural Africa shows that illustrations that incorporate perspective lead to some typical misunderstandings:

Relative size

An object that is smaller because it is in the background is wrongly interpreted.

Picture 3: Fetching wood

This woman is so small because she is inferior to the man. The man is knocking the bundle of wood off the woman's head with his axe (Federation of Village Cooperatives, BOUAKE).

Superimposing

When objects are partly concealed, people misunderstand what is meant, either because the visible part is interpreted as the whole object or because the object in the foreground and the object behind it are seen as joined together.

C 3

Picture 4: Transporting beams
(South African poster on safety at work)

30% of the South African workers questioned took the person in the background to be a boy and not an adult.
(WINTER in RAMM, p. 118).

Picture 5: The football player

This picture makes people laugh. How can he play football with only one leg? (GRAAP).

Picture 6: Flies on food

(detail from a poster warning against cholera)

The bowl of food in front of the man's foot is seen as a part of his foot. What's wrong with the poor man's foot? (tested by Service Animation et Formation, Kibuye, Rwanda).

Picture 7: The cyclist

Superimposed images are not only difficult to interpret in drawings; they create problems in photographs too, an example being the cyclist who caused amazement by riding his bicycle with one leg. The fact that it was an action photograph was not appreciated (see below "Movement")
(FUGLESANG).

It makes just as much sense to draw something as we know it rather than as we see it – like the African schoolboy's drawing of a lorry showing all four wheels because he knows a lorry has four wheels (FUGLESANG).

Picture 8: The lorry

In Cubism too the artist shows the different sides of an object at the same time because he knows they exist.

Shadow

In illustrations with perspective, the shadows cast by objects and people are also significant. We know from using pictures in Africa that they can hamper perception, because they break up the structural features that help people to understand a picture. Thus they try to interpret the shadow as an object in itself.

C 3

Picture 9: Fetching water

(detail from a poster warning against cholera)

The jug for the water cannot be clearly recognised in the picture. A bird? A duck? Or is it an object I am not familiar with? (tested by Service Animation et Formation, Kibuye, Rwanda)

Conclusions

Illustrations that use linear perspective are more difficult to understand. Overlapping objects and objects shown bigger or smaller because of perspective should be avoided. The relative dimensions of figures and objects should be the same as in real life. Shadows cast by people or objects interfere with the interpretation of pictures because they break up structural features that are essential for recognition.

2.3 Movement

Showing movement in static pictures is difficult and uses certain conventional devices that are widely understood.

For example, tracks running along a path indicate that something is moving forwards.

Picture 10: Comics tell their stories through pictures and use a large number of devices to indicate motion (lines following a moving figure or object, stars indicating impact, clouds of smoke or dust to show speed).

Similarly, we understand lines that make the invisible visible, for example fumes, the movement of air, etc. Anyone not familiar with this convention tries to interpret them in the same way as visible objects.

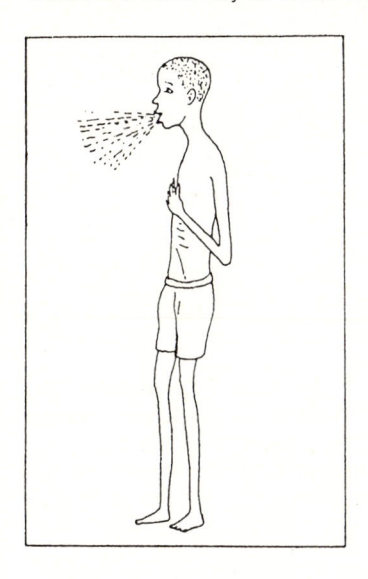

Picture 11: Coughing

That person is vomiting or swallowing gnats.
(BIMENYIMANA, GÖRGEN).

In technical instructions, arrows are used to show the direction of movement. Experience of using this convention in developing countries has clearly shown that,

Picture 12: Compost heap

None of the people questioned could understand the meaning of the arrows that show how the central rod in the compost should be moved.
(BIMENYIMANA/GÖRGEN).

where it is unknown, people try to interpret the arrows differently or they simply ignore them. Nobody realised that the star shaped lines in the safety at work poster (→ Picture 4) were supposed to illustrate movement and impact (WINTER in RAMM p. 119).

Another common way of illustrating movement is the use of picture sequences, but this method also has many pitfalls.

Picture sequences

We know from using series of pictures that people do not automatically read them in the right order, from upper left to bottom right (in the same way as most European written languages). It is also by no means obvious that characters in a story told in pictures are doing jobs one after the other. It is often assumed that quite different people are doing or experiencing different things at the same time. The object of illustrated stories is not just to show a sequence over time but to underline a chain of cause and effect (if..., then...) as in the following example from Rwanda: (→ Picture 13)

The aim of this poster, that was shown all over the country by the Rwandan Ministry of Health in 1983, was to inform people about the dangers of cholera infection. The story told by posters was as follows:

1. One man answers a call of nature in the open, while another man is scooping water out of the nearby river.

2. It is well known that flies settle on faeces and now they settle on food. The polluted drinking water is in the calabash.

3. Eating contaminated food and drinking dirty water leads to diarrhoea and vomiting.

4. Diarrhoea and vomiting cause loss of fluid and the infected person has to seek treatment.

5. In hospital the lost fluid is replaced by infusions.

6. Unless he is treated, the patient dies.

But the way people saw and interpreted this series of events was in fact quite different.

Picture 13: Cholera poster

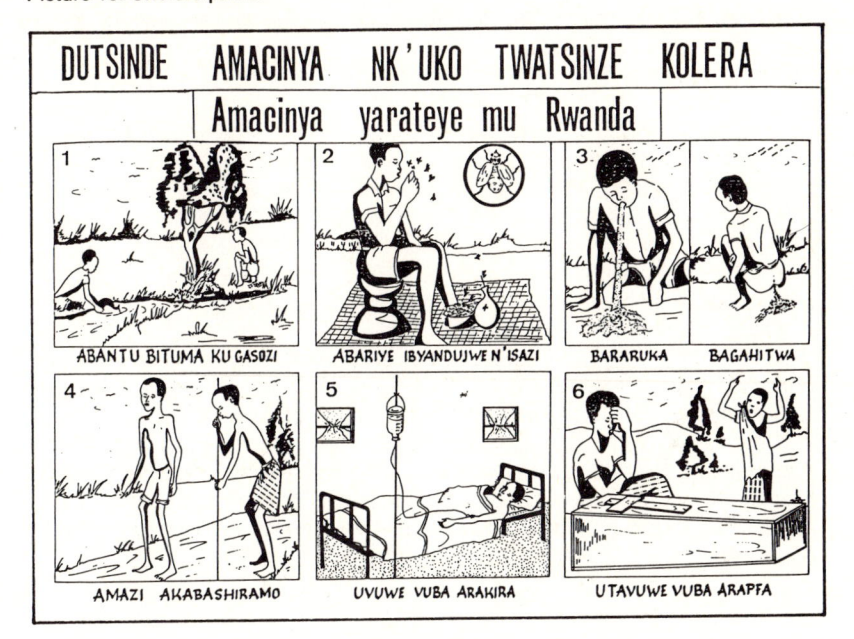

1. Someone is squatting under a bush with his intestines hanging out.

2. The man's foot is in a very bad state.

3. One man's intestines are hanging out; the other man is chewing a rope or a stick.

4. A blind man is going for a walk with his guide.

5. This is a man in hospital.

6. A woman with an eye complaint is sitting by her table. Her neighbour is waving to her.

The final message: "So you see now what can happen to you too."
(But the people responding to the pictures were as little able to read and understand the message of the text as German readers).

This complicated series of pictures involves temporal and causal relations that are difficult for the uninitiated to grasp. It is further complicated by the style (figures casting shadows and superimposed images) and the use of unknown symbols and unfamiliar objects (vomiting, coffin with crucifix). Nevertheless this is by no means an extreme example.

Conclusions:

A series of pictures is usually only worthwhile in the context of group discussions, because the conditions of time and space and the causal relations have to be explained and discussed. The poster box or felt picture series (Boite à image, flip-over, flanellographe) are methods of illustration adapted to these needs. Using this equipment the next picture, the next stage in a story, can be presented as the discussion progresses.

2.5 Symbols borrowed from the written language

Crossing out is often just as unfamiliar as "ticking"; people seek to explain the lines as objects (beams, ropes, etc.).

Picture 14:
Fetch water above the latrine

The drawing clearly shows a woman fetching water. But why attention was drawn to this obvious fact by means of a cross was not understood by the majority of those who saw the picture.
(FUSSELL/HAALAND)

A circle drawn round something to focus attention is also unknown; the circle is overlooked altogether or interpreted as a circular object (see → Pictures 6 and 13). The circle round the enlarged fly was thought to be a window (since traditionally huts have round window apertures) with a very large mosquito.

Like the other signs, arrows are also associated with objects of similar shape or size (beams, ropes, etc.) or they are overlooked (→ Picture 12).

Symbols with historical roots, social conventions

The symbols that signify abstract concepts like danger or illustrate natural phenomena like the sun, storms or fire are in such common use that we are taught them as children. Thus we consider these symbols to be so simple and obvious that we are often unaware that they are characteristic of our culture only, and we try to use them as basic illustrations in other cultural settings. Surveys have shown that they are by no means "international".

Picture 15: Skull and cross-bones as the symbol of danger

In Nepal 410 farmers were asked what this symbol means, and only 4 knew that it referred to danger
(FUSSELL/HAALAND p. 34).

Picture 16: The sun

In Egypt the setting sun was interpreted as half a water melon or a flower.
(ROSSER p. 10)

Picture 17: Burning weeds

The (reddish-yellow) flames were taken to be flowers; a woman picking flowers.
(BIMENYIMANA/GÖRGEN)

Conclusions:

Take care with symbols. They are only understood as a "reflection" of reality because we have been brought up to recognise them. In other cultures different

C 3

symbols are commonly used and we should take note of and use them. Materials for self-instruction, however, should not contain symbols if they can be avoided.

2.6 "Simple" and "realistic" as culture-dependent descriptions

We have pointed out obstacles to understanding pictures. But can we remove the barriers if we use simple pictures like those in children's picture books or reduce them to essentials as in line drawings or pictograms (examples being international traffic signs)?

Picture 18: Various telephone pictograms

(AICHER, KRAMPEN p. 126).

Picture 19: Three sports in pictograms

(Triple jump, long jump and high jump.) Would you have recognised them?

Picture 20: Animal sketches (reduced to their unmistakable essentials) (STEINER)

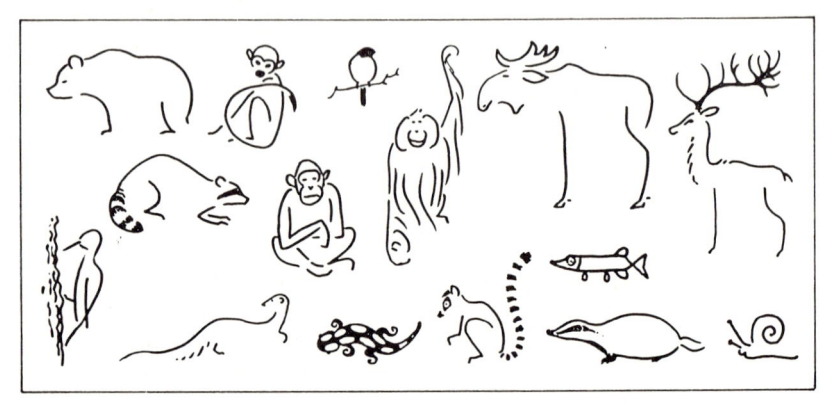

Or should we only work with photographs, slides and films, because they are realistic and show things as they exist in nature?

The literature indicates the following conclusions:

Good pictograms and sketches emphasise a few characteristic features that typify the appearance of the subject and distinguish it from cognate or similar subjects. This can simplify and shorten the process of recognition, provided the drawing captures the permanent key features and strikes a chord in the memory of the people looking at the picture. This is the real problem in fact: line drawing and pictograms are not "simple". Reduction to a few basic structural features has to take into account the society where the drawings are to be shown. What we regard as essential features are obviously not those that are recognised by rural societies in developing countries. Both the study of FUSSELL in Nepal and the surveys of COOK in Papua New Guinea have shown that line drawings of figures and silhouettes (as used in pictograms) are least recognisable. Different cultures regard different features as characteristic. We hope we have demonstrated this point clearly with → picture 21. It shows that the communication value of ostensibly convincing sketches of animals (→ picture 20) is in fact relative and that they cannot be used indiscriminately in all cultures.

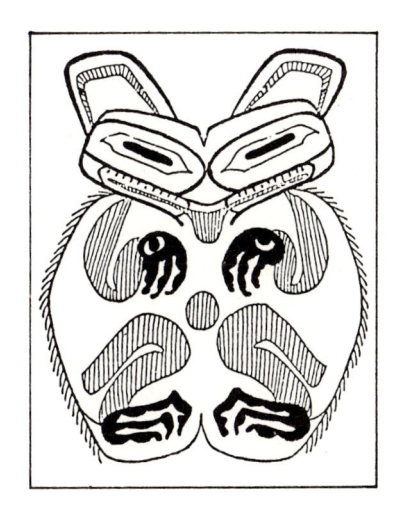

Picture 21: A bear

Drawn by a Tsimshian Indian.
(BOAS in MANGAN p. 248)

We know from studies of the comprehension of photographs and films that perception, as in the case of drawings, is affected by the problem of subject and background, perspective and excessive detail, causal relations in the sequence of pictures, etc. Thus the relationship between subject and background is the factor that decides whether the picture is understood, not the faithful reproduction of reality. In particular, the background in photographs is full of detail and, unless it is blocked out, it is difficult to see the point of the picture. This is illustrated by, for example, → picture 22. Drawings are a better method of expressing a specific message than photographs.

C 3

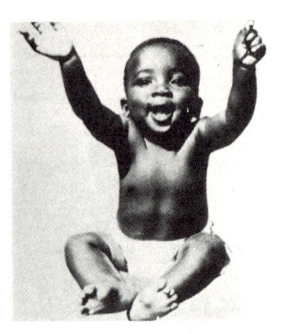

Picture 22: Baby

A photograph with and without background.
(FUGLESANG P. 95)

Films are complicated and rich in detail but they are also made incomprehensible by modern techniques of shooting and editing. Panning shots and zoom shots are disorientating for anyone unfamiliar with these filming techniques. It is not obvious that it is the same car that drives out of the picture on the right and reappears on the left. People who are not used to watching films find it impossible to interpret flashbacks. It helps if we recall the history of the film: in the early days scenes were filmed with a static camera in the same way as they are seen by a static observer.

It is important to emphasise once again that we cannot assume a universally applicable principle of simplicity. "Simple", "easily understood" have to be redefined in each and every cultural context.

From traditional methods of illustration in cultures that use pictures, we know what readily comprehensible material looks like. We think of advertisements at hairdressers, photographers, in bars and on lorries.

Conclusions:

Simplicity and "true to nature" are not criteria that apply in all cultures. Line drawings and pictograms are not simple. In this context, simple means pictorial representation that can be readily understood. Photographs do not satisfy this criterion. And finally, films are often extremely complicated because they are full of detail and can manipulate time and space in a way that is often beyond comprehension in certain cultures. Producing comprehensible, regionally adapted films is a costly undertaking.

Further information on this topic can be found in → Chapter III.5, → Chapter III.11, → Chapter V.5 and in → C 1, → C 2 and → F 2.

Bibliography and sources:

Otl AICHER, Martin KRAMPEN: Zeichensysteme der visuellen Kommunikation. Handbuch für Designer, Architekten, Planer, Organisatoren. Stuttgart 1977

B.BIMENYIMANA, R. GÖRGEN: Perception et compréhension du matériel didactique par la population rurale au Rwanda. Kibuye, Rwanda, 1983

F. BOAS: Primitive Art. H. Aschehoug & Co. Oslo, Norway, 1927, p. 225.

Fédération des groupements villageois de la région de BOUAKE: Perception et assimilation du visuel par les populations rurales. No date.

B. L. COOK: Understanding pictures in Papua New Guinea; what kinds of pictures communicate most effectively with people who can't read? Elgin, David C. Cook Foundation, 1981

Andreas FUGLESANG: Applied communication in developing countries. Ideas and observations. The Dag Hammarskjöld Foundation. Uppsala, 1973

FUSSELL, D.,HAALAND,A.: Communication with pictures in Nepal. Report on a study by NDS and UNICEF. Kathmandu, 1976

Regina GÖRGEN: Didaktisches Bildmaterial für die Landbevölkerung Rwandas. Eine Untersuchung über Wahrnehmung und Verständnis von Plakaten und Bildern für die Flanell-Wand. Kibuye, Rwanda, 1983

R.GÖRGEN, Ch. KAYIBANDA: Conception du matériel didactique à l'écoute des paysans. Kibuye, Rwanda, 1983

A. GOSH: Media and rural women. In: Adult education and development. 27, Bonn, 1986

GRAAP: Dessiner. Grammaire du dessin au tableau feutre pour une pédagogie de l'autopromotion. Bobo-Dioulasso, Burkina Faso

J.MANGAN: Cultural conventions of pictorial representation. Iconic literacy and education. In: Educational Communication and Technology. 1978, pp. 245–267

Gabriele RAMM: Unterschiede der Bildperzeption in Kulturen der Dritten Welt. Master's thesis, Osnabrück, 1985

Marc ROSSER: Preliminary perception survey (for development of self-explanatory graphic illustrations for birth control pill usage). DSC Project, Mariut, Egypt, 1980, 20 p.
Chrisje M.E. van SCHOOT: In the picture. Pictorial perception and communication in rural development. Master's thesis, Reading, 1985

Gerolf STEINER: Tierzeichnungen in Kürzeln. Stuttgart 1982

D. A.WALKER: Understanding pictures. A study in the design of appropriate visual materials for education in developing countries. Centre for International Education, Univ. of Massachusetts, 1979

A. and F. ZIMMER: Visual literacy in communication: designing for development. Indiana University, Hulton Educational Publications, 1978

C 3

Compiled by:

Regina GÖRGEN, Volker HOFFMANN, Rolf SÜLZER

C 4

Illusions of communication between projects and their target groups: a cautionary example in Nigeria

The German development sociologist Peter Ay produced a description and analysis of social processes during the planning and implementation of a development project in West Nigeria. He carried out a random sample survey of the cropping system of 240 farmers in 6 villages. During a stay of roughly three years in the village of Badeku, between 1974 and 1978, he concentrated on collecting information from farmers, project planners and personnel on the dynamics of running a project. His sources of information were participatory observation, informal interviews and group interviews with selected informants.

The Badeku Project of the University of Ibadan was established as a pilot project to test extension systems and to accelerate the transfer of technology. Thus it is comparable with a whole series of projects set up to modernise agricultural production in developing countries. However, there is relatively little information on how these projects are regarded by the farmers themselves. The reason for this paucity of information may be that the survey methods are time-consuming and presuppose an understanding of the local language. They are therefore obstacles, since it is virtually impossible to repeat and check such surveys in the same project.

The following excerpt is intended to be a cautionary tale and to stimulate discussion of the topic.

1. Project targets

1. To create a testbed for innovations. The idea was that the villages should be used to test experiments on the speed and permanence of technological change in agriculture, health and nutrition. The change and the methods devised to achieve it should be capable of being repeated elsewhere in the country.

2. To set up a kind of laboratory situation in which students and staff of the faculty and the university study and observe rural development.

3. To create a link between the university's researchers, other organisations and the rural population in whose interests they are working. In this way they were to be systematically brought into closer contact with the villagers so that they could understand their problems and reactions and therefore set up research that was more relevant and directly applicable to problems of rural development.

4. To create a basis for local initiatives, self-sufficiency, self-confidence and participation in the planning and implementation of rural development programmes.

2. Organisation of the project and its main activities

At the top of the project's hierarchy are scientists; there are links with other organisations, and the Rockefeller Foundation provided the finance. In the formal organisational structure there are no representatives of the farmers or of the rural population.

Agricultural innovations are directed principally at improving maize cropping by using different varieties, mineral fertiliser and keeping the crop in special storage facilities. There are also experimental programmes for sweet potato and legumes and chemical weed control. This was supplemented after 1976 by a poultry and small livestock programme.

As well as agricultural activities, there is also a health programme and women's programme incorporating domestic science.

3. Phase of project development

3.1 Initial contacts, mutual expectations and their significance for the project.

Usually very detailed reasons are given for selecting a particular village in preference to others for a survey. But if we look more closely, it soon becomes clear that chance plays an important part in this decision. It may depend, for example, on who provides information and who were the first contacts sought by the project.

There are, however, typical conditions when making initial contacts and they certainly apply to other development projects as well.

The way in which the university personnel see their role determines the initial stage of the project. They assume that the project will benefit the farmers. A closer examination shows that the first contacts on both sides are not radically different. The project personnel turn first to the advisers who have already worked with farmers, and the farmers turn to their "experts" to get information about possible courses of action.

Whereas the farmers, if no information is forthcoming, rely on their experience of previous contact with institutions, the project personnel, if they have no data, keep to the theoretical models of farmers and their development.

C 4

The farmers' experience of official institutions may go back for decades and may not be simply the product of recent years. Whereas the negative effect of institutions (for example, taxes collected in cash) tended to be felt by everybody, there were always some farmers who benefited from their positive effects. But programmes like renewing cacao plantations, the extension service, cooperatives and individual development projects always applied to a fraction of the farmer population only, because of the capacity available, even if it was officially claimed that far more farmers had been reached. We have to remember that farmers are independent producers who make decisions in keeping with their individual production conditions, and positive or negative intervention by the administration is usually felt to be aimed at individuals.

But the representatives of the project assume that the farmers are a homogeneous group characterised by, for example, backward production methods, ignorance, poverty and the need for help. Even if differences are perceived, in the eyes of the project planners they are differences between poor and very poor, backward and very backward, etc. They also regard it as axiomatic that the project will help farmers to escape from their desperate plight – which gives the project personnel a sense of power to shape and influence their development.

The farmers also see the power wielded by the project and how it can affect them. But in their experience this potential influence is diffuse and may well be more to their disadvantage than their benefit. This is also true of those institutions that – officially – were founded and administered "in the interest of the farmers".

Whereas cooperatives and marketing organisations have been founded on behalf of the farmers, and failure could be explained by the decisions and the administration being in the hands of outsiders, even institutions that the farmers have organised themselves have not become established. These organisations have been exploited by other groups, especially political parties, for their own ends.

When the new university project was launched, the attitude of the majority of farmers was therefore to wait and see if the anticipated advantages would really materialise. In their view it was quite likely that the university would pursue its own interests but that they would benefit indirectly (a better road, water, electricity and possibly a job). The fact that the university was interested in coming to Badeku was confirmed again and again for the farmers by the visits and interviews, the maize demonstration fields and the work of university people in the village. But the farmers showed no enthusiasm for information from the university on how they could improve their cropping system and become "successful farmers". They were mainly interested in the fact that the university would soon create permanent jobs in the village.

Even six years after the start of the project, these hopes were still alive. When I moved into the village, many farmers regarded my arrival as the beginning of this institutionalised relation between university and village, and they expected the building of a house and laboratory to start straightaway.

It can be said that project planners and workers have a diffuse sense of power. It is diffuse because they do not know with any degree of precision how things will turn out in practice. At the outset they even tend to dismiss the misgivings of the farmers and assert their own ideas, because they see themselves acting in the (true) interest of the farmers. Farmers with different views from their own are felt to be an inconvenience, and they are quickly dismissed as backward. Planners and personnel see the project only from their own point of view and act in the belief that it will automatically benefit the farmers.

This is the reason why project personnel and planners are largely ignorant of the motives and expectations of the farmers — we can even go as far as saying they will always remain ignorant despite frequent contact with farmers. Because they are convinced they are acting in the best interest of the farmers, they are tempted, in the typically uncertain early phase, to make promises. They do not, however, consider the implications; they are confident at the time that these promises will be fulfilled in the future.

The reason why the views of the farmers are not taken into account is the assumption that their views will in any case change and, of course, conform with the project. Thus official reports on contact with farmers often imply that farmers were in total agreement with the decisions of the project.

It was assumed to be obvious that the farmers wanted to expand the cultivation of maize, but in fact this was an invention, because what the farmers really wanted was credit. In their experience maize cropping was simply the precondition for receiving credit. The reports even give the impression that the farmers would not have been in a position to act in their own interest without the project.

Since the project's stated objective is the success of the farmers, their success means the project has been successful and praise for the farmers is basically self-congratulation confirming the importance of the project and its personnel.

The project takes the credit for all developments in the area and claims that they are significant for the development of Nigeria, for which the project representatives have the required expertise. It is additionally maintained that the maize project in Badeku is helping to prevent migration from rural regions to the towns, and that the production changes were, moreover, achieved without any noteworthy distortion in the rural economy. Thus what is basically a revolution is being offered without the usual side-effects of revolution.

This line of argument even gives the project the right not to bother with deviant views of farmers, because it is acting not only in the best interest of the farmers but of the whole nation. The project presents itself as a way of converting these higher interests into the subjective interest of the farmers.

This interpretation of project management seems to be confirmed beyond doubt by events in the second year of the project: the farmers applied on their own initiative to take part in the project, more and more new groups were formed, group farms were laid out to crop maize using the new methods, consumption of mineral fertiliser rose, etc. How far the official view is from that of the farmers is shown, for example, by the fact that some farmers had in the meantime only been fulfilling the project's conditions because they wanted to avoid possible sanctions.

Whereas the Badeku farmers thought it was quite "normal" for selected farmers to be involved in the university's maize programme, the project assumed that the programme would have a demonstration effect on all farmers. But in the eyes of the inhabitants of Badeku, the two farmers with the experimental fields were employees of the university rather than local farmers.

This is in fact what the farmers told project workers at the beginning. Individual farmers told them that their own system was good and that maize could not be grown in the way proposed by the project. But the project personnel did not pursue this line of argument: instead they tried even harder to prove that the usual cropping method in the village was inferior, backward and no longer viable. It became clear in the minds of the villagers involved in these exchanges that the university's workers did not want to understand why the farmers used their particular cultivation method. They reacted by praising the new cropping method and accepting the arguments of the project workers without demur. Their justification for not actually applying the new method was that the farm would have to be extended and wage labour employed. The project workers did not realise that this argument was no different than the usual argument, i. e. the farmers did not want to abandon their traditional methods in favour of a new technique.

The project workers assumed that the farmers had now learned how effective the new method was. But all they had in fact learned was what to say to curtail the constant interference by the project's personnel. When large numbers of farmers actually tried out the new varieties of maize, because they were supposed to produce a high yield, they did so within their own traditional farming system. For the project this partial adoption was a "mistake" and evidence that the farmers had clearly not understood the new system. Thus they tried to intervene yet again to tell the farmers to adopt the new system in its entirety, since this was the only way to achieve success.

The project workers again felt completely justified in their demands, because after all the farmers had been convinced by the higher yields of the superiority of the modern method. All they needed to do was to search for the causes of the problems and eliminate them, and the farmers would then accept any innovation. For the project there were no problems with the new methods, since they were dealing with the results of scientific research. but for the farmers adoption of the new methods meant a whole series of important decisions. They would have to change the whole process of planning and run risks. In their view, however, it was pointless to get involved in discussion or even to express their misgivings. If they did so, they would suffer disadvantages:

- The project workers would immediately continue their efforts to convince the farmers.

- The farmers who expressed doubts would be considered backward or used as examples of what to avoid.

They would also suffer the threat of sanctions, since it was pointed out that the project preferred to work with farmers who were progressive and willing to adopt innovations.

The project's field staff became aware of the discrepancy between what the farmers said and the cropping method they used in practice. However, the fact that everything was not going according to plan did not result in the project concept being revised at this stage. On the contrary, the project workers regarded it as further confirmation that it was their duty to work harder to persuade the farmers to adopt the new method.

In their estimation, if the project did not exist, the farmers would never be able to accept the innovation. Accordingly, there was even a potential willingness to accept the conditions named by the farmers for adopting the cropping method (money for wage labourers).

The farmers could point out how difficult it was for them to get the necessary inputs for the new method. For example, if they themselves tried to get seed or other agricultural supplies, it would mean hours of waiting. They had to try and find the people in charge, the stocks in the state-run stores were limited, and by no means all needs could be met, etc. This (in fact, realistic) illustration of the farmers' helplessness in the face of officialdom fits the project's philosophy. On the one hand it shows that the farmers are interested in the innovation, and on the other it confirms the need for help to be supplied by the project. The offer by project workers to organise the supplies of seed and mineral fertiliser for the farmers is regarded as a demonstration of how production inputs should be bought and as a lesson in how farmers could help themselves.

But the project has completely overlooked the fact that farmers — especially those in the higher income groups — have been solving problems of the supply of other items for decades. Farmers have bought their own spraying equipment to combat cacao diseases. Even if they only have small fields, they acquire and spray the correct chemicals. They have even been known to fetch their own mineral fertiliser, and many farmers go back and forth between their village and Ibadan to do shopping.

When the farmers emphasise that inputs can only be acquired by the project, they mean that they do not want to do it for themselves. On the other hand, the project also demonstrates in the course of time its power to organise and exert influence, which is proved by concrete examples like well construction and the inoculation campaign against cholera. The project arranges for the usually remote bureaucracies to send their representatives to the villages, an example being the state health organisation. Such actions make the farmers more willing to take part in the project's activities, even if the individuals expect to gain little from the subprogrammes.

But, by participating, farmers can perhaps benefit from the demonstrated power of the project and gain advantage over other farmers when the project has privileges to hand out.

The project workers assume that the farmers' initial expectations are not significant, since they will be convinced by demonstrations and changes in agricultural practice in the course of the project and thus change their minds. A comparison of different groups shows, however, that initial expectations can be crucially important for the rest of the project. For example, these expectations determine to a large extent whether a farmer takes part in the project at all.

In Badeku, for example, it was still assumed, even after the project had been running for 6 years, that the university would put up buildings in the village. The groups that had formed in other villages, so that they could receive the same level of credit as Badeku farmers, expected this credit even though the link between credit and farm size had been repeatedly emphasised at the regional meetings in Egbeda. Thus when far less credit was allocated, the members could still not understand the reason, because in their view they had fulfilled the same conditions as the Badeku farmers.

The project reports tell us that the farmers had learned to apply for credit themselves. If this was true, the farmers must have realised when they applied how small the amount would be. According to the reports, the farmers completed the formalities under the supervision of the project. But in fact it was the field staff who drew up the applications, with the farmers simply appending their thumb print. They wanted to take the application forms to the relevant office as quickly as possible, and most of the groups' representatives could in any case neither read nor write. In all the interviews on this problem area in 1977 the farmers emphasised that they could not apply for credit without the help of project personnel.

In the view of the project, it is important for farmers to receive some credit, so that they are motivated to seek more for themselves, because farmers are thought to accept innovations only when tangible benefits accrue. Decisionmaking processes that lead to a farmer participating in the programme are ignored and specific information is not provided, even when conflicts and contradictions arise. On the other hand, the farmers' groups feel no need to approach the project administration directly for information because they have been given information by the farmers in Badeku who, as they noted, had received their money.

3.2 From random to institutionalised contact

Chance plays a major role when a particular region or village is selected. But from the perspective of the villages themselves there are many factors that determine whether it is this or that village which is chosen. Villages that are already in contact with official organisations are more likely to be chosen. In Badeku it was the cacao programme of the Ministry of Agriculture; in Apoku, for example, it was another development project that had links with the Badeku project.

This is not unusual, since development projects often cover a limited area, but, considering the low level of inputs in relation to the total number of farmers, it becomes important at the national level. As a rule, contact is first made through the traditional power structures in the village. New structures are formed relatively quickly. The project workers make what can be called institutionalised contact with some of the villagers. The villagers with the best chance are those who already have experience of institutions — for example, if they have attended school, worked in towns or other regions of Nigeria, taken part in cooperative organisations or have been leaders of religious groups, etc.

The project naturally turns to these people when newcomers arrive. This is sometimes done for very practical reasons. For example, several project workers did not speak the Yoruba language and automatically they relied on those villagers who could interpret for them. These people thus became the obvious choice to liaise between the project and the farmers. The project workers had no difficulty in communicating with them and relied on them to pass on their information. The standing of these intermediaries in the villages was enhanced by the fact that the project workers turned mainly to them. They rapidly became important purveyors of information. The villagers wanted to know what they could expect from the project. The project workers gave their information to the chosen intermediary since he was the only person they knew well in the village.

Such intermediaries benefit personally from everyday events, like being driven into town or getting medical supplies. The project workers are willing to satisfy their wishes without question because it does not create extra work and it gives them an opportunity to do something informally in return for services rendered or to be rendered.

Other everyday experiences have their effect: the intermediary notices that the project workers will reward him by calling him "progressive" and "cooperative" if he simply confirms that they are doing a good job. Usually all he needs to do is repeat the words of the project workers themselves.

3.3 Creating and reinforcing illusions

At the beginning of the project both sides possess their own stereotyped ideas based on their experience or derived from other people's reports. These stereotyped views become more significant as the project advances and help to create erroneous ideas in the minds of both the farmers and the project staff of the targets and the way the project is progressing. In this respect, the intermediaries in the villages and the field staff play a decisive role in creating illusions. The intermediaries tell the other villagers about their interpretation of the project and their expectations. In the case of Badeku, for example, this took the form of descriptions of the work being carried out on the university farm. The intermediary is in a position to draw on his own experience and to provide authentic information, since he knows more about the farm than about the project itself. He influences the expectations of the listeners so that they are different from the project's actual aims and the measures it is employing to achieve those aims. Some farmers are willing to cooperate with the project simply on the basis of expectations that are in fact misguided.

The project workers tend to transfer their positive experience of the intermediaries in the villages to other farmers. Their mainly verbal support for the work of project personnel, confirmed in the meantime by other farmers, gives them the impression that the project is developing according to plan. The success of their own operations is corroborated. The field staff can then present the intermediaries in the villages to the project management and other institutions as "typical farmers" who confirm the "importance" and "appropriateness" of the project measures. However, the intermediary is far from being a typical farmer; in truth, he is very much the exception in the village.

By telling the villagers about their experiences and expressing their own views on the project, the intermediaries can even find themselves guaranteeing the effectiveness of the project. They can substantiate their claims partly with the personal advantages that they have derived from cooperation with the project's representatives and partly with the tangible benefits enjoyed by the villagers (wells, combating cholera, credit). The result can be that the intermediary arouses even more unrealistic expectations in his fellow villagers. This can be partly explained by the fact that the contacts feel themselves to be under social pressure. For example, the villagers want to know why it takes so long for their expectations to be fulfilled. Because the intermediaries have been the principal link with the project, the villagers think they can influence the project to their advantage. The intermediaries are delighted when they are regarded as instrumental in bringing benefits to the village or creating them through personal intervention or influence, and they never miss an opportunity to remind the farmers of their "important position". But in the long run this means that the villagers call the intermediaries to account if their expectations are not fulfilled. The villagers put pressure on the intermediaries to do something to make the project keep its promises.

However, the project employees also play their part, because they are more than willing to go along with the expectations that the intermediaries have of the university. This gives them the chance to demonstrate to the farmers what an important position they have, and they tend to make exaggerated promises about the project's measures. From the perspective of the farmers, these employees are the most important project personnel, whereas in fact theirs is a subordinate role in the project hierarchy. This is why they do not feel inclined to tone down the exaggerated expectations, and they simply put their faith in the project as an institution able to live up to these expectations.

Thus, without being aware of the roles they are playing, the project workers and the intermediaries in the villages help to create myths about the project.

Contact with other villages also contributes to misconceptions of the project. A number of factors are involved. Contact with the university also means prestige, especially when it brings the village material benefits. Several Badeku villagers were not slow to point out in neighbouring villages that these contacts would be to their advantage (e. g. road building, water supply and electricity). Wishful thinking joined forces with what the project had actually organised (e. g. well construction).

In this way, both project farmers and project workers find themselves in a similar position — they are under pressure to succeed. To justify the project, the project workers have produced reports for the university, government and financial backers that underline its success. These reports contain much about how they would have liked the project to progress rather than how it was actually progressing. A particularly important point is that the project workers vouched for the farmers when dealing with other institutions, the Credit Corporation, for example, but without telling the farmers themselves or asking their opinions. The project workers were acting, in their own estimation, for the good of the farmers. In return for this service on their part, they "simply" expected the farmers to accept innovations, to comply with their requirement that maize production should rise, to appreciate the help of the project workers, and to be grateful.

The farmers assume that they are serving the project by cooperating with it and that they can expect something in return. Especially those farmers who have already invested their labour or even cash in the project (for example, farmers who offered their fields for maize cropping experiments) want to see at long last some of the rewards to which they have a right. Despite the high yield, they regard the maize harvest on the experimental field as justified payment for their special efforts in the service of the project. But since the other farmers in the village cannot see any tangible benefits from the project, they ask the intermediaries to urge the project to get on and fulfil their expectations.

In this phase in Badeku there was increased activity among the farmers, which can be explained partly by their dissatisfaction with the project and partly by their desire to secure possible future advantages. There was a corresponding increase in activity by the project workers, who by working harder wanted to remedy the obvious discrepancies between what they expected of the project (which was in their reports) and what had really happened. In this situation there are far more opportunities for the farmers and project workers to make contact with each other. The idea of forming groups now suggests itself to both sides. In retrospect, each side claims the idea for itself. In the interviews in 1977 in Badeku, people stressed that groups were formed on the initiative of the farmers and particularly of the intermediaries in the villages. The project workers claimed that formation of groups was a fundamental part of project philosophy and played an especially important role in the project strategy that had been devised by the university staff. The concept of groups, however, fits well in the strategy of extension and spreading innovations, and precisely who can claim to have originated the idea is irrelevant. As mentioned above, forming groups for particular purposes is an everyday occurrence among Yoruba farmers. When credit was paid out, it benefited groups in many ways, and it reinforced their readiness to do something for the project. In the meantime they have learned from personal contact that the project workers are very interested in seeing maize grown with the new methods. In these circumstances the groups are anxious to respond as required and to confirm the expectations of the project workers. But we must not assume that they are deliberately telling lies to deceive the project workers. On the contrary, the project workers formulate their questions in such a way that the response they are looking for is virtually preprogrammed. Investigating and analysing the way a project is running thus becomes a search for confirmation that the project's measures are correct.

3.4 Maintaining the illusion

We might well expect that the contradiction between expectations and actual events would lead to the farmers and project workers realising that they have been indulging in wishful thinking, and that this in turn would lead both sides to revise their ideas. But this does not happen. The intermediaries between the farmers and the field staff of the project again play a vitally important role. Any problems the project has will primarily affect them. The farmers will then put pressure on the intermediaries in the villages on account of what has become an "official role". In the case of the Badeku group this took the form of the members questioning the position of the chairman and the secretary of the group. Many people left the organisation; others threatened to withdraw or refused to work on the group's farm.

The project's field staff are given work that is no longer in line with either the project's basic concepts or their own positive reports. In this phase the representatives of the farmers and the project employees are very interested in achieving something for their members to encourage their continued cooperation or to keep them in the group. In Badeku this was done by procuring credit that gave the members financial advantages. In the groups that had formed in other villages, a low level of credit had been paid out from the start, and heightened tension resulted from the maize marketing plan, so that it proved impossible to stabilise them. Several groups disintegrated completely, although they were still nominally members of the project, which resulted in the critical situation not being recognised by the project management.

The farmers turn to the field staff with their problems and expectations, but this means they pass through a kind of filter and are amended before being passed on to project management. There are several reasons for this process of modification:

- Positive reports on their practical work that conform with the aims of the project are expected. If they mentioned discrepancies in their reports, it could be interpreted as an admission of incompetence. Moreover, as subordinates in the project hierarchy, they have no right to criticise the project.

- Field staff have little use for reports on discrepancies and unexpected reactions by farmers, because instead of the project being modified, management reacts by issuing new duties and instructions to solve existing problems. This means more work, more labour input, because the project management would like to receive reports of problems being overcome.

- The project management tends to interpret reports on deviating views of farmers, their wishes and criticisms as necessarily coming from uncooperative and backward individuals. Thus if farmers express critical views, the answers tend to be dogmatic and they discriminate against their critics. Field staff increasingly avoid reporting serious situations in order not to expose themselves to further criticism and to conceal the fact that they have far less influence on project management than they had pretended.

In summary, these three points mean that the project employees would call their own position into question if they emphasised the discrepancies. Consequently there is a tendency for them to conceal conflicts from both the farmers and project management, to ignore them or to play them down. Thus they go through the motions of carrying out instructions and then file them away as having been dealt with. In reality, conflicts continue to exist.

The employees react by trying to reduce their workload so that they can at least cover the formal requirements of their posts. For example, they have to keep minutes of meetings of the extension committee and write reports for the project management; they have to arrange the dates of discussions in the villages. It is easy to stress the positive aspects, to confirm fulfilled expectations and either to leave out critical points or to report them in such a way that they do not appear to call for further action. But we have to remember that these comments and oral reports eventually find their way into the official reports on the project. The following example illustrates what happens in practice.

During a trial demonstration of a tropical variety of bean ("cowpeas", vigna unguiculata), the project planned to let the farmers spray the experimental fields to control insects. The field staff were supposed to tell them how to carry out this work. When they appeared in the village and asked the farmers to help on the experimental fields, not one of them was at first prepared to do so. There were lengthy discussions and time passed. Finally one came forward, to be joined much later by two others. But because so much time had elapsed, explanations were kept to a minimum and the project workers did the spraying themselves, so that they could return to Ibadan before nightfall. When it was time to spray again, they did all the work themselves without even asking the farmers in the village if they wanted to be involved. They were finished in about one hour compared with about three hours when they had sprayed for the first time. The project management was told that the fields had been sprayed according to the technical instructions. The fact that not one single farmer participated was not mentioned.

The farmers are not without blame for helping to perpetuate these illusions of communication. Even though the project workers repeatedly stressed that the new cropping methods were to be applied on the group farms, the Badeku farmers still cropped maize and cassava together. This happened on a part of the farm that could not be seen from the access paths. The representatives of the project, who often came to the village with visitors from other institutions, were only shown the nearest plots and, in the experience of the villagers, that was all that the visitors wanted to see. A kind of ritual programme quickly developed for visitors. They were always taken to the well, shown the medical post and they inspected the maize store and local soap production. Then they went to the farm that in 1976 was about 2 km from the village. Different groups of visitors came, but this programme was repeated time and again; the villagers had become accustomed to visitors and had the appropriate information ready.

3.5 Withdrawal

The Badeku project was still operating in 1978, although officially it started to wind down in 1976. The stated reason was that the project had given the farmers the ability to manage their own affairs and to represent their own interests. It was claimed that they had learned to make contact with the administration and to negotiate on their own behalf and further that they would apply the new cropping methods with modern inputs. Since they had learned all these things, they would be in a position to accept more innovations in future. The eventual official withdrawal is not important for our understanding of the various phases of the project. During the whole course of the project there are in fact signs of withdrawal both by the farmers and the project: at the outset both sides anticipated success and showed therefore a high level of commitment, but this commitment diminished when the expected benefits were not forthcoming. The intermediaries in the villages and the project's field staff were among the first to be affected by this loss of enthusiasm.

C 4

Personal reactions:

Both the intermediaries and the project employees soon realised that their interpretations were incorrect and that they could not keep their promises. When directly approached, they pointed out that it was the responsibility of the project management or other institutions and that the situation being criticised was beyond their control. For example, at a meeting of group representatives in Egbeda in the spring of 1976, the project management repeatedly pointed out that the credit institution was to blame for the late payment of credit and that the project was in no way responsible. However, this weak link in the organisation had been apparent from the start, and it could have been analysed and taken into account in planning.

There are also more subtle reactions. The field staff are dependent on the cooperation of the farmers, but, since they have a great deal to do, they prefer to work with farmers who appreciate their efforts and produce positive results. They pay less attention to groups that make demands and criticise or doubt the usefulness of the work of field staff. They justify this neglect by claiming that the critical and demanding farmers are backward and unreasonable. Some of the intermediaries in the villages have put a great deal of effort into forming groups and their organisation in the hope of greater personal influence or a permanent job. Many of their smaller requests having been granted, if new requests and demands are rejected, some of them take it personally and are no longer prepared to do anything for the project. These are not calculated personal reactions; they are undirected and unpredictable and can give rise to conflict. Some groups reformed themselves as a result of personal reactions of this kind. The intermediaries were changed and new group representatives sought direct contact with the project in Ibadan without relying on the previous intermediaries and also without reference to the project's employees. However, the opportunity to investigate what had happened was never followed up.

Reactions of the institution:

Such personal reactions also provoke reactions by the project as an institution. First, the project employees are encouraged to intensify their instructional work in the villages. But then we find that the project will no longer act as general guarantor and that the farmers are no longer free to use their credit as they wish. The project exercises controls, demands security in the form of the group farm and in this way develops its own credit institution with conditions that are even more stringent than those of the Credit Corporation. The farmers' motivation for joining the groups is ignored.

There are further important changes that affect the project as an institution. In the initial phase the planners and managers went on fact-finding visits to the villages; they wanted to consolidate existing contacts and make new ones. They worked closely with the field staff — which strengthened their motivation. The visits to the villages influenced the decisions taken by the project managers. But in the course of time, contact with the villages is left increasingly to the project's employees. The situation in which these people now have to work is one of more and more criticism by the farmers, at a time when groups are breaking up, instructions not being carried out, etc. The project management also leave negotiations and decisions increasingly to the employees. Since they do not have the formal competence to take these decisions, they tend to avoid them. The interviews showed that the farmers expected very little of the project employees. Some farmers' groups had, for example, asked to be allowed to negotiate directly with the project management, but, since the managers did not appear in the villages, the farmers assumed that the field staff had not passed on their request.

The project managers give as their reasons for withdrawal the workload at the university, the fact that the project employees have received sufficient training to work independently and the farmers have learned in the meantime how to approach particular institutions. But when they justify their action in this way, they overlook the fact that the project employees are still bound by the instructions of the management and that they are held responsible for, and therefore have to bear the consequences of wrong decisions.

There is some truth in the official explanation for withdrawal of the project, namely that the farmers have learned to handle their affairs for themselves. Some groups get seed and fertiliser for maize themselves from the appropriate government research station in Ibadan. One group even made contact on its own initiative with the International Institute of Tropical Agriculture to obtain information on new varieties of cassava. Through reference to the project they managed to secure advantages for themselves and they did not even inform the project workers of their action. Nevertheless, we are not justified in attributing these independent actions simply to the influence of the project. There are instances elsewhere of farmers organising themselves in order to pursue particular interests.

Some members of groups argued in the spring of 1977 that the university project was perhaps hampering progress, because people in the area were saying that Badeku was not a progressive village. Despite a severe shortage of water in the village in 1977, the Badeku villagers refused to sink new wells because they felt that this would only delay a piped water supply even longer. Construction of the pipeline was finally begun in 1978 after a direct appeal to the local government. However, it was another six years before the pipeline was finished, and it was finally connected up in 1985. No one in the village even bothered to inform the pilot project of the actions and preparations leading up to this significant event.

It could be argued that the farmers were only able to take action because the pilot project had made them more aware. But even this line of argument is not totally convincing, because the Badeku farmers organised, for example, the construction of an advice centre for mothers before the project was started in the village. For decades roads have been repaired annually by communal effort, and there is no

C 4

doubt that Badeku farmers have been influential in the political sphere, in the Agbekoya Movement, for example.

For reasons of space, we conclude our selected extracts at this point. In his article, Peter AY goes on to give detailed analyses of the interests of the people affected by or participating in the project, the areas of conflict and the strategies for action. For further information, the reader is referred to the source we have used for this contribution.

Source:

Peter AY: Agrarpolitik in Nigeria – Produktionssysteme der Bauern und die Hilflosigkeit von Entwicklungsexperten. Ein Beitrag zur Revision agrarpolitischer Maßnahmen in Entwicklungsländern. – Feldforschung in Westnigeria –. Arbeiten aus dem Institut für Afrika-Kunde, Nr. 24, Hamburg 1980. 337 p. (Largely verbatim from pp. 140 – 185, with some cuts).

Compiled by:

Volker HOFFMANN

C 5

Experience of technical demonstrations in agricultural development projects

Demonstrations play a key role in many development programmes. In a successful project in **Ghana,** the most progressive farmers were identified and asked to try some innovations on a small area of their fields. They were simple innovations that had been carefully tested on research stations and did not involve financial risk. The selected farmers were given intensive back-up by advisers. In **Kenya,** the expansion of tea cultivation depended largely on the demonstration effect of farmers who were already cropping tea. By observing tea cultivation, the farmers not only became interested in the crop but also learned the basic techniques at the same time. In **Zambia,** a vegetable project was successful because interested farmers were given the opportunity to establish small experimental plots on common land. Thus there was hardly any risk involved, and the farmers had their first experience of growing vegetables. The projects in **Puebla,** and many others as well, make use of demonstrations and exploit the demonstration effect in their extension programmes.

In **Nigeria,** all the production means required for demonstrations were distributed with instructions in prepared packages. This simplified distribution and ensured that all the production inputs were available in the right quantities for all the demonstration plots. In each village, leaders of the village selected a demonstration farmer to receive this package. The demonstration then consisted of four improved and one local variety of maize. Thus the demonstration also became a field trial. The demonstration plots were visited regularly by advisers and research staff to ensure continuous checking and the exchange of ideas. This model was applied successfully in other countries too.

The use of demonstration in extension has many advantages. Visits to farms with successful field trials were shown in **Puebla** to be much more convincing and persuasive than the explanations of the advisers, and subsequent extension work was made appreciably easier. Here too demonstration proved to be a good way of testing under field conditions. Innovations are introduced on a wide scale only after demonstrations have been successfully carried out, and the risk level is thus kept low.

Demonstrations are not, of course, the solution to all extension problems. The **Barpali Village Service in India** had some success when demonstrations were used to motivate farmers to adopt innovations. The advisers started growing vegetables, and thus gave the farmers some incentive to grow vegetables themselves. But in this case adoption of this innovation was made easier by extending the area of irrigated land and by creating new markets. As production rose, however, there was a considerable fall in price that made vegetable cultivation uneconomic, and the project was finally wound up.

C 5

The same extension service then tried to improve local poultry by distributing cock birds for breeding. But the advisers did not consider the needs and capabilities of the village population, with the result that most farmers refused to exchange their birds for the better quality cock birds. There is a practical explanation for this behaviour, namely the much higher costs for coops for improved cock birds, feed and veterinary checks. Poultry cooperatives established by the extension service were a failure, and they were abandoned when the foreign specialist lost interest in poultry keeping.

These examples show that the farmers recognise the desirability of a useful and profitable innovation demonstrated by advisers or other farmers and that they will adopt it. Other innovations, that were not to the advantage of the villagers and were planned without involving them in decisions, were most definitely failures.

Demonstrations are no compensation for the inadequacy or inappropriateness of technology or an institution, and they are also no substitute for involvement of farmers in working out extension topics. They are particularly effective when it is a question of persuading farmers that they will benefit from using new technology. This is the case when target groups have already expressed an interest in adopting an innovation. These demonstrations are more likely to be successful when they are carried out by farmers on their own land. Demonstrations in **Gambia** that were carried out solely by advisers were a failure. It proved impossible to continue the project until two villages had laid out their own experimental plots and seen how successful they were. These villages only implemented the experiments because the production inputs had been made available at low cost, subsistence production was not endangered by the innovation and the farmers had no alternative income. Demonstrating an innovation on a peasant holding is always more convincing than a report of trial results, demonstrations on experimental stations or demonstrations by advisers themselves. Farmers have learned to be suspicious of anything that they have not experienced personally. Because of this mistrust the word "demonstration" was replaced in the **Puebla** project by "high yield cropping". Planting was always left to the farmers, the advisers simply giving guidance on how to proceed.

An important reason why demonstrations should be undertaken as far as possible by the farmers is that advisers do not usually have any time to spend on this job, or at least not enough time to do it properly.

For further information, see → Tables 1 and 2 in → Chapter III.14 and → E 6 and → E 7.

Bibliography:

A. WATERSTON: Managing Planned Agricultural Development. Washington: Governmental Affairs Institute, 1976.

Compiled by:

Gerhard PAYR, Rolf SÜLZER

C 6

Problems of working with contact farmers

Again and again attempts have been made in many different ways to involve farmers directly in extension work. One of the best known endeavours to involve contact farmers in extension was undertaken in Comilla in Bangladesh. In this case the functionaries of the cooperatives and the contact farmers were selected by the members of the cooperatives.

Only outstanding and trustworthy farmers were to be accepted. In addition, individuals were chosen to be responsible for women and young people. They were given instruction once a week in agriculture and the functioning of cooperatives. They were expected to pass on what they had learned to the target groups. At the same time they were supposed to look out for difficulties in implementation, listen to farmers' comments on the extension packages and recount them at the weekly training sessions. If the contact farmers were particularly successful, they were made into controllers in charge of up to four cooperatives. These farmers were then given additional weekly training, but this proved to be yet another demand on their time.

The assumption underlying this programme was that farmers accept information from agricultural advisers but not instructions. Thus the farmers would be much more likely to follow the advice of trustworthy farmers. Such farmers do not normally belong to the official elite in a village. These assumptions were formulated and agreed in the Comilla research centre.

But problems nevertheless arose in practice. In particular, there were disagreements between the functionaries in the cooperatives and contact farmers. As a consequence, the two areas of activity were amalgamated. In most villages only about half the villagers participated in the cooperative and the wealthier farmers benefited disproportionately. Expansion of the project over the region was prevented by escalating total costs, and it was finally abandoned.

An attempt was made later to revive the approach. Once again the cooperatives were rapidly dominated by the relatively large-scale farmers and used for their purposes. In 1974 the number of contact farmers taking part in weekly training was usually lower than 30%. The reason given was the irrelevance of such training to the real needs of the majority of farmers.

A simple concept was tried in **Daudzai in Pakistan.** The farmers were first organised in cooperatives to solve problems. Later, obligatory savings programmes and weekly gatherings were introduced. In addition, contact farmers had to take part in training every two weeks, and they also took charge of the farmers' weekly meetings. The project failed because the contact farmers had to spend too much time on extension activities.

C 6

A similar project was tried by **CADU in Ethiopia.** Of five candidates proposed by the farmers, one was chosen by the adviser to be the contact farmer. One adviser with two assistants was in charge of 15 contact farmers. Instead of giving them formal training at a centre, the advisers supervised the contact farmers during extension work. The programme functioned well at first, but in this case too it eventually led to the contact farmers neglecting their own farms. As a consequence, they became less willing to be involved in extension work.

Contact farmers were also used in the **ZAPI project** in **Cameroon.** They were chosen by the advisers, the main criteria being knowledge of French and contact with the administration. The status of these farmers in the rural community was practically ignored. Because hardly any attention was paid to the overall technical and institutional conditions, the project foundered.

Summary

There are very few cases where the use of contact farmers as advisers has met with lasting success. The reasons for this state of affairs seem to be as follows:

- In Comilla one contact farmer per village was supposed to have the trust of all the farmers and to take over the work of extension. It later transpired that in one village there were up to 14 leaders of opinion, and logically therefore the same number of contact farmers should have been chosen. Of course, this would not have been a practical proposition.

- The main mistake in the Cameroon project was that outside advisers often chose contact farmers who most resembled themselves. Consequently, the contact farmers were often too young, too well educated, too prosperous or too progressive to serve as credible examples for the mass of poorer farmers.

- Contact farmers were often used simply to keep down the cost of extension. The problem of limited input by contact farmers and the fact that time used for extension was needed for other purposes was usually ignored.

- Contact farmers were normally only given the task of relaying prepackaged information on behalf of the advisers. Experience has shown that the interest and enthusiasm of contact farmers rapidly decline unless they and the target groups can participate in problem solving and decisions on the measures to be taken.

- The concept of formal training was also largely misguided: by first training advisers and contact farmers, information was supposed finally to reach the mass of farmers. But because of illiteracy and unfamiliarity with texts and

C 6

lectures, practical demonstrations have proved to be much more suitable as a means of communication.

Contact farmers often tend to use information and extension measures principally for themselves and relatives. There is greater danger of this happening the less the farmers are involved in deciding who should be the contact farmers and what should be the content of extension.

We have pinpointed real weaknesses, but at the same time we can see possible remedies. The more the target groups participate in choosing contact farmers, and the more practical their preparation, the more likely it is that they will support extension work in an effective way.

For further information on working with contact farmers, the reader is referred to → E 4 and → F 9.

Source:

A. WATERSTON: "Managing Planned Agricultural Development". Washington: Governmental Affairs Institute 1976.

Compiled by:

Rolf SÜLZER, Gerhard PAYR

C 7

Problems of leadership style in organisations

Since being an organiser calls for a large measure of skill in dealing with people, the style of leadership in organisations is of vital importance. As described in → Chapter III.14, performance and job satisfaction in organisations depend largely on the view of people on which senior staff base their dealings with subordinates. Thus notions of how to behave and why such behaviour is desirable determine the approach, the style of leadership.

It is customary to classify systems of leadership as follows:

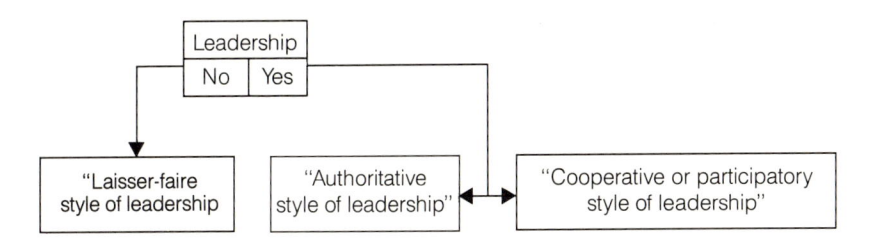

```
            Leadership
            No   Yes
    ┌────────┘    │
    ▼             │
┌──────────────┐  ├──────────────────┬──────────────────────┐
│ "Laisser-faire│  │  "Authoritative  │◄────►│ "Cooperative or participatory │
│ style of      │  │  style of        │      │ style of leadership"          │
│ leadership"   │  │  leadership"     │      │                                │
└──────────────┘  └──────────────────┘      └──────────────────────┘
```

The classifications "authoritative – cooperative" represent the ends of a scale and are theoretical extremes. In reality, however, styles of leadership are almost always hybrid forms and lie somewhere along the scale. We can identify these styles of leadership by, for example, the methods used to persuade people to comply:

	Method of leadership	Reasons for complying
Ethically and morally not acceptable	Force Threat of force Emotional pressure Suggestion Trying to impress	Compulsion Fear, Worry Emotional dependence Mental subjugation Intimidation or admiration
Authoritative Cooperative	Insistence on rank Insistence on duties Promise of reward Promise of recognition Personal concern Personal request, taking into confidence Sympathetic model Idealising the job Revealing motives Putting trust in others Rational orientation and reasons Joint discussion	Obedience and humility Interpretation of job, obligations Striving to earn more Wanting to impress Gratitude, loyalty Helpfulness, responsibility Respect Enthusiasm Trust Proving worthy of this trust Insight, shared resonsibility Personal decisions, shared responsibility

C 7

In general the style of leadership determines:

- the form of contact;
- the attitude of the leader to the led and his leadership behaviour;

Social-psychological effects other systems of leadership		
	Authoritative	Cooperative
I. 1. Form of contact	Distant, hierarchic	Close, egalitarian
II. 2. Personal behaviour of leaders 3. Attitude to subordinates	Stress on authority, demonstrating rank. Likes obedient, willing individuals. Values obedience and discipline	Straightforward, avoid ceremony and formality Values free, independent thinkers
III. 4. Emotional reaction of subordinates 5. Motives for action 6. Attitude to leadership	Often does not feel fully understood and appreciated, feels restricted or suppressed according to his level Sense of duty Respect, deference	Feels personally appreciated and understood, liberated or privileged according to his level Insight, feeling of responsibility Affection, familiarity
IV. 7. Communication on an intellectual level and bond with the system of leadership 8. Social climate created	Little Slight tension. Danger of mutual mistrust, formation of cliques	Large measure of participation in all planning and intentions Trust, cohesion and harmony

System of leadership	Authoritative	Cooperative
1. Preconditions	Big difference in education between leaders and subordinates	Same level of education in leaders and subordinates
2. Advantages	Quick decisions	Correct decisions, because checked by those who carry them out, stability, natural selection of potential leaders
3. Dangers	Collapse of group unless there is constant leadership	Slow decision making, collapse of cooperation in complicated situations
4. Requirements	High level of personal responsibility and self-monitoring, foresight, tact	Receptivity to ideas, mental agility, willingness to trust others, foregoing personal privileges

- the reactions of the subordinate partner, his motives and attitudes to leadership and to his superiors;
- the degree of mutual communication and the social and psychological climate (working atmosphere).

Depending on the particular circumstances, each system of leadership has advantages and disadvantages. When we recommend cooperative and participatory leadership, it must not be forgotten that adequate preconditions for this style of leadership have to be created. We should also remember that, in special situations,

Managerial functions	Role interpretation in different styles of leadership		
	Authoritative	Combination	Cooperative
1. Making plan		Inspirer Initiator	Group member
2. Implementation of plans, break-down into tasks		Isolated specialist	
3. Allocating jobs to suitable people	Leader	Organiser	Group coordinator
4. Giving instructions on implementation	Commander	Manager	Responsible senior partner
5. Showing how to implement plans: demonstrate, explain, let workers practise, encourage independence		Master Instructor	Adviser Friend
6. Supervising implementation	Controller		Helper
7. Evaluating the result	Critic		Expert
8. Correction, adjustment	Judge		Encouragement of self-discipline and group discipline
9. Maintaining discipline	Holder of power		

C 7

if time is short or action imperative, there may be no alternative to an authoritarian approach if solutions are to be found. This deviation from the usual practice of cooperative leadership is acceptable if the leaders in question are trusted individuals and have genuine authority.

The style of leadership is determined not only by the image of colleagues but also by the leader's interpretation of his own role.

The key to the cooperative and participatory style of leadership is the transfer of skills and responsibility from the leader to the workers who accept the spirit of cooperation. Thus delegation of duties becomes the most important principle of successful management.

Finally, we illustrate the above once again by contrasting the basic features and types of behaviour across the range of styles of leadership.

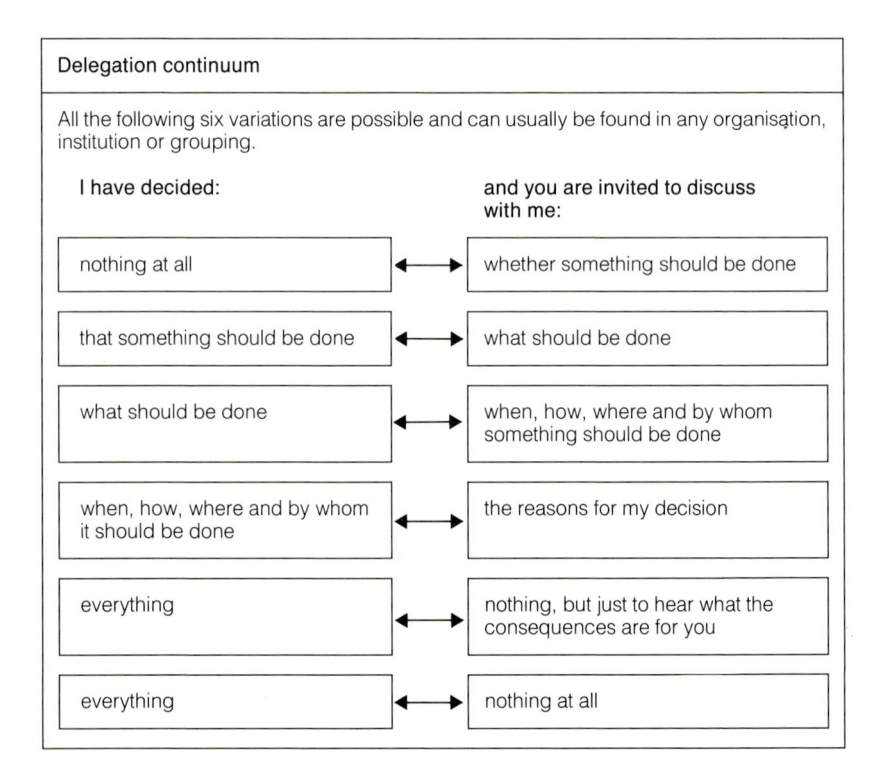

Delegation continuum

All the following six variations are possible and can usually be found in any organisation, institution or grouping.

I have decided:		and you are invited to discuss with me:
nothing at all	⟷	whether something should be done
that something should be done	⟷	what should be done
what should be done	⟷	when, how, where and by whom something should be done
when, how, where and by whom it should be done	⟷	the reasons for my decision
everything	⟷	nothing, but just to hear what the consequences are for you
everything	⟷	nothing at all

Features of different styles of leadership

Dirigistic/authoritative	Cooperative/participatory
1. A boss taking all decisions is most effective.	1. Decisions that draw on the knowledge of everyone involved are most effective.
2. Managerial staff decide as much as possible on their own (isolated decisions).	2. Workers are encouraged to think about solutions, even for difficult cases, and to put them forward.
3. Senior staff constantly try to extend their influence.	3. Senior staff work hard to improve the status of their colleagues.
4. Senior staff use pressure and fear to make colleagues work.	4. The performance of colleagues improves throgh recognition and further training.
5. Senior staff constantly check the work of all colleagues.	5. Colleagues develop a sense of personal responsibility because of jointly formulated targets and procedures.
6. Senior staff take credit for good work by subordinates.	6. Senior staff give credit for good work by colleagues and tell superiors who was responsible.
7. In discussions and in conversation workers are on their guard and reticent, because they fear blame or disapproval.	7. Discussions and conversations are lively and draw on the workers' expertise, because there is no fear of sanctions if they express themselves clumsily or make mistakes.
8. Criticism takes the form of personal blame and rebuke, without discussing the real cause.	8. Senior staff justify criticism and give colleagues the opportunity to reply.

Sources:

K. ANTONS: Praxis der Gruppendynamik. Übungen und Techniken. Göttingen: Hogrefe, 4th Ed., 1976, Delegation continuum after G. SCHWARZ, T. JOHNSTADT, p. 174.

E. BORNEMANN: Sozialpsychologische Probleme der Führung. In: Kölner Zeitschrift für Soziologie und Sozialpsychologie, 1962, pp. 105–123.

C. M. PRINCE: Creative meeting through power sharing. In: Harvard Business Review, 1972.

Compiled by:

Volker HOFFMANN

C 8

"Extension", an international terminology problem

There are many problems of terminology in the international discussion of extension. We find that in practice standard translations have become established, but if we examine them more closely it can be seen that certain concepts that are regarded as synonymous have very different meanings. As a consequence, communication on the subject of extension is difficult or in some cases even impossible. In → Table 1 we have compiled examples from various European languages. Since we do not have either the knowledge or the means of transcribing non-European languages, they have to be excluded from this comparison.

The range of terminology is matched by the range of interpretations and underlying philosophies of extension.

Some thoughts on "word development"

If we turn our attention specifically to the vocabulary of German, we find that even the term "beraten" (to advise) has various meanings, although at first sight it appears to be quite unambiguous. Our everyday use of the word in the context of extension as a verb taking a person as a direct or indirect object is a relatively recent phenomenon in the history of the language.

beraten (to advise)

Person as direct or indirect object		No 'third party' as direct or indirect object	
jemanden beraten	– to advise someone	sich beraten	– to discuss/consult
einen Rat geben	– to give advice	mit sich zu Rate gehen	– to consider
einen Ratschlag geben	– to give a piece of advice	etwas gemeinsam beraten	– to discuss together
		etwas beratschlagen	– to discuss

The original meaning of the word appears to show that it was used without a direct or indirect object in the form of a person addressed.

C 8

Table 1:

Extension and adviser: internationally incompatible expressions			
Language	Term denoting giving advice	Content of term	Term denoting the person giving advice
German:	Beratung	give advice, assistance for problem solving	Berater, Ratgeber
French:			Conseiller
British and American English:	Advisory work		Advisor
	Counselling	psychologically advising	Counsellor
	Consultation	consult	Consultant
	Extension	disseminate	Extension-Agent
Spanish:	Extension	spread out	Extensionista
Portuguese:	Extensao		Extensionista
French:	Vulgarisation	to make popular	Vulgarisateur
Italian:	Divulgazione	spread out	Divulgatore
French:	Encadrement	to frame to incorporate to check in to file in	Encadreur
French:	Animation	to motivate to activate	Animateur
French:		indicator monitor commander	Moniteur
Dutch:	Voorlichting	to light ahead illuminate	Voorlichter
Danish:	Oplysning	enlighten	Consulent
Italian:	Assistenza tecnica	technical assistance, help	Assistente tecnico

The unspecified recipient of advice

If you have needed to write about extension, you must have come across the difficulty of what to call the person being addressed by the adviser.

Berater (adviser)	?
Berater (adviser)	Beratener (person being advised)
Berater (adviser)	Beratungspartner (extension partner)
Ratgeber (person giving advice)	Ratnehmer (person receiving advice)
Ratbietender (person offering advice)	Ratsuchender (person seeking advice)
Therapeut (therapist)	Klient (client)
?	Kunde (customer)
?	Zielperson/Zielgruppe (target individual/target group)

All the terms in common use are inadequate, cobbled together, and do not quite express what we want to say. If our view on the different use of verbs is correct, it helps to explain the dilemma. If "beraten" was originally used in the way shown in the second column, there was no direct object in the linguistic sense and therefore no person addressed. It was only used in the sense of "pondering", thinking things over in the company of others.

As the meaning changed to "giving advice to others", the word "beraten" was retained but the people involved in the process of giving and receiving became active and passive participants. The word for the active partner was easily derived (Berater = adviser), but for the recipient of advice there is still no unequivocal, generally accepted term in German. Because he receives advice, the terminology used denotes his passive role, his position of weakness.

Negative connotation in the change of meaning

Critics who are sceptical about the increasing professionalisation of all service activities have pointed out that, with the shift towards the transitive use, people are more likely to be deprived of the right to manage their own affairs. "Ratschlag geben" (giving a piece of advice) becomes in this sense an aggressive act, because "Schlag" means literally to be beaten with advice. We can detect this kind of aggression in the current use of extension "being applied to target groups". In French the military connotation is particularly clear. When the term "groupe – cible" is used, we realise that "cible" or "cibler" are derived directly from aiming at targets. Also "encadrer" could be of military origin; under Napoleon a "cadre" was the smallest military unit under common command.

Finally, we sometimes find people in irrigation projects being forced to cultivate particular crops – which is euphemistically called "production under close supervision" and referred to as an "extension approach". "Beratung", in the sense of of-

C 8

fering advice, sounds good and everyone lays claim to the word, even if what they do in practice is far from "advising". So, be careful! Be on your guard against misleading labels.

The reader will now appreciate why we were at such pains to define the concept of extension and its precise application in → Chapter I.2.

Source:

Volker HOFFMANN: Beratungsbegriff und Beratungsphilosophie im Feld des Verbraucherhandels. − Eine subjektive Standortbestimmung und Abgrenzung. In: Die Qualität von Beratungen für Verbraucher, Campus Forschung. Band 462, Frankfurt, New York, 1985, pp. 26 − 47.

Compiled by:

Volker HOFFMANN

Cases and examples of method

D 1

Problem-solving method of RIP in Botswana

"Rural Industries Promotions" (RIP) is a non-commercial company that runs a "Rural Industries Innovation Centre" in Kanye, Botswana. It **works together** with the people to develop production methods that will attract workshops and small-scale industry to rural regions.

Anyone who tries something new is still regarded even today as an outsider by the various Bantu tribes. In the Innovation Centre, the staff have developed the method of permanent dialogue with the people, to persuade them to use different equipment and tools. Dialogue comprises the following:

(1) To find out who has problems, what the problems are and what solutions the people would like, experts from the Innovation Centre regularly visit and hold detailed discussions with:

- tribal chiefs;
- village communities;
- cooperatives;
- individual artisans;
- government officials.

(2) After discussing with them which problems are urgent and should be given priority, the staff at the Centre look for solutions — in the literature, by contacting experts inside and outside Botswana and in practical development work in the Centre's own workshop.

(3) Prototypes are then constructed in the Centre and tried out (e.g. pasture fencing, millet threshers, carriers for bicycles).

(4) The staff take these prototypes to the people who sought their help. They then get them to judge the effectiveness of the prototypes.

(5) They discuss together how the objects can be produced (materials, tools required, methods) and together with the village communities they look for small production facilities.

(6) When the small-scale manufacturers have accepted the work, the design is adapted to their facilities, they are given help with the first few items, and where necessary they are also given initial training.

D 1

(7) While the manufacturer is busy with production technology problems, the representatives from the Centre try to organise a healthy production base: credit, purchase of raw materials, marketing the products.

(8) The Centre continues to observe production over a fairly long period and watches out for any problems that may occur.

Compiled by:

Rolf SÜLZER, Gerhard PAYR

D 2

Problem-solving approach in the "Tetu Extension Project" in Kenya

The Tetu region lies in the Kikuyu highlands in Kenya's Central Province. The extension project is a part of the larger "Special Rural Development Programme" (SRDP). In this programme, innovative methods to promote rural development are tried out. They are supposed to be experiments that can be replicated and transferred to other regions.

The Extension Project in Tetu began with a **basic survey** of the current production methods, innovations that had already been introduced, farm types and communications (situation analysis).

The **diagnosis** based on this survey established that none of the previous development efforts in the region had reached the small farmers, who lacked the know-how to turn proposals into actual innovations on their farms.

The result of the situation analysis and the diagnosis were presented at several levels, so that a **strategy** could be worked out. Thus the first draft of the situation analysis was discussed in the project territory with officials at Province, District and Division level. Attention was drawn to bottlenecks, inequalities and the importance of specific communication techniques for particular groups of farmers.

In the course of the discussions, the officials became increasingly familiar with the difficulties faced by the region, so that they eventually agreed to change the orientation of the already existing Farmer Training Centres to cater for the needs of small farmers. The results of the situation analysis were not published or presented for consideration until these discussions had been concluded.

The plan of action comprised a special training programme for the staff of the training centres in communication techniques, criteria for selecting advisers (Junior Agricultural Assistants), establishing a card index record of farmers and farms, developing the curriculum, teachers testing the curricula on the Junior Agricultural Assistants, recruiting farmers, training and supervising them, special advisory work and evaluation. This plan had to be implemented at widely differing levels. It became apparent after only a short time that there was no point in trying to do this in Nairobi. Officials did not have enough time to read the proposals or even to come to the programme of seminars.

Thus the plan was explained, using transparencies and an overhead projector, at meetings in the countryside. After each presentation of the plan, experts, local functionaries and District leaders from various ministries sat down together to discuss the possibilities. In the process, some proposals even took on a life of their own. A report of successful meetings and the idea of not confining training pro-

D 2

grammes to agriculture even got as far as the cabinet in Nairobi. Officials at Province level were then asked how they had arrived at these proposals, which they had in fact not made! The approach came to a temporary halt when the impetus was lost. But because of good contacts and relations with the population, the project group finally succeeded in gaining renewed access to the people.

The situation analysis, diagnosis and strategy were presented at various conferences and seminars: "Nyeri Workshop on Co-ordinating Education", "Kampala Social Science Conference", "The Rural Development Seminar" and "Wamalwa Commission on Training". After three months things had settled down, and the plan could be put into practice in the first training centres.

This short introduction to the method adopted makes two conditions clear:

(1) The problem-solving approach can be tedious, but it nevertheless mobilises many people and makes an impact over a wide area.

(2) Time and again programmes are ruined because they do not have the agreement and political backing of everyone involved. Resources are withdrawn or not made available, people refuse to cooperate or − as in this case − permission to enter the region is cancelled.

Compiled by:

Gerhard PAYR, Rolf SÜLZER

D 3

Deciding on extension methods in the "Kawinga RDP" in Malawi

1. General development policy situation

A National Rural Development Programme (NRDP) has been operating in Malawi since 1976. The aim of the programme, which encompasses the whole country, is to improve the living conditions of the rural poor. To fulfil development policy, both indirect and specifically devised and targeted measures are employed. The following principles underlie the attempt to implement this concept of a mass development programme to combat rural poverty:

(1) Target groups participate in planning and implementing the programmes through target group organisations that are set up at village, area and district level.

(2) Phased project planning and implementation is to be achieved by splitting the project into extensive and intensive phases and by appropriate control mechanisms.

The planned timescale for the implementation of projects in the NRDP is 15 – 20 years. In the first phase the project takes stock of the situation, investigates development possibilities and at the same time begins to build up the infrastructure and administration. In the second phase (extensive phase over 5 years), basic agricultural services like extension, credit and marketing are expanded. Far-reaching innovations in production technology are not introduced until the third phase (intensive phase). Finally, in the fourth phase (consolidation), rural trades and industries are developed.

To put this development concept into practice, Malawi was divided into 8 agricultural development regions, each consisting of 6 – 10 project regions. The further subdivision of these project regions then represented the lowest level for planning, implementation and control. Each of the 8 development regions was allocated a central management unit that consisted of specialists, administrative personnel and a project monitoring and evaluation department.

2. Planning the project territory of Kawinga

To help understand the methodology used in the Kawinga project, we first give a brief account of the planning stages. We then explain how decisions were made to use particular extension methods.

D 3

- Basic information was collected about the project territory and the population covered by the project.

- The major factors impeding the use of available production methods were investigated (analysis of obstacles).

- Steps were taken to establish which population groups were in a similar position regarding resource provision and obstacles (target groups).

- Drafts of possible measures were prepared to show target groups how to make better use of production methods with their given factor provision.

- The possible repercussions of these measures were quantified, and the costs of implementation were established.

- The micro and macroeconomic benefits of the various alternatives were calculated, and a decision was made on the package that offered the best combination.

- The best way to implement the chosen measures was devised.

3. Procedure for deciding on extension methods

a) Extension-specific situation analysis

The aim of this analysis is to gather information from the target groups and the existing extension organisation. The procedure adopted was as follows:

- evaluation of existing surveys by planning departments, research posts, donor institutes;

- evaluation of existing data in statistical offices, ministries, regional and district administration;

- study of documents of regional, district and field offices regarding Kawinga (programme planning, monthly reports, records of discussions, information from field advisers, files on personnel);

- comparison with documented experiences of similar projects inside and outside the country;

- discussion with experts in the ministries, other levels of administration, research establishment, traditional leaders, party functionaries, missionaries;

- interviews with 176 farmers in the project area to establish and define specific extension problems.

b) Analysis of weaknesses

Weaknesses in the extension organisation can be pinpointed with the help of data in the situation analysis. This indicates where improvements could or should be made. Typical weaknesses of a quantitative and qualitative nature are:

- adviser density;
- advisers' qualifications;
- applied methodology;
- content of extension;
- organisation and management;
- material resources.

c) Deciding on the content of extension

Extension measures (in the first year) were the result of interdisciplinary decisions by all the planners involved in the project, with the participation of the target groups and advisers. The following example illustrates the relation between the objective of development aid, extension measures, the extension concept and the actual process of extension work.

From the microeconomic angle, the gross margin from hybrid maize cultivated under optimal conditions is appreciably higher than that of single strain local varieties that can be grown again and again. But, as surveys in neighbouring territories have shown over the years, optimal cultivation conditions rarely exist in small farmer agriculture, even when the average level of advisory work is high. Thus, in the light of the limited extension capacity, variations in soil fertility and low profitability, single strain maize was preferred to hybrid maize in the first phase of the project.

d) The extension concepts

By adopting the right approach, innovations were to be spread to cover the mass of small farmers. Thus with an adviser ratio of 1 : 500 the common practice of targeting aid at progressive farmers was abandoned, since it was shown to be fairly ineffectual. Instead, priority was given to group extension with the help of target group organisations (committees) at village and regional level.

e) Deciding on extension methods

The village development committees are the driving force behind extension and disseminate the packages of innovations. Thus, one of the first tasks of extension is to create and train a committee in every village that represents all target groups and decision makers. Depending on their level of efficiency, these committees also take charge of complementary measures (credit, reforestation, seedbeds for rice, erosion control, etc.) as well as extension itself.

Individual extension work is restricted to the following groups:

- contact farmers of the committees;

- powerful local people who have been identified as resisting extension and therefore have a negative effect on the extension effort as a whole. Advisers try to change their attitude to one of support for extension work.

- progressive farmers should only be advised on an individual basis when they are given untested innovations to try out for general use and to see if they can be transferred to other target groups.

The following group methods are recommended:

- demonstrations and group discussions;

- laying out demonstration plots;

- field days;

- group seminars in schools or village halls;

- exhibitions and demonstrations;

- campaigns involving politicians and leaders from outside;

- contacts with school teachers and pupils (communicating the latest extension information, school gardens, documentation).

D 3

The following methods can be used to disseminate information:

- use of the mobile cinema to bring people together for a film show, after which information is given and group discussion takes place;
- distribution of brochures and up-to-date extension circulars for committees (in the local language);
- putting up noticeboards in every village;
- cooperating with the local media department to devise posters, slide series, films, radio programmes and brochures.

Source:

Project Appraisal, Kawinga Rural Development Project (Malawi). Eschborn: GTZ 1979

Compiled by:

Gerhard PAYR, Rolf SÜLZER

D 4

Committees as intermediaries between target groups and development organisations in Malawi

Committees that were set up to act as intermediaries in the implementation of development measures have proved their worth in such countries as Pakistan, Nigeria and Ghana. There now follows a summary of what happened in Malawi, where these committees have operated successfully since 1969 in several regional projects of GTZ and the World Bank.

1. Reasons why committees were founded

In most cases, rural development only has a lasting effect if the target groups are given the opportunity to contribute their opinions and proposals when programmes are planned and implemented. But, because the number of advisers is limited compared with the number of those seeking advice, the extension service has to create the right conditions for group work. This means that mediating organisations have to be created that can take charge of some aspects of extension work.

The farmers' clubs that have existed in Malawi since colonial times have proved unsuitable to take on the role of intermediary because:

- members of the farmers' clubs were almost always progressive farmers;

- the clubs were mostly organised on a wider scale than the village;

- members benefited greatly (credit, joint ordering, special advice etc.), but the poorer population was hardly helped at all;

- thus only a small proportion of the rural population derived benefit from the development aid institutions, and they were principally farmers who were already privileged in terms of factor provision, know-how, and access to know-how, and production inputs.

In contrast, the committees set up after about 1969 embodied the spirit of holistic rural development and were organised so that every group in a village was involved in decisions and given the chance of participating in development. Every group had therefore to be represented on the committees. These committees concerned themselves with health, schools, road building, credit, etc., in addition to measures in the agricultural sector. By involving the target groups in decisions on measures and their implementation, the advisers were able to gauge the farmers' reactions more quickly and more accurately. In this way, both the measures and the methods were continuously assessed and adjusted.

2. The network of committees

In the Lilongwe Project (World Bank), a hierarchical structure with five levels of committee was created, although only the first three levels became fully operational:

- Village committees:

    They have between 13 and 18 members and include the village leader plus a representative of the party, of women, the church and every extended family in the village. The field advisers explain the procedure and the committee members are then elected under their guidance.

- Section committees:

    A section comprises about 5 villages with a total area of about 1 000 ha. A section is identical to the extension territory of an adviser. The membership of a section committee comprises the village leaders and the chairmen of all village committees and their deputies.

- Regional committees:

    50 villages with about 10 000 ha form a region that is supervised by a senior adviser. The functionaries of the committees at section level and the traditional headmen are represented on this committee. Important party members and prominent local people can be elected "ex officio".

- Group committees:

    A group consists of 4 – 5 regions with about 200 villages and a total area of 40 000 ha. The membership is analogous to that of the regional committees. The group's committees are supposed to meet twice a year and to be involved in decisions on fundamental issues like the general orientation of annual programmes. (These committees have scarcely had any effect, however, because of legislative difficulties).

- Project committees:

    The chairmen of group committees, headmen, the district commissioner, the chairman of the party, the project manager and top management staff meet once a year on this committee to discuss basic questions of development aid. (This committee has only an advisory function, since its decision-making powers are still unclear.)

3. Duties and achievements in the agricultural sector

- Village committees participate in extension work and relieve the burden on advisers. After instruction and practical training by advisers, the committee members give the villagers information and show them new technology. They pass on the wishes, suggestions and reactions of the target groups to the advisers and thus guarantee two – way communication. The work of the committees comprises, for example, demonstrations of protection of stores, telling farmers when to start tilling the fields, organising group work, advertising events (market days, fertiliser distribution, film evenings, field days, exhibitions). The advisory work of the committees is carried out by individual functionaries contacting particular farmers or by means of group demonstrations that are initially prepared and carried out with the advisers and later by the committee alone.

- Other activities are the distribution of maize seed and the communal production and storage of seed for the whole village – which reduces costs considerably.

- Fertilisers can be ordered jointly through the committees. This has the added advantage that the fertilisers can be taken by lorry into the villages, and the rebate on bulk purchase greatly reduces the price paid by the farmers.

- Since the committees became instrumental in granting group credit, the number of borrowers has risen considerably and the administrative costs have been reduced. 99% of borrowers repay their loans, this level being achieved by the sustained solidarity of the credit groups. If a farmer cannot repay for reasons beyond his control, the other members of the group come to his assistance. But if he is in arrears because of his own negligence he is immediately excluded from the group.

- By giving the names of farmers interested in receiving production inputs, the committees help to estimate requirements.

- The committees are becoming increasingly influential in decision making at section and regional levels, examples being the siting of markets and drinking troughs for cattle, formulating the focal points of extension work, arranging the time and place of field days, agricultural shows, etc.

4. Other functions

- setting up local markets near advisers' offices – formerly farmers had to go 12 km to the nearest market;

- improvement of sanitation in the villages by providing 200 latrines in a few months;

D 4

- insistence on beer halls staying closed during the day in the peak season;
- organisation of further training courses in agriculture for women and the appointment of a female agricultural adviser in each section;
- settling social, ethnic and religious issues, examples being the clarification of grazing rights, the allocation of land to outsiders and respect for religious groups.

General evaluation

The target population and development aid institutions have more contact with each other, and the quality of communication is much improved. This applies particularly to committees at village, section and regional level. These committees are a forum in which politicians, officials in the administration and members from all the development aid institutions can make direct contact with the target groups or their representatives.

As the committees gain more experience, they relieve the work load of the development services. As they become more efficient, the committees take responsibility for more areas of activity, such as arranging discussions, drawing up agendas and formulating requests. The advisers are increasingly being invited by the committees to take part in discussions. Gradually the committees are developing into independent self-help organisations and, as such, they have more and more influence on the objectives and strategies of programmes.

But it is not easy for the extension organisation to create committees and then to give them assistance once they are functioning. Sometimes problems arise that are similar to those encountered when working with contact farmers (→ C 6). → F 10 describes some of the points that have to be taken into account when committees are formed.

Compiled by:

Gerhard PAYR, Rolf SÜLZER

D 5

The role of stimulation in the CFSME extension system in Kibuye, Rwanda

1. Introduction

Stimulation is an essential ingredient in agricultural extension. The reasons why it cannot be dispensed with are:

1. A society can only accept a new technology when the social values that it incorporates become an integral part of that society. Thus the adviser must not see his role as simply recommending new technologies; he must go a stage further and help to introduce any new social values associated with technology.

2. Most agricultural holdings in Rwanda have less than one hectare of land, i.e. today many families can no longer satisfy basic human requirements from agriculture alone. If a new and unknown technology is introduced, it represents yet another risk for the large agricultural section of the population. It is obvious that a population at the limits of survival will not be prepared to run even more risks. Thus, these people prefer to continue and repeat what they know, i.e. they still use the same farming methods and exploit every opportunity to extend the land under cultivation.

3. If these farmers adopt new technologies, like those recommended by technical experts, they always have to bear the extra burden. Considering the target population's low level of nutrition and health, it is not surprising that people are unwilling to accept the heavier burden that the experts require.

4. The target population has a somewhat naive perception of problems; their mentality tends to be submissive. Problems are surrounded by an aura of mystery and are felt to be inevitable: instead of being called problems, they are therefore regarded as immutable facts of life to which they are helplessly exposed. Of the need for improvement or change they have only the faintest awareness or none at all (D 6).

The aim of stimulation is therefore to help remove these obstacles to development by:

– reinforcing those social values that would be conducive to development but which are not held in sufficient esteem (honesty, diligence, entrepreneurial spirit, dynamic behaviour, being well informed, sociability, etc.) by ensuring that people who have internalised these values and demonstrate them in their daily lives enjoy more prestige;

- compensating people who incur extra costs and run higher risks by giving them tools or production inputs;

- creating an atmosphere of tolerance and mutual trust between advisers and the population so that "positive stimulation" can be practised.

If this stimulation is successful, we can try to introduce, use and retain new technologies so that:

- farmers gain confidence in new techniques and grow accustomed to them;

- farmers feel a need to find, test and improve the new techniques – which has the effect of making society more and more dynamic;

- being a progressive farmer becomes more and more a question of prestige and even of survival.

Stimulation is an indispensable element in the CFSME extension system. But it can only be effective if it is fully integrated with the other major elements of the system (→ A 8).

Stimulation cannot be undertaken at random but has to be carefully planned and prepared. It is not a question of "to stimulate or not to stimulate". By simply appearing on the scene, we provide stimulation in one way or another. In this sense the only question is: "How should we provide stimulation?" What should the means be and how should those means be used to create coordinated and effective stimulation? The following points should help to answer the above questions.

2. The various forms of stimulation and their characteristics

a) **Artificial positive** stimulation

- increases trust between advisers and farmers;

- increases the prestige of progressive farmers in society;

- develops the imagination and creativity of farmers, encourages them to look for appropriate solutions themselves;

- creates a dynamism in the population;

- can be replaced in phases by positive natural stimulation that accords with the aims of extension work;

- is effective in the short, medium and long-term;

- is completely in the hands of the extension organisation in terms of the measures and implements employed.

b) **Artificial negative** stimulation

- creates mistrust between advisers and farmers;
- is conducive to rejection of recommended technologies or the extension service;
- produces only short-term effects;
- causes farmers to see recommended technologies in a negative light. If people are against or prejudiced towards a particular technology, they are incapable of seeing its advantages, even if these can be demonstrated objectively.
- creates virtually insoluble problems of control. The adviser can issue orders and threaten a farmer, but he has no sure way of exercising effective control, and he has no effective sanctions if the farmer disobeys his instructions.
- reduces the advisers' credibility. If they apply these methods of stimulation, they soon look ridiculous, their words are soon ignored by the people and the advisers lose all credibility;
- is difficult to develop into natural positive stimulation, since the farmer only follows orders if he is threatened by punitive sanctions.

Thus the ostensible improvement is founded on fear and not on the will or know-how of the farmers. Therefore artificial negative stimulation

- encourages farmers to oppose individuals and organisations;
- stifles individual and communal initiatives;
- makes it more difficult to introduce further innovations.

c) **Natural positive** stimulation

- corresponds in terms of measures employed with our general targets (increasing production);
- encourages a multiplication effect when farmers imitate each other;

D 5

- is conducive to an inner dynamism in the system;

- is an incentive to farmers to think more deeply about the technologies they have successfully adopted;

- encourages farmers to continue working with advisers and searching for solutions to other problems.

d) **Natural negative** stimulation

- is ineffective wherever there is a simplistic view of problems, because events are naively perceived as inevitable (like fate or the will of God). Farmers see nothing significant in a change or improvement.

- often leads, because of a feeling of impotence in the face of problems, to even greater inertia in the population.

→ Figure 1 shows the methods of stimulation appropriate to the four categories described.

3. Deciding on general strategy and stimulation measures

We start with the general strategy of stimulation. When a new technology is introduced, the aim is to mobilise sufficient driving force by means of artificial positive stimulation to induce a farmer to adopt. As positive natural stimulation becomes effective, artificial stimulation must be correspondingly reduced. As soon as natural positive stimulation has developed its full potential, artificial stimulation must cease. This is the only way to guarantee that an innovation is retained for its own intrinsic value and advantage over possible alternatives.

→ Figure 2 is a general illustration of this principle. It shows how the composition of stimulation varied over six years. The height of the right-hand column corresponds with the total level of stimulation or motivating force required for adoption of a new technology. We distinguish between two main groups of incentives: those that can be used as short-term stimulation, and permanent incentives.

Short-term stimulation can only play a significant role in the first three years; in the medium and long-term it gives way more and more to the second category of permanent incentives. Among these, medium and long-term natural incentives are the most important (e.g. good harvest, good food, cash income). The effects of awareness creation and training and encouragement by advisers become in the long-term permanent features at a constant level.

We can establish through surveys what inducements are most likely to lead to adoption of innovations in each case.

Figure 1:

A suggested typology of stimulation		
	Positive stimulation	Negative stimulation
Artifical stimulation	Visits to the farmers by the extension commission	Criticism
	Visits to the farmers by officials	Fines Conditions
	Awareness creation/ training	Punishment
	Winning prizes in the agricultural competition	Ridicule, etc.
	Public display of photographs and names	
	Announcing the names of prizewinners on the radio	
	Visits by other farmers who are interested in adopted innovations	
	Public praise and general recognition, etc.	
Natural stimulation	Good harvest	Poor harvest
	Better nutrition	Malnutrition/deficient diet
	Healthier family	Sickness
	Good returns on sales	Poor returns on sales
	Lighter workload	Excessive workload
	Reduced risk, etc.	High, incalculable risks, etc.

Artificial positive stimulation, accompanied by awareness creation and training, induces the farmer to try innovations. This provides the initial incentive and motivates the farmer to accept new initiatives.

Programmes to create awareness and to train farmers and constant encouragement by the authorities and advisers have to be continued over a sufficiently long period.

D 5

Figure 2:

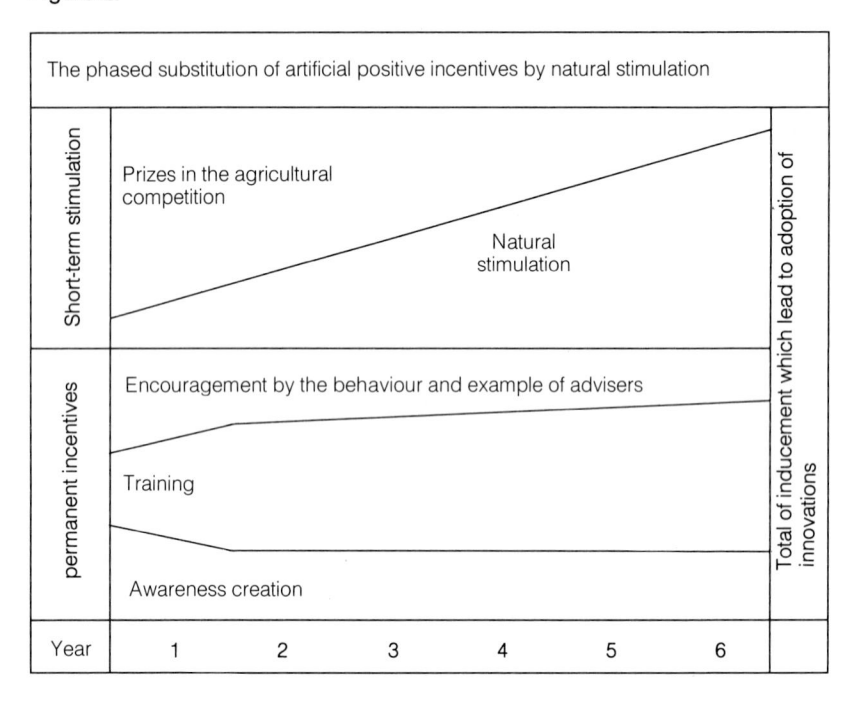

```
The phased substitution of artificial positive incentives by natural stimulation
```

Short-term stimulation	Prizes in the agricultural competition ⟶ Natural stimulation	Total of inducement which lead to adoption of innovations
permanent incentives	Encouragement by the behaviour and example of advisers / Training / Awareness creation	
Year	1 2 3 4 5 6	

On the other hand, prizes and awards soon have to be superseded in stages by the tangible results of an adopted innovation.

In this sense, stimulation cannot be treated like a present to be handed out but should be linked to clearly defined conditions (for example, the rules of the agricultural competition).

→ Figure 3 shows the introduction and permanent adoption of an innovation in the rural community. Artificial stimulation, awareness creation and training are outside stimuli that set an independent, self-sustaining process in motion, i.e. natural stimulation. Extension in keeping with the CFSME system operates mainly in the first four stages.

Stimulation can only achieve its objectives if the recommended technologies that the farmers adopt have been properly adapted to specific circumstances and prove to be a real benefit. If this is not the case, we risk the spread and application of innovations coming to a halt as soon as we stop applying artificial stimulation.

Figure 3:

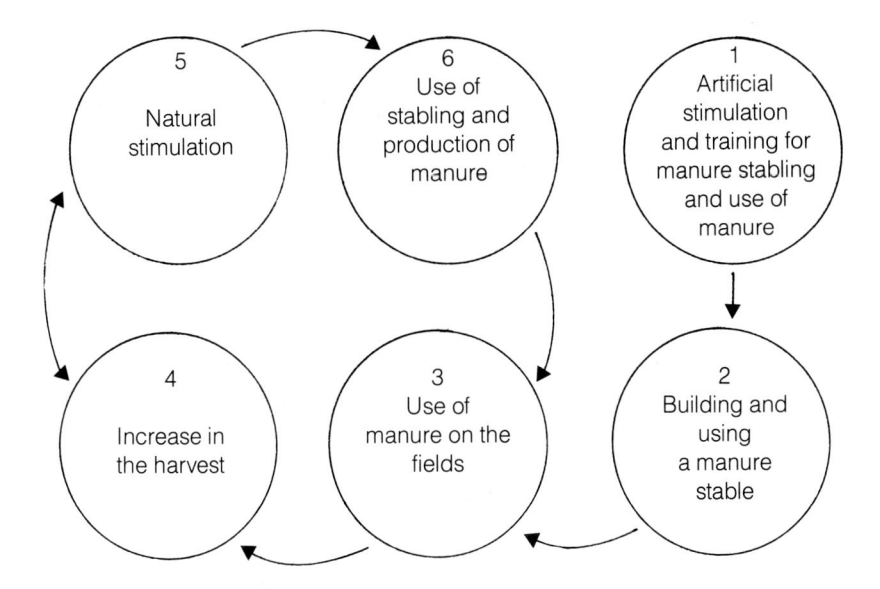

```
    ┌─────────────┐    ┌─────────────┐      ┌─────────────┐
    │      5      │──▶ │      6      │      │      1      │
    │   Natural   │    │   Use of    │      │  Artificial │
    │ stimulation │    │ stabling and│      │  stimulation│
    │             │    │production of│      │ and training│
    │             │    │   manure    │      │ for manure  │
    │             │    │             │      │ stabling and│
    │             │    │             │      │use of manure│
    └─────────────┘    └─────────────┘      └─────────────┘
                                                    │
                                                    ▼
    ┌─────────────┐    ┌─────────────┐      ┌─────────────┐
    │      4      │    │      3      │      │      2      │
    │ Increase in │    │   Use of    │      │ Building and│
    │ the harvest │    │ manure on   │      │    using    │
    │             │    │ the fields  │      │  a manure   │
    │             │    │             │      │   stable    │
    └─────────────┘    └─────────────┘      └─────────────┘
```

Effective stimulation should be planned as follows:

- The process of adoption should be divided into phases and a timetable drawn up;

- The three most difficult activities should be noted, i.e. where farmers are most likely to become discouraged or to give up altogether.

- We should then note activities that determine ultimate success (for example, increasing production).

- Next we determine which of the most difficult activities are also those activities on which success depends.

- We then decide on ways of encouraging and stimulating the farmers to overcome the critical thresholds that these activities represent.

→ Figure 4 illustrates this process.

D 5

Figure 4:

An example of how to plan stimulation		
Activity	Date	Stimulation
Initial information	1. 7.	●
Training	7. 7.	●
Decision to adopt	15. 7.	● ← Visit by agronomist
Marking out building site	21. 7.	●
Tree felling and removal	25. 7.	●
Building the stable	26. 7. 29. 7.	← Support from "Monagri"
Litter and manure preparation	1. 8. 1. 9.	← Visit by extension commission
Removal of manure and composting	1. 9. 9. 9.	
Transport of manure to fields	9. 9. 12. 9.	← Final visit by extension commission, giving points for the agricultural competition
Harvest	26.12.	● ← Evaluation, "Monagri" with farmers

4. Choosing the methods of stimulation

a) The competition

   The agricultural competition is effective short-term stimulation that can easily be combined with the other elements of the CFSME extension system. Only one competition should be organised, otherwise it could lose its appeal and effectiveness. A competition is particularly suitable for launching new ideas.

b) Prizes

   Prizes in the form of tools and other production inputs are awarded. They may be given to individuals or whole communities. At all costs a demoralising effect must be avoided, i. e. prizes should not be in the form of food aid. They should also be reserved for farmers who have demonstrated that they have used and have continued to use or maintain an exemplary innovation.

c) Incentives and encouragement

   Good examples are visits by people in authority to progressive farmers and the publication of their names and photographs at central meeting places. Both measures cost little but raise the standing of farmers in the community. However, these incentives have to be repeated over a period of time if they are to be appreciated generally and to increase the prestige of the progressive farmers sufficiently for other farmers to follow their example.

d) Awareness creation/training

   The act of creating and nurturing awareness is an act of stimulation. The teaching material itself often has a very stimulating effect (drawings, posters, felt pictures, demonstration fields, etc.). This kind of stimulation should not be confused with the compelling interest that prompts people to analyse problems, causes and consequences. It is usually of short duration, but it can be used to lead people from one stage to the next. The only deep and lasting stimulation is awareness creation/training that leads to the analysis of problems and creates problem awareness. Awareness creation/training awakens needs that farmers then try to satisfy by adopting concrete recommendations (the need to transform an unsatisfactory situation into a satisfactory state of affairs).

Awareness creation/training produces elements of permanent stimulation.

5. Encouraging adoption that only produces tangible results in the longterm

Innovations that produce only long-term results are not readily adopted, and they therefore create special problems for advisers. The farmers cannot see direct results, become despondent and give up. Erosion control is one of the commonest instances. In situations of this kind stimulation can intervene and perform an important role. The process is illustrated by → Figure 5.

The first two stages (A and B) are the preconditions for applying mineral fertiliser and lime. At the end of the third year, prizes of mineral fertiliser and lime are awarded for the best erosion control measures.

D 5

Figure 5:

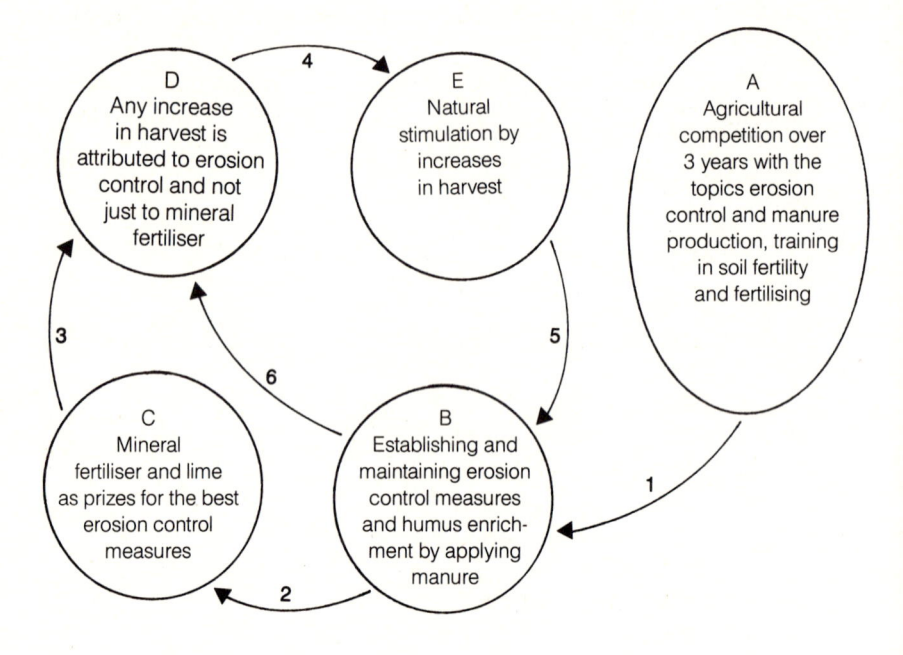

```
        4
    D ──────► E                    A
Any increase   Natural        Agricultural
in harvest is  stimulation by  competition over
attributed to  increases      3 years with the
erosion        in harvest     topics erosion
control and not                control and manure
just to mineral                production, training
fertiliser                     in soil fertility
                               and fertilising
  ▲                    5
3 │      6                         │
  │   ◄──                          │ 1
  C                B          ◄────┘
Mineral       Establishing and
fertiliser and lime  maintaining erosion
as prizes for the best  control measures
erosion control   and humus enrich-
measures        ment by applying
                  manure
        ◄── 2
```

The aim is to make people aware that the use of mineral fertiliser and lime is closely linked to the erosion control measures (D). The increase in harvest should be seen as the result of erosion control. In this way, an activity that can by its nature only bring long-term benefits is turned into an activity linked to success in the medium term. Thus the circle of natural stimulation (B,D,E) is closed more quickly and the self-sustaining forces can develop at an earlier stage.

6. Conclusions

Stimulation is an indispensable element in extension. It must be a permanent feature in any extension concept. The ways of creating incentives have to be carefully defined and programmed. A stimulation plan should be drawn up to link stimulation to the rest of the CFSME extension system (when and how to stimulate). Unplanned and careless stimulation can have serious consequences that cannot be put right. In general, we should only operate with positive stimulation so that we can create and maintain a basis of trust between advisers and farmers.

Sources:

Ernst GABATHULER: Le rôle de la stimulation dans la vulgarisation CFSME. In: Bulletin Agricole de Rwanda, H.1, 1980, pp. 20 – 24

Ernst GABATHULER: Résumé du cours de formation sur le Système National de Vulgarisation (SNV) du Rwanda, donné aux Agronomes et Vétérinaires des Communes, appuyé par le Projet Agro-Pastoral de Nyabisindu. Nyabisindu, 8, 1982, 26 p.

Compiled by:

Volker HOFFMANN

D 6

Awareness creation and training in the CFSME extension system in Kibuye, Rwanda

1. Introduction

Extension work is not confined to organising the dissemination of new means of production and production technologies. It must go further and strive to let the farmers in a region and their social communities (families, cells, sectors, community, etc.) gain experience, learn and acquire the skills to master the new inputs and technologies for themselves.

This calls for:

- simple technology;
- organisation which is simple and clear for the farmers;
- reasonable costs for purchase and maintenance;
- an open socio-cultural milieu that is dynamic, prepared to innovate and able to adapt its social values to new technologies and new inputs, but conversely is also able to modify new inputs and technologies and adapt them to its social values.

Thus extension is not only a structured organisation but also a driving force for socio-cultural and economic developments. The whole process of extension includes awareness creation and education whose aim is to ensure that recommended technologies and measures are mastered by the target population, in other words function as integral parts in rural life. Within the CFSME system (→ A 8), these elements combine with extension services and infrastructure, methods of stimulation, recommended methods and measures and the evaluation process to form a total unit.

2. What is awareness creation/training?

It is difficult to draw a distinction between the two activities. As awareness is developed, the desire to find solutions through education increases. When solutions to problems are proposed, this encourages people to broaden and deepen their thinking: they become increasingly aware. Although awareness creation and training complement each other, we are nevertheless going to characterise them individually.

D 6

Awareness creation begins when a problem is defined aptly and with precision, which is the starting point for analysis. Analysis goes on to reveal the structure, nature and details of the problem and helps those involved to distinguish clearly between these basic factors. The object of the analysis is to make people more interested and motivated to examine the basic factors in more detail and to arrive at a fuller understanding. However, this is only possible with special training that provides the necessary knowledge and information.

Reliable problem analysis enables us:

- to determine the direct and indirect causes of problems;
- to estimate the direct and indirect consequences in the short, medium and long term;
- to work out how to start tackling problems and under what conditions this can be done.

After the analytical phase, the search for solutions begins. This involves combining the elements of a solution found in analysis and training to produce a final solution that is fully adapted to the particular circumstances. Thus training constitutes one aspect of awareness creation. On the other hand, people can go through training and not develop problem awareness, i.e. if we do not provide an opportunity for them to formulate and analyse the problems. Programmes that are devised by people without a developed problem awareness can hardly be called integrated and tend to be technocratic and to be written from a narrow specialist viewpoint.

Awareness creation/training is an open-ended activity; it is a continuous process and develops in parallel with the changing situation.

Awareness creation develops in phases, and we can distinguish four levels that are shown in → Figure 1.

It is the aim of awareness creation/training to develop liberating awareness and thus to encourage initiative and problem-solving behaviour.

Success in this sphere of activity is dependent on:

- the organisation of work;
- the teaching materials;
- the teachers and advisers.

Figure 1:

Stages of awareness				
Stage of awareness	Submissive awareness	Pre-critical awareness	Critical awareness	Liberating awareness
State of mind attitude	– Mystification of problems	– More or less explicit problem formulation	– Observing the environment	– Search for solutions
	– Fatalism	– Dissatisfaction with the current situation	– Analysing problems	– Individual and group creativity
	– Allowing oneself to be dominated by the problem	– Vague, sweeping resentment	– The will to build on one's own strengths and potential	– Readiness to experiment
	– Submitting to fate	– Need for exchange of ideas	– The will to create one's own future	– Analysis and synthesis
	– Resignation			– Initiative and problem-solving actions
	– Feelings of guilt			
	– Preserving tradition			
	– Many rituals and recurring activities			
	– Little innovation			

3. Organisation of work (taking a sector as an example)

3.1. Basic data

a) Priority extension topics (for 1981/2)

Defining extension topics on the basis of development strategy, developing targets and fixing priorities are important processes within the CFSME system. For this reason they are described in detail, the results providing the basic data that underlie awareness creation/training. Five topics were selected for the year in question and they appear at the top of Figure 2.

D 6

b) Intervention strategy

Overall goal:
- improving the living conditions of the population

Objective:
- improvement of the food supply and reduction of supply deficiencies by 10% a year.

Results:
- increase in agricultural production by 5% a year.
- diversification of production.

Resources:
- budget for an agricultural competition (CA)
- a social development centre (CSD)
- a nutrition centre (CN)
- the "Umuganda"
- groups in the target population
- an agricultural expert for two days a week
- female social worker for one day a week
- the extension commission consisting of:
  the sector advisers, the cell representatives,
  technical personnel working in the sector,
  a female social worker and three progressive farmers
- a tree nursery
- six seed-propagation fields.

c) Methods of intervention

Intervention is a part of the CFSME extension system that is described in → A 8.

3.2. Drawing up a programme for the educational work

The plan of action for training is drawn up on the basis of the data derived from the extension system, the selected topics and the intervention strategy. The programme reproduced in → Table 1 was drawn up at the annual meeting of cell representatives and the technical personnel of the communities.

→ Table 1 calls for further clarification

- Practical activities in the fields and the events to promote awareness creation and training are coordinated and belong together.

- A precisely defined topic is prescribed for each month and is the focus of all

D 6

Table 1:

Annual programme of events in 1981/2 to create awareness/train the population of the Ngoma sector							
Priority extension topics		1. Manure stable	2. Reforestation	3. Improvement of the banana grove	4. Vegetable garden and fruit trees	5. Erosion control measures	
Activity	Duration	Themes of events	Timetable of events in the Ngoma sector				Work in the field	Timetable of visits to the cell by extension commission
			Umuganda in cells	CSD-groups	CN	Cooperatives / Classroom		
Awareness-creation	1 April - 14 May 1981	The population problem	A 3. 4. B 10. 4. C 17. 4. D 24. 4. E 8. 5.	1. 6. 4. 2. 7. 4. 3. 8. 4.	2. 4.	1. 7. 4. 7. 10. 4. 2. 8. 4. 8. 17. 4. 3. 9. 4.	– Preparation of tree nurseries and seed propagation fields – Personnel become familiar with the area	
Stable	15 May - 31 July 1981	Circulation of minerals and nutrients	A 15. 5. B 22. 5. C 29. 5. D 5. 6. E 12. 6.	1. 4. 5. 2. 5. 5. 3. 6. 5.	7. 5.	1. 5. 5. 7. 15. 5. 2. 6. 5. 8. 22. 5. 3. 7. 5.	– Building a model stable with the extension commission	A 27. 7. B 28. 7. C 29. 7. D 30. 7. E 31. 7.
		Stable building, preparing and using stable manure	A 19. 6. B 26. 6. C 3. 7. D 10. 7. E 17. 7.	1. 1. 6. 2. 2. 6. 3. 3. 6.	4. 6.	1. 2. 6. 7. 12. 6. 2. 3. 6. 8. 19. 6. 3. 4. 6.	– Helping the farmers to build a stable	
Reforestation	1 Aug. - 30 November 1981	Making people receptive to reforestation	A 31. 7. B 7. 8. C 14. 8. D 21. 8. E 28. 8.	1. 3. 8. 2. 4. 8. 3. 5. 8.	6. 8.	1. 4. 8. 7. 10. 8. 2. 5. 8. 8. 17. 8. 3. 6. 8.	– Marking out future reforestation	A 23. 11. B 24. 11. C 25. 11. D 26. 11. E 27. 11.
		Where can we reforest?	A 4. 9. B 11. 9. C 18. 9. D 25. 9. E 2.10.	1. 7. 9. 2. 8. 9. 3. 9. 9.	3. 9.	1. 8. 9. 7. 11. 9. 2. 9. 9. 8. 18. 9. 3. 10. 9.	– Digging planting holes	
		Choice of trees	A 9.10. B 16.10. C 23.10. D 30.10. E 6.11.	1. 5.10. 2. 6.10. 3. 7.10.	1. 10.	1. 6.10. 7. 9.10. 2. 7.10. 8. 16.10. 3. 8.10.	– Planting cuttings	
Improvement of banana groves, vegetable garden and fruit trees	1 Dec. - 15 Jan. 1981/2	How do you improve a banana grove?	A 4.12. B 11.12. C 18.12. D 8. 1. E 15. 1.	1. 7.12. 2. 8.12. 3. 9.12.	3. 12.	1. 8.12. 7. 11.12. 2. 9.12. 8. 18.12. 3. 10.12.	– Improvement of a banana grove with the extension commission	A 25. 1. B 26. 1. C 27. 1. D 28. 1. E 29. 1.
	16 Jan. - 14 Mar. 1982	The three categories of food	A 22. 1. B 22. 1. C 29. 1. D 29. 1. E 5. 2.	1. 4. 1. 2. 5. 1. 3. 6. 1.	1. 1. 2. 6. 3. 7.	1. 5. 1. 7. 8. 1. 2. 6. 1. 8. 15. 1. 3. 7. 1.	– Seed distribution – Establishing a vegetable garden with the extension commission	A 8. 2. B 9. 2. C 10. 2. D 11. 2. E 12. 2
		Fruit and vegetable husbandry	A 12. 2. B 12. 2. C 19. 2. D 19. 2. E 26. 2.	1. 1. 2. 2. 2. 2. 3. 3. 2.	4. 2.	1. 2. 2. 7. 12. 2. 2. 3. 2. 8. 19. 2. 3. 4. 3.	– Helping farmers to establish a vegetable garden and to plant fruit trees	
Erosion control	1 March - 30 Apr. 1982	Soil fertility, loss of humus, leaching of nutrients	A 5. 3. B 5. 3. C 12. 3. D 12. 3. E 19. 3.	1. 1. 3. 2. 2. 3. 3. 3. 3.	3. 3.	1. 2. 3. 7. 12. 3. 2. 3. 3. 8. 19. 3. 3. 4. 3.	– Marking out ditches along contour lines – Planting 500 m of hedge for wind protection with the extension commission	A 26. 4. B 27. 4. C 28. 4. D 29. 4. E 30. 4.
		Erosion control measures	A 26. 3. B 26. 3. C 2. 4. D 2. 4. E 9. 4.	1. 5. 4. 2. 6. 4. 3. 7. 4.	1. 4.	1. 6. 4. 7. 9. 4. 2. 7. 4. 8. 16. 4. 3. 8. 4.	– Helping farmers to set up erosion control	
Conclusion of agricultural competition	1 May - 15 May 1982						– Final visit by the extension commission – Final celebration and presentation of prize winners	A 3/4. 5. B 5/6. 5. C 7/8. 5. D 10/11.5. E 12/13.5. 14/15. 5.

225

extension activities. These topics make up the basic programme for awareness creation and training. In the CSD/CCDFP the basic programme can be extended, but the first meeting each month is reserved for the topic of the month.

- Training by means of the Umuganda takes place cell by cell. Every month, one Umuganda-day is devoted to awareness creation and training. This training is the job of the agricultural field adviser in the sector.

- The weekly meetings in the CSD/CCDFP are chaired by the female social adviser. The first meeting each month is reserved for the topic of the month. Later meetings are for other topics, ideally supplementary ones.

- The monthly meetings of the nutrition centre (CN) are chaired by a female nutrition adviser. Among other things, the monthly topic is discussed.

- The monthly meetings with various cooperatives are arranged by the community adviser. These meetings deal, among other things, with awareness creation and the training of members of the cooperative on the various monthly topics.

- The meetings for awareness creation and training in schools can be arranged by the senior teacher in the zone.

- The teaching materials to be used at these meetings are prepared at the CCDFP level.

- Three training staff per community are instructed in the use of the teaching materials by the "Service d'Animation et Formation" (SAF).

3.3. Organisation of a session for awareness creation and training (July: stable manure)

a) Discussion of the population problem (stagnating production with high birth rate):

- relate the importance of stable manure to the development problems;
- how is the preparation and use of stable manure related to other problems?

b) Recapitulation of topics dealt with at the earlier session on: "circulation of minerals and nutrients" followed by discussion.

c) Discussion of the main topic of the day using a montage on a felt board.

- building a manure stable

- preparing and using stable manure

d) Inspection of a composting unit belonging to a progressive farmer and then discussion.

3. 4. Teaching materials for awareness creation and training

The teaching materials are the tools of the trade for the staff in charge of training. They help them

- to involve the group in defining and analysing the circumstances prior to discussion;

- to present problems in a precise and graphic form;

- to repeat and summarise important statements and interrelations at the end of a session.

The teaching materials help the farmers to grasp and think about the topic under discussion and they also make the meetings more enjoyable occasions. But to be successful, they have to be adapted to the group and the specific circumstances of the rural environment. The following points have to be borne in mind:

- the composition and size of the group;

- the educational level of those taking part;

- the venue (open air or specially equipped rooms);

- the level of education of the training staff using the teaching materials;

- the facilities for transporting teaching materials;

- the ways in which they can be used and how easy they are to handle, etc.

3.4.1. Producing teaching materials

We now describe picture materials for use on felt boards and written instructions for the training staff.

a) The advantages of the felt-picture method:

- illustrations can be built up stage by stage;
- pictures can be altered and regrouped in the course of presentation and discussion;
- these materials are easily transported on a bicycle (the felt board rolled up or folded and the pieces of felt kept in a bag);
- they can easily be combined with other teaching aids (blackboard, natural objects, etc.);
- very low purchase and maintenance costs;
- simple technology, easy to use;
- encourages dialogue; groups can be actively involved by the training staff in placing the pieces on the board and moving them around; the groups can interpret the pictures for themselves.

→ Picture 1 shows the felt board method being used at an open air training session on a hill in Rwanda.

b) Explanatory text

The text that accompanies the felt board materials is always an excerpt from the same basic story: "The story of the Family Majyambere". Each topic can easily be related to all the others (circulation of nutrients in the soil, population problem, food, family planning).

Each explanatory text has the same format:

- first page: introduction to the topic
- second page: the general aims of the session
- following pages: text organised as follows:

Picture 1:

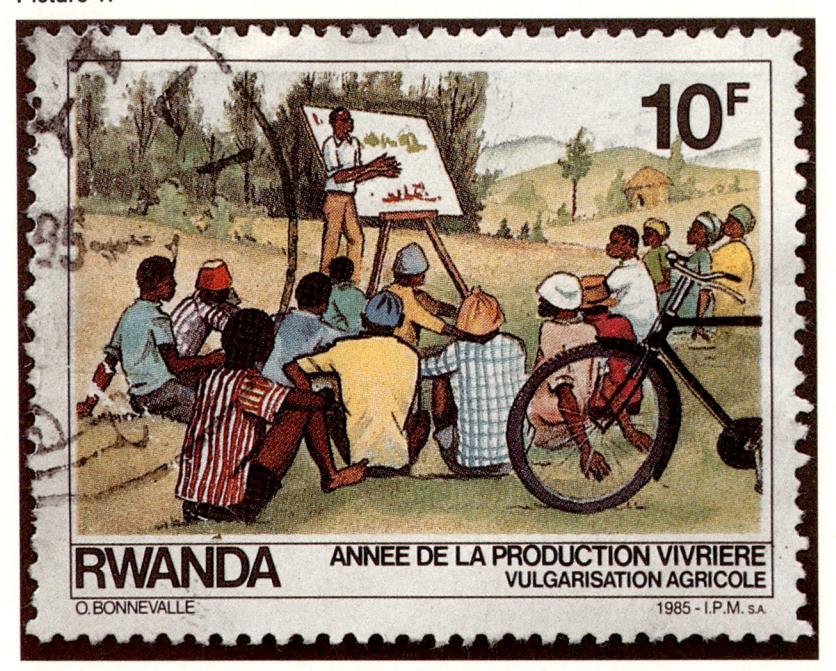

Number of felt pieces and short description	Aims of individual pieces	Important details to be discussed or explained	Model text

– last page: suggested questions to stimulate discussion.

When the training staff and group chairmen are provided with a statement of aims, details to be explained and model texts, they find it much easier to monitor their own work. The sample text gives them the appropriate vocabulary, suitable examples and handy comparisons.

3.4.2. Teaching materials for creating awareness of the population problem: "The Story of the Family Majyambere"

The history of this particular family and their hill is unfolded as in a novel. By juxtaposing the good and bad brothers, each on his half of the hill, a dramatic effect is achieved and the whole story is made more entertaining. The audience can identify with what they see, view it objectively and then apply it to other situations. The materials used are shown in → Picture 2.

D 6

A second run-through is used to show how the story of the family relates to the history of the country in general and to the specific situation of the group. The scope of the topic is broadened as follows:

1st Aim:

To show and discuss the development of culture and society from the beginning of this century.

Details to be dealt with:

1910 – 1960:

– establishment of a large number of foreign mission stations in the country – creation of a colonial administration – setting up hospitals and health centres – importing a wide variety of technologies – road building and importing vehicles – beginning of extensive export production (coffee, natural resources) – appreciable population growth – opening the country to all nationalities in the world.

1960 – 1980:

– independence – emancipation of the peasant population – rise in aid from abroad – rapid population growth – shortage of agricultural land – resorting to land of lower fertility – reduction of fallow – accelerated urbanisation – increased dependence on other countries – social problems – start of industrialisation – many new desires and needs of the population – change in social values and explanations of this phenomenon – considerable undernourishment and malnutrition – new social class of functionaries.

2nd Aim:

Working with the participants, to find and analyse the connections between the different aspects of this development.

Details to be discussed:

– hospitals reduce the mortality rate – population growth increases water pollution – education encourages crafts and industry – more schools mean more migration from the land – flight from the land creates social problems – population growth creates supply problems, etc.

3rd Aim:

To develop with the participants the thesis that all progress, all improvement, demands change, the adaptation of people to the new situation, if development is to be harmonious.

D 6

Picture 2:

D 6

Details to be discussed:

– if the agricultural land available per family decreases, the farming methods must be changed to raise the yield per unit of area – if more sophisticated and more complicated tools and machines are introduced, precision and punctuality become important social values if the system is to function properly – if medicines reduce the death rate, it also becomes necessary to reduce the birth rate – if the population lives in closer proximity, hygiene becomes a vital precondition for survival, etc.

4th Aim:

To develop and discuss with the participants what the consequences would be of technical and economic developments without adaptation of social values and the prevailing mentality.

Details to be discussed:

– corruption – environmental pollution and an increase in certain diseases – low productivity in relation to the available production means – waste of resources – impoverishment of the soil – social tension, etc.

5th Aim:

Summary: 5 prerequisites of harmonious development and discussion of how they complement each other:

1. provision of good quality food for all the family;
2. increasing agricultural production;
3. increasing production in crafts and industry;
4. school education for children;
5. family planning.

3.4.3. Teaching materials for training on the topic: manure stable

1st Aim:

Clarifying the role of manure in the development process

D 6

Details to be discussed:

− manure helps to increase and diversify agricultural production − increasing and diversifying agricultural production helps to improve the food supply − development is not possible in a poorly fed population, because malnutrition debilitates health and prevents full development of physical and mental abilities.

2nd Aim:

Discussion of the technical construction of a manure stable

Details to be discussed:

− choosing and preparing the site − levelling to prevent urine flowing away from the stable, since this would be a loss of valuable nutrients − measuring out the stable (4 m^2 for the first large livestock unit and 2 m^2 per additional animal) − making supports out of charred wood (to prevent wet or dry rot) − digging holes for corner supports − measuring the height − digging a pit to prevent loss of nutrients and to keep the area round the stable clean − building a fodder rack − making the stable door − use of roof gutters − trough − building costs.

3rd Aim:

Discussion of the techniques of stable manure preparation

Details to be discussed:

− importance of litter − the various materials that can be used instead of straw, their absorption properties and their mineral salt content (swamp straw, wood shavings, sawdust, husks of maize cobs, millet, etc., dried grass, etc.) − storing and composting manure.

4th Aim:

Discussion of the technique of using stable manure

Details to be discussed:

− season and dates for applying manure − losses through ammonia evaporation − immediate digging into the soil − ways of delivering manure to the fields − crops to be manured − including fertilising in rotations − dosages, etc.

5th Aim:

Exchange of experience of stable manure

Details to be discussed:

- increasing yields (example of farmers, results of evaluation of farmers' fields, model plots, etc.) – erosion-inhibiting effect of manuring through better soil cover, better take-up of water and water retention by the soil (sponge effect) – calculating the value of stable manure by comparison with mineral fertilisers and also from yield increases.

→ Picture 3 shows most of the visual materials used in training on the topic "manure stable".

After the general aims of the session and the details to be discussed have been agreed, the next step is to make pictures and visual aids and to write the explanatory text for the training staff's brochure. The special characteristics of the target group and the specific situation in which the material will be presented must be borne in mind all the time.

To develop good teaching materials, it is essential that:

- texts and pictures are compatible with the socio-cultural context of the region, so that the group has no difficulty in identifying with the material.

- the target group perceives and interprets the material correctly. For this reason systematic testing is essential (→ E 13).

4. The training staff

Taken together, the organisation and methodology of extension and the teaching materials provide a clear operational framework and indicate the content of extension work. But the success of extension depends largely on the good will, the attitudes and abilities of the training personnel (community agronomists, social workers, advisers, etc.). Since extension without general education of the population is condemned to failure from the start, the training of advisers in methodology and teaching techniques is of crucial importance. A good adviser must of necessity be a good teacher.

Induction and training of teaching staff

The main aims of this training are that training staff should:

- learn more about methodology and teaching techniques;

- practise using teaching materials;

- develop positive views and attitudes to educational work;

D 6

Picture 3:

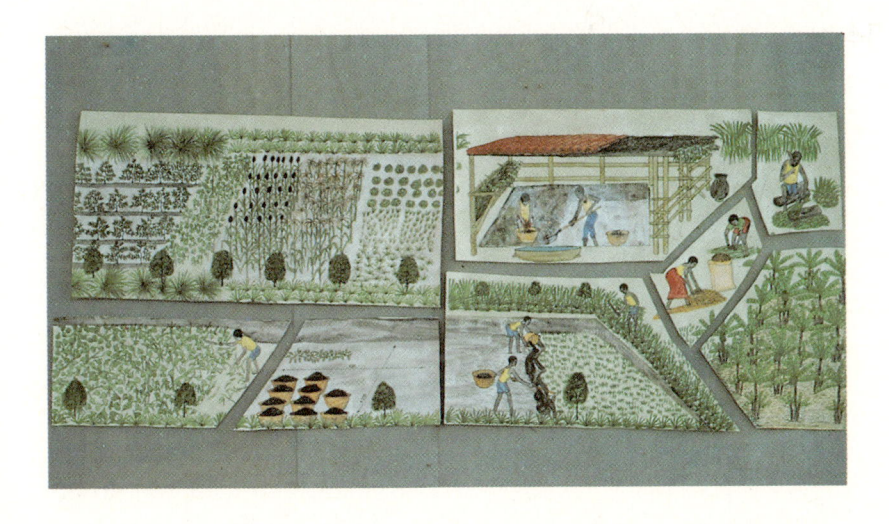

– thoroughly work through and think through the major topics dealt with in the teaching materials.

Training personnel are inducted and trained mainly by CPDFP/CCDFP, the centre for development and continuous training in the prefecture or the communities. The programme should always be as concrete and relevant as possible. → Figure 3 is an example of such a programme.

Afterwards the three participants return to their own communities, where they organise a seminar for their colleagues in keeping with the plan drawn up on the fourth day. Meetings with the target population are also planned between 8 and 10 o'clock on day 4.

Figure 3:

Model training programme for advisers on the introduction of new teaching materials		
Day 1.	10 – 12.00 14 – 16.00	Presentation of new teaching materials Group work on various aspects of the topics
Day 2.	8 – 10.00 10 – 12.00 14 – 16.00	Presentation of the results of group work and other contributions to the theme Second presentation of the teaching materials and general discussion. Group activities with the teaching materials.
Day 3.	8 – 10.00 10 – 12.00 14 – 16.00	Continuation of group activities Training session with a group of farmers. One adviser is in charge of this group session and uses the new teaching materials. The others observe their colleague. Evaluation of the morning group session with discussion of the approach of the adviser in charge, his way of conducting the session, how he handled the materials, assessing the behaviour and reactions of the group of farmers (→ E 12).
Day 4.	8 – 10.00 10 – 12.00	Devising a programme for introductory seminars at community level (CCDFP) for technical and social personnel in the communities. Handing out the teaching materials. Further information.

The question of evaluation, the fifth component of the CSFME method, is described in the same detail as awareness creation and training. The basic aims are explained. The special considerations involved in evaluating training events are given in working paper → E 12.

When we have the results of evaluation, we can turn our attention to the specific task of improving the organisation, the teaching materials and the training of teaching staff. Awareness creation activities and training should be evaluated once a year by the community personnel and the CCDFP.

D 6

Finally, → Table 4 lists the teaching materials that were made by the "Service Animation et Formation" up to 1982 in Kibuye.

Table 4:

Topics of felt-board courses and posters in PAK up to July 1982				
	Course	Poster	Text Kin.	Text French
Topics to increase awareness				
1. The population problem	x		x	x
2. Circulation of nutrients	x		x	x
3. Reforestation	x		x	x
Agricultural topics (included in the agricultural competition)				
4. The fight against erosion	x	xx	x	x
5. Compost: compost pit, compost heap		xx	x	x
6. The manure stable and use of manure	x	x	x	x
7. Fodder cropping		x		
8. Small animal breeding:	x	x	x	x
hares, chickens	x		x	x
9. Integrated tree plantation	x	x	x	
10. Growing vegetables and fruit	x	x	x	x
11. Improved banana growing	x	x	x	x
12. Coffee	x	x	x	x
13. Growing potatoes		x	x	x
14. Improving living conditions, building latrines		x	x	x
Other topics				
15. Nutrition I (Three categories of food)	x	x	x	x
16. Nutrition II (Feeding babies)	x		x	x
17. Water hygiene	x		x	x
18. Family planning	x		x	x

→ Table 5 shows the logical order in which the topics are treated. To increase the target group's sensitivity, they are preceded by the course "The population problem". The topics are then dealt with in detail in keeping with the "5 prerequisites of harmonious development". Also, when special topic areas are treated, awareness creation courses are held before solutions to problems are proposed. The unequal distribution of materials over the five main groups is explained by the differing areas of emphasis in this project. There are special organisations and projects for developing crafts, for family planning and school education in Rwanda.

D 6

Table 5:

Topic areas and topics in PAK, Kibuye, in the recommended order (July 1982)				
The population problem				
Increase and diversification of agricultural production	Development of rural crafts	Development of health	Development of family planning	Development of school education
x The circulation of nutrients o Maintenance and improvement of soil fertility x The fight against erosion x Compost x Manure stable and use of manure x Fodder cropping x Reforestation **Further topics to be appended in any order** x Vegetable and fruit growing x Improved banana growing x Coffee x Growing potatoes o Intensive large stock keeping o Crop rotations and green manuring	o Crafts	x Water hygiene x Improvement of living conditions x Building latrines x Nutrition x Feeding babies o Feeding children o Inoculation o Deficiency diseases	x Family planning	
x = existing materials o = materials in preparation				

Sources:

Ernst GABATHULER: La conscientisation/formation dans le processus de vulgarisation. In: Bulletin Agricole de Rwanda, H. 4, 1983, pp. 223–236

Ernst GABATHULER: Résumé du cours de formation sur le Système National de vulgarisation (SNV) du Rwanda, donné aux Agronomes et Vétérinaires des Communes, appuyé par le Projet Agro-Pastoral de Nyabisindu. Unpublished manuscript, Nyabisindu, 1982, 26 p.

Regina GÖRGEN: Übersicht über das didaktische Material, das zur Sensibilisierung und zur Ausbildung der Landbevölkerung in der Präfektur Kibuye eingesetzt wird. Projet Agricole de Kibuye, Service Animation et Formation, Rwanda, 7, 1982

Photographs:

Regina GÖRGEN, Volker HOFFMANN

Compiled by:

Volker HOFFMANN

"Majeutics" — GRAAP's pedagogic approach to self-development

GRAAP is the abbreviation of "Groupe de Recherche et d'Appui pour L'Autopromotion Paysanne" — a group to research into and promote self-help in the peasant population. GRAAP was founded in 1975 in Bobo-Dioulasso in Burkina Faso where it still operates today and can be contacted via P. O. Box (B. P.) 785.

The founders of GRAAP were the last three technical advisers of the "Fédération des Groupements Villageois de la Région de Bouaké". When it was founded the basic pedagogic approach and the first batches of teaching material had already been developed. The methodology and the materials aim to encourage self-help among villagers so that they can themselves improve their living conditions. The following description of method is a free translation of excerpts from the two GRAAP texts to be found in the bibliography at the end of this contribution.

1. What does majeutics mean?

Majeutics is about helping rural people to stop passively submitting to the pressures of the modern world and to become dynamic participants in the development of their country. It is about, in a way, helping the villagers to give birth to a new life, springing from the life of their ancestors but adjusted to present conditions. This is what majeutics means, the method that we are going to describe for helping villagers in their self-advancement. The original meaning of majeutics is in fact the art of midwifery.

Majeutics thus refers to a pedagogic method that helps people to discover truth. By using a dialectic discussion arising from a number of carefully selected questions, people are prompted to use their own inner resources to arrive at a deep level of truth.

2. What is this method based on?

Considering what we have just said about majeutics, its starting point, its foundation and form are all dependent on the life and culture of the rural people.

Village culture:

African rural cultures are in general oral civilisations. This means that people express themselves and exchange ideas principally through the spoken word. This oral expression is supplemented by physical and artistic expression (dances, postures, gesture, paintings, sculpture, carvings). Through these forms of expression thought is expanded, the life of the community and the people is enlarged.

This oral culture permits all adults to express themselves to anyone about the realities of life (family, marriage, land, work, etc.). In this way a reservoir of diverse knowledge is created which belongs to the community as a whole. Thus, the "palaver" occupies a position of central importance in village life.

Here we see one of the major differences from western cultures, which are dominated by writing and audio-visual communication. These are mass means of communication that affect many individuals, but in isolation. They do not give rise to dialogue; there is no mutual exchange and discovery. What is worse, these means of communication allow only a few people, generally the intelligentsia, to express themselves, as if they were the only possessors of knowledge, while the masses have no means of expressing their point of view in return. This creates a mentality that divides people into classes: the teachers, the intellectuals who cast knowledge in their own mould, and the taught who submit to it.

Consequences of this pedagogic method

This method was constructed gradually, showing respect for the cultural realities of village life and resolutely turning away, for the moment, from modern communication methods and the mentality that they have created.

It is based above all on the spoken word — the means of expression at the heart of the community. It involves helping villagers to express as a group the realities of their lives, with all the changes occurring at present, and their ideas and wisdom.

With this method we seek to make maximum use of concrete style, the poetic language of the village, comparisons and proverbs. Verses, proverbs and folktales can have the effect of questions put to the listeners and forcing them to think. An example is the proverb below:

"When you are roasting something,
if you fear to let it get hot
it won't get cooked."

D 7

This method uses visual representation but only as a supplement to the spoken word. The objectives of these visual aids are:

- to help people remember and internalise what has been said;

- to stimulate the villagers to express themselves;

- to render explanations or new ideas more comprehensible.

For example, to generate discussion about health problems, one can present a picture of a sick man next to a healthy man. In the same way, the vitality of the village can be discussed by comparing a diseased tree with a fruit-laden, healthy tree.

This teaching method, beginning with oral expression, sometimes gives rise to spontaneous physical expression in the form of personal gestures or songs and dances.

3. The pedagogic approach

Villagers are dynamic, active people. It is their way of life that must be observed, since it is their way of life that has to be renewed and constantly improved. That is why the first step in this approach is to get the villagers used to **looking, observing** their lives and behaviour patterns in a conscious way and sharing their observations with each other.

The more this act of sharing allows different social groups (male or female, young or old) to say what they understand about the reality of life, the closer the group comes to a true recognition of reality. But, as we all know, reality has many sides to it and the villagers sometimes say: "A roof must have two sides for it to be complete."

Sharing experience entails discussion, which should in turn lead to an analysis of facts and situations. Analysis and **thought** constitute the second step in this approach. Analysis must be carried out in such a way that it brings out as much as possible the truth of the facts and situations studied together with their consequences. It should also lead to deep thought in order to uncover the roots and causes of situations. "You must pull a weed out by its taproot, if you don't want it to grow again", say the villagers.

It is often impossible to complete analysis without outside help in the form of extra information and basic knowledge. The GRAAP method gets the villagers used to looking for this supplementary material themselves.

Some basic knowledge (biology, economics, geography, etc.) is indispensable for the villagers' understanding of the "why and how" of the phenomena that touch them. It prevents them from looking for solutions in magic, or executing technical instructions without understanding them. On the contrary, this training will give the villagers a chance to participate in the development of their village and their country in a responsible and intelligent manner.

Reflection should help the villagers to make more profound judgements on the meaning of facts and situations and to discover what to do to improve the life of the whole community.

The solutions they discover have next to be realised through **action**, which is the third step in this approach. So that this action can be carried out, it is necessary to determine priorities, to assess the real potential of the community, to undertake technical and practical training, etc. To achieve all this, the community must organise itself.

This teaching method is not set and invariable. Indeed, it is always changing in response to changing reality. It inspires new actions which in turn bring about new

D 7

situations that must be analysed and acted upon in a never-ending spiral of seeking and acting by the community to improve its own life.

4. Three important elements of majeutics

This method has three major components: questions, groups and sub-groups, and the "Animateur". They are all linked by teaching materials in the form of felt board pictures accompanied by detailed instructions for the Animateur.

4.1. Questions

People who live their whole lives in a certain environment often find it difficult to see and analyse objectively the various aspects of their lives in that environment. But we can help them to do so by the skilful use of questions.

Questions are an essential part of the pedagogic method that we are proposing. In this approach questions are our major tool. In order to make each villager feel that he is being addressed personally, the questions are as simple and direct as possible. They are always open questions so that the villagers cannot respond with "yes" or "no" but are compelled to discuss, search and think.

Sometimes questions have to be posed that do elicit only a brief response, but then we always follow them with "why?" or "how?" so that each person is forced to explain his point of view.

When the prepared training topics and pictures are used, the introductory questions are grouped under the heading: questions for stimulating awareness. Others are suggested as the investigation proceeds. These questions can be modified as the need arises, according to circumstances and the stage reached in the investigation. The Animateur should be able to replace these questions with proverbs, tales or comparisons whenever appropriate. Using this method, the villagers should ask each other questions during discussions.

4.2. Groups and sub-groups

This teaching approach aims to get each person to express himself so that there will be an interchange of ideas among members of the community. One of the essential elements of this method is therefore the group and especially a relatively homogeneous group. Such a group is not always easy to constitute. The customs of the people often militate against it.

Sometimes certain groups in the community cannot express themselves freely in front of others, for instance women in front of men, the young in front of the old.

One helpful way of giving everyone the opportunity to express himself is to create sub-groups of the various categories of participants. Also, when there are too many participants to allow each individual to speak, sub-groups of no more than ten people are a good solution.

After discussion by sub-groups, it is essential that the results are shared with the whole group, and for this purpose each group should nominate one or two spokesmen who can report the results of their group's discussion to all participants. This may sometimes be the only way to establish dialogue between the various categories of people in the community.

This method of reporting is generally very animated and promotes further discussion. It is enlightening because each sub-group contributes facts and points of view that are sometimes very individualistic.

When it is a question of selecting from several alternatives and getting down to action, the group and sub-group enable all those in the community to involve themselves equally and to share responsibility. Thus there is less risk of the burden of responsibility falling on one man or sub-group.

This also prevents the solution to problems becoming the province of a few individuals who could try to exploit opportunities for their own benefit at the expense of the community.

4.3. The Animateur

If village communities are to benefit from this teaching method they must be helped by an Animateur. The role of the Animateur can be likened to that of a **mirror**. As a result of the questions he asks and which are discussed in the groups, the community is given the chance to see all the positive and negative aspects of its life as we see the reflection of our faces in a mirror. By asking questions, he can help the community to analyse its situation and find ways of changing it.

As well as using majeutics, the Animateur can provide some basic education and technical and practical training for his fellow villagers. We would like to emphasise that "basic education" means the scientific explanation of phenomena, permitting people to understand the "how and why" of human, animal and plant biology, economics, etc.

The Animateur has felt board pictures to help him to achieve these objectives, but they can in no way be a substitute for the dynamic qualities and drive that a good Animateur needs. Since the programmes deal with problems in a general manner, each Animateur must adapt the material to his particular area and circumstances. He may, therefore, have to reformulate the questions and translate them, look for proverbs and comparisons and bear in mind events and specific situations in his region.

The Animateur can only be successful in this work if he is thoroughly familiar with his community. For this reason the Animateur should ideally be a man or women

D 7

from the village in question. Otherwise, if he or she is a stranger, the individual must make every effort to become acquainted with the area and as quickly a possible train "Animateurs" from the area. In cases like these, the role of the Animateur is therefore only to back up locally recruited personnel.

After all that has been said about the role of the Animateur, it is obvious that he is not the fount of all knowledge, who imposes his ideas and solutions on others, but someone who helps the community of which he is a member to observe its life, to reflect upon its problems, to take the initiative and commit itself to building a better life.

5. Topic-based training packs for tackling specific problems

When we speak to villagers about their problems, we find that a number of topics frequently recur, for example:

- lack of money;
- lack of water;
- problems of communication with better educated people;
- the exodus of young people to the cities;
- lack of health facilities;
- high rates of infant mortality.

The village people who experience these problems every day are naturally fully aware of them. But the pedagogic approach just described should help them to become aware of the causes of those problems and thus to resolve them.

To help them, we propose teaching aids or picture packs on a variety of specific themes. Others can be devised in the same way on the same or other topics. Thus, we propose two programmes to help villagers tackle the problems of:

- communication with better educated people;
- the exodus of young people to the cities.

Together with the villagers we have also devised and worked out:

- the role of rural people in the nation;
- the part played by the rural economy in the nation's economy.

These two programmes try to bring the villagers to the realisation that they are the roots, the foundation on which the whole life of the nation rests. This should strengthen their self-confidence and remove their feeling of inferiority in the face of modern life, so that they can take their own life in hand and organise themselves to take their place on an equal basis with other categories of citizens in the nation.

As well as these and similar picture series that aim to promote awareness, there are also topics that are more solution-oriented, whose aim is to communicate basic knowledge and practical training. But the goal of all these picture materials is always the same: to give the villagers an effective mental stimulus to tackle their problems in a dynamic and critical manner and to encourage them to assume a responsible position in the evolution of their village and their nation.

6. Summary

We leave the reader with → Table 1 as a summary of the majeutics of GRAAP.

GRAAP's materials are now being used in 17 African countries, and there are now training packs on a wide range of topics. Three books are available from GRAAP that introduce this method of training – one for teachers, one for Animateurs and one to show how educational picture series are produced. Together with CESAO (Centre d'Etudes Economiques et Sociales d'Afrique Occidentale), GRAAP publish a magazine "Echanges", whose aim is to broaden and deepen know-how in peasant communities.

An example of training packs focussing on awareness creation and dealing with the topic "Living in a Green Environment" can be seen in → G 11.

Sources:

GRAAP: Towards teaching self-development, Bobo-Dioulasso, GRAAP, No year given.

GRAAP: 12 questions sur le GRAAP. 12 réponses de son auto-évaluation. Bobo-Dioulasso, GRAAP, 1986

Bibliography:

GRAAP: Pour une pédagogie de l'autopromotion. Trainer's book. Bobo-Dioulasso, GRAAP. 4th edition, 1984

GRAAP: Pour une pédagogie de l'autopromotion. Animateur's book, Bobo-Dioulasso, GRAAP, 1st edition, 1985

GRAAP: Dessiner. Grammaire du dessin au tableau de feutre pour une pédagogie de l'autopromotion. Bobo-Dioulasso, GRAAP, 1st edition, 1984

Compiled by:

Volker HOFFMANN

D 7

Table 1:

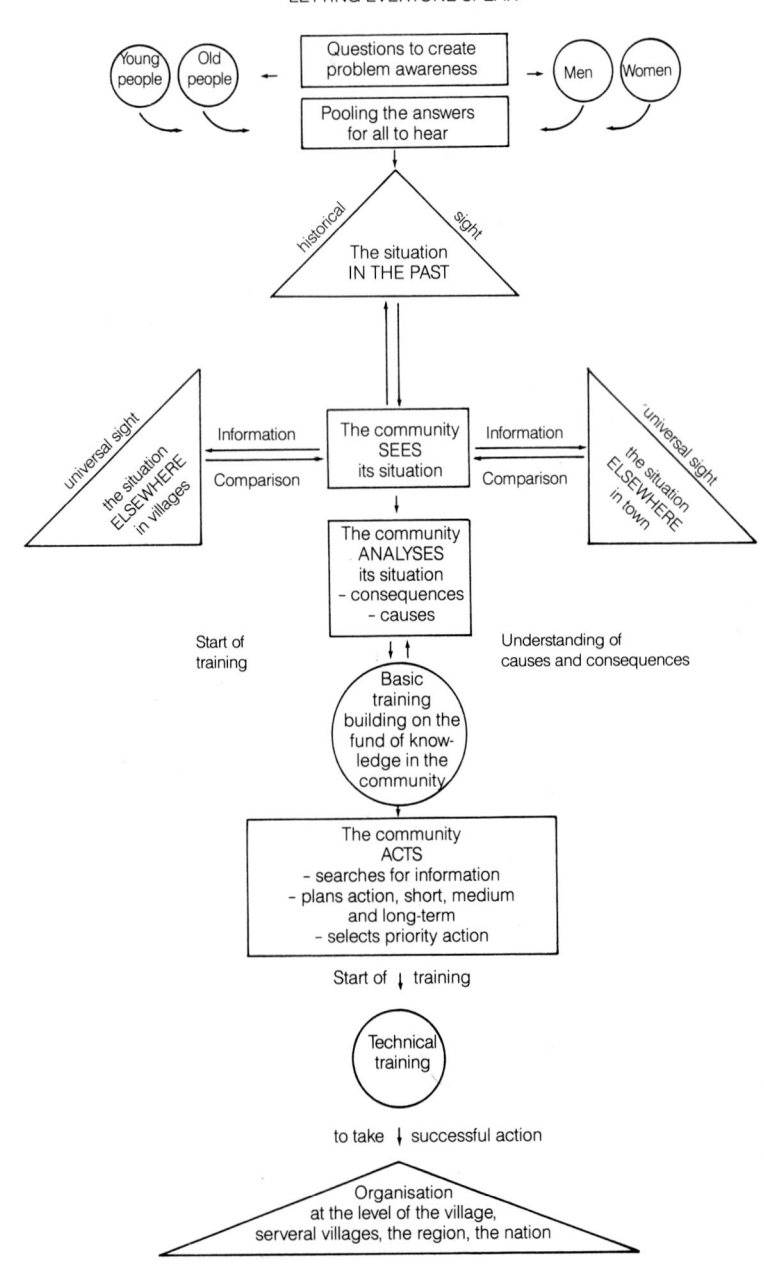

— LETTING EVERYONE SPEAK —

```
Young people → Old people → Questions to create problem awareness ← Men ← Women
                             Pooling the answers for all to hear
```

The situation IN THE PAST (historical sight)

The situation ELSEWHERE in villages (universal sight) — Information / Comparison → **The community SEES its situation** ← Information / Comparison — *The situation ELSEWHERE in town* (universal sight)

The community ANALYSES its situation
- consequences
- causes

Start of training — Basic training building on the fund of knowledge in the community — Understanding of causes and consequences

The community ACTS
- searches for information
- plans action, short, medium and long-term
- selects priority action

Start of ↓ training

Technical training

to take ↓ successful action

Organisation at the level of the village, serveral villages, the region, the nation

A table of contents of an extension programme: the "Goat Project" in Ngozi, Burundi

Extension projects or extension departments of development projects are repeatedly faced with the task of keeping a written record of an extension programme. However, they are often not sure what belongs in this kind of report. It is hoped that the following, freely translated breakdown of the extension programme in a project to develop goat keeping in Ngozi in Burundi will provide some guidance.

Extension programme in the project to develop goat keeping

1. Introduction

1.1. Outline of the evolution of the project
1.2. The current situation in the project
1.3. Reason for this report and its objectives

2. The target groups and their situation

2.1. The economic and social importance of goat keeping in the region
2.2. The state of goat keeping in the project territory
2.3. Characteristics of the goat keepers
2.4. Where and how to start improving goat keeping, and the potential adopters of innovations

3. Objectives-oriented project planning (ZOPP)

3.1. Resources, potential and preliminary achievements by the project
3.2. The people involved, the people affected and their probable interests
3.3. The hierarchy of problems of the target group
3.4. The hierarchy of aims
3.5. The project planning matrix
    3.5.1. The project purpose
    3.5.2. The overall goal
    3.5.3. The results
    3.5.4. The activities
    3.5.5. The important assumptions
    3.5.6. The objectively verifiable indicators
    3.5.7. The sources of verification

D 8

4. The project organisation

4.1. Important organisational principles
4.2. The organisation chart of the department of training and extension
4.3. Job descriptions
    4.3.1. National director
    4.3.2. German project leader
    4.3.3. Leader of the department of training and extension
    4.3.4. Province adviser
    4.3.5. Leader of the specialist group for monitoring and evaluation (M&E)
    4.3.6. Community adviser
4.4. List of institutions with which the project collaborates
4.5. Organisations whose cooperation is sought

5. Technical extension topics (in most cases shown without detailed breakdown)

5.1. Description of local breeds of goats and cross breeds
    5.1.1. General description
    5.1.2. Meat yield
    5.1.3. Milk yield
    5.1.4. Reproductive capacity
    5.1.5. Use of carcasses and hides
5.2. General problems of goat keeping in the project territory
    5.2.1. The traditional form of goat keeping
    5.2.2. Constraints on goat keeping in the region
5.3. Feeding goats
5.4. Stabling goats
5.5. Breeding
5.6. Milk yield
5.7. Herd management
5.8. Animal health and hygiene

6. Methodology of training and extension

6.1. The extension approach
6.2. Information and feedback
    6.2.1. Translating technical information at three levels (the project, community advisers, goat keepers)
    6.2.2. Training and advanced training for advisers
    6.2.3. Training programme for newly appointed advisers (six-month practical on the breeding station)

6.3. The extension and training system
    6.3.1. Discernible phases of adoption and dissemination of innovations
    6.3.2. Extension and training measures
    6.3.2.1. Awareness creation and training
    6.3.2.2. Incentives to adopt innovations
    6.3.2.3. Practical training and complementary extension
    6.3.2.4. Provision of resources
    6.3.2.5. Selecting extension aids
    6.3.2.6. Purchasing, making and using extension aids
    6.3.2.7. Model programme for extension meetings
    6.3.2.8. Description of the advisers' duties at meetings
    6.3.2.9. Description of the advisers' duties when supervising innovations
    6.3.2.10. Description of the advisers' duties when visiting farms
6.4. The monitoring and evaluation system
    6.4.1. The important indicators and their classification
    6.4.2. The system of reports
    6.4.3. Continuous up-dating of tables and diagrams
    6.4.4. Decision-oriented and action-oriented surveys
    6.4.5. Interpretation of data and corrective action

7. Operational planning

7.1. Programme for expanding the extension organisation to other territories
7.2. Annual programme
7.3. Monthly programmes for province advisers
7.4. Monthly programmes for village advisers

8. Appendix

Sources:

HOFFMANN, V., SCHULZE ALTHOFF, K., NGENDAKUMANA, S., NIYONZIMA, G.: Programme de Vulgarisation au Projet de Développement de l'Elevage Caprin. Ngozi, Burundi, 1984

Projet Caprin: Guide de l'Elevage Caprin au Burundi. Ngozi, Burundi, 1986

Compiled by:

Volker HOFFMANN

"Extension Centre Day": festivities and agricultural exhibition by CARDER Atlantique, Benin

With the help of a GTZ project, the agricultural extension service in the Atlantic Province of the People's Republic of Benin was reorganised. A detailed account is given in → B 5. The creation of 27 extension centres (CVA = Centre de Vulgarisation Agricole) had repercussions on the agricultural exhibitions planned by CARDER's audio-visual unit.

Originally only seven exhibitions were to be organised in the main villages in the sectors, but after detailed discussion it was decided to decentralise arrangements and thus come into closer contact with the target groups. The "agricultural exhibition" thus became an extension centre day (journée du CVA). The council (conseil consultatif) took on its first important duty and it was an indication by the project that it was taking seriously the idea of participation by target groups in the new extension structure.

1. Planning

In August 1984 the following plan was drawn up:

Title

Extension centre day (agricultural exhibition 1984)

Aims

1. to demonstrate the services available from CARDER and to make them better known throughout the province;

2. to encourage greater exchange of ideas and information between CARDER personnel and the target groups;

3. the exhibition to be planned and carried out in such a way that it can be used by the consultative councils of all the extension centres as a method of increasing sensitivity to problems, of advising farmers and stimulating discussion;

4. thus the organisation and running of the extension centre day to become the first real task of the newly created councils;

D 9

5. the experience of preparing and running the extension centre days to tell the councils whether they should think in terms of one large-scale central exhibition (CARDER day) in 1985.

Timing

1. The exhibition is officially opened at the same time as the new headquarters of CARDER.

2. It then travels round to each extension centre in CARDER Atlantique.

Target groups

1. the workers and farmers in each extension centre (members of the extension contact groups and other farmers);

2. the personnel of CARDER;

3. guests and visitors at the official opening of the new headquarters.

Budget

Two million Francs CFA for 1984

Content

1. The content of the exhibition was chosen from the following services offered by CARDER:

    - the 11 service units available from CARDER
    - marketing
    - plant protection
    - supply of production means
    - the extension system and extension centres
    - storage facilities
    - literacy programmes

- the cooperative programme
- the vaccination campaign
- fishing

2. Interesting innovations for the farmers and the rural population, such as:

   - new varieties of seed;
   - plant protection treatment (beans, grain storage);
   - use of mineral fertiliser;
   - improved fallow;
   - etc.

3. Presentation of the harvest results of the season 1984/5 (or only of the main season 1984) achieved by production cooperatives and extension contact groups.

Method

It is important to devise a methodology that allows the councils in the extension centres to develop a common strategy. Building on the agricultural exhibition, the extension centre day could also comprise:

- an agricultural competition between the various extension contact groups of the centre;
- an intensive discussion of the successes and failures in the last cropping season;
- a discussion between the farmers and authorities to analyse the needs of the target groups and to identify where attention should be focussed in the following season.

The display articles must therefore be accompanied by written instructions describing the aims, methods and running of the extension centre day. The actual programme of the day is decided by the councils after receiving proposals from CARDER.

D 9

Running the extension centre day

Responsibility for implementing the programme lies with the audio-visual unit of CARDER working together with the relevant departments, service units and individuals.

2. Implementation

The audio-visual unit began preparations on the basis of this planning.

The overall concept was defined in more detail and discussed at length in the four extension centres and modified to take account of local wishes and requirements. The topics for fourteen display boards were decided, designed, tested and produced.

To back up the national literacy campaign in which CARDER is also involved, it was decided to draw up all textual material for the exhibition in the national language (Fon). To ensure correct translation, the project sought the assistance of the "Provincial Service for Literacy and the Rural Press" (SPAPR).

The extension centres used one of the display boards to advertise their own activities. Texts and ideas on presentation were worked out with the representatives of the centres; the final format was then decided by the extension centres alone.

Finally a transportable circular tent with stout bamboo posts and a heavy tarpaulin to protect the display boards from wind and rain was constructed.

The exhibition was mounted for the first time on 29th November 1984, coinciding with the opening of CARDER's new headquarters. After the opening ceremony, a special meeting was held of all 29 leaders of centres, who were shown the exhibition again and given more detailed explanations. They were also given carefully worked out teaching guidelines (Fiches pédagogiques) for each display board. Then proposals for planning an extension centre day were worked out at a joint session. This plan was immediately written up as "Technical Instructions" (Fiche technique), the text of which we reproduce in free translation.

3. Technical instructions for an extension centre day

What is an extension centre day?

An extension centre day is an event that is planned and carried out by all the councils of extension centres in our province. The aim of the day is to make the services of CARDER Atlantique better known and to encourage the exchange of ideas between CARDER personnel and the target groups, i. e. it is a way of making people sensitive to problems, giving advice and generating discussion.

The extension centre day is coupled with an exhibition prepared by the audiovisual unit of CARDER. This exhibition is for the use of extension centres and consists of fourteen display boards illustrating the organisation of CARDER, the extension centre and the services that they make available for the rural population.

The high point of an extension centre day is the meeting attended by the various groups: the extension contact group of farmers, members of production cooperatives, farmers not in any organisation and the personnel of CARDER. When the council of a centre organises this kind of meeting, various activities can take place: discussions on the situation analysis, evaluation and planning of extension work, a competition, entertainments, the announcement of farmers' successes and awards, etc.

The extension centre day is rounded off by a film show using the film bus belonging to CARDER.

How is an extension centre day organised?

The exhibition is being shown for the first time at the opening of the new headquarters of CARDER Atlantique in Abomey-Calavi on 29th November, 1984.

During December and January it will travel to all the extension centres in the province. Each sector and each extension centre will be notified well in advance when the event is to be held.

1. The extension centre chooses a suitable location for the exhibition, preferably next to the extension centre itself. If access to the extension centre and the site is difficult, the alternative location must be central, so that the extension centre day will run smoothly.

2. The extension centre team, with the help of council members, must ensure that the extension centre day is adequately advertised. Posters advertising the day should be prepared by the audio-visual unit. On the day of the event, the cinema bus should advertise it over loudspeakers. It is important to inform and invite all official representatives well in advance.

3. The council is responsible for the preparation of the programme in detail. The following is a possible schedule:

    11.00 – 12.00 Declaring the day open and tour of the exhibition

D 9

12.00 – 17.00 Exhibition open to visitors, demonstrations and explanations by the staff of the extension centre.
Exhibition of the produce of extension contact groups and production cooperatives.
Exhibition of the production inputs and equipment available at the extension centre.

17.00 – 18.00 Second organised tour of the whole exhibition

18.00 – 20.00 Discussions, games, talks, dancing, awarding prizes won in the agricultural competition

20.00 – 22.00 Cultural programme, film, slide show, music, dance, etc.

Demonstrations can be of improved seed and maize cobs of the Poza-Rica variety, the seed dusting drum, spraying equipment, maize grinder, oxen for ploughing and transport, and whatever else the centre makes available to farmers.

All councils, except the one in the first centre, can get more information by taking part in other extension centre days in their area.

4. The exhibition comprises:

   – a tarpaulin 10 x 10 m and bamboo posts for constructing a tent;

   – 14 display boards on stands;

   – sundry items.

   Early on the morning of the extension centre day, the materials are delivered to the site. Under the guidance of an experienced technician sent by CARDER headquarters, the council sets out the exhibition. The extension centre is responsible for the security of the materials and objects displayed.

5. The extension department and the audio-visual unit of CARDER will give the council all the help needed to make the extension centre day a great success.

   This help consists of:

   a) a practical introduction for everyone involved before the day starts;

   b) technical instructions on running the whole day's programme and detailed instructions on all 14 display boards;

c) the presence and help of a member of the audio-visual unit's staff throughout the day. He is assisted from time to time by other colleagues from headquarters;

d) a budget from which the CARDER management subsidises the costs of the day. If other costs are incurred, they have to be borne by the individual extension centre or finance has to be planned by the council and raised during the day itself.

How should we use the extension centre day to improve our extension system?

Whether an extension centre day is successful or not depends above all on the commitment of the council. It should regard the day as its primary task in the first cropping season when the new extension system is used. The extension centre thus has the opportunity to make itself and CARDER known to the rural population as an organisation with popular appeal in the service of farming.

By commenting on the services of the extension centre and making proposals, the farmers can become actively involved in the extension system. Our aim is to make the target group realise that the extension centre is their concern. A well organised extension centre day can make our work substantially more effective, because on the one hand the target groups find out what services are being offered, and on the other hand CARDER staff learn more about the needs of farmers.

4. Evaluation

The evaluation of the whole campaign was overwhelmingly positive, but it also revealed many points where improvements could be made in future.

Preparation for the extension centre day was the biggest and most complex job ever undertaken by the audio-visual unit, which does not have a specialist trained in the use of media. The personnel, building on a general agricultural training, have had to acquire their skills largely unaided. In this sense, the preparation and implementation of 28 exhibitions was a huge on-the-job training programme. The weaknesses and deficiencies that it revealed were dealt with in a training programme run in 1985/6.

By being actively involved in the extension centre day's programme, the staff of the audio-visual unit had ample opportunity to test their own media material and their skill in presentation to the target groups. The feedback gave them important clues on how to improve their materials and how to plan future extension centre days.

D 9

The extension centre day was very well received by the target groups. The leaders of the extension centres have estimated that more than 25 000 people in the whole province took part. The exhibition was often seen by more than 2 000 people, especially in the more remote regions. The councils in all the centres have taken over planning and organisation with great enthusiasm. Without exception, the farmers have not objected to sacrificing a working day and have taken an active part in folk activities and exhibiting produce in the agricultural competition.

The exhibition itself, showing the services offered by CARDER and the extension centre, was very well attended, but it became clear that more explanation was essential. Even people who could read the keyword texts and explanations often did not understand the meaning. The carefully devised illustrations on their own were even less effective in communicating the message. Thus, if misunderstandings were to be avoided, each display board had to have its own carefully worded explanatory text, and the public had to be given a chance to ask questions. This was not always possible in view of the mass of visitors.

It is advisable to reduce the number of display boards in future exhibitions and they will have to be tested more thoroughly to check that they are fully comprehensible. A well informed individual should stand by each display board to answer questions.

All centres complained that the 50 DM subsidy provided by headquarters was too low. Food and drink for the staff involved and the fee of the obligatory folk music and dance groups cost several times this amount and could not simply be recovered from the visitors or the farmers' groups. Also some extension centres claimed that good folk groups would only perform and successful farmers would only exhibit in the competition if they were provided with transport.

Since most investment in materials has been made in the first year, it seems reasonable to raise the level of subsidy for the running costs in the following years.

With unanimous agreement, the extension centre day was repeated the following year. This event, held after the first cropping season, has played a very important role in the reorganisation of the extension system and has been a positive factor in the rapid adoption of the extension system by the target groups.

Sources:

Volker KNERSCH, Uwe Jens NAGEL: La journée du CVA, une nouvelle approche dans la vulgarisation agricole. Projet Bénino-Allemand de développement rural, CARDER de l'Atlantique. Cotonou, 1985

CORREZE, A., HOFFMANN, V., LAGEMANN, J., MACK, R.P., NEUMANN, I., YEBE, C.,: Evaluation du projet CARDER Atlantique, République Populaire de Bénin. Unpublished appraisal for GTZ, Eschborn, 1986

Compiled by:

Volker HOFFMANN

Practical guidelines

Identifying target groups and differentiating sub-groups

A working party, "Rural Development", commissioned by the Federal Ministry for Economic Cooperation, has devised a method for producing a "reduced regional analysis" in which target groups are investigated according to a set procedure.

To analyse target groups, the following criteria are applied:

- possessions/occupation;
- household income;
- level of food supplies;
- level of risk;
- social structure;
- division of labour;
- norms and values.

This target group analysis provides the framework for a problem-oriented, differentiated analysis of target groups or subgroups from the point of view of extension. The characteristics of the total target population and the identification of more specific target groups on the basis of their general level of deprivation enable the extension organisation to assess how these groups will react to extension measures.

Already existing groups and other associations in a particular society/region are the starting point for project activities. Here an overall analysis to establish social statistics (reduced regional analysis) acts as a check. Indeed, it tells us whether starting project activities with existing groups is compatible with the overall project goal.

To obviate lengthy planning and preliminary phases, a project can, by specifically addressing people who **can be reached** and are **capable of being mobilised**:

- link up with communal activities already undertaken;
- tackle problems that have previously been ignored;
- appeal to groups that have not been touched by development activities.

E 1

Here too the analysis of social statistics acts as a check on whether the groups are representative of the target population and their problems.

With the **problem-oriented approach** (→ Chapter II.1) the following groups have to be differentiated in the **feasibility study:**

(1) **total population** of a region;

(2) **target groups,** i. e. all people encompassed by the development policy and the project's aims, even though they may fall into social categories rather than groups in the sociological sense;

(3) **subgroups,** i. e. groups within the target groups, who are defined according to observable criteria, for example, women with access to markets;

(4) **mediating groups,** i. e. existing active associations (neighbourhood help groups, savings clubs for men or women, cooperatives; groups already formed by the state extension service, etc.);

(5) **groups providing services,** i. e. the people who have to devise the extension programme, take responsibility for it and carry it out (government departments, research, training, radio, cooperatives);

(6) **indirectly affected groups,** i. e. individuals or groups in the population who are not specifically addressed by the programme. They may be cooperatives, traders, large-scale farmers, creditors or women, who in West Africa are traditionally the key figures in marketing crops and in East Africa are almost totally responsible for growing crops.

The main object of the feasibility study is the identification of such groups from the point of view of their potential and ability to take part in the extension programme. In particular, we have to look at factors that could further the autonomous spread of innovations. The larger extension projects will in many cases have to design specific measures for specific groups.

Investigation of channels of communication and contact reveals, for example, that women in strict Islamic societies can hardly ever be reached via the men. If the project addresses the women separately but only in domestic matters, this approach misses the realities of life in peasant society in most countries, because women are in fact very much involved in agricultural production. Thus changes to agricultural practice and ways of reducing physical labour have to be aimed just as much at women as men.

We should concentrate on the bottlenecks occurring in typical types of farm when we identify the various subgroups.

E 1

An example from Java:

The farm in question is small and short of capital (0.5 ha, 6 people). In this situation the farmer:

- is compelled to lease land;
- is dependent on landlords and mainly Chinese money lenders;
- is compelled to take another job to earn cash, e. g. porter, betjak (3-wheeler) driver in the towns;
- has a shortage of labour on his farm despite the high level of unemployment;
- has a poor and unbalanced diet because all the products that bring in cash have to be sold for consumption in the towns (beef cattle, eggs, etc.).

In this situation, raising the rice yield may seem to both the project and the target group to be a good starting point for development measures. But we still find typical constraints that enable us to divide the target group into subgroups with a common problem (in this case, producing more rice). Specific packages of measures have to be compiled for each of these subgroups.

By working together with the target group, we find it relatively easy to differentiate these sub-groups – on which we base the later analysis of farming systems – if we weigh **resource potential** against **constraints**.

Resource potential	Constraints
Reduction of total losses in the case of traditional varieties (during cultivation, ripening, harvesting, marketing, processing, preparation).	Training and level of know-how, labour available, pest control only if used by all farms, fertilising scarcely possible.
Introduction of new varieties	Increase in the farmers' burden of debt and rising land prices and farm rent, labour available, giving up subsidiary employment, marketing and credit facilities.

E 1

Resource potential (continued)

Technical measures (fertilising, plant protection, use of machines, consolidation of plots).

Constraints (continued)

In irrigated farming, fertilising only possible with participation of neighbours — same applies to plant protection, fish breeding not possible with plant protection, capital bottleneck, level of training and know-how, setting up a land registry.

A joint discussion of these interacting factors helps us to distinguish the following subgroups:

- farms that can introduce technical measures because of their low level of debt;

- farms that can systematically reduce their debt by introducing fish breeding, planting embankments, etc.;

- farms in existing village "cooperatives" (so-called water cooperatives) that can organise the use of machines (contract threshing, hand pumps, etc.);

- farms for which work must be created in such activities as water management, harvesting; farmers can therefore solve the problem of a lack of work on their own farms and at the same time earn extra cash.

Source:

K.M. FISCHER, et al: Ländliche Entwicklung. Ein Leitfaden zur Konzeption, Planung und Durchführung armutsorientierter Projekte. Bonn: BMZ 1978, English edition Bonn: BMZ 1980

Compiled by:

Rolf SÜLZER

Participation of target groups

In the "Chilalo Agricultural Development Project" in Ethiopia an attempt was made to link the participation of target groups to the wider issues of rural development. The following diagram illustrates the theoretical links:

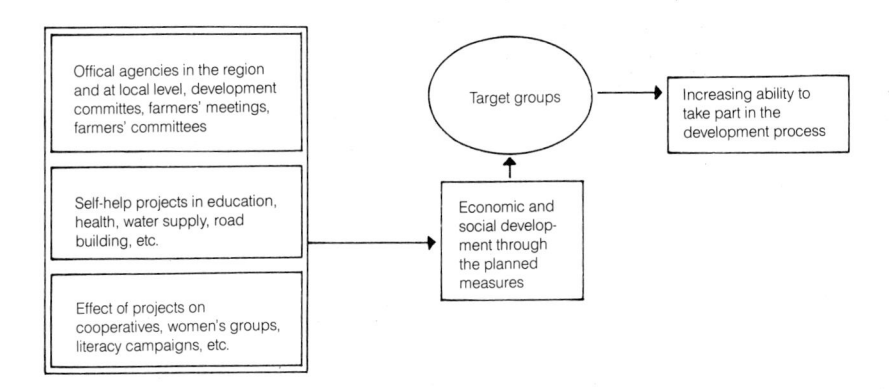

```
┌─────────────────────────┐
│ Offical agencies in the │
│ region and at local     │
│ level, development      │         ┌──────────┐    ┌─────────────────┐
│ committees, farmers'    │────┐    │  Target  │───▶│ Increasing      │
│ meetings, farmers'      │    │    │  groups  │    │ ability to take │
│ committees              │    │    └──────────┘    │ part in the     │
└─────────────────────────┘    │          ▲         │ development     │
                               │          │         │ process         │
┌─────────────────────────┐    │    ┌─────────────┐ └─────────────────┘
│ Self-help projects in   │    │    │ Economic    │
│ education, health,      │────┼───▶│ and social  │
│ water supply, road      │    │    │ development │
│ building, etc.          │    │    │ through the │
└─────────────────────────┘    │    │ planned     │
                               │    │ measures    │
┌─────────────────────────┐    │    └─────────────┘
│ Effect of projects on   │    │
│ cooperatives, women's   │────┘
│ groups, literacy        │
│ campaigns, etc.         │
└─────────────────────────┘
```

However, this situation was not achieved in the project, because the planners and the front-line project workers did not involve the target groups in the decision-making process. An evaluation of the degree of participation in the various areas of decision making revealed shortcomings. Thus the brief statement of results in → Figure 1 also shows where and how participation could be initiated. For this reason we show the analysis of the situation both as it was and as it should have been.

When involving target groups, we regard the following procedures as important:

1) in discussion, concentration on feasibility;

2) formulation of targets and measures and keeping a written record of them;

3) ensuring that all participants are informed about their duties and know precisely what they have to do.

4) direct testing and the implementation of trial programmes;

5) regular contact with decision makers and people with responsibilities (both in the subgroups and the service groups).

6) observation of the reactions of other people in the vicinity of the project;

7) consistent detailed planning and implementation of the programme after discussion (ideally without delay between decision and implementation);

8) constant supervision of operations and regular coordination with all participants.

Figure 1:

Influence of various groups in the decision-making process						
Where the groups can participate	Population		Local leaders		Government personnel	
	Actual situation	Target situation	Actual situation	Target situation	Actual situation	Target situation
Initial decision on						
Target groups	None	None	None	None	None	P
Needs and priorities	None	P	None	P	None	None
Aims of the project	None	None	None	None	None	P
Location of the project	None	P	None	P	None	P
Cropping systems	None	P	None	P	None	P
Ongoing decisions on						
Needs	None	P	None	P	None	None
Project measures	None	P	None	P	None	P
Project locations	Requests	Requests	Influence	Influence	Influence	None
Reorientation of the project	None	P	None	P	Influence	Influence
Place/time of meetings	None	P	Joint decision	Joint decision	Influence	P
Criteria for participation in the programme	None	P	None	P	None	P
Selection of model farmers	5 local people propose	All local people propose	5 local leaders propose	All local leaders propose	Influence who is chosen	None
Selection and appointment of personnel	None	None	None	None	None	None

P = participation and shows where the involvement of each group is both possible and desirable

E 2

Source:

J. M. COHEN, N. T. UPHOFF: Rural development participation. Concepts and measures for project design, implementation and evaluation. Ithaca, N.Y. Cornell Univ. 1977, (Rural Development Monograph 2) pp. 204 ff.

Compiled by:

Rolf SÜLZER, Gerhard PAYR

E 3

Deciding on target groups and development measures

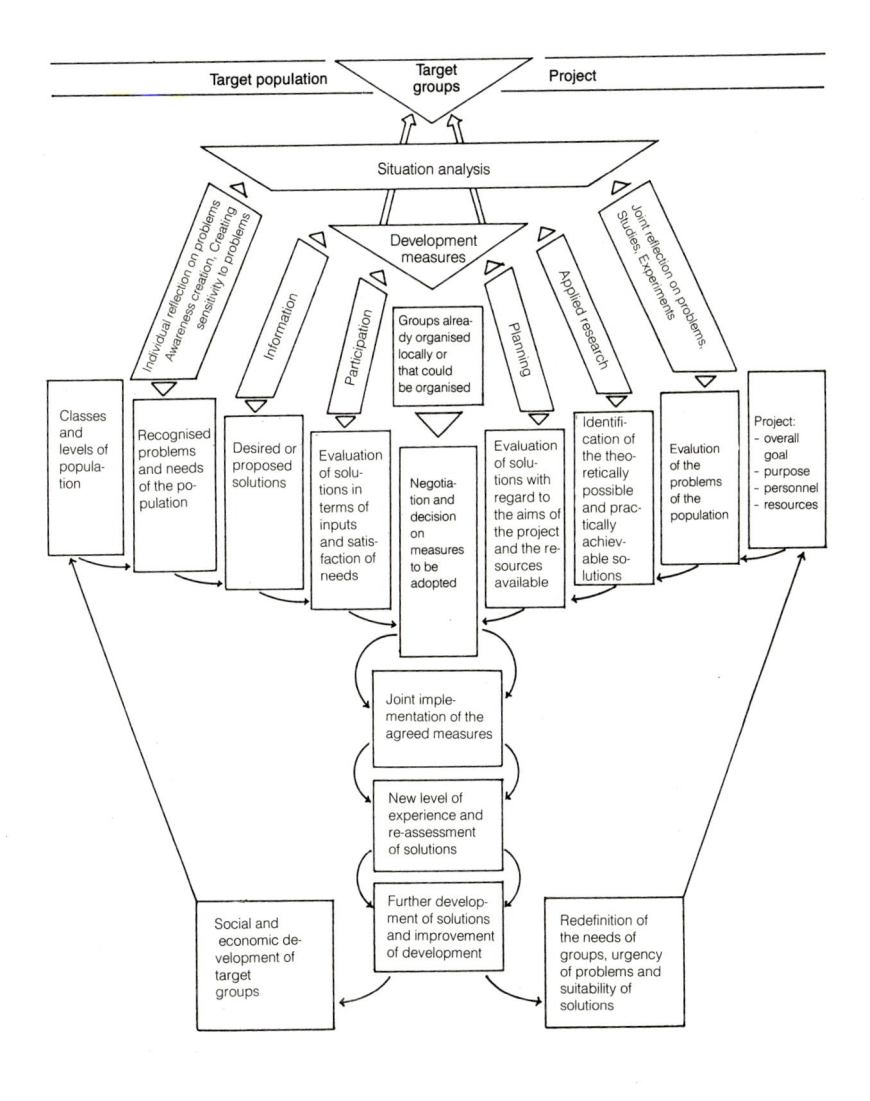

Target population | Target groups | Project

Situation analysis

Development measures

Individual reflection on problems. Awareness creation. Creating sensitivity to problems

Information

Participation

Groups already organised locally or that could be organised

Planning

Applied research

Joint reflection on problems. Studies. Experiments

| Classes and levels of population | Recognised problems and needs of the population | Desired or proposed solutions | Evaluation of solutions in terms of inputs and satisfaction of needs | Negotiation and decision on measures to be adopted | Evaluation of solutions with regard to the aims of the project and the resources available | Identification of the theoretically possible and practically achievable solutions | Evalution of the problems of the population | Project: - overall goal - purpose - personnel - resources |

Joint implementation of the agreed measures

New level of experience and re-assessment of solutions

Further development of solutions and improvement of development

Social and economic development of target groups

Redefinition of the needs of groups, urgency of problems and suitability of solutions

E 3

Source:

Volker HOFFMANN: Identification des groupes cible et des mesures du projet. In: LAGEMANN, HOFFMANN, RAUSCH, SCHREINER, YEBE: Evaluation du projet CARDER Atlantique, République Populaire du Bénin. Unpublished appraisal for GTZ, Eschborn, 1984.

Compiled by:

Volker HOFFMANN

E 4

How to select contact farmers

Since both individual and mass extension prove impossible in certain projects, we often find it necessary to make use of contact farmers. For individual extension there are too few advisers; for mass extension it is usually impossible to standardise and pass on the content of extension unless personal contact is made and the farmers are shown how to apply the measures. Thus the contact farmer should act as an intermediary between the adviser and the farmer. We now examine what determines the success or failure of the contact farmer.

Definition

In both the literature and projects many similar terms are used to denote this farmer but, when we examine their meaning more closely, we find that they fall into two categories: terms that stress personal contact and terms that refer to the farm situation:

1. **Personal contact**

    Key farmer
    Contact farmer
    Key individual
    Opinion former

2. **Farm situation**

    Progressive farmer
    Model farmer
    Master farmer
    Demonstration farmer

The concept of contact farmer applies to group 1 only. These are people who already have a multiplier effect within the community, who can be regarded as "central individuals" (on the analogy of "central locations"). The terms in group 2 indicate farms or farming systems that are already well ahead of the average farmer in a region or that are systematically programmed by the extension organisation to be so.

Conditions for success

Many surveys have shown that deliberately producing progressive individuals does not induce others to follow. A "radiation effect" only occurs in an established contact situation or in group situations. These are characterised by:

(1) possession of know-how that can be passed on;

(2) motivation to pass on know-how;

(3) ability to pass on know-how;

(4) positive relations between individuals and sources of information;

(5) trust in the credibility of the contact farmer and his technical competence;

(6) guaranteed regular meetings;

(7) groups that are relatively homogeneous as regards production potential, the mentality of the group, ability to comprehend, their system of values.

Reasons for the failure of group extension by contact farmers

(1) The "groups" are not groups in the sociological sense (→ see point 4 above) but a number of individuals with the same or similar characteristics (social category).

(2) "Contact farmers" are people who prefer to cultivate relations only with elites – especially in the non-agricultural sector.

(3) When they are chosen, their agreement to act as contact farmers is confused with their actual willingness to pass on know-how. There are no contractual obligations or social controls.

(4) Their originally positive relations with neighbours or colleagues are eroded by their advancement and replaced by mistrust.

(5) Contact farmers regard themselves as "representatives" of the others but pursue their own goals and distance themselves socially, and eventually also economically, from the group.

(6) They are not given preliminary advice, nor are they given ongoing back-up.

Finding contact farmers

Contact farmers have to be chosen with a great deal of care to ensure maximum benefit and to avoid negative effects. It is best to combine a variety of methods, since each has its own shortcomings. There are four possible approaches, each of which should involve the target group:

(1) grouping together farms with a similar resource base and similar constraints;

(2) observation and evaluation of gatherings and meetings;

(3) investigation of the contact situation by means of sociometric surveys (e. g. the situation analysis);

(4) appeal to the target groups to use their own initiative.

Grouping farms together

This method forms part of the situation analysis. Farms are categorised according to particular features in household and farm surveys; farms in similar problem situations are grouped together in types of farm.

Evaluating meetings

This method is sometimes used in the situation analysis too, but it can also be applied while the project is running. We observe which people meet at particular places, what topics and problems they talk about and whether people in similar farming situations meet each other. Observation is supplemented by asking well informed individuals about existing group relations.

Investigating the contact situation (sociometric survey)

This method involves asking people, in interviews and questionnaires, with whom they would cooperate, whom they would ask for advice, etc. The answers to the questionnaire are entered on a matrix with rows and columns for the names of everyone interviewed. It can be applied, for example, to village surveys. → Table 1 shows what this kind of matrix looks like.

The important factor is the choice of contact questions relating to the situation and the problem. Simply asking about prominent people proves to be unproductive – the question must refer specifically to problems. In the case of agriculture, the contact question could be: "Who would you prefer to cultivate a field with?" or "Who would you hire a pair of oxen with, etc.?"

The answer, entered in the matrix, is in this example: A and B have both named C. Since C has given A, they have chosen each other, indicating a close mutual relationship.

After examining the choices in a matrix, the best method is to illustrate the network of relations as in → Figure 1. The arrows show the direction of choices and the number of circles round individuals represent the frequency with which they are chosen.

E 4

Table 1:

Evaluation of a sociometric survey in tabular form						
	The people chosen					
The people making a choice	A	B	C	D	E	F
A			x			
B			x			
C	x					
D		x				
E		x				
F				x		

From a purely sociometric point of view, C would be the best contact farmer since he was chosen by A and B; B is mentioned by D and E and D by F as the individuals they would prefer. With this pattern, B would only be suitable if the A – C relationship allowed it, but this is clearly not the case.

Figure 1:

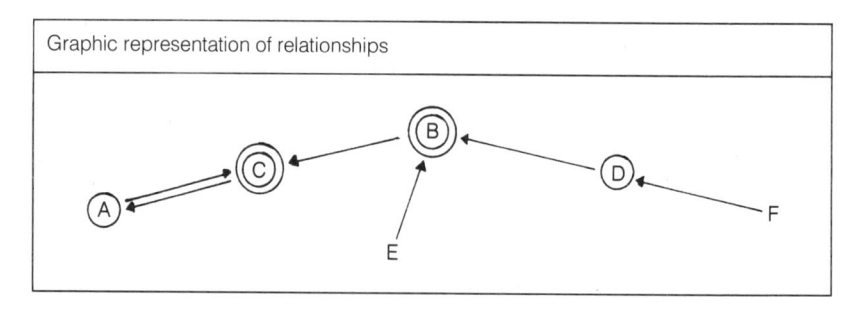

Graphic representation of relationships
A ↔ C → B ← E, D ← F (with B ← D)

Appeal to use initiative

The fourth way might involve asking groups to work independently in the preliminary phase of projects. The first groups to be helped are those that have formed themselves. The project and the groups commit themselves contractually to mutual obligations: the activities of the project and the contribution of the groups are laid down precisely in the contract. This approach depends on:

E 4

(1) the project's contribution and measures being made known on a sufficiently wide scale;

(2) the clear definition of which groups are to be helped by the project and under what conditions (target group definition);

(3) guaranteed measures for the groups in need.

This method — extension on request accompanied by the target group's own input — has often been tried out; for example, the Swiss development agency SATA operates according to this principle that requires the target groups to take a share, albeit a small share, in the financing of the programme. In Chile, approaches similar to the German ring extension method have been employed. Groups finance "their" adviser. This is common in crisis situations in all regions, examples being villages that employ teachers at their own expense, farms with cash cropping that join forces in one production unit and appoint their own adviser (→ B 4 also).

Final choice

These various methods should be combined to create groups and to select extension contact partners in these groups (contact farmers, etc.). Farm surveys are necessary to determine what measures should be applied and to categorise farm types. Surveys at meeting places and finding out how best to establish contact are important if extension strategy is focussed on individuals who do not enjoy general prestige but who do have a reputation as "good farmers" or even "good maize farmers", etc. Finally the appeal to people to use their own initiative shows what groups can form themselves and which people in the target group have to be approached as problem cases through individual advisory work as well.

The same problem is dealt with in working paper → F 9.

Bibliography:

H. W. SCHÖNMEIER: Agriculture in Conflict. The Shambaa Case. Bensheim: Kübel Foundation GmbH 1977, p. 288.

Compiled by:

Rolf SÜLZER, Gerhard PAYR

The methodology of extension talks

I. Introduction

"Giving advice is a difficult business," said Goethe, "and, when we see how the most promising endeavours come to nothing and how something quite absurd can have a happy conclusion, we recoil from wanting to give advice. Basically the man who seeks advice is often displaying his own limitations and the man who gives advice is displaying arrogance."

This statement recorded by ECKERMANN in his conversation with Goethe (12.3.1831) sets the tone for our discussion, because it is a widely held but erroneous view that the main task of the adviser in an extension talk is to give advice.

This paper deals with the basic questions of conversation technique between people seeking and giving advice. We do not refer specifically to agricultural extension in developing countries, but the psychological starting point for conducting discussions can easily be applied to other contexts including agriculture. Apart from farmers and advisers, we might apply the principles to conversations between advisers, married couples, parents and children, teachers and pupils, etc.

When we talk about discussion as a method, we tend to regard the technique, the superficial efficiency with which a discussion is conducted, as the central issue. In so doing, we easily overlook the fact that a conversation between two people consists of far more than simply seeking and supplying information.

The extension talk aims to:

- help in a situation of ignorance;
- help in conflict situations;
- help to overcome problems.

Thus, in terms of its function and methodology, there is a clear distinction between the extension talk and simple information, conversation, enquiry and interrogation.

The factors that determine the function and structure of an extension talk are that:

- the problem is recognised;
- the extension partner is given some insight into the causes of problems;
- solutions are worked out together.

E 5

II. Four basic functions

1. Clarification of the problem and its causes

The extension talk revolves round the attempt to clarify the problem situation and how it came about. During the dialogue we must never forget that the problem experienced by the farmer is in fact a part of his everyday life. The farmer's perception of a problem often does not coincide with what the adviser considers to be the heart of the problem. We often find that the farmer and the adviser either do not speak the same language or have different perceptions of reality or may have to contend with both disadvantages. Extension is only likely to be successful if we are able to see the world through the eyes of the extension partner. A discussion will not be fruitful unless there is at least some common ground between the different perceptions of reality (→ Chapter III.5 and III.7).

Problems are experienced subjectively, but for the person concerned they represent objective reality and as such determine his behaviour. These subjective perceptions will usually be quite different from the perceptions of advisers.

2. Grasping the nature of the problem

Extension practice has shown that all manner of difficulties can serve as the starting point for discussion. The extension partner sometimes has no understanding of his problem and simply feels a vague need to talk about it, although sometimes he is able to articulate his difficulties clearly and with precision.

The extension partner often has a feeling of agonising uncertainty or pressing disquiet that he can hardly express in words, let alone formulate as a precise question. In particular, deep existential issues affecting all aspects of human life are often so complex that they are beyond the powers of language. The client is looking for a way out of this confusion. He still does not know how this is to be achieved or whether his opposite number will be sufficiently patient and receptive.

Simply by his presence the adviser is offering support; by listening attentively he encourages the farmer to articulate his problems. The farmer thus expresses what has been on his mind – which may of course be right or wrong – but once he has given expression to what has been preoccupying him, topics can be taken further and dealt with in depth.

These two scenarios show clearly that there are many starting points for an extension talk. The adviser must keep the starting point in mind all the time if he is to offer genuine help to solve problems.

Clients perceive problems from a subjective point of view; thus the structure of problems and the clarity of perception will vary from one person to the next.

3. Understanding problems as an incentive to act

The extension discussion must be a phased process of clarification before the adviser can finally suggest solutions. This process calls for a high degree of concentration and patience on the part of the adviser. Often he thinks he is being helpful by providing an answer before the discussion partner has clarified his own thoughts on the matter. But this "help" is premature and jeopardises the further development of discussion. The man seeking advice appears to display a lack of ability, whereas the adviser is astute, has a quick mental grasp of problems and is therefore superior. The self-esteem of the farmer suffers as a consequence. Moreover, the premature attempt to solve problems runs the risk of distracting the farmer from the real problem and causing him unwittingly to abandon the path he had spontaneously followed – namely, the gradual identification of the causes of his difficulties (→ Chapter III.7).

The extension talk must be conducted in such a way that the client can himself gain an insight into the causes of problems and the overall structure of the problem situation. Only in this way will the client develop the psychological powers needed to take fully independent action.

4. Mobilising initiative and dynamic behaviour

Insight into the nature of problems automatically acts as an incentive to take independent decisions and actions. Solutions offered by the adviser can have the same effect when they are presented in such a way that they are accepted subjectively as solutions by the client. If this is to occur, the discussion must be conducted to ensure that the solution fits the operational frame of reference of the discussion partner. For example, adherence to a particular rotation – for which there are good reasons from the angle of plant protection and soil science – has to be fitted into the relevant frame of reference of the farmer, namely "long-term high yields". Similarly, technical language has to be converted into the everyday language of farmers – which must not be confused with manipulation of language (falsifying the message). Only if we take a farmer's operational frame of reference and his everyday vocabulary fully into account can the motivation and alternative strategies to overcome difficulties be developed.

The extension talk must be conducted in such a way that, simply by showing how issues are interrelated, the client's initiative and inner dynamism is stimulated.

II. Non-directive counselling even in technical extension work?

The approach described above is in keeping with the concept of non-directive or partner-centred counselling.

E 5

1. Even non-directive counselling exerts influence.

When we talk of non-directive extension or counselling, it would be a fatal mistake to assume that it excludes bringing influence to bear on the extension partner. → Figure 1 illustrates the extension process in a way that would satisfy both adviser and client.

The illustration shows clearly where influence is exerted (indicated by the word **"induction"**). From the point of view of extension methodology and extension discussion technique, the question is simply what form this induction is to take. Influencing the client is a good idea, but the question remains as to how it should be done. In our scheme the method of non-directive counselling gives attitudes, strategies and techniques that should allow the extension partner maximum scope to think through and clarify his own situation.

As well as the objection to influencing people, there is another objection connected with technical extension work. This criticism usually takes the following form: "This non-directive counselling work may well be effective where interpersonal problems of a predominantly psychological nature are dealt with − after all, this method was developed by psychology − but we are giving technical advice and therefore we are working under totally different conditions."

It is certainly true to say that technical extension operates under quite different conditions. The adviser is an expert in a particular subject and he is consciously sought by the client. Despite the partnership approach, the levels of know-how and experience of the adviser and farmer remain unequal and characterise the extension situation. The consequence, in our view, is simply that in technical extension non-directive and directive discussion phases should alternate. If directive technical extension is used exclusively, it is highly likely to end in failure.

When the expert with his specialist technical knowledge is approached for advice, he must never appear reluctant. As he points out particular circumstances and gives information to his client, he naturally takes the initiative and directs the extension discussion. This is quite normal. At this stage there is no immediate threat to the client's sense of responsibility for his actions. The general question − when should an adviser use the non-directive method; when is a directive approach appropriate − is answered in the next section with the help of a phase model from → Chapter III.7.

2. The method of conducting a discussion varies according to the functions of the discussion in the problem-solving process

The definition of extension adopted in this handbook (→ Chapter I.2.1) regards advisory work as non-material help in the search for solutions to problems. Since we have earlier recommended an approach to problem solving (Chapter III.7), we

Figure 1: Flow chart of successful counselling

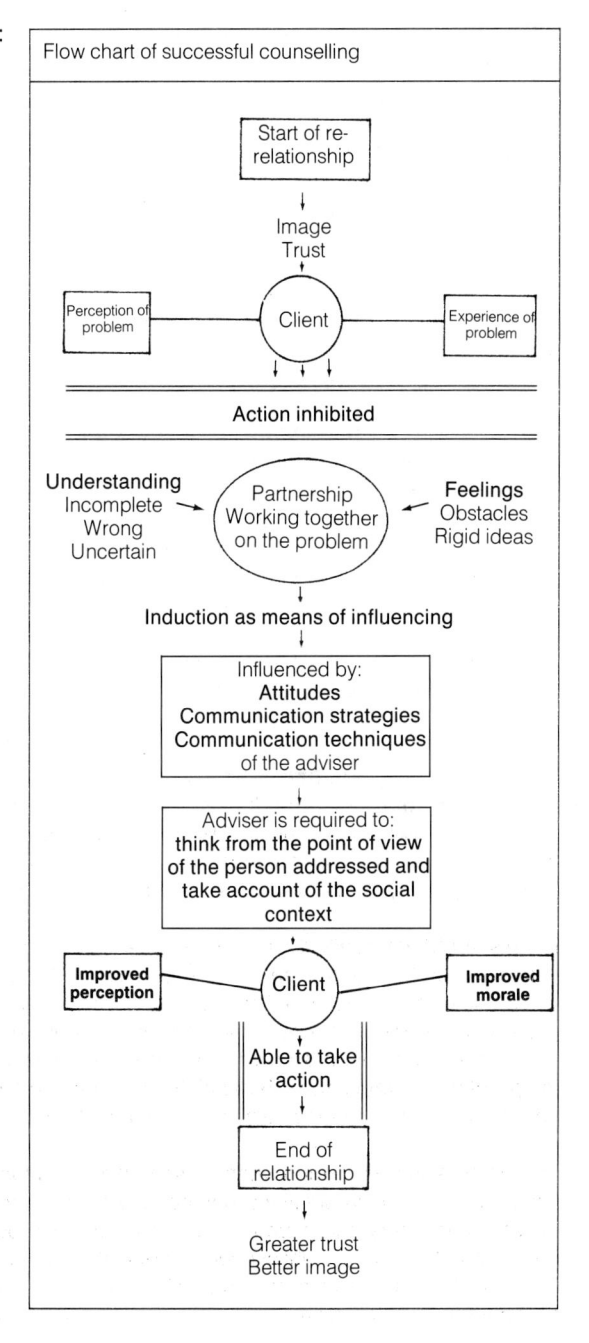

```
                    ┌──────────────┐
                    │ Start of re- │
                    │ relationship │
                    └──────┬───────┘
                           ↓
                         Image
                         Trust
  ┌──────────────┐      ╭───────╮      ┌──────────────┐
  │ Perception of├──────┤Client ├──────┤ Experience of│
  │   problem    │      ╰───┬───╯      │   problem    │
  └──────────────┘        ↓ ↓ ↓        └──────────────┘
  ══════════════════════════════════════════════════════
                     Action inhibited
  ══════════════════════════════════════════════════════

 Understanding      ╭────────────╮       Feelings
 Incomplete   ────→ │ Partnership│ ←──   Obstacles
 Wrong              │Working together    Rigid ideas
 Uncertain          │on the problem│
                    ╰──────┬───────╯
                           ↓
              Induction as means of influencing
                           ↓
                  ┌──────────────────┐
                  │  Influenced by:  │
                  │    Attitudes     │
                  │Communication strategies│
                  │Communication techniques│
                  │  of the adviser  │
                  └────────┬─────────┘
                           ↓
                  ┌──────────────────┐
                  │Adviser is required to:│
                  │think from the point of view│
                  │of the person addressed and│
                  │take account of the social│
                  │     context      │
                  └────────┬─────────┘
                           ↓
 ┌──────────────┐       ╭───────╮       ┌──────────────┐
 │   Improved   ├───────┤Client ├───────┤   Improved   │
 │  perception  │       ╰───┬───╯       │    morale    │
 └──────────────┘           ↓           └──────────────┘
                      Able to take
                         action
                           ↓
                     ┌────────────┐
                     │   End of   │
                     │relationship│
                     └──────┬─────┘
                            ↓
                      Greater trust
                      Better image
```

will now use our recommendations to illustrate the phases into which the extension process can be divided.

When the client and the adviser meet, the first step is **to find out** what **the issue** really is. It may be that the client sees his problem clearly and consciously seeks out the extension officer or the adviser. But it is equally possible, and sometimes desirable, for the adviser to approach the client first, in order to draw his attention to current developments and the problems these could create for him.

A farmer may increase his **awareness of problems** by thinking back and realising that his conditions have deteriorated or by looking to the future and hoping that his circumstances will improve. He measures his situation and expectations by comparing himself with other people and the situation in other locations.

It is vitally important to **register and analyse the prevailing situation** before the search for solutions begins. With our problem-solving approach, this takes place in several phases. The client describes his situation, which is naturally his subjective perception of his circumstances. He may overlook important factors or he may, in the opinion of the adviser, interpret situations and interrelations in an unusual way, so that the adviser will want to discuss and examine his perceptions. Occasionally problems can be solved simply by changing the perception of the client.

Once the situation has been examined, the **search for realistic,** attainable **targets** begins, bearing in mind actual needs, followed by the attempt to define the problem.

As far as possible, a non-directive approach should be used throughout the examination and analysis of the client's situation. So that we can understand his personal position and appreciate his experience and degree of comprehension, we have to give him as much support as possible and encourage him to think about his circumstances and express his own opinions.

In the **search for targets,** the adviser may have to point out that in his professional judgement certain targets are impossible to attain. His expertise is again called for when problems are defined. But more important is the methodological point that problems should not be given final definition too soon and the adviser should think for as long as possible in terms of several parallel definitions. **The final definition of the problem contains more than half the solution,** and which solution is the right one should not be decided hastily at the stage of problem definition.

The expert is always needed when the **search for solutions** begins, especially if he can propose technical solutions that are not known to the client. In the **choice between alternatives,** the expert should also point out possible risks and consequences that the client might overlook. On the other hand, the final choice is a purely personal decision and must be made freely by the person who will later bear the consequences on his own.

Unfortunately, most advisory sessions end with the preparation for decision making. Thus both the usual **post-decision conflicts** and the inevitable **problems of implementation,** when the decision is put into practice, receive scant attention. Much effort and time spent on extension up to the point of taking decisions is often wasted, because no advice and further support is given when the solution is being carried out. Extension workers find it particularly frustrating that they hardly ever receive feedback about the success or failure of their advisory work.

If the advisers observe the process of problem solving, they can usually see if a positive **result is achieved.** This then enables the client to **evaluate the result** for himself. Only if the solution to his problem is felt to be positive is the danger of relapse eliminated. In this case, extension can be regarded as successful.

If the adviser finds that solutions are regarded as a failure, he can at least try to find a more satisfactory way of tackling the problems. In fact, if the adviser goes through the whole process in this way, he is much more likely to learn from mistakes and gain genuine experience which he can pass on to the next client.

3. What basic mistakes should be avoided in an extension talk?

Every difficulty that a person cannot overcome on his own without professional advice reduces his self-confidence. Thus an extension partner is very sensitive to the remarks and reactions of the adviser. Subconsciously the client is intent on warding off further damage to his self-esteem. Unsubstantiated criticism, bias, disapproval, moralising reprimand, demonstrations of superiority and playing down difficulties all provoke defensive reactions. At the very least they give rise to helplessness, discouragement, resignation or aggression rather than the initiative to overcome difficulties and modify behaviour.

Every individual is a complete personality in any situation. Thus a person feels more impelled to mobilise his inner resources to overcome difficulties, the more he is treated with consideration, i.e. the more he feels he is respected as an individual human being.

This is why a good adviser avoids all kinds of manipulative techniques in extension discussions, such as:

- refusing to put his cards on the table, not being straightforward, using rhetoric, showing off and trying to impress, putting people down;

- moral judgements, value judgements, praise, criticism, taking sides, admonishing, reprimanding;

- laying down the law, sophistry, penetrating questions, premature proposals to solve problems, persuasion, a final piece of advice.

E 5

So we conclude our contribution by not giving advice. Instead, we take a quick glance at philosophy. Labels can be empty sounds; reality is the product of deeper communication. "No discussion can touch the essence of things or people. Discussion is merely a way of comparing and adjusting horizons and perspectives. That is in itself an admirable achievement and one can hope for nothing more than many good, honest discussions" (Bruno Baron von Freytag Löringhoff).

Further information can be found in checklists → F 11 and → F 14.

Sources:

FREYTAG LÖRINGHOFF,B.: Über einige Wesenszüge des Gesprächs. In: Studium Generale, 8, H. 9, 1955, pp. 449 – 555

HENNIS, Wilhelm: Rat und Beratung im modernen Staat. In: Nachrichtendienst des Deutschen Vereins für öffentliche und private Fürsorge, 1963, pp. 8 – 13

HOFFMANN, Volker: Beratungsbegriff und Beratungsphilosophie im Feld des Verbraucherhandelns – Eine subjektive Standortbestimmung und Abgrenzung –. In: Die Qualität von Beratungen für Verbraucher, Campus Verlag, Frankfurt, New York, 1985, pp. 26 – 47.

HRUSCHKA, Erna: Methodische Aspekte des Beratungsgesprächs. In: Der Förderungsdienst, (1974) Sonderheft 2, pp. 44 – 48.

Bibliography:

BANG, Ruth: Das gezielte Gespräch. I. Teil: Gespräche als Lehr- und Heilmittel. Munich/Basle, 1968.

BÜRGI, A.; RUTISHAUSER, B.: Die Gesprächsführung in der Berufsberatung. In: Handbuch der Berufspsychologie, Hogrefe Verlag, Göttingen 1977, pp. 478 – 530

FITTKAU, B. et. al.: Kommunizieren lernen (und umlernen). 2nd ed. Westermann Verlag, Braunschweig 1980

GORDON, Thomas: Familienkonferenz. Die Lösung von Konflikten zwischen Eltern und Kind. Verlag Hoffmann und Campe, Hamburg 1972

GORDON, Thomas: Lehrer-Schüler-Konferenz. Wie man Konflikte in der Schule löst. Verlag Hoffmann und Campe, Hamburg 1977

GORDON Thomas: Managerkonferenz. Verlag Hoffmann und Campe, Hamburg 1982, 2nd ed.

HOFSOMMER, Wolfgang: Stichworte zum Beraterverhalten. Beratung als helfende Kommunikation. Unpublished document of BfA (Bundesanstalt für Arbeit, Nuremberg), No year given.

HORNSTEIN, Walter: Beratung in der Erziehung, Ansatzpunkte, Voraussetzungen, Möglichkeiten. In: Funkkolleg: Beratung in der Erziehung, Belz-Verlag, Weinheim and Basle 1975, pp. 33 – 68

HRUSCHKA, Erna: Psychologische Grundlagen des Beratungsvorgangs. In: Probleme der Beratung, Ulmer Verlag, Stuttgart 1964, pp. 107 – 135

HRUSCHKA, Erna: Versuch einer theoretischen Grundlegung des Beratungsprozesses. Psychologia Universalis, Bd. 16, Verlag A. Hain, Meisenheim am Glan, 1969

KRAPF, Bruno: Die Aufgaben des Beraters im partnerzentrierten Beratungsgespräch. In: Zeitschrift für Gruppenpädagogik, 6. 1980, pp. 189 – 194

LIPPIT, R.: Dimensions of the Consultants Job. In: Bennis; Benne; Chin (Eds.): The Planning of Change. New York 1961, pp. 156 – 162

MUCCHIELLI, Robert: Das Nicht-Direktive Beratungsgespräch. Otto Müller, Salzburg. No year given.

ROGERS, Carl: Die nicht-direktive Beratung. Kindler-Verlag, Munich 1972

ROGERS, Carl: Lernen in Freiheit. Kösel-Verlag, Munich 1974

ROGERS, Carl: Therapeut und Klient. Kindler-Verlag, Munich 1977

SCHÖPPING, Wolfgang: Die nicht-direktive Beratung. In: Schwalbacher Blätter, 102, H. 2. Jg. 25, 1974, pp. 42 – 50

STAHL, Claus D.: Was geschieht zwischen dem Berater und seinem Klienten? Kommunikationstheoretische Überlegungen zum Prozeß der psychosozialen Beratung. In: Blätter der Wohlfahrtspflege 124, 1977, pp. 263 – 268

WEISBACH, CH. R.: Das Beratungsgespräch. Lexika-Verlag, Weil der Stadt 1982

Compiled by:

Volker HOFFMANN, Gerhard PAYR

E 6

Laying out and using plots to demonstrate crop rotations

Demonstration plots are an especially good method of showing how yields are affected by new varieties, different plant intervals, the use of fertiliser and pesticides, etc. These plots are either laid out and tended by the advisers themselves or sections of farmers' fields are chosen for demonstration purposes with the farmers continuing to cultivate them.

In the first case the amount of time involved is a disadvantage. It is therefore usually better to mark out sections of the farmers' fields for demonstrations (using poles and unplanted strips to indicate the edges of plots) (→ Chapter III.14).

Maintenance of soil fertility is a key issue in many extension programmes. Target groups have often lost their familiarity with traditional soil-conserving land-use systems and methods, like shifting cultivation and mixed cropping, on account of the pressure of a rising population and the introduction of nonadapted "modern" techniques. By means of demonstrations, target groups have to be shown why appropriate rotation systems and adapted cropping techniques are necessary and how they are applied.

In many cases demonstration plots can be established which are used, under the supervision of the field adviser, for practical demonstrations and field days. These plots are ideal for demonstrating rotations, the benefits of which can only be seen over long periods of time.

→ Figure 1 illustrates how such a rotation demonstration plot might be laid out.

1. Basic intention

The basic intention is to place the right and wrong cropping systems and practices side by side on a small plot. This is done by cultivating half the garden correctly (Mr Right) and half incorrectly (Mr Wrong). In addition, two plots are reserved for demonstrating new crops and varieties. Be careful: in some Asian countries the use of "Mr Wrong" would not be the best way to approach extension work. We also have to bear in mind that when demonstrating the wrong alternative we run the risk that the farmers will misunderstand the experiment's aims and feel their inappropriate behaviour has been confirmed (C 1).

2. Area, position and number

The plan in → Figure 1 shows the relative size and positions of the plots:

E 6

Figure 1:

Plan of a rotation demonstration			
Mr. Right		Mr Wrong	
250 m² groundnuts	1	250 m² cotton	
250 m² cotton	2	500 m² maize	
250 m² maize	3		
150 m² sunflowers		150 m² soya beans	

Rotation Mr Right	Year 1	Year 2	Year 3
Plot 1	Groundnuts	Maize	Cotton
Plot 2	Cotton	Groundnuts	Maize
Plot 3	Maize	Cotton	Groundnuts

— An area of about 2 500 m² is necessary for rotation plots.

— The subplots should not be so small as to emphasise the model nature of the garden.

— There should be a grass strip of about 7 – 10 m between the fields of Mr Right and Mr Wrong; this area is needed for demonstrations and field days.

— A noticeboard giving explanations should be erected so that advisers do not have to be on the spot all the time.

— The rotation plots should be arranged in such a way that they can be easily inspected from the roads and paths.

— The number of demonstration plots is dependent on the settlement density, the aims of extension, the number of farms that can be used for demonstrations and the resources available.

— When the plots are being created, costs are incurred for renting land, erecting a strong fence, workers' wages, production inputs and making a noticeboard. Income from the sale of crops produced on the land is low.

E 6

3. Demonstrations and results

In plant production the methods and the results cannot normally be observed at the same time, but in demonstrations methods and results have to be shown side by side. → Figure 2 gives some examples.

If we demonstrate all the recommended measures at the same time, the different results can certainly be seen, although we have to accept that it may be impossible for observers to decide which results are linked to particular methods.

4. Possible uses

- Demonstration plots must be easily accessible. A noticeboard must present, in the local language if possible, the most important facts and figures (comparisons of yield, varieties, fertilisers and implements used). The adviser can also chalk up on the board his most recent observations and other information.

Figure 2:

Possible topics in a demonstration of plant production	
Fields of the progressive farmer (Mr. Right)	Fields of the inefficient farmer (Mr. Wrong)
Demonstration of method	
– Early cultivation of fields – Correct plant intervals – Use of improved implements – Keeping to a rotation – Tested seed – Early weeding – Mulching with harvest residues – Use of compost – Early harvest – Improved harvesting techniques – Composting harvest residues	– Late cultivation of fields – Plant intervals too wide – Use of traditional implements – No particular rotation – Poor quality seed – Late weeding – No soil cover – No fertilising – Late harvest – Traditional harvesting techniques – Burning harvest residues
Demonstration of results	
– All seeds germinate – Good plant growth – Low level of pest infestation – Little competition from weeds – Loose, moist topsoil – Soil fertility maintained	– Not all seeds germinate – Poor plant growth – High level of pest infestation – Much competition from weeds – Hard, dry topsoil – Soil fertility in decline

- At regular intervals the adviser demonstrates cultivation techniques and changes made to them.

- These rotation plots are an important item on the programme of field days.

- If there are target group organisations and contact farmers, the advisers should keep them informed about the possibility of giving demonstrations and, if required, produce and distribute leaflets.

- The functionaries of groups and contact farmers can then carry out demonstrations themselves.

- Women and children must be encouraged to attend demonstrations. Similarly, school teachers should be invited to bring their classes along.

- Wherever possible the advisers should work with the research stations to measure yields, so that cropping techniques can be assessed.

5. Experience of rotation plots

- To show the effects of rotations, demonstration gardens have to be a long-term undertaking, but their success can sometimes be jeopardised by farmers demanding the return of their land, poor supervision and the lack of interest on the part of senior advisers.

- It is important to protect gardens from domestic and wild animals. The gardens often have to be fenced off with barbed wire.

- It is important to continue showing farmers which techniques are correct and which are wrong. The differences should be unambiguous and instantly recognisable.

- Signboards have to be erected if demonstration plots cannot be inspected from roads and paths.

- It is essential to demonstrate rotations on soil of uniform quality that should also be typical of local conditions in terms of nutrients, water balance and soil type.

For general information the reader is referred to → C 5.

Compiled by:

Gerhard PAYR, Rolf SÜLZER

E 7

Demonstrating the use of portable sprays for pest control

1. Content and aims of the demonstration

- operating and servicing a portable spray for pest control;
- explaining the need for pest control;
- making up spray mixtures;
- the demonstration serves to enable farmers to see the point of pest control, to gain some experience in operating sprays and to motivate them to buy sprays for the following cropping season.

2. Preparatory work

Target group

- farmers who have never worked with a spray;
- drawn from one village;
- no more than 8 – 12 people in each group.

Location of demonstration

- the field of a good cooperative farmer in the target group;
- the demonstration field to be within easy reach of the village.

Timing the demonstration

- in the relatively slack period after weeding;
- repeating the demonstration for the same group after three weeks;
- starting the demonstration each time at 9 am.

Demonstration aids and extension aids

- a well prepared back spray;
- tools to dismantle the spray;

E 7

- the liquid to be sprayed;
- instruction sheets on how to operate the spray;
- approximate proportions for making up the mixture;
- board or felt board;
- pictures of pests or models in casting resin.

Technical preparation of the adviser

- going through the operating instructions of the spray;
- practising the demonstration under the guidance of the senior adviser: taking it apart, repairing it, care and operation of the spray; the cost-effectiveness of pest control; getting, storing and using insecticides; safety measures when working with poisons.

3. Carrying out the demonstration

The demonstration takes about 2 – 3 hours. After welcoming the participants, the adviser explains briefly why portable sprays should be used to combat pests:

- using illustrations and insects prepared in casting resin, description of the pests and the damage they cause;
- discussion of the loss of yield and income through pest infestation with the help of illustrations, blackboard and felt board;
- the reasons why it is necessary to use pesticides to combat pests;
- brief explanation of the effects of poisonous insecticides and information about the danger to people and domestic animals.

When he explains the backspray the adviser should not go into details of its components and how it works. It is important to restrict the explanation to essentials only:

- First, the correct spray concentrations have to be demonstrated, for which the recommended receptacles and mixing buckets are needed. In demonstrations substitutes for the insecticides can be used. After mixing the correct concentration, the liquid is poured into the spray and then pressure is produced by pumping.

- After adjusting the spray nozzle, the adviser goes at walking pace through the field, pumping all the time.

- Masks or a cloth over the face must be worn as protection against poisonous substances.

- Immediately after the demonstration, the participants should be given the opportunity to try out the spray for themselves.

Then a semi-circle is formed round the adviser, and the farmers are given the chance to ask questions:

- At this stage it is important to deal with the farmers' questions very carefully, because farmers make their decision to accept or reject the innovation at this point.

- After answering questions, the adviser should demonstrate basic servicing and such operations as cleaning the nozzles, opening and closing the tanks, fixing the hose connections and greasing moving parts. The farmers should practise these operations as well.

- The adviser must tell the farmers exactly how much the spray costs. Since many farmers can only buy a spray with credit, the conditions for granting credit have to be explained: cropping a minimum area, filling in an application form, adhering to schedules.

- If brochures or leaflets are available, they should be handed out when the demonstration is finished.

4. Follow-up work

These demonstrations are backed up by other activities like field days, exhibitions, training contact farmers, poster campaigns or film shows. Once the decision has been taken to acquire a backspray, further extension measures have to be carried out:

- demonstrating how to establish the degree of pest infestation by using a counting board (to help non-numerate farmers a small board with holes, pieces of wood and coloured bands should be used. A marker is removed every time a pest is found. If used along a prescribed row of plants – for example, 50 paces long – the coloured band reached indicates whether spraying is necessary and how it should be done);

- avoidance of harmful effects on people, animals and plants by correct sealing and storage of containers;

E 7

- calculation of the amount of insecticide required on the basis of area or degree of pest infestation;

- carrying out the less demanding repairs and servicing;

- drawing up a spray plan and keeping a record of pest infestation and the amount of insecticide used.

A model calculation of the time spent on demonstrating a portable backspray is given in → G 7.

Compiled by

Gerhard PAYR, Rolf SÜLZER

E 8

Programming field days

Programming field days must be prepared systematically. A programme has to take into account changes occurring during a cropping season. Thus a programme may stay the same for 2 – 4 weeks and such issues as establishing erosion control strips, animal sheds or the allocation of fields in a rotation may well be on the programme for the whole season. But the advisers must also be ready to include in the programme of a field day an unexpected case of pest infestation, the effects of fertilising, the use of a machine that has only just become available, etc.

1. Checklist for the preparation of a field day

Content

- What is to be communicated?
- Is the content currently relevant to the target groups?
- Have target groups taken part in deciding the content?
- Is the content intended to be effective in the short, medium or long term?
- Is the content in keeping with the overall development target?

Participants

- Must the group be homogeneous (criteria of homogeneity)?
- Have the participants been informed about the date of the field day?
- Have the time and place of the meeting been fixed?
- How can the participants be informed if the field day has to be postponed or cancelled?

Programme

- Have all the people on the farms, in research stations, etc., been informed and prepared?
- Is the day's schedule realistic?

E 8

- Has information material been prepared on the issues that are likely to arise?

- Have equipment, models, display boards, etc., been prepared?

Transport

- Is it necessary to provide transport?

- Is transport available on the appointed day and has it been booked?

- Can the places to be visited be reached by the transport available?

- How many people can be transported?

- Can the participants be expected to make a contribution towards cost?

2. Programme planning

→ Figure 1 shows how a field day could be planned. We have intentionally devised a simple programme comprising a wide range of items, because this is what is usually encountered in practice. The programme is comprehensive because it needs to cover in a short time locations that are geographically close together with a variety of issues of current value and interest to the participants. Such a wide variety of topics can naturally do no more than arouse interest — it cannot bring about full understanding or changes in behaviour. This is the role of follow-up advisory work.

4. Evaluation of field days

Field days are a good opportunity to observe the reactions and problems of farmers. But, before this can occur, advisers must note their difficulties and questions. The adviser must ascertain whether the issues raised apply to the majority or only to particular individuals. The evaluation of field days meets the following specific aims:

- identifying problems in the target groups;

- examining extension topics and methods;

- deciding where to put the emphasis in the further training of advisers;

- estimating adoption rates for the following season;

- improvement of field days and coordination with other extension methods;
- improving the preparation of advisers for further field days. Advisers must consider the target groups' problems with senior staff and specialists in discussions and training seminars and think out suitable solutions and responses.

Figure 1:

Example of a field day programme			
Time	Place	Activity	Remarks
7.00	Binga, adviser's house	– Participants meet – Adviser explains programme – Departure by lorry	Keep to schedule Return probably between 12.30 and 13.30
7.15 8.40	Binga, research station	– Inspect rotation experiments – Inspect the station's model farm – Demonstration of composting – Demonstration of a maize peeler – Departure	Maximum 35 participants Discussion of each item on programme Have illustrations ready on the station
9.00 10.30	Chisangu Peter Mwale	– Visit to a farm with integrated stock keeping – Farmer and adviser introduce the farm – Demonstration of mulching – Demonstration of intercropping – Demonstration of a new hoe – Demonstration of poultry keeping – Continue journey	Prepare farm data Note farmers' questions Conduct discussion so that the farmer has to provide answers Have maize, groundnuts, plants and hoe ready Discuss egg marketing and feeding
11.00	1 km from Bangu	– Inspection of a badly eroded maize field	Discussion of causes of erosion and protection measures
11.15 12.00	Bangu	– Inspection of a communal cashew nut unit – Demonstration of intercropping – Discussion with village committee – Tea break – Return home to Binga	Inform village committee Prepare cashew data 50 g tea for the committee Distribute brochure
 13.00	Mwona Binga	– Short stop on the journey at the rice field of farmer Timothy near Mwona – Return and farewell	Point out excellent protective embankment

E 8

In conclusion, we list a number of questions that farmers put to advisers at field days:

- Why don't small farmers get credit?
- Why does the price of fertiliser go up practically every year?
- Why does the farmer get less for 1 kg wool than for 1 kg groundnuts?
- How can farmers pay back loans when drought causes the harvest to fail?
- By how much can we raise the yield if we use improved seed?
- Why can't we see any increase in yield even though we have been using the recommended rotation for two years?
- What are the correct plant intervals for millet and cassava?
- What must I do to qualify for a further training course?

Since farmers expect clear answers to questions like these, advisers should think about them and similar questions and prepare their answers in joint discussions well before the field day.

Compiled by:

Gerhard PAYR, Rolf SÜLZER

E 9

Example of extension work at markets

Agricultural advisers should always be present when the farmers go to market to sell their produce.

Their general duties are:

1) to check whether the products brought to market by farmers are correctly sorted into prescribed qualities;

2) to help farmers in disputes and disagreements with the market personnel and credit assistants;

3) to report serious problems like late opening of the market, defective scales, irregularities in payment for farmers' produce, shortage of sacks for the produce, etc.

Special extension programme

1. Demonstration of a new portable spray:

    – explaining how it works;

    – dismantling and cleaning the spray;

    – farmers trying it out themselves (→ E 7, → G 7).

2. Information on how to buy a new spray:

    – subsidised cash price: 150 Shs.;

    – subsidised credit price: 200 Shs.

When bought with credit, a downpayment of 50 Shs. has to be made to the credit assistant. The remaining 150 Shs. are then paid in two instalments of 75 Shs. in the following year. The benefits of cash sales should be made clear to the farmers. Applications for cash and credit sales should be prepared and checked by the adviser and then passed on to the credit assistant.

E 9

3. Demonstration of cotton picking sacks

- The amount of cotton picked can be increased by 50% when picking sacks are used.
- They make it much easier to grade the cotton according to quality.
- Cotton picking sacks can be bought for 10 Shs. each at the market.

4. Grading groundnuts

To get the maximum price for groundnuts, the following points have to be taken into account:

- The red skin on the shelled nuts must not be damaged.
- The colour and size of the nuts must be uniform.
- Crushed, misshapen and rotten nuts reduce the quality grade.
- To prevent the poisonous effect of aflatoxins when they are consumed, the nuts must be dried for a sufficient period after harvesting.

5. Fertiliser vouchers

Since farmers cannot save enough during the cropping season for the cash purchase of mineral fertiliser, vouchers can be bought at markets and then exchanged for mineral fertilisers from December onwards. The adviser must tell farmers about this method of buying fertiliser.

6. Campaigns

When campaigns are being run, every market is visited once a week by the loudspeaker van and a lorry with tools, models and illustrations. The adviser concerned is given the dates of these visits in his weekly programme. It is his duty to be present on such occasions.

Compiled by:

Gerhard PAYR, Rolf SÜLZER

E 10

Preparing and running local agricultural exhibitions

At local exhibitions extension back-up can be provided by:

1. Extension service display stand

- Illustrations and posters should be as traditional as possible to ensure that the message is understood by the target population. Figures and text should be kept to a minimum.

- Solid objects are better than illustrations or photographs. Being able to compare objects is best of all. Thus we can easily explain the difference in yield from traditional and improved farming methods by piling up the sacks. When a new crop is introduced, each visitor could be allowed to take samples of the seed.

- The visitors should be allowed to touch and try out all the demonstration objects, including tools.

- Another possibility might be to make scale sand-table models of farms. But we must first check the level of comprehension of the target groups and how they are likely to react.

- An adviser must be in attendance at every display stand to answer visitors' questions and to explain the objects on display by means of a felt board, blackboard, etc. The use of loudhailers is recommended for this work. The adviser chosen for this job should be technically well qualified and an uninhibited individual.

- A record should be kept of the names and village of the visitors, so that follow-up work can be carried out by the adviser.

- The more attractive the display stand, the more interest it will arouse. We should not hesitate to use such proven means of attracting attention as little badges, balloons or boxes of matches carrying advertisements. We could also exhibit an unknown animal or organise a guessing game with prizes (how many grains of rice in a glass or the exact weight of a sack of groundnuts) (→ C 2, → C 3).

2. Media room (tent, school, community centre, etc.)

A room or tent that can be darkened can be used in a number of ways:

- **film shows:** it is advisable to show a combination of entertainment and instructional films;

- **slide shows** with recorded commentary: the same recommendation applies as in the case of films;

- **dances:** if possible new dances should be created with symbolic agricultural themes;

- **songs and music:** there is even more opportunity than in the case of dances to follow tradition but also to include instruction, or to compose new pieces.

- **theatre:** depending on local tradition, there are many ways in which theatre can be used to demonstrate agricultural problems and show different aspects of agricultural life.

- A **media tent** can be shared with firms, but details of the programme must be coordinated in advance.

3. Demonstrations

Practical demonstrations are an essential ingredient of all agricultural exhibitions. The kind of demonstration determines whether it is held on the exhibition site or in the vicinity. As many currently relevant demonstrations as possible should be carried out, giving the visitors every opportunity to operate a backspray, pull sowing equipment along, start up a water pump, to lead a team of oxen, etc.

4. Competitions

Competitions are popular and an attraction. The prospect of winning a prize is an important incentive for many people to visit an exhibition. There are two kinds of competition:

- exhibiting and giving prizes for agricultural produce;

- competitions involving physical performance like ploughing, hoeing, digging up groundnuts, etc.

The focus of agricultural exhibitions is usually the display of crops, animals, domestic and craft products. When shows of this kind are being organised, the following points should be noted:

- The advisers should tell the farmers some time before the exhibition what products may be displayed and in what form and quantity.

- Only farmers and rural craftsmen in the extension territory should be allowed to take part in the competition.

- Advisers, officials and their families should not normally be allowed to take part in the competition, although they are fully entitled to exhibit.

- The prizes to be awarded for each product group should be announced in advance. The prizes should be neither too grand nor too small. In most cases, a fairly large number of small prizes is preferable to a few expensive prizes.

- The composition of the panel of judges can be a problem. It should be left to the organisation committee to choose the judges. Then the adviser must ensure that the judges are familiar with the standards and assessment criteria that have to be applied.

- A system must be worked out for recording and identifying the items to be put on display (plants, animals and craft products).

Similar principles apply when judging the performance of competitors taking part in ploughing, ox-cart racing, etc. An effort must be made to ensure these competitions are happy occasions and good fun. Tests of skill in general can prevent agricultural competitions becoming too serious.

Enough time should be left for awarding prizes, which should ideally be performed by a dignitary who is held in high esteem by the farmers. At the prizegiving ceremony, the relevant adviser for each category should be presented.

Sometimes it is possible to combine elements of an agricultural show, a field day and a demonstration (→ E 6, → E 7, → E 8).

Compiled by:

Rolf SÜLZER, Gerhard PAYR

Establishing a school garden

Teaching programmes to create awareness of the environment in rural regions are greatly helped by the observation, experiments and demonstrations that can be carried out in school gardens. The following points should be considered when school gardens are created and used:

1. Position

A school garden should be located as near as possible to the school. The soil should be suitable for a variety of crops. It should be at the disposal of the school for at least a few years.

2. Size

The labour input has to be calculated when the size of the garden is decided. About 20 – 30 m^2 per pupil are required.

3. Type

It is not advisable to prepare and cultivate small plots "incorrectly" in a school garden to demonstrate the difference between the right and wrong methods. Experience shows that people often become confused and no longer know what is right and wrong. However, it is a good idea to cultivate a section of the garden strictly by traditional methods. In this way the teacher and adviser get to know the traditional methods, to use them and to form an opinion about them. The parents also appreciate it if their children learn the "good old ways" and not just modern techniques.

4. Crops

Only those crops should be cultivated in the garden that can be grown by all farmers now or in the immediate future. But there is no reason why a corner of the school garden should not be clearly marked off for experimenting with exotic plants, demonstrating the excessive use of fertiliser, the effects of insufficient watering, etc.

5. Cropping plan

The advisers and teachers should work together to draw up the annual cropping plan, which should always include a rotation.

E 11

6. Means of production

If production inputs cannot be obtained through the school authorities, projects can often get fertiliser, spraying equipment, etc., as a gift or by taking out credit. It is important to ascertain needs, to order and distribute production inputs at the right time.

7. Schedule and operational plan, records

Deadlines for sowing, fertilising, weeding, harvesting, etc., should be displayed in the classrooms and shown on charts. A record must be kept of work already carried out, observations and notable incidents. This information is important if there is a change of teacher and is also essential teaching material.

8. Duties of the adviser

Advisers must inspect the gardens regularly and if necessary point out to the teacher where work needs to be done. If special measures have to be carried out, like pest control and watering, the adviser can demonstrate the use of spraying equipment to the teachers and pupils. If problems arise in school gardens that the teachers cannot solve, they should turn in the first instance to the adviser.

9. Use of the garden

The main function of school gardens is to give practical relevance to teaching and to acquaint schoolchildren with improved techniques, but they can be put to other uses as well, for example school field days. They also have a demonstration effect on the adults in the locality.

The crops produced in school gardens can be sold and the money used to finance the school, books or excursions. Model kitchens set up to use the crops from the gardens are an ideal way of teaching practical domestic science.

10. Misuse of gardens

Sometimes school gardens are used as means of raising funds to run the school. In most cases, this is asking far too much of school children. Similarly, making schoolchildren work in the private gardens and fields of teachers is a practice that should be condemned.

Compiled by:

Gerhard PAYR, Rolf SÜLZER

E 12

Evaluating training events

Training events should always be adapted to the specific conditions of a location. In this sense, what is required of a training event is also required of evaluation, namely that the special conditions of the social situation and the environment are taken into account.

Evaluation and self-criticism help the Animateur to assess the effectiveness of his work. A poor Animateur judges his work in terms of the hours the participants spend with him, without trying to find out whether the training he gives has actually had any effect on them.

He measures the success of his training only in terms of quantity, just as a farmer thinks of his sweet potato harvest in kg per hectare. But training in the true sense of the word is more even than increasing the "amount of awareness" — it is a question of changing the quality, the character and the pattern of awareness. This forces us therefore to work out criteria to register this qualitative change in the awareness of groups or individuals.

Because the success of training cannot be quantified (or perhaps it can, but only in the long term), we have to evaluate training carefully and regularly. We evaluate a training event by assessing the teaching aids used, the role of the Animateur and the reactions of the participants during and after training.

I. Evaluation of the teaching material

We distinguish between three types of criteria:

1. Socio-cultural, pedagogic and psychological criteria

- Which of our senses is the teaching material directed at? Material that appeals to more than one of our senses makes it easier to take in and store information in our memory. Thus we perceive in a variety of ways, and an abundance of associations working together with our memory creates links with other topics, problems, observations, past experiences, etc.

- Does the teaching material also appeal to the emotions? If there is something in the information that touches the emotions, it makes a deeper impression on the minds of the participants.

- Can the participants identify with at least some of the teaching material? If they can identify, it will be easier for them to discover parallels between their training and their own situation.

- Does the teaching material allow the participants to discover problems for themselves? Does it encourage dialogue and group discussion, or does it reduce them to mere consumers who only listen and watch?

- Does the teaching material encourage the participants to relate what they see to their own situation, and does it stimulate their imagination and ability to see problems? The more the teaching material "allows projections", the less danger there is of its being prescriptive and inhibiting creativity. Good material is creative in the sense that it helps people to formulate and develop ideas and to see the links with allied problems.

- To what extent does the teaching material conform with the culture of the country? The more it is in keeping with the local culture (songs, poems, theatre, etc.), the better it will be understood. The teaching material should not be something alien and imposed from above but should be an integral and integrating element.

- Can the participants recognise and understand the information that the teaching material is intended to communicate (pictures, photographs, slides, films, etc. → E 13)?

- To what extent does the teaching material present a challenge, compel the participants to take a stand and formulate their problems? Does it motivate them to solve their problems?

- Do the materials address a real problem? Do they refer to problems clearly enough for the participants to recognise them as their own?

2. Target criteria

- Is the material intended to develop awareness, to create sensitivity to problems, or is it material that helps to find a solution to a precise problem that has already been defined by the participants?

- Is the material targeted towards a special group (men, women, farmers, old people, children, etc.)?

- Do the people take part in training sessions regularly, occasionally or rarely?

- Is the teaching material aimed at people with a particular level of education (illiterates, primary school, secondary school, higher level schools, etc.)?

E 12

- Is training carried out in the open or in a special centre?
- How many people take part in each training session?

3. Logistical criteria

- cost of purchasing and maintaining teaching materials;
- mobility (transport in the field);
- possibility of combining with other teaching materials;
- time for devising and making the materials;
- time for preparing a training session;
- availability of the materials in the hands of field advisers;
- the provision of technical equipment;
- level of education required of the Animateur;
- Does the material provide the Animateur with a central theme and to what extent does it suggest the methodological approach?
- How easily can the material be reproduced and copied?

II. Assessing the role of the Animateur in the training process

It is up to the Animateur to exploit the teaching material to the full. If he is not thoroughly acquainted with his material and its potential, he will not make the best use of it, and his efforts will be of little benefit. Whether the training session is a valuable experience or a waste of time depends on the Animateur and his use of the materials, and for this reason his performance must be assessed.

1. Use of the teaching materials

- Has the Animateur mastered the topic he is dealing with? Is he aware of the complexity of the problem?
- Is the Animateur capable of exploiting the full potential of the teaching material? Does he know how to handle the material correctly?
- Does he speak loudly enough for all to hear and understand him?

- Does the whole group understand the language spoken by the Animateur?

- Does he use gesture and facial expression to emphasise what he is saying?

- Does the Animateur encourage discussion? Does he know how to lead a discussion? Is he able to draw attention to important points during the discussion and then to summarise them?

- Can the Animateur make constructive use of the negative reactions of the group?

- Does the Animateur help the participants to identify with the teaching material, for example with characters in a play?

- Does he make it easier for participants to project themselves on to the teaching material?

- How does he help them to see parallels between the teaching material and their own problems?

- Does he use enough concrete examples to help them to discover parallels between discussions and their actual situation?

- Does the Animateur ask the right questions at the right time?

    - questions to establish the level of group development;

    - questions to encourage the participants to follow ideas presented and to discuss them;

    - questions that encourage them to think more deeply about what has been said;

    - questions to check whether they have followed the discussion;

    - questions that force them to formulate problems;

    - questions that enliven discussion.

2. The relationship between the Animateur and the group

- How does the Animateur introduce himself to the group? Does he emphasise his position as a state official? Does he make a point of his official nomination? Does he line up the participants so that they can listen to his monologue or does he allow a group discussion to develop, like a conversation in which he also takes part as the recognised authority, a position deriving from his intelligence, experience and the good example he sets for everyone around him.

- Does the Animateur maintain his reserve and an "artificial" distance between himself and the group? Are there any signs that he is nervous of the group or that the group undermines his confidence?

- Does the Animateur mix with the group, and is he acknowledged as a member?

- Does the group pay attention to the Animateur simply because he has a position of power in the hierarchy and they are afraid of the consequences if they do not listen to him?

- Do people listen to the Animateur because he convinces his listeners that what he says is true, intelligent and authentic?

- Is the relationship between the Animateur and the group based on mutual trust or mistrust? How does mutual trust manifest itself?

- Does the presence of the Animateur make the group unsure of itself?

- Do the members of the group feel at ease in the presence of the Animateur? What indications are there?

- Does the Animateur create "negative uncertainty" in the participants, so that they lack the confidence to express themselves freely, or simply say what the Animateur wants to hear?

- Does the Animateur create "positive uncertainty" that acts as an incentive to express their own thoughts?

- Can the Animateur devote enough time to his group?

- Is he open and flexible enough to go into the ideas and thoughts of those taking part in the discussion?

- Is he sufficiently acquainted with the locality where he is working?

3. The Animateur's capacity to appraise his own performance (the ability to question what he is doing)

- Is the Animateur able to accept criticism and to turn it to constructive use?

- Is he sensitive enough to interpret the reactions of the group of individuals correctly? Can he draw conclusions from their reactions?

- Is he capable of self-criticism?

- Is he capable of modifying his own behaviour in the light of reactions by the group?

4. Ability to use initiative to solve problems

- Has the Animateur enough imagination to make use of the resources available when solutions are proposed and to integrate them into existing structures (solutions that lend themselves to advice)?

- How does he handle solutions proposed by the group?

- Is he willing to cooperate with other functionaries to work towards solutions?

- Can the Animateur fit a proposed solution into the wider context (national, worldwide) and assess its advantages, disadvantages and consequences? Can he make the group more aware of these issues?

- If the Animateur has practical skills, would he be able, for example, to hold a demonstration of proposed solutions in the same way as dealing with a training topic or a problem awareness course?

- Has the Animateur organisational ability and planning skills?

III. Evaluating the reactions of participants during and after training events

This aspect of evaluation is the most important since it records the actual results of training. It is a question of spotting and interpreting the indicators that tell us the results of training. What are these indicators?

- apathetic silence after a question or proposal;

- mechanical repetition of the "Animateur's" words;

- talking among themselves about other topics;

- questions that have nothing to do with the topic;

- questions that are asked to curry favour with the Animateur;

E 12

- remarks that have nothing to do with the topic;
- remarks to catch the attention of the Animateur;
- provocative questions (to catch the Animateur out or make him look ridiculous);
- provocative, disruptive behaviour;
- surly silence;
- ostentatious and provocative silence;
- aggression towards the Animateur and others;
- scepticism;
- critical questions;
- provocative but constructive remarks;
- questions that genuinely seek to add to their knowledge;
- a sense of expectation in the participants;
- questions that call for answers;
- questions that seek to deepen the subject matter;
- remarks that advance the subject under discussion;
- comments that make proposals;
- participants make use of ideas derived from previous discussions;
- participants begin to make demands on their environment;
- participants become creative, discover their own potential;
- they begin to make use of their newly discovered potential;
- participants give reasons why this or that is the real issue;
- they realise that a problem is linked to other problems in their environment;
- they develop initiatives that have been created by their own needs;

E 12

- they ensure that problem-solving measures are continued;
- they now feel the need for emancipation;
- they begin to see their needs and solutions, their very existence in a wider context (national, continental, worldwide).

These various reactions and responses can occur at any point during the development of groups.

This is not a comprehensive list of indicators that need to be interpreted, because all groups develop their individual ways of expressing themselves, acting and reacting. Thus it is the job of the Animateur to extend the above list.

When we interpret these indicators, we must always take account of the particular circumstances under which training was carried out. The participants do not react to training alone; there is a host of other factors that give rise to reactions in the group. The Animateur must therefore investigate the reasons for a particular reaction. If a group reacts to the training session itself, it is obviously important from the point of view of evaluation. If something else causes the reaction, it interests us because we may want to incorporate it in our training programme.

To interpret a reaction properly, we must always ask why, how and when aspects of training had an effect and what that effect was. In other words, we should try to relate the effects to the particular conditions of the training session (role of the Animateur, the teaching materials, etc.). In this way we are given valuable clues as to how training can be improved.

Source:

Ernst GABATHULER: Evaluation d'une session de formation. Projet Agricole de Kibuye, Service Animation et Formation. Rwanda. 4. 1979.

Compiled by:

Volker HOFFMANN

Pre-testing pictorial material

What one man takes for granted can be surprising to the next man, which means it can prove costly to leave things to chance when using media. This is why it is **imperative to pre-test** picture material. In most cases it can be done relatively easily with just a few basic test procedures.

A "free test" on a small number of individuals is often sufficient. Each individual is shown the whole picture and asked: "What can you see?" We can learn a lot from the order of what they say, what they omit to say and also from following their gaze and observing facial expression. If they have no further comments to make, we can ask: "Can you see anything else?" Finally we ask: "What is the whole picture trying to say?"

Sometimes, especially when a large number of copies or expensive pictures are planned, it pays to go further than this necessary routine check and to test more intensively. We now give details of how to tackle more thorough testing of pictures.

Even **before the first drafts** of pictures have been created and sample photographs taken, some basic questions have to be asked. They must be answered conclusively not later than the preliminary testing stage:

- Who is the message trying to reach (target groups)?

- What message is to be communicated (content)?

- What is the message trying to achieve (aims)? Is it supposed to inform, train, create problem awareness, indicate solutions, induce a change in behaviour?

- Are pictures the best method, and what kind of pictures should we choose (→ F 12)?

- Are the target groups familiar with the medium, what are the conventions regarding pictorial illustration, what colour preferences exist, etc.? Are there any local artists, how do they work, what do children's drawings look like, etc.?

- How is the message received by the target group? Is the situation depicted realistically for them, do they agree with any value judgements, are the proposals considered meaningful?

Discussions with colleagues, experts and representatives of the target groups can provide much useful information on these issues. The artist or photographer should take part in discussions as early as possible.

Then an **"aide mémoire"** should be drawn up that **describes** the **use of pictures as a teaching aid**; aims, content, method, medium, sequence, combination of picture and text or pictures and the spoken word, etc.

Following these guidelines (very much like a script), the first **sample pictures** are made and have to be tested. If the pictures contain many details, it is sometimes helpful to test in **two phases**:

1. Are the **elements** of the picture **recognised** and is their significance understood? For this kind of testing, the rest of the picture is covered and the same question asked about each individual element: "What is that and what does it mean?" Responses should not be corrected and no explanation given, because that would interfere with the second part of the test.

2. Has the **total picture** been **understood**? Now the subject's interpretation of the whole might enable him to correct wrong interpretations of the parts. Conversely, he may have interpreted the parts correctly but nevertheless still cannot understand what the total picture is saying.

If a series of pictures or elements are shown, we have to check whether they have been understood. In the case of single pictures, we asked, for example: "What is going on here?" or "What does this picture tell us?" Now we ask: "What is happening in these pictures, what does the whole series tell us?"

A small and if possible mixed group is best for initial testing. The test subjects can then help each other to interpret the pictures. The next step is to show the pictures to individuals representing the categories in the target group (for example young women, old men, illiterates, farmers, craftsmen, etc.). It is easier to undertake this test with people who are accustomed to pictures – it is obviously more difficult if they are not familiar with the kinds of pictures being tested.

Representative samples and quantitative results of testing are a waste of time and money. It is not helpful to know what percentage of the test subjects have misunderstood. As far as possible we should simply remove from pictures anything that could lead to misunderstanding. It is better to keep on modifying the picture and then testing it again.

Who should test pictures?

It is not advisable to let outsiders carry out this vital work. We should avoid using interviewers, as well. On the other hand, it is most important that the artist or photographer and those responsible for the technical content are present in all cases. Thus they can learn from their own mistakes and have another chance of making direct contact with their target groups. If they take part in the test, they are more likely to accept the need to modify their own work.

A series of pictures should, if possible, still be amended even if it has been reproduced in large quantities. If a participatory approach is used, we get a good deal of feedback about the pictures and they can therefore be improved.

If the tester is still unsure how to ask his questions, he can write down a few guidelines. Such guidelines are particularly helpful in group discussions to ensure that he does not lose the thread. We now give an example of relatively detailed discussion guidelines.

Example of discussion guidelines for use in picture testing

The pictures should be hung up one at a time. Only one element of each picture should be shown and the following questions asked:

1. What can you see here? What does it mean?

The same question is asked for every detail of the picture. No comment is to be made on the intended message of the picture.

After dealing with the picture detail by detail, the whole picture is shown and the following questions asked:

2. What can you see, what does the picture mean, what message does it have for us?

3. Is the picture telling us to do a particular thing? If so, what?

4. Can you express the message of this picture in your own words?

5. Are there people in this picture who remind you of friends or who look quite different from your friends? If they are different, what are the major differences?

6. Does this (a detail in the picture) look like yours or is it different? If it is, what are the differences?

7. Is there anything in the picture that disturbs or annoys you or that could offend friends and neighbours? If so, what and why?

8. Is there anything about this picture that you particularly like? If so, what and why?

9. Is there anything in this picture that is not clear? If so, what?

10. Have we forgotten anything important in this picture? If so, what and why?

E 13

11. Is there any message in this picture that you find hard to believe? If so, what is wrong?

12. Are there any particularly pleasing colours in this picture? If so, which colours?

13. Are there any colours in this picture that you do not like? If so, which colours?

14. What could we do to improve the picture?

With group discussion, a note should be made at the end of the test of how many people and what categories have taken part. If the pictures were shown to individuals, we should keep a record of the test subjects' age, sex, religion, language and level of reading ability.

These features will have to be recorded for the various categories within the target group.

We have naturally given only a very general example of discussion guidelines. They can be shortened, amended or supplemented according to the aims, content, target group and situation.

Bibliography:

J. T. BERTRAND: Communications pretesting. Chicago: University of Chicago, Community and Family Study Center 1978. (Media Monograph. 6.)

Ingo BINNEWERG: Landwirtschaftliche Beratung, Strategie, Inhalt, Methode, Mittel. Zentralregion Togo, Sokodé, 1986

Regina GÖRGEN, Charles KAYIBANDA: Conception du materiel didactique à l'écoute des Paysans. PAK, Kibuye, Service Animation et Formation, Kibuye, Rwanda, No year given.

Compiled by:

Volker HOFFMANN

E 14

Circulars for advisers

Circulars for advisers aim to provide the following:

- organisational, technical and methodological information on the current programme **(up-dating function)**;

- further training by giving information about measures that are not directly related to current programmes **(training function)**;

- information of a personal nature like births, football matches, photographic clubs, etc. **(social function)**.

Circulars help field advisers and their superiors to communicate with each other. They are usually issued monthly and distributed and explained at programming discussions. We often find the following typical weaknesses in the production, distribution and use of circulars:

- The lowest level of advisers have frequently had inadequate schooling and technical education so they often find it difficult to read technical texts, especially when circulars are written in a European language and pay no heed to the level of understanding of the readers.

- They are often produced and distributed late and irregularly.

- The content is often decided by senior staff without any direct involvement of advisers or even the representatives of the farmers. Technical information not infrequently takes the form of directives that are not regarded by the advisers as "assistance".

- Since field advisers are not consulted regarding content and production, the circulars mostly do not meet the technical requirements of current programmes.

Since these are common faults, we now suggest ways in which to improve the preparation of content, distribution and use of circulars:

(1) Circulars should never be produced without involving the target groups and the field advisers. If direct participation is not possible, they must be involved at least indirectly (by talking over content at advisers' discussion sessions and by providing a special column for advisers' contributions).

(2) Circulars should always be issued at project and district level, thereby ensuring that they offer practical guidelines for advisers in regions of the same kind and with the same type of organisation.

E 14

(3) Great care must be taken to make the content of circulars clear and comprehensible. The messages must be geared to the lowest level of advisers.

(4) Circulars should ideally appear once a month and cover all extension activities and complementary measures like credit and marketing.

(5) Even with unsophisticated methods, the layout and printing of circulars can be made attractive. Little drawings, bold type, readers' letters, family news and anecdotes can all contribute to lively presentation.

(6) Wherever possible, circulars should be written in the local language. This point is particularly important when representatives of target groups are addressed.

(7) Circulars must be explained at the weekly training sessions for advisers, so that they all have the same information for implementing programmes.

(8) When senior advisers go on field visits, they must check that circulars are being correctly used. Testing the advisers' level of expertise by means of questionnaires, however, is only recommended when it is done voluntarily and does not become a part of the appraisal of advisers' performance.

(9) We recommend issuing folders in which a year's circulars can be kept.

(10) Regional handbooks can be based on circulars, and later circulars can refer the reader to such handbooks.

In → G 6 there is an example of a circular for advisers.

Compiled by:

Gerhard PAYR, Rolf SÜLZER

How to prepare and deliver a speech in the context of mass extension

During campaigns advisers, alone or in the company of politicians and leaders, have to address large crowds of people at village meetings. We offer the following advice to help them structure their speeches at mass meetings more effectively:

(1) The content of the speech must be up-to-date and interesting. The adviser must bear in mind the composition of his audience when he prepares his speech.

(2) The audience must be told at the beginning what points the speech is going to cover.

(3) People with little education can only take in a limited amount of information. Thus speeches should be limited to one basic theme and be guided by local practice regarding language and duration.

(4) Speeches should not begin with apologies for mistakes and misunderstanding.

(5) The speaker must always try to speak to his audience as individuals and not at them.

(6) The speaker must be able to justify what he is saying. Only if he can defend his own assertions will he be credible and self-assured. The key to this kind of performance is conscientious preparation.

(7) The speaker should address his audience in a loud, clear voice. He should avoid violent gestures but, on the other hand, not behave too casually. If he is going to use a loudspeaker, it should be checked in advance to make sure it is properly adjusted.

(8) Interesting examples and anecdotes can give speeches a lighter touch, but the speaker must not exaggerate or be too intent on putting on a good performance.

(9) A speech must not be learned by heart – hardly better than reading from a script. The speaker should try to express himself as freely as possible, using only keywords for reference.

(10) Advisers should not be too formally or ostentatiously dressed. In a harvest campaign, a field adviser wearing a dark suit and tie would create a barrier between himself and his audience.

(11) Direct personal attacks on people, whether present or absent, must be avoided. The same principle applies in the discussion that follows. Also advisers must not allow themselves to be provoked by irritating questions.

(12) Before he starts, the speaker must decide whether questions can be asked during or after his speech. With all speeches, enough time must be left for discussion and, although it is wise to impose a time-limit, discussion should not be stopped if important problems are brought up.

(13) When the speaker comes to the end of his speech, he should summarise the most important points.

(14) If copies of the speech, brochures or leaflets have been prepared, they should not be handed out until discussion has finished, to avoid unnecessary interruption.

Bibliography:

"Extension Training Bulletin" of the Ministry of Agriculture and Natural Resources, Nigeria. No year given. No place of publication.

Compiled by:

Gerhard PAYR, Rolf SÜLZER

E 16

Structuring group sessions to identify problems

The object of such discussions is to structure the knowledge of the participants and to "visualise" it (to make it visible), so that problems can be identified and their importance assessed, and finally solutions can be found. In practice we adopt the following approach:

1. Compiling a list of problems

It is best to begin by compiling a list of all the problems known to be associated with a particular issue. The question is introduced in written form and if necessary discussed in advance. Then there is a pause for thought with everyone maintaining silence. Thus everybody has the chance to sort out the problems he knows of and to define them in his own mind. He should then write them down legibly in the form of keywords on cards that are collected on a pinboard. It is worthwhile to compile the list in a plenary session. This method prevents talkative individuals from dominating the discussion, and information cannot go astray.

2. Sorting

The next step is to structure the problems, not with the intention of evaluating but of categorising them in problem areas. The frequency of problems is an initial indicator of relative importance.

3. Supplementing the list

Once categories of problems have been established, we can see whether the initial list was complete or whether we should add further categories or aspects of problems.

4. Discussion

We now discuss the various categories of problem to establish their relative importance. For this stage, it is advisable to create small groups of 4 – 6 people. It is the job of these working groups to discuss the problems thoroughly, to reveal further aspects and to decide on and give reasons for an order of priority. This process should be recorded on pinboard charts or demonstration blocks (flip-charts).

E 16

5. Presentation

After the small groups have worked on the problems in the different categories, the results are presented to the plenary session. Thus the assembled group has a chance to comment on the results before they are re-examined as the starting point for the formulation of solutions. → E 17 gives more details about moderation and visualisation techniques.

Bibliography:

B. PÄTZOLDT: Didaktisches Seminarkonzept und methodischer Ablauf. In: MUNZINGER P.: Beratung als Instrument der ländlichen Entwicklung in Westafrika. Bericht über das 1. Regionalseminar der GTZ/DSE in Kamerun 1978. Eschborn: GTZ, 1979, pp. 3 – 5

METAPLAN: Metaplan – Gesprächstechnik. Kommunikationswerkzeug für die Gruppenarbeit. Quickborn, 1975. Überarbeitete Neuauflage 1982, (Metaplan-Reihe, Heft 2).

E. SCHNELLE: Metaplanung – Zielsuche Lernprozeß der Beteiligten und Betroffenen. Quickborn: Metaplan GmbH, 1973 (Metaplan-Reihe, Heft 1).

T. SCHNELLE-CÖLLN: Visualisierung, die optische Sprache für problemlösende und lernende Gruppen. Quickborn: Metaplan GmbH, 1975 (Metaplan-Reihe, Heft 6).

R. SÜLZER: "Seminarorganisation, Arbeitsverfahren und Arbeitsablauf". In: DSE/ GTZ (Ed.): Beratung als Instrument der ländlichen Entwicklung in Südostasien. Bericht über das 2. Regionalseminar 1979 in Chiang-Mai, Thailand, Eschborn und Feldafing 1980, pp. 7 – 14.

Compiled by:

Volker HOFFMANN, Rolf SÜLZER

E 17

Using visualisation to improve group communication

The most common way of communicating in groups is by word of mouth. However, when the oral method is used, the following problems often occur:

- some people contribute more than others and some get no chance at all to make a contribution;
- the memory is overtaxed, people cannot retain everything, there is a lot of repetition, misunderstanding, waste of time and losses of information;
- the more factual communication is impeded, the more problems of personal relations between the participants come to the fore. Ostensibly factual topics are misused for personal attacks or defending oneself;
- It becomes increasingly difficult for the discussion leader to keep the group to the point.

By means of visualisation and suitable techniques of moderation, everyone is more able to take part and the job of leading the discussion becomes easier. Thus, if the materials and techniques of visualisation are properly used, better results can be achieved in a shorter space of time.

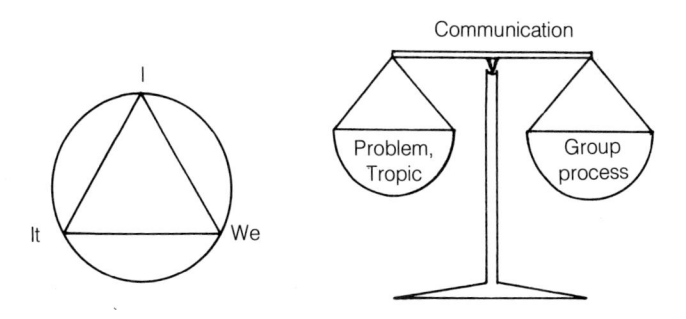

The aim of visual communication is to achieve a better balance between the various aspects of group communication. In "topic-centred interaction" we speak of the tension between "I", "We" and "It", with "It" referring to the factual information, the topic itself. By analogy, the issue could be, for example, the balance between the problem or topic and the group process — a balance that has to be achieved by the appropriate methods of communication.

E 17

If we apply the materials and techniques of visualisation, the four essentials for comprehension in communication automatically come into play:

- simplicity, comprehensibility;
- brevity and conciseness;
- structure and good organisation;
- further stimulation.

Simplicity and comprehensibility are achieved when people are asked to express themselves in a few keywords on a small card, and this is also automatically conducive to brevity and conciseness. To make sure that everyone has understood, the cards can be read out later and if necessary explained and commented on.

Structure and good organisation of visual material result from the arrangement of the cards on a pinboard or wall chart and from the choice of suitable colours and shapes for the cards.

Further stimulation arises from the choice of materials and how they are combined in visual composition plus the act of presentation in which all the members of the group are involved. Thus there is variety, there are changes of scene and visual links between information and the individuals providing it. The group dynamic, far from disrupting the group session, now encourages and stimulates communication – it gives the visual method that little bit of extra impact.

The aims, content and methods of visual communication in groups are shown in → Figure 1.

→ Pictures 1 – 5 show further aspects of the visualisation approach and the rules we have to apply. The posters try to demonstrate, through the manner of their own visualisation, the correct application of the rules and recommendations they present.

The technical and material input required by this kind of visual technique is frequently overestimated. Even if the services available are used and fully prepared materials are bought, the costs are insignificant compared with the other costs involved (the participants' work time, possibly board and lodging), and they are easily outweighed by the time saved and the far greater effectiveness. If there is reluctance to spend money on materials, or if expensive imports and the expenditure of foreign exchange are to be avoided, local materials can easily be used instead. Wrapping paper, waste paper, wax crayons or felt-tip pens, drawing pins and boards covered with corrugated cardboard instead of proper pinboards all serve the same purpose. We can even manage without a pinboard at all, if we use strips of adhesive tape to fix the cards on blackboards and to move them around.

Figure 1:

Visual communication as a means of problem solving in groups		
what	how	why
Defining the problem Analysing the problem ↓ ↑ Working out alternative solutions ↓ ↑ Evaluating and taking decisions ↓ ↑ Putting into practice Planning	In each case: – compiling – explaining – substantiating – evaluating – categorising Alternating between: – individuals – small group – whole group Visual presentation with cards of various shapes and colours on pinboards	More participation More interaction More clarity In stages Structured Categorised Comprehensible External memory bank Can be checked Can be corrected Reorganise Supplement Remove Change Can be documented

Visual techniques also make it easier to keep a record of discussions. If good materials are used and technically sound work is done, the record can simply consist of photocopying photographs of wall charts. As an alternative, the details are simply noted down in a written record.

It is hoped that this contribution, in conjunction with paper → E 16, will arouse interest in the techniques of visual presentation. Detailed further reading and relevant training opportunities are available for anyone who decides to apply these methods and experiment with them.

E 17

Pictures 1 and 2:

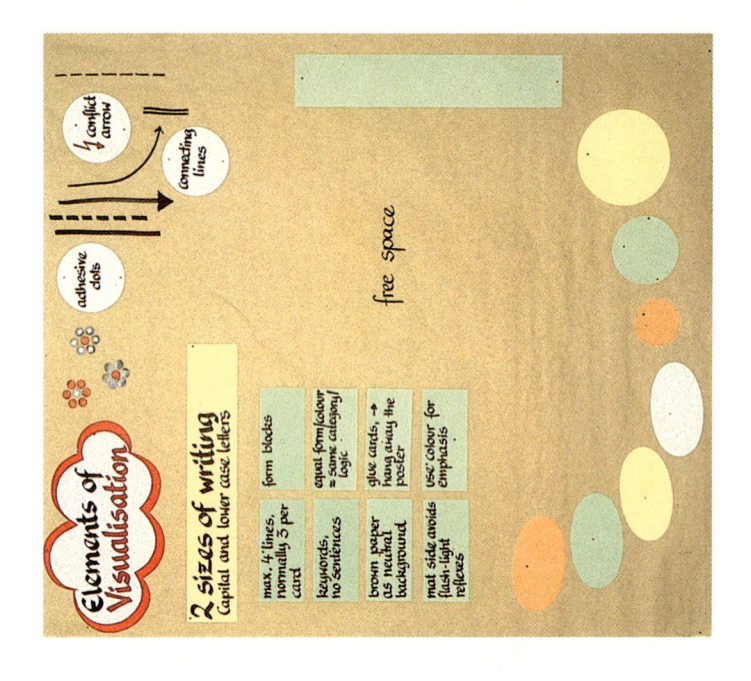

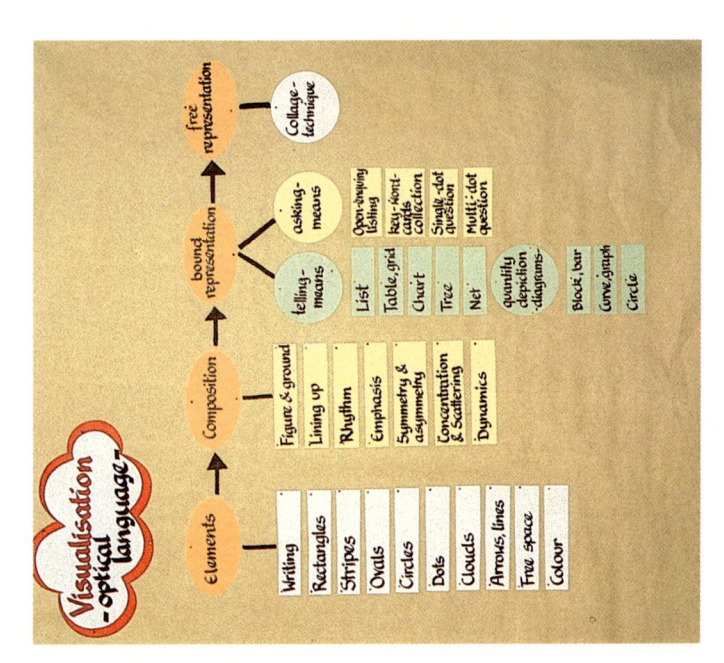

E 17

Proposal for Presenting group posters

Group:
1. maintain eye contact with plenary — to focus plenary / to catch all attention
2. the whole group presents — no spokesman / show agreements and disagreements
3. read the text of all cards — Visualisation does not speak by itself / point out holes and limitations
4. point to the card you are reading — to coordinate ear and eye / unified impression of poster, voice & body
5. avoid long comments — explain what is written / don't add all missing

Plenary:
1. hold back questions until end of presentation — perhaps it will be shown later on
2. agree on the procedure for discussion — for not getting muddled

Pictures 3 and 4:

Proposal for Small group work

1. Arrange work place — sit in a round / free access to working material
2. Clarify task, subject — reformulation is possible
3. Assure coordination — for procedure and visualisation

joint silence

4. Collect ideas on cards — individually without talking
5. Jointly discuss, order and arrange cards — assign conflict and go on, don't fight / show contradictions and limitations
6. What is missing? — find new aspects, supplement elements
7. Prepare presentation — distribute the tasks and roles / nobody remains without "job"

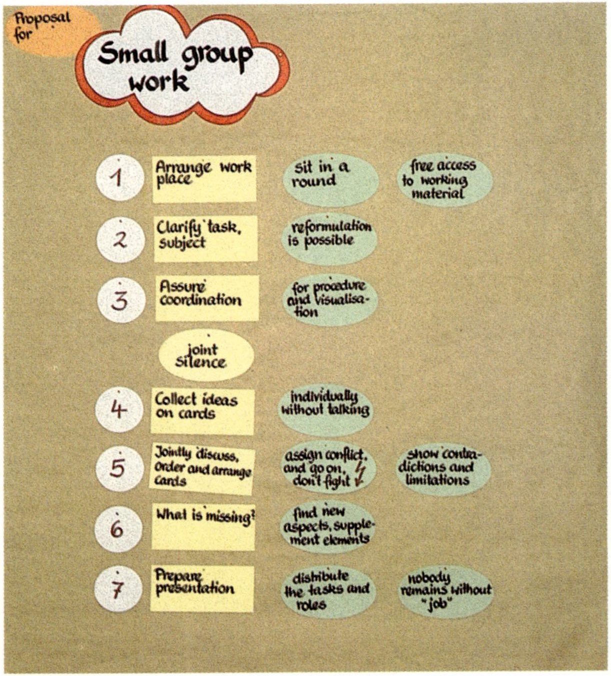

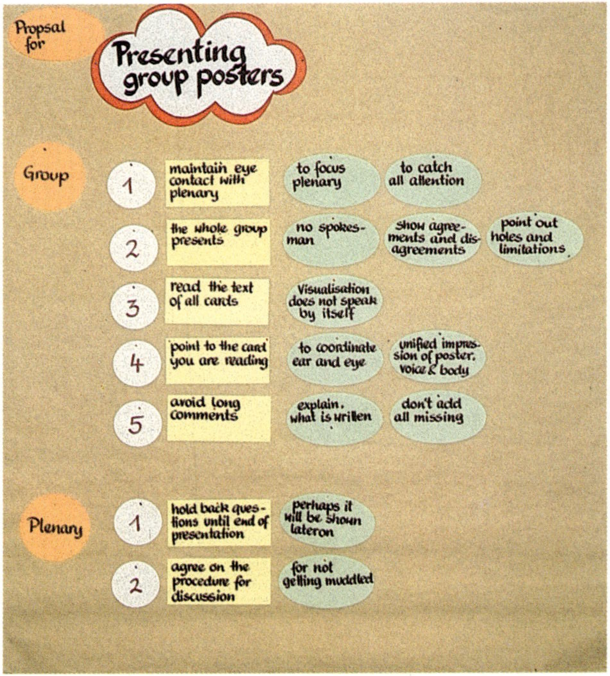

Picture 5:

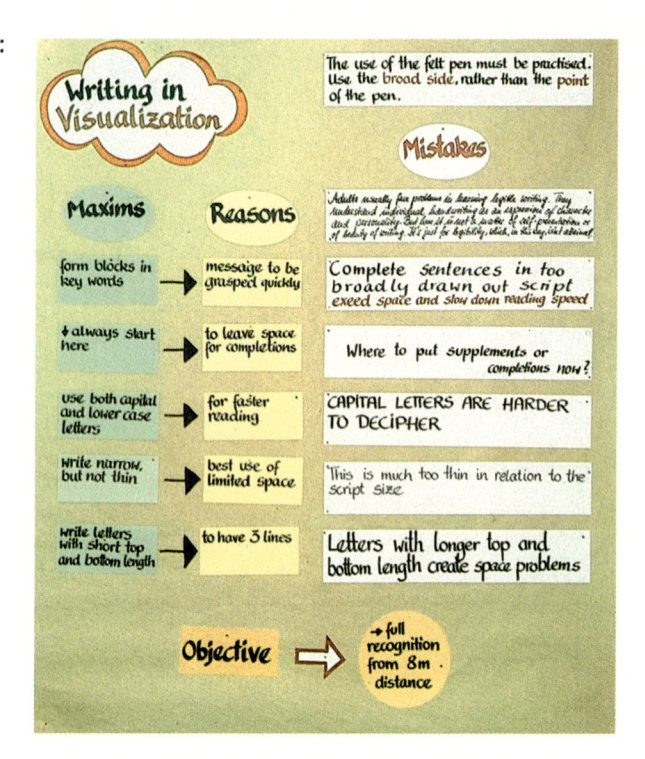

Sources:

Metaplan: Metaplan-Gesprächstechnik. Kommunikationswerkzeug für die Gruppenarbeit. Quickborn 1975. Überarbeitete Neuauflage 1982 (Metaplan-Reihe, Heft 2)

E. SCHNELLE: Metaplanung – Zielsuche Lernprozeß der Beteiligten und Betroffenen. Quickborn: Metaplan GmbH 1973 (Metaplan-Reihe, Heft 1)

Telse SCHNELLE-CÖLLN: Visualisierung, die optische Sprache problemlösender und lernender Gruppen. Quickborn: Metaplan GmbH, 1975 (Metaplan-Reihe, Heft 6)

K. KLEBERT, E. SCHRADER, W. STRAUB: Moderationsmethode. Gestaltung der Meinungs- und Willensbildung in Gruppen, die miteinander lernen und leben, arbeiten und spielen. Zweite überarbeitete und erweiterte Auflage 1984, Preisinger, Verlag, Rimsting am Chiemssee

G. ULLRICH, U. KRAPPITZ: Participatory approaches for cooperative group events – introduction and examples of application, DSE, Feldafing, 1985

Compiled by:

Volker HOFFMANN

Suggestions for setting up participatory external evaluation missions

Every so often, external evaluation missions descend on projects out of the blue, like natural disasters. They come to assess important phases of projects while they are still running. They are dispatched for this purpose by the organisation implementing or financing the project. For this reason, projects have scarcely any defence against such visitations. All they can do is hope that at the end all will be well, that the expert appraisers will be benevolent and overlook any serious weaknesses, will not report too critically on faults or will refer to them only in terms of general proposals for improvement. Of course, these hopes are not always fulfilled, and external evaluation can turn into an explosive situation. The project workers (and usually the experts, too) are subjected to a month of excessive strain and many opportunities to benefit from the evaluation visit are lost through insensitive behaviour.

We know from experience that a different approach is possible. The following principles and methods are therefore our recommendations for these occasions:

- The underlying principle of the evaluation mission should be teamwork using "ZOPP" (Objectives-oriented project planning), moderation and visual presentation techniques.

- The terms of reference of the evaluation mission should have been agreed by both the organisation sending the experts and the project.

- The work of the evaluation mission should be primarily problem-oriented and not recommendation-oriented. It should concentrate on perceived problems and their assumed causes and should guard against proposing instant solutions and recommended courses of action.

- The evaluation mission should comprise the nominees of both the sending organisation and the national sponsoring organisation of the project.

- All important aspects of the project to be reported on by the evaluation mission should be covered by an expert (or certain areas of activity should be specifically excluded from the report).

- The leader at least of the evaluation mission must be familiar with ZOPP, moderation and visualisation techniques, and he should introduce the other members of the mission to the fundamentals of these methods at the outset. When evaluation has commenced, he must be on hand to give practical assistance.

- After this introduction to basic work techniques, the members of the evaluation mission should begin to study project documents and papers individually.

- At this stage, the evaluation mission's members and selected project workers can be formed into specialist groups to work on particular technical problems. The composition of these groups can change in the course of evaluation and should be determined by the technical experience, the areas of responsibility and the information background of the individuals to be included.

- The work of evaluation should continue, alternating between individuals, specialist groups, the whole evaluation mission and special meetings of the evaluation mission with other project workers.

- The specialist groups should draft an initial plan of action and decide on the first steps to be taken in their investigations. These plans should be coordinated and displayed in wall newspapers for all to see.

- The work programmes should be continued and adapted to the increasing level of information. The leader of the evaluation mission should coordinate all steps and methods with the project management. He should make sure that information travels in all directions and that everyone can see what is going on.

- For practical as well as psychological reasons, it is of the utmost importance not to begin the process of evaluation with the search for problems but to start with the aims of the particular phase of the project and by listing the positive preconditions which the project work can build on. These include the natural resources and the socio-economic project environment, the achievements of the target groups and the achievements of the project.

- After three weeks at the latest, the evaluation mission should have reached the stage of prioritising the project's problems.

- It is advisable to discuss the "problem hierarchy" in a 4–6 day ZOPP workshop and to develop it further into a project planning matrix for the next phase of the project. All directly involved project workers should take part in the workshop.

- The evaluation report, the offer and the negotiations about the next project phase should then be based on this jointly produced and agreed project planning matrix.

- After the ZOPP workshop, the organisational, staffing and financial consequences of the project planning matrix (based on objective criteria) are discussed in smaller groups. Evaluation personnel, the project management, project sponsors, the organisation implementing the project and the financers should all be adequately represented. As soon as binding decisions are made, the people affected by them should be informed.

- The evaluation report describes the process of evaluation, the steps taken and the methods of investigation. The presentation of results follows the material already produced in the form of wall displays and visualisations through to the project planning matrix for the next phase of the project.

- Where compromises cannot be found, the people concerned should be free to have their differing views recorded in the report. However, this should only apply where there is a serious case of disagreement. It is primarily the members of the evaluation commission who should make use of this right if they feel they want to bring a particular view to the attention of the organisation commissioning the report.

Where the methods of moderation and visualisation are used, it has become established practice to keep a written record of deviating views or conflicting results (→ E 17).

If this approach to external evaluation is used, there is more chance of the proposals for the next project phase being regarded by all concerned as a desirable and practicable step towards a better future. They will therefore be able to identify fully with the proposals and they will do their utmost to turn the plans into reality.

Source:

Regina GÖRGEN: Projektevaluierung und ZOPP. Erfahrungen – Probleme – Vorschläge. In: BASLER, A. et al: Unveröffentlichter Evaluierungsbericht zum PAP, Nyabisindu, Rwanda. GTZ, Eschborn, 1986, Anhang 4.

Compiled by:

Volker HOFFMANN

E 19

The use of vehicles in extension organisations

Since the costs of fuel and materials are constantly rising, it is essential to take good care of motor vehicles and to use them economically. We now give some advice on how to look after and make the best use of vehicles.

Vehicles are a source of prestige and a rare convenience, especially when vehicles in the private sector are scarce and expensive. Thus the way in which they are used can give rise to envy, rivalry and dissatisfaction in the organisation.

It is therefore all the more important that the regulations are clear and felt to be fair.

1. Vehicles at headquarters

- Journeys have to be planned on a weekly and daily basis. One person at headquarters must be given responsibility for this planning. The vehicles, their readiness for use, the routes and the purpose of the journeys should be displayed for all to see.

- To ensure that vehicles are used to best effect, it is advisable to set up a pool at headquarters.

- Journeys should be planned to cover several different jobs.

- A logbook must be filled in regularly before and after journeys. If the next driver notices anything wrong, he should report it to the vehicle administration before he sets out on his journey.

- Official vehicles should be driven mainly by professional drivers, to increase the useful life of vehicles and to ensure that faults are spotted early and repaired.

- When vehicles are used for private purposes, the social customs of the country have to be observed. Private use must not get in the way of work and should not give rise to unfair advantage. The display chart makes the use of vehicles sufficiently public to create social controls. Any costs involved should also be paid according to local custom; perhaps they can be covered by labour or payment in kind. Abuse of the system should be prevented by making the user personally liable for the vehicle in his charge.

- A check must be made to ensure that servicing is carried out regularly (logbook, stickers).

E 19

- The loan of vehicles to other institutions should be kept to a minimum.

- If vehicles cannot be repaired and serviced locally and are known to be out of action for long periods, serious thought should be given to setting up a repair department.

- Headquarters should guarantee the supply of fuel for use in the field, paying particular attention to the regularity of supplies and proper storage.

2. Transport at field offices

- Government credit should be made available on favourable terms so that advisers can buy bicycles and motorbikes. They are more likely to be treated properly if they are privately owned. Lump sums or mileage payments are another way of encouraging private purchase.

- So that they are always ready for use, bicycles and motorbikes must be checked for roadworthiness once a month.

- Motorcyclists in particular must receive regular training in vehicle maintenance and must be told why it is so important to have vehicles serviced at the appropriate intervals.

- It is advisable to establish a stock of spare parts and tools at field office level, so that small repairs can be carried out on the spot.

- Since newly appointed advisers often do not have a bicycle, each field office should have a few available for use until they can buy their own.

Compiled by:

Gerhard PAYR, Rolf SÜLZER

Checklists

Checklist of constraints on participation of target groups

A number of factors militate against the measures devised to promote systematic participation by target groups. The obstacles to participation can usually be overcome, but extension work has to take account of them from the outset, so that ways and means can be found to eliminate them. When we aim to achieve target group participation, we have to bear in mind the following areas of influence:

Factors influencing participation	Effects and interrelations
Physical/biological	Climate, weather, soil composition and cropping dates, etc., affect participation in meetings (poor road conditions, heavy work on poor soils).
Economic	Poor land tenure conditions, limited land ownership and availability of other production factors are typical of small farmers. Since they are in a position of dependence, participation often makes them fear social sanctions, loss of credit opportunities and of marketing their harvest.
Political	Rural elites, parties and bureaucracies stand in the way of participation. Instructions are issued by national or provincial centres. Nothing can be done about central planning. Provision for decentralised decision making is deliberately circumvented.
Social	Family/clan structure, group relations, rules of inheritance, social stratification, class structure and different forms of settlement make participation more difficult to achieve. Because target groups do not own certain production factors and because more prosperous groups exercise control, their chances of participating in decisions are reduced.
Cultural	Values and norms of a particular society, target group or sub-group; division of labour between the sexes, looking to the future, communal work and the role of women and other sub-groups in decision making affect whether women are even allowed to leave the house, whether it is the men who make decisions on food cropping, competition between families in place of communal labour, etc.

F 1

Historical | An appeal for participation is often greeted with mistrust, because of relations with national or state-run institutions, experience of government powers and the extension organisation, traditional rivalry between town and country or recommendations that proved to be of no benefit.

Bibliography:

J. M. COHEN, N. T. UPHOFF: Rural development participation. Concepts and measures for project design, implementation and evaluation. Ithaca, N. Y. Cornell Univ. 1977. (Rural Development Monograph 2)

Compiled by:

Rolf SÜLZER, Gerhard PAYR

F 2

Checklist of weaknesses in extension work

In 1975 the FAO carried out a comparative survey in eight countries in East Africa to try to establish where weak links occur in extension. Similarly, experts taking part in extension seminars run by DSE and GTZ have taken stock of the situation on a number of occasions.

The following list of identified weaknesses acts as a **warning signal**. With the help of this list we can ask the following questions wherever extension work is being carried out:

(1) Is this weakness likely to occur or does it already exist in the planned project?

(2) What is the **cause**?

(3) What **effects** will it have?

(4) What is the best **way of remedying the situation**, and how can it be accomplished?

Wherever weaknesses are found, these four questions reveal the priorities to be pursued.

Weaknesses:

- lack of trained personnel?

- poor opportunities for marketing agricultural produce at adequate prices?

- inadequate transport facilities?

- communication difficulties?

- lack of credit programmes for small farmers?

- inadequate supply of inputs?

- rapid turnover of extension staff?

- poor administrative support (rooms, materials)?

- too many local languages – resulting in problems with written materials?

- too dependent on foreign donors?

F 2

- no understanding of the extension concept or no extension concept at all?
- ratio of farmers to field advisers too high?
- no extension work directed towards women?
- problems of land ownership?
- poorly defined extension targets?
- inadequate job description for extension staff?
- lack of a personnel and programme policy?
- no annual extension plan?
- no instructions, brochures, materials for advisers?
- little idea about further training for extension personnel?
- little effort to survey the farming systems of small farmers?
- insufficient awareness on the part of economic planners of the tasks, importance and problems of extension work, especially regarding field advisers?
- no monitoring and evaluation system?
- inadequate exchange of information between research and extension?
- no specially trained senior staff to assist field advisers (supervision)?
- lack of supplementary services and/or problems of coordination with extension?
- past developments unfavourable, poor image of extension?
- hierarchical and control-oriented extension organisation?
- directive behaviour on the part of field advisers?
- duties unconnected with extension and role conflict in field advisers?

Compiled by:

Gerhard PAYR, Rolf SÜLZER, Volker HOFFMANN

F 3

Checklist of features of successful development work and extension

In this paper we present a whole range of points that can be used to establish the state of a project. They can be applied at the stage of the feasibility study, operational planning and ongoing evaluation.

Important general conditions

(1) The development aid and extension measures have not created any economic, social and political inequalities. The living conditions of those receiving development aid have at least not deteriorated.

(2) The measures as planned and implemented did not exceed the economic capacity of the farm, household and family. The effects were positive, not just as abstract data but as tangible, microeconomic benefits.

(3) The innovations were technically fully developed and capable of being applied under the given conditions – even if farmers used them wrongly or in a different way.

(4) The development aid measures were socially acceptable, i.e. the offer of help was compatible with the existing social organisation and gave rise to a self-sustaining spread of innovations.

(5) The administration was able to cope with the organisation of development aid measures and to implement them. There were enough staff and materials available. There were also links, horizontal and vertical channels of communication, to exchange information with back-up institutions at all levels.

(6) The target groups were able to comprehend the proposed innovations (mainly devised with their cooperation). They had the necessary technical knowhow, the capacity to take in information and were able to see the main interrelations.

(7) The planned improvements often related to existing endeavours by the population itself. Thus the advisers and experts found a way of lending support to efforts already being made by the people and mobilising them. They took into account existing social relations, groupings and interests.

F 3

Features specific to extension

(1) The advisers were able to concentrate on extension and did not have to undertake unrelated work. Thus, instead of just receiving and carrying out orders, the members of the target group had the opportunity of genuine dialogue with the advisers.

(2) The advisers had not only received technical training but had been instructed in methodology.

(3) Training was not conceived as a single act of instruction for advisers; it was continued as an integral part of practical work (on-the-job training, in-service training).

(4) Advisers were given regular, planned support in technical matters and methodology by people inside and outside the development organisation (supervision). The object of this supervision was not primarily to check on advisers but to create a supportive relationship with the aim of improving operations.

(5) The aims of extension were clearly defined and all advisers were aware of them.

(6) It was made absolutely clear how advisers in different subject areas and/or different organisations were to work together and how their work was to be coordinated (unambiguous job descriptions).

(7) The satisfactory work situation was reflected in the stability of personnel; there was little turnover of staff.

(8) The extension organisation used its own experts, or brought in outside experts, to guide the communication processes, supervise campaigns and carry out continuous evaluation of social and economic developments.

(9) The authoritarian approach was slowly but surely transformed into leadership based on partnership.

(10) Extension work was frequently organised towards a specific target, which was attained in the scheduled period.

(11) This target was felt by the target group to be a real need and a direct contribution to improving their situation.

(12) The advisers and extension organisation have found ways of playing down their contribution to improvements in order to underline the role of

the target group. Thus the extension partners can feel proud of acting independently and taking responsibility.

(13) The advisers are in touch with agricultural and social research and in case of doubt can make enquiries. They can therefore always check to see whether recommendations are sufficiently developed to be put into practice.

Compiled by:

Rolf SÜLZER, Gerhard PAYR

F 4

Checklist for information gathering in the situation analysis

This list is intended to serve as an example only. It has to be evaluated and used selectively in relation to specific problems. → G 1 shows how a data plan for the situation analysis can be made from this check list.

1. **Subject of survey: project environment**

    (1) Basic physical and demographic data

    - geo-climatic conditions and their change over time;

    - population, settlement, migration patterns, distance to markets and administrative units;

    - land use and attitude of the population to agricultural production;

    - production methods, means of production and how and where they are made;

    - type and structure of employment.

    (2) Production and income generation

    - production factors: soil, climate, water, seed, fertiliser, draught animals, tools, fuel, labour, etc.;

    - economic factors: transport, storage, processing and marketing, credit, prices, levies and taxes;

    - social and institutional factors: ownership and land tenure conditions, farm size, structure of labour, organisation of activities in the household and on the farm, multi-farm cooperation, labour obligations and prohibitions, division of labour on the basis of sex and age;

    - organisational factors: cooperatives, service institutions, general administration, education and level of training;

    - off-farm sources of income: migrant labour, seasonal wage labour, sale of tools, equipment, household articles, clothes, etc.

(3) The use of products

- crops are used for: food, cash, animal keeping, subsistence, sale at markets, social obligations, storage, seed;

- use of cash income: consumer goods and food, house building, bride price, investment in agriculture, capital assets, taxes, education.

2. Subject of survey: dynamic of the social system

(1) Level of know-how in the target groups

- technical knowledge of plant and animal production: soil, plant breeding, etc.;

- economic know-how: elasticity of production, labour input, farm organisation, credit, etc.;

- knowledge of politics: agricultural policy, influence of the administration in general, influence and power structure of formal and informal leaders;

- general level of education: literacy, formal and informal socialisation, learning processes.

(2) Social structure and decision-making behaviour

- family structure: roles, obligations, participation in certain activities;

- family relationships and friendships: mutual dependence and help, hierarchies, communal work, etc.;

- social structure in larger units (villages): group formation, influential individuals, systems of values and norms, etc.

(3) Socio-cultural characteristics

- aspects of life influenced by religion: production methods, cropping systems, land use, etc.

- traditional and modern laws: processes for conflict solving;

- systems of values: "decent" behaviour, dealing with things in the "right" way, etc.;
- an idea of the connection between cause and effect (see also: level of know-how);
- certain behaviour patterns rooted in the social system, and their sphere of influence: validity for persons of the target group, sanctions, alternatives, degree of tolerance, etc.

(4) Structures of communication and the spread of innovations

- informal channels of communication: meeting places, gatherings, markets, migrant labour;
- formal communication channels: newspaper, magazines, brochures, radio, folk groups, etc.;
- spread of innovations: innovations already adopted, inhibiting and driving forces, effects on social and economic processes, etc.

3. Subject of survey: project organisation

(1) Methods of financing: microeconomic and macroeconomic, credit, etc.

(2) Composition of the project: establishing independent research and extension departments, media departments, etc.

(3) Structure of the organisation: relation to the target groups, man-management, guidelines for decision making, areas of responsibility and communication within the organisation, planning procedures, etc.

(4) Equipment and staff: the personnel required, materials, buildings, etc.

(5) Integration in existing organisations: changes in organisational structure, intervention in existing areas of responsibility, etc.

4. Subject of survey: complementary institutions

(1) Research and training: applicability of research in the locality, relevance to small farmers' systems, qualifications of trained staff, motivation to work in the agricultural sector, etc.

(2) Farmers' associations: cooperatives or self-help organisations or informal groupings.

(3) Marketing facilities: capable of handling the produce of small farmers – small quantities, poor infrastructure, etc.

(4) Credit: traditional savings groups, rotating credit systems, bank finance, etc., and their appropriateness for small farms.

(5) Administrative/political institutions: participation in setting the aims and implementing the project; willingness to cooperate, financial and personnel/material support, cooperation with the target groups, etc.

5. Subject of survey: participation

(1) The extent to which the target or sub-groups can be reached and mobilised: communication channels, how to address them (dialects, level of education, behaviour of advisers, etc.).

(2) Risk situation of the target groups: dependence on physical or social factors (landlords, traders, etc.).

(3) Specific obstacles for target groups: political or social barriers, economic barriers, motivation and level of know-how.

(4) Social and political ability to articulate their own interests and problems.

(5) Willingness and ability of participating organisations to involve target groups: methods of participation, schedules and locations, areas of responsibility, etc.

6. Subject of survey: target groups' scope for action

(1) The connection between the whole process (the content of extension and measures) and the social and individual abilities of the target groups.

(2) Ecological compatibility: the possibility of integrating innovations in traditional cropping systems, the reliability of recommendations.

(3) Socio-cultural suitability: benefit to the target groups, increasing their ability to take action, reduction of constraints, relative freedom from conflict, etc.

(4) Political and legal acceptability: land tenure system, autonomy of the relevant groups, etc.

F 4

(5) Link with traditional forms of organisation: extended family groups, mutual neighbourhood help, etc.

(6) Taking account of all members of the target group: women, men, young people, etc.

(7) Effects on sub-groups and other associations in the existing social system.

Compiled by:

Rolf SÜLZER, Gerhard PAYR

F 5

Checklist of assumptions about the extent and speed of the diffusion of innovations

During feasibility studies or the ongoing planning of extension measures, certain assumptions are made about the speed with which innovations spread. These studies must make a special point of listing and examining the following issues:

(1) Is the extension organisation able to convey the innovations to the target group?

(2) In what way were the target or sub-groups involved in formulating the measures? Is there any competition between targets?

(3) What relations currently exist between advisers and target groups?

(4) Are the target groups already familiar with the innovations in principle?

(5) What changes in behaviour and learning processes are called for by the innovations? To determine their complexity, list the changes that will be necessary.

(6) What material or social risk is involved in the innovation or package of innovations?

(7) What are the benefits of the innovation in material, social or personal terms (for example reduction of workload)?

(8) Have the consequences of changes in the division of labour (social and between the sexes) been discussed with the target groups?

(9) What are the predictions of the speed of dissemination based on (adoption rate)?

The reader is referred to → F 6 for criteria to evaluate innovations.

Compiled by:

Rolf SÜLZER, Gerhard PAYR

F 6

Checklist for evaluating innovations

In **feasibility studies** or continuous planning, priority is often given to collecting data for an economic evaluation. But this is only one of many aspects. An extension-oriented situation analysis or operational plan must, if it is to follow the procedure we recommend, answer the following questions with the use of empirical evidence wherever possible:

(1) Can the measures help to reduce existing inequalities (or at least not make them worse)?

(2) Are they beneficial at both microeconomic and macroeconomic levels, and can they be financed within the project?

(3) Are they technically feasible with the given target group, i.e.

– does the target group have the necessary tools and equipment,

– the required know-how and the practical skills to cope with the measures,

– or can these preconditions be created?

(4) What is the current method of problem solving? What methods are being used and why? What insights, what learning processes, what adaptation are called for as the target group moves towards adoption of the innovation?

(5) Are the measures socially acceptable, i.e. do they fit the existing system of norms and values in a particular culture?

(6) Who is affected directly and indirectly by an innovation?

– What reactions do we expect if an innovation is adopted?

– What reactions are likely in the case of failure?

(7) Can the measures be coped with organisationally?

– Are the financial and human resources available?

– Are the institutions/organisations/firms who will have to supply the production inputs both informed and equal to this task?

F 6

(8) Will it be possible to spread the innovation with the active participation of the target group?

(9) Will it be possible to use existing groups and communication networks in the population to spread the innovation?

(10) Is the way of communicating the measures (the methodology and the content) adapted to the level of comprehension of the target group?

(11) Is the proposed measure understood by the population as an answer to a perceived problem?

→ F 5 gives information on checking important assumptions about the extent and speed of the dissemination of innovations.

Compiled by:

Rolf SÜLZER, Gerhard PAYR

F 7

Checklist for selecting contact farmers

Contact farmers are used when innovations undergo practical testing in field trials. In addition to this function, they are the partners of advisers, and in this capacity they pass on information and techniques to other farmers. As representatives of the target groups, contact farmers see that the wishes, proposals and criticisms of the farmers are taken into consideration when extension measures and programmes are formulated.

When contact farmers are chosen, the following conditions should be fulfilled:

Relation to the target group

− The selected farmers must not be different socially or economically from the target group.

− Contact farmers must be identified in every target group.

− Contact farmers must be integrated in the target group in terms of caste, family, religion, tribe, etc.

− They must have the same basic agricultural practices and the same level of production factors as the farmers in target groups.

− Innovative farmers who have moved into the area are not usually integrated and are therefore unsuitable as contact farmers.

Status

− Contact farmers should have sufficient status in the target group to help counter the sanctions that could be applied when somewhat unconventional innovations are tested.

− It is a great advantage if the contact farmers have sufficient status for the target group to accept their role in testing innovations.

− Great care is necessary if people are brought in from outside the village society, even for setting up field trials.

Communication

− The farm should be suitably located to give easy access to the maximum number of target group members.

F 7

- Contact farmers should always be socially integrated and outgoing personalities.

- They must be willing to establish and maintain communication with farmers and institutions.

Know-how and skills

- A good formal education is an advantage but must not be a condition.

- More important than formal education is the willingness and ability to take in new ideas and information.

- They must have the ability to carry out trials and interviews correctly (time, content, observations).

- Contact farmers must be capable of advising farmers and giving them factually correct information and advice at the right time. They must also be in a position to interpret farmers' reactions correctly.

- An important precondition of selection is the willingness to undergo further training, either by means of courses, training by the adviser or with the aid of brochures and information circulars.

Personal characteristics

- Contact farmers must not be motivated simply by personal advantage, such as the cost-free provision of operating funds or transport.

- The development aid organisation should be able to rely on agreements being kept.

- Contact farmers should always behave in solidarity with the members of their target groups.

Selection procedure

(1) The field advisers are the people who are most likely to know suitable individuals. The field advisers should be told about the requirements at a seminar.

(2) The field advisers and the representatives of the target group organisations jointly nominate suitable individuals. If necessary, a brief sociometric survey should be undertaken (→ E 4).

F 7

(3) The people chosen by this preliminary selection procedure undergo training to prepare them for their role as contact farmers.

(4) There must be no element of compulsion when individuals are selected. It must be made quite clear to the contact farmers that their new role will entail extra work. Not until this point is a final decision made regarding who will participate in the programme.

(5) The contact farmers should be suitably recompensed for significant costs in terms of time or money that they incur by working for the extension organisation. But it is imperative not to give the impression that contact farmers enjoy special privileges.

(6) Contact farmers require constant, careful back-up in the form of:

- preparatory courses;
- regular training;
- participation in advisers' discussions;
- visits by advisers and specialists;
- brochures and books.

See also the information given in → C 6 and → E 4.

Compiled by:

Rolf SÜLZER, Gerhard PAYR

F 8

Points for the field adviser to bear in mind when forming village committees

Introduction

The keywords and information in this paper can be regarded by the adviser as examples when he is called on to form village committees. They have to be explained to the target groups in great detail. There is little point in expecting functionaries to take charge of newly created committees unless they have been trained and are supervised (→ D 4).

1. What is a committee?

A committee is a group of people who are elected by the village with the agreement of the village head. The villagers select these individuals because they are considered capable of representing the interests of the whole village in the community and in dealings with the outside world. The committee endeavours to improve the living conditions of all the men, women and children in the village.

2. What should be the functions of the committee?

It is the job of the committee to examine critically the situation of the village and its inhabitants and to consider which of its problems could be solved by the village itself.

- What problems exist in the village?
- Are the houses in good repair?
- Is enough food produced?
- Is enough clean drinking water available?
- Are the children well fed and healthy?
- Are there any schools?
- Are the women overworked?
- Is there adequate health care?
- What would we like to change in the village?
- What can we do about it ourselves?

3. How does a committee work?

- The chairman calls a meeting for a specific purpose (at least once a month) and draws up an agenda with the functionaries.

- The village committee invites other individuals to take part in the discussions, if it is deemed necessary, e. g. the field adviser, the domestic science adviser, the local party chairman, the health inspector, the teacher, etc.

- The committee may first discuss a problem and then propose a solution. If, for example, a new plant disease has been spotted, the adviser is called on to suggest remedies.

- For his part, the adviser will introduce new methods to the committee members, tell them about opening times of markets, give out posters, etc.

4. Duties of the committee members

Chairperson

- he or she is the spokesperson of the committee;

- convenes the meeting;

- invites guests and introduces them;

- ensures that all the participants have a chance to speak;

- makes the final decision if opinions are divided;

- makes sure that the areas of responsibility for adopted measures are clearly defined;

- sees that decisions are minuted;

- represents the village committee on the higher level committee;

- can be removed by ballot at a village meeting, if he fails to carry out his duties.

Secretary

- minutes the decisions of the committee and reads them out at the next meeting;

- keeps minutes, letters, brochures, etc., in files and makes them available to the villagers if they wish to inspect them;
- tells all committee members about deadlines and any information received, and if there is a noticeboard in the village he is in charge.

Treasurer

- administers money being paid out and received (cash book);
- issues receipts and records outgoings;
- has payments authorised by the committee;
- opens a bank account and administers it;
- must at any time be able to inform the committee of the current balances and the flow of monies;
- draws up the balance sheet at the end of the year.

Duties of all committee members

- to inform the villagers about decisions;
- to advise and train the villagers;
- to discuss current problems with the villagers;
- to support decisions taken by the committee, even if they do not personally agree with them;
- to help the field advisers and other field staff to carry out development programmes.

5. The behaviour of advisers towards village committees

- Committee members should always be treated politely and with respect by the adviser.
- If an adviser wants to say something at a committee meeting, he must ask the chairperson for permission to speak.

F 8

- If an adviser introduces a new extension programme at a meeting, he must prepare himself carefully and, where appropriate, hand out brochures.

- If he comes across resistance at meetings, he must never use pressure. He must take objections seriously, try to understand the reasons for them and deal with them objectively.

- When measures are to be implemented in the village, he must always inform the committee in advance about content, location and timing.

- The adviser can only expect help with his extension work if he succeeds in building up trust and friendly relations with the committee members.

Compiled by:

Gerhard PAYR, Rolf SÜLZER

F 9

Points to bear in mind when preparing and conducting individual extension talks

Basic principles and advice:

(1) On account of the high time input, individual extension work has to be planned particularly carefully. Wherever possible, the farmer or his wife should be informed in advance about the adviser's visit. A visit to another farmer should also be planned in advance or another activity held in reserve in case the extension talk has to be called off for reasons of sickness, bereavement, celebrations or family matters.

(2) The relationship between the adviser and farmer may suffer if an appointment is arranged and then not kept. If this happens for reasons beyond the control of the adviser, he should try to tell the farmer as soon as possible why he did not appear. An apology after the event is better than simply not turning up or offering no word of explanation.

(3) The adviser must prepare carefully for every single extension visit and take note of the following points:

 – He should recapitulate previous visits. What questions and problems were addressed? What solutions were worked out?

 – What questions can be anticipated? What solutions can the adviser propose?

 – What written materials and extension aids must he bring with him?

 – What practical demonstrations could be required?

(4) The adviser must pay due regard to tradition during extension visits, for example addressing words of greeting, typical courtesies, prayers, eating and drinking. The adviser must be very careful about accepting presents, since both acceptance and refusal can be problematic. Requests to attend drinking sessions should if possible be refused.

(5) The adviser must be careful about how he uses information that he collects during extension talks. He must not give people the impression that he passes on rumour and gossip.

(6) He should make brief notes of his discussion to remind himself of action to be taken and further visits to be made.

(7) If the adviser makes promises that he cannot keep, like sending extension materials or negotiating credit, the effects can be disastrous. The basis of trust is destroyed, which is particularly serious in the case of contact farmers or representatives of the target group organisations.

Techniques of conversation management

(1) The adviser must create an atmosphere in which the farmer does not feel he is there to beg favours or to receive orders.

(2) The adviser must not behave submissively or arrogantly.

(3) It is often not customary in traditional societies to restrict discussion to practical issues. On the other hand, time is at a premium for the adviser, who must therefore try to find a middle way.

(4) The adviser should listen attentively, not lecture the farmers; he should not constantly interrupt or give the impression that he knows best.

(5) Discussions should never begin with criticism; if he detects resistance, he should never try to overcome it with complete and final solutions. He should try to find the causes of problems by asking searching questions and then work out ways of solving the problems with the farmers.

(6) The adviser should never encroach on the private lives of farmers or taboo subjects. If he makes this mistake, the value of future extension discussions will be reduced, or they may not be possible at all.

(7) The farmer seeking advice should always have the feeling during a discussion that the adviser is genuinely interested in his problem and in finding a solution. But the adviser must be careful not to take the side of the farmer, especially when the issues are not his responsibility and beyond his power to decide. He must pass on problems to the appropriate level if he cannot find solutions himself.

(8) The adviser should not decide on a particular solution immediately but must give his client the opportunity to discuss and weigh up the solutions with his family, the group or at village level.

(9) All extension talks should be concluded on a positive note. Even if the discussion has not produced a solution, it is nevertheless important to decide how to carry on working towards a solution.

→ E 5 and → F 10 give further information on extension talks.

Bibliography:

Erna HRUSCHKA: Methodische Aspekte des Beratungsgesprächs. In: Der Förderungsdienst, Sonderheft 2 (1974), pp. 44 – 48.

R. KRISHAN: Agricultural Demonstration and Communication. London: Asia Publishing House 1965.

Compiled by:

Gerhard PAYR, Rolf SÜLZER

F 10

The advisory process: questions for guidance

Making contact and initial assessment of the situation

Contact is made either because farmers approach the adviser or the adviser himself takes the initiative.

When the adviser first makes contact, he must make every effort to establish good relations. By means of discussion ("active listening"), observation and investigation, he gets an initial impression of the situation and problems.

From the point of view of the adviser, extension is a process consisting of four main phases (situation analysis, planning, implementation and evaluation of results). Sometimes phases or parts of the extension process have to be repeated.

Situation analysis

(1) Have the basic data relevant to the situation been collected (household, family/people, farm, social environment)?

(2) How does the adviser see the situation and future developments, what basic problems are responsible for the given situation and what are the causes of these problems?

(3) How do the people affected by the problems see their own situation and future development, to what extent do they understand basic problems and causes, and what aims or scope for action do they have and what difficulties (obstacles) do they see?

Problems

(4) What solutions and scope for action exist and what can actually be achieved?

(5) What advantages, disadvantages and consequences would the various alternatives have for population, and in what way would they have to change their behaviour?

(6) How can the population be actively drawn into the extension process, will colleagues also be involved and what should the extension approach be (extension concept)?

Implementation (and decisions by the extension partners)

(7) Is the whole target group included in the extension process, and are they being taught in a manner that is appropriate to their situation which often means using a phased, gradual approach to appreciate the problems and their causes in the current circumstances, the probable developments, the action they could take and its consequences?

(8) Is it made clear that the decision is theirs and that they bear the consequences?

(9) Once one of the alternatives has been selected (decision), is the approach worked out jointly in such detail that the chosen path can actually be followed, and will implementation require the adviser's follow-up?

Evaluation of results (intermediate evaluation for each phase is also very useful)

(10) Is the adviser able to recognise differences between the actual extension process and the planned process (and if the deviations are significant, to record them), and are conclusions drawn from this appraisal for the case in hand, and possibly also for future extension endeavours?

Source:

Peter DENZINGER: Organisationsfragen der landwirtschaftlichen Offizialberatung. In: Bericht über Landwirtschaft 59, pp. 93 – 104.

Compiled by:

Volker HOFFMANN

F 11

Checklist for preparing and running a meeting during a campaign

1. Planning

- What information is to be communicated?
- Is a meeting a suitable method?
- What other methods could be used?
- What are the reasons for and against a mass meeting?
- Are the measures:
  - of direct appeal to the target group?
  - unattractive?
  - useful only in the long term?
- Are the target groups involved in formulating the information and drawing up the programmes?
- Has the right time been chosen for the meeting?
- How is participation by the target group being achieved:
  - early invitation;
  - influential individuals passing on information;
  - announcement in the media;
  - inviting popular speakers;
  - attractive events (music, theatre, lotteries with prizes)?
- Is there enough money to finance the programme?
- Is participation by local decision makers guaranteed?
- Have the messages in the various speeches been coordinated?
- Have the transport problems been solved?

F 11

2. Duties of the participants

The extension service

- informing radio stations;
- informing the chairmen of all village committees, village heads and party functionaries about the meeting;
- preparation of equipment and visual material for a demonstration;
- providing leaflets and loudspeakers;
- coordinating leaflets and loudspeaker announcements;
- preparing the speech to be given by a senior adviser;
- organising field advisers to marshal the crowd;
- distributing leaflets.

Farmers' representatives

- inviting the local population to take part;
- preparing the meeting place (setting up benches and chairs, providing drinking water, sanitary facilities, etc.);
- crowd control;
- preparing the speech of the farmers' chosen representative;
- inviting local dancers and musicians.

Traditional and modern functionaries and dignitaries

- information gathering and inviting the people via existing organisational networks (parties, administration, clubs);
- preparation of speeches;
- help with transport and finance.

Complementary institutions (credit, marketing, etc.)

- provision of information material;
- help with transport;
- help with finance;
- preparation of speeches.

3. Implementation (example of how a meeting could be organised)

    9.00 Everyone sets out for the meeting

    9.30 Local dances by various groups

    9.45 Prayers

    9.50 Opening speech by the head of the local administration

    10.00 Main speaker (minister, member of parliament, etc.)

    10.30 Speech and demonstration by the extension service

    11.00 Acknowledgment of outstanding farmers' representatives

    11.15 Local dances and music

    11.30 Speech by a representative of the farmers

    11.45 Lottery with prizes

    12.00 End of meeting

When running a meeting attention must be paid to the following:

- keeping to the schedule;
- speeches to be easily understood;
- programme items to be of limited duration and closely coordinated;
- people given the opportunity to ask questions after every speech;

F 11

- observing the reactions of the participants;
- using any aids and resources available.

4. Follow-up measures

Analysis of the results of the meeting by means of:

- weekly discussions with advisers;
- target group organisations;
- evaluation department;
- identifying the need for supplementary measures, like field days, group demonstrations, further training programmes for target group functionaries, use of the media;
- any changes necessary in further meetings during the current campaign.

Compiled by:

Gerhard PAYR, Rolf SÜLZER

F 12

Checklist for using media

When media are used, they must be adapted to the situation of the target group. In each individual case we have to decide how best to adapt the media and the message.

The checklist below consists of groups of questions and individual questions that have to be worked through in the project. They help to reveal the facts of the situation. The best method is to take several sheets of paper, write at the top which of the media is being checked, for example "slides", and then go through the list, noting answers and problems. The five groups of questions deal with "aims", "general conditions", "rationalisation effects", "adaptation to target groups" and "situations".

Group 1. Aims

- Has the content been clearly delineated and how does it relate to the aims of the whole project?
- Should the attention of people in the target group be drawn to any particular facts?
- Is the object of the media input to mobilise and motivate?
- Are the media being used as a means of stimulating activity on the part of the target group?
- Is the aim to show processes and events over time?
- Is the intention to give concrete help to solve problems?
- Do certain innovations require technical or social back-up?
- Do the objectives of the media input seem operationally feasible, and will we be able to check that they have been achieved?

Group 2. General conditions for the use of media

- Are the conditions satisfactory in terms of organisation, time, finance and personnel?
- Are there enough media staff, equipment and materials available to reach the members of the target group?

F 12

- Do all the people in the target group have radios or access to radios?
- Is special building work necessary before information media can be used (rooms, seats, etc.)?
- Can the planned media be easily transported to other locations?
- Are technical facilities available for use by media staff at each location?
- What is the quality of the repair and servicing facilities?
- Are there any special requirements regarding storage (dust, heat, humidity, etc.)?
- Are there any special requirements regarding the production of media aids (experts and foreign teams necessary, or can they be produced without outside help)?
- Is electricity necessary?
- How complicated is equipment to operate? Are experts needed?
- Are already available media facilities being fully utilised?
- Who decides on the use of media (who controls access to media)?
- How much and what kind of pre-testing is necessary?
- Is the media service connected organisationally or through its personnel with the target group?
- Can the target group influence the content and the input of media?
- What is the level of training and qualifications of the staff using media?

Group 3. Rationalisation effects created by the use of media

- Can the media be reproduced (how often)?
- How long and how safely can the material be stored (under what conditions)?
- Are the materials always available (for which individuals, under what conditions)?

- Is repetition possible (for the same target group, at the same place)?
- What are the costs of equipment and materials (total and per head of the target group)?
- What are the costs of producing films, slides, broadcasts, etc. (total and per head of the target group)?
- What costs are created by the dissemination process (personnel, transport, etc.)?
- How big is the target group?
- Do the members of the target group really have enough in common to be reached by a single means of communication?
- Are the people in the target group already in touch with each other (through cooperatives, self-help groups, village communities, etc.)?
- Are there already multipliers who can be approached to spread the message among the target group?
- Are existing multipliers being supplied with supplementary information (individuals or institutions, e.g. branches of cooperatives, hospitals, etc.)?
- Have tests shown that the planned media are useful and effective? Have the right methods and messages been chosen for communication, i.e. does the target group talk about them?
- In summary: are the media really more cost-effective, and is the learning effect greater than the use of manpower alone?

Group 4. Adaptation to the target group and to problems

- What are the criteria for determining the content?
- What methods have been used to test the material in the target group (with what results)?
- How is the media input evaluated (the methodology and the content; what are the criteria of success or failure)?
- Have the best methods of communication been chosen, bearing in mind the target group and their problems (give reasons)?

F 12

- Are moving pictures necessary?
- Is it necessary to use colours?
- How faithfully is reality reproduced?
- Is the target group able to form opinions about the messages?
- Are their opinions noted and taken into account when the media are used again?
- Has the material been specifically developed or appropriately adapted for the recipients and local conditions?
- Is the training of the media staff relevant to the problems and the situation?
- Is the content concrete or abstract?
- Do the solutions shown to the target group really correspond to their scope for action, given their material, psychological, social and political constraints?
- How and where is information about the know-how, the practical skills and the motivation of the target groups stored (who is it available to) (→ C 2)?
- How do communicators and members of the target group work together (place, individuals, topics)?
- How is an information unit produced? What is the production process in detail?

Group 5. Adaptation to various situations

- Does the use of media depend on the seasons (technically or in terms of the content)?
- Can the information be easily adapted to new situations?
- Is the use of media tied to instructors?
- How are language barriers overcome (several dialects in a small area)?
- Can the media be adjusted and adapted (after the first time they are used in the field)?

F 12

- What transport is required?

- Can the media materials be reproduced at local level (in local studios, by existing staff, etc.)?

Bibliography:

Rolf SÜLZER: Medienstrategien und Entwicklungspolitik. Anwendungsbezogene Forderungen für Medienprojekte im ländlichen Raum. In: Rundfunk und Fernsehen, 28, 1980, pp. 55 – 69.

Rolf SÜLZER: Information Systems for Propagating Rural Innovations in African Countries. Audiovision Workshop 1979, pp. 55 – 79 and Appendix I – XII.

Compiled by:

Rolf SÜLZER

**Presentation and structure:
examples and suggestions**

G 1

Data plan for the situation analysis – sub-section extension

Discussion of methods	Reason for and use of data	Method of data collection[3]	Accuracy[4]	Survey carried out by:	Timing
Subject of survey[1]					
B 1 Level of know-how in the target groups	Point of contact for extension measures, creating demonstration programmes and media input.	Group discussion, interviews and observation, tests using pictures, evaluation of secondary material.	If no new crops, etc., are introduced, a good knowledge of traditional methods is essential for making improvements.	Trained experts for group discussion and observation. Trained interviewers for surveys in larger agricultural regions.	Essential before deciding on extension measures.
1.1 Technical knowledge of plant and animal production					
1.4. General level of education, formal and informal socialisation, learning processes[2]	Basis for creating extension aids and deciding on extension methods, especially group work.	Tests using pictures and texts, observation of group behaviour, intensive discussion with individuals and personal accounts of lives, secondary material.	A general assessment is sufficient at the beginning. It must be made more specific as tests and measures are carried out.	Trained experts. During implementation advisers carry out this job with the help of already formulated criteria for observation.	Essential before deciding on extension measures especially when using contact farmers; continuous.

1 The subjects of the survey are taken from paper → F 4.
2 Socialisation is the process of learning how to relate to people, animals and things; behaviour patterns are formed.
3 The choice of methods of data collection also depends on the quality of the secondary material.
4 Accuracy largely determines the time, personnel and financial requirements. Limited finance has a direct effect on the practical design of the survey.

Compiled by:

Rolf SÜLZER, Gerhard PAYR

G 2

Suggested structure of feasibility studies for extension

We can only create the right conditions for successful extension work and problem solving by target groups if we can answer the following questions as early as the feasibility study stage:

1. Detailed identification of problems:

- the circle of individuals (and groups) who have the problem and who are aware of it (politicians, experts and organisations, small farmers and their families, large-scale farmers);

- description of the undesirable existing situation, i.e. concrete, if possible quantifiable details of the current scope for action and the use of resources by the target population;

- deciding what the target situation should be, i.e. analysis of the developments in living conditions and specifying objective targets (resource potential) and subjective targets (desirable from the point of view of the population); discussion of "unrealistic" expectations and aims;

- definition of obstacles (physical and/or economic, cultural, social, political barriers) that stand in the way of target attainment.

2. Discussion of general conditions

- details of the methods of problem identification: people involved, method of enquiry, discussions with politicians, local sponsoring institutions, target groups;

- definition of who is **affected directly or indirectly** by the problem (for example traders, large-scale farmers, institutions);

- estimating the urgency of the problem and stating the reasons for giving priority;

- analysis of solutions already tried (resources, the people involved, the degree of success).

3. Formulation of basic solutions

- demonstrating how the obstacles identified can be systematically tackled;

- description of who can profit from the proposed solutions and how;

- discussion of possible reactions by other groups or of changes in the ecological system; discussion of anticipated new problems.

4. Deciding the extension methods

- levels of discussion with the target groups;

- methods of communication in extension work;

- participation of target groups in decisions;

- coordinating the approach with everyone concerned (politicians, authorities, development aid organisations) to ensure agreement and active support;

- deciding the methods of monitoring and control.

5. Drafting the extension concept

- reasons why the extension approach will be conducive to a largely independent (autonomous) and rapid spread of innovations; changes in the behaviour of the defined target group;

- exploiting and systematically influencing the existing scope for action of the population;

- methods of actively involving the target population in planning and above all in the final drawing up of programmes.

Compiled by:

Gerhard PAYR, Rolf SÜLZER

Excerpt from a card index of terms

We can learn much about a culture, perception, thinking and actions from how a language is used to describe and to differentiate between concepts. Thus it is advisable for all foreigners to note the major terms in the local language in their specialist areas and to compile a card index of these expressions. They should do this even if they are unable or unwilling to acquire a thorough knowledge of the language. The following example is taken from an index of terms relating to social organisations in Yemen.

ain, pl. ayyan	bayt
is the head of a production unit; but in the plural the word refers to village elders, heads of extended families.	also refers to such an extended family but refers more to the place, is often used as a name and is a kind of honorary title of an extended family (badanah).
'aquil, pl. 'oqual	qebar
is the chairman of a village; he is elected by the meeting of ayyan who as heads of extended families represent them.	is the word used to denote the "important people" in the settlement; it is not a family relationship.
badanah	shaykh, pl. mashaykh
means members of a tribe, who live in one place (extended family). It is an association of core families (asrat).	denotes the leader of a tribe, tribal area or sub-tribe; but it is also the most common term used for "leader" in general. (For example, shaykh al qaryah = leader of the village; shaykh as-suq = responsible for running the market properly).

Compiled by:

Rolf SÜLZER

G 4

Example of a routine report form for a target group organisation

Target group organisation .... Extension territory ....
Place .... Field adviser ....

1. Comments on the current extension programme:
1.1. The majority of farmers find the current extension work:
   - satisfactory
   - satisfactory in some aspects only
   - totally unsatisfactory

1.2. Reasons for dissatisfaction with extension:
   ....
   ....
   ....
   ....

1.3. Suggested improvements:
   ....
   ....
   ....
   ....

2. Other suggestions, wishes, complaints, problems of target group organisations:

Date ....
                                                Signature of the target group representative

Note: This report should be given to the senior field adviser every month. A copy remains with the target group organisation.

Compiled by:

Gerhard PAYR, Rolf SÜLZER

G 5

Example of a circular on the introduction of improved weeding

The context

In close cooperation with field advisers, target groups and research stations, a project developed and tested improved weeding techniques. A newly developed hoe was shown to be superior in all respects to the traditional hoe, so that its introduction in large numbers was included in the extension programme. The field advisers were prepared at a two-day course for the campaign to introduce new weeding methods. We now reproduce the brochure that was issued to help advisers to carry out extension discussions and demonstrations.

No. 21	Extension circular	March 1980

Introduction of a new weeding hoe

(1) Reasons for introducing the new hoe

One of the greatest problems experienced by our farmers is coping with the peak in labour demand caused by keeping the fields free of weeds. Many farmers get behind in this work, resulting in fields full of weeds, poor and retarded crops and little benefit from the use of fertiliser. The low yields mean a shortfall in food production and a lack of profitability in cash-crop cultivation.

Techniques must therefore be found that enable farmers to keep up to schedule with their husbandry. The new hoe is one such tool. After being successfully tested by selected farmers, it is now going to be introduced on a wide scale.

(2) What are the advantages of the new hoe?

— With the new hoe, farmers can save 40% of the time spent using the traditional hoe.

— The work is less tiring, since the new hoe is only half the weight of the conventional hoe.

— Work in the fields is therefore much easier, especially for women and children.

G 5

- The hoe will last 2 – 3 years, because it is made of a particularly tough material that can still be worked by the local blacksmiths.
- Despite being made of better material, the hoe does not cost more than the traditional hoe.

(3) What are the general points to note in weed control?

- Hoeing should be started when the weeds are 2 cm high; while weeds are still low the work is easy and quick.
- Schoolchildren can help with weeding.
- Weeding has to be repeated until the crops can suppress weed growth.
- Cut weeds should be used as soil cover.

(4) How should the hoe be introduced?

- From now on every field adviser must keep the demonstration hoe with him (tying it to his bicycle with the hoe end pointing backwards).
- The first step is to train all contact farmers by means of a demonstration if they are unfamiliar with the new hoe.
- After the training session, the contact farmers are given a free hoe by the adviser, so that they can carry out their own demonstrations. They can buy more hoes at the standard price of 20 Escudos.
- The contact farmers must be encouraged not to use any other hoe when weeding.
- At first, the field advisers must help the contact farmers at demonstrations and observe the reactions of the farmers.
- The advisers must show the hoe to the farmers during the current programme of demonstrations at field days.
- The new hoes are recommended with the help of the film vehicle, the radio and posters.
- Local blacksmiths have already been shown how to repair the new hoe at a training session in the village crafts school.

G 5

(5) How can farmers get the new hoe?

- The hoes are obtainable at all the distribution outlets of cooperatives.

- The cash price is 20 Escudos, which is normally not beyond the means of the farmers.

- For this reason hoes are only available on credit if bulk orders are placed by village committees. At least 10 hoes have to be ordered. The credit applications are checked by the field adviser and passed on to the credit inspector who issues a letter of credit. This is given by the adviser to the village committee, who can then get the hoes from the cooperatives. The price of a hoe bought on credit is 24 Escudos.

(6) Possible difficulties

Even though the hoe has been tested for more than a year, unforeseen problems might occur. All field advisers must therefore note the reactions of the people using the new hoe and report positive and negative observations at their weekly discussions or inform their immediate superiors straight away.

Compiled by:

Gerhard PAYR, Rolf SÜLZER

G 6

Example of calculating the time needed for demonstrating a portable spray

Mistakes are often made when the time required for a job has to be estimated. People usually underestimate the time to be spent on development measures, resulting in unrealistic programmes and targets that are impossible to achieve. Consequently, field advisers and the benefit of their experience should be included in the planning process.

The following example draws on the method described in → E 7; it gives a detailed breakdown of the demonstration and draws attention to problems of time input.

Activity	Time spent (minutes)
1. Contact farmer passes **invitation** to a group of 10 – 15 farmers:	
– journey to the village by bicycle	30
– the contact farmer announces the object of the demonstration and arranges the time, place and participants	30
– return journey	30
Subtotal	90
2. Carrying out a demonstration	
– journey to the demonstration	30
– preparation of equipment	15
– explaining how it works	30
– preparing the insecticide solution	15
– demonstration of spraying	15
– participants operate the equipment	45
– discussion and information	30
– return journey	30
Subtotal	210
Total 1 and 2	300

If there are no contact farmers, the adviser must inform the farmers individually. This could obviously take much more time. Noticeboards should only be used when extension has been successfully introduced and the level of literacy is high.

G 6

The breakdown shows clearly how much time is spent on individual activities. If 300 farmers per adviser are supposed to adopt the portable spray, the problem of time becomes obvious.

Rationalisation can be achieved by:

- demonstrating to a larger group;
- the adviser carrying out the first demonstration only; further demonstrations and explanations are then given by the contact farmers;
- linking demonstrations to extension discussion or other events;
- handing out simply and clearly illustrated leaflets.

Bottlenecks are caused by the fact that many demonstrations are tied to specific seasons and have therefore to be accomplished in a short period of time.

Compiled by:

Gerhard PAYR, Rolf SÜLZER

G 7

Example of the personnel requirements of a regional agricultural administration in Malawi

The following information is taken from the "Management Unit Liwonde", Malawi 1979. It undertakes the planning, implementation and evaluation of eight rural development projects with a total of about 1.1 million people.

	Qualifications		
	No. of management staff	No. of technical staff	No. of field and auxiliary staff
1. Manager of the regional administration	1		
2. Head of the Extension Services department	1		
– farm economics	1		
– plant protection		1	
– wildlife control		1	
– animal husbandry	1	1	2
– special crops	2	2	
– domestic science	1		
– stores management	1		
– extension aids		1	5
– training and further training	1	2	
– forestry	1	1	
– marketing	1	1	
– credit	1		
3. Head of the rural services department	1		
– rural institutions	1	1	
– evaluation	1	3	52
– land development	2	4	
– experimentation	1		
4. Head of the finance department	1		
– book keeping	1	2	7
– credit accounting	1	1	4
5. Head of the department of administration	1		
– personnel		1	1
– transport (including drivers)		1	27
– stores		1	1
– registry		1	3
– administrative staff of the department			17
– auxiliary staff of the department			11
Total required	22	25	130

Compiled by:

Gerhard PAYR, Rolf SÜLZER

G 8

Three examples of structuring work programmes for field advisers

Example of a weekly programme for field advisers

week: ..
month: ..

Project: .... Extension territory .... Field adviser: .... year: ..

Day	Location (village)	Duties	Notes	Comments on implementation: (fill in after completion of work)
Mon. 1.11.	Village 1 Village 2	1. Hold a village meeting: – explain the new maize seed – fix dates for issuing seed – collect credit applications – announce when the film vehicle will arrive to demonstrate cropping maize and groundnuts	Fix date with village committee	– no meeting in village 1 because of funeral, meeting postponed to Saturday morning – credit office had handed out the wrong applications – all committee functionaries informed about film show
Tues. 2.11.	Village 3	as above	ethnic problems in village 3	– Moslems in village 3 did not attend meeting. Spoke with religious leader and informed him about the programme
Wed. 3.11.	Village 5 Village 6	1. Village meeting: – repair of embankments – dates for exchanging seed – bulk order for fertiliser – announcement of the film vehicle 2. Selection of 2 demonstration plots	Villages 5 and 6 grow mainly rainfed rice	– seed requirement village 5: 2 400 kg village 6: 3 850 kg – position of demonstration plots: see sketch enclosed – dates of film show announced
Thurs 4.11.	Village 7	1. Group discussion with local leaders: – explanation of current extension programme – arranging a village meeting for the following week – announcing when the film vehicle will arrive to demonstrate cropping maize and groundnuts	No committees in villages 7 and 8, traditional leaders are against committees	– local leaders agree to found committees – village meeting on 9.11. agreed – date of film show announced – a local trader is selling poor quality maize seed
Fri. 5.11.	Field office	1. Programming 2. Training for the programmes		– applications filled in for internal inspection – no notebooks available
Sat. 6.11.	Village 1 Advisor's house	1. Village meeting, planned as on Monday 2. Training the committee functionaries 3. Administrative work	For villages 1 – 6	– seed requirements: 3 050 kg – all committees were represented

399

G 8

Example of a monthly programme for field advisers

Month: ....
Year: ....

Project: .... Extension territory: .... Field adviser: ....

Measures	In cooperation with	Target (indicator)	Notes	Week 1	2	3	4	Complementary measures
1. Programming and further training seminar	Plant production specialists		Every Friday					
2. Introduction of a new maize variety		200 farmers should adopt						
– seminar for committee functionaries	Senior adviser	1 x						
– village meeting	Functionaries and village head	1 x	In week after training of functionaries					
– use of film vehicle	Audio-visual specialists	2 shows	select film and slides					Announce date on the radio and notice-boards
– seed distribution	Credit/marketing personnel	4000 kg 200 small loans	Issue at stores					Deliver seed on 15th Prepare credit cards
– group extension, cropping	Plant production specialists		Extension via commitees					

G 8

Example of an annual programme for field advisers

Project: .... Extension territory: .... Field adviser: ....
Year: ....

Measures	In cooperation with	Target (indicator)	J	A	S	O	N	D	J	F	M	A	M	J	Notes
1. Introduction of new variety of maize		Adoption by 40% of the target population													Innovation was demonstrated in the previous year
– seminar for commitee functionaries	Senior adviser														About 20 people, once a month
– village meetings	Comittee functionaries														Every second month
– use of film vehicle	Audio-visual specialists														Once a month
– provision of seed	Credit/marketing organisation	5000 kg seed													Check availability
– group extension work on cropping	Specialists														
– laying out demonstration plots	Specialists	1 per village													Including monitoring
– field day	Village committees	3 per week													Combine with other activities
– group extension on harvest	Specialists	1 model barn per village													
2. Promoting mixed cropping of groundnuts	Research station	3 demonstration plots per village													Benefits proved by field trials
3. 4. 5. . List the measures for all extension activities, as in 1!															
8. Further training															
– 1 week course	Regional training centre														With examination
– 1 day per week	Senior adviser														After programming
9. Holiday															

Compiled by:
Gerhard PAYR, Rolf SÜLZER

G 9

Instructional material for creating awareness and for training in the central region of Togo

Following the mobile picture method, we use pictures and shapes that can be moved around the board. To avoid trouble with wind, we use a folding metal board, instead of the common felt board, and the pictures are held on by magnets.

1. Examples of picture series: awareness creation Kabyé

This series of pictures is used at the beginning of the annual programme. It is a problem analysis in picture form. It does not indicate solutions but is intended to make people think! Basic information is then given in the subsequent series: "circulation of nutrients" and "soil fertility". It is not until this stage that solutions are proposed!

Description of picture series

Aims of the pictures:

After taking part in training, every participant should be aware that:

- there is only a limited amount of arable land available for each family, each village;
- the environment is changed by the activities of man;
- people can control this change;
- the environment determines men's lives.

Picture 1:

The Kabyé family in their place of birth

- poor harvest of maize and sorgho;
- the men return empty-handed from hunting;
- malnutrition and sickness;
- little vegetation;
- shortage of water;

G 9

Pictures 1 – 4:

404

- uncontrolled bush fires;
- life has become very difficult.

Picture 2:

The Kabyé family leave their place of birth

- only sparse vegetation;
- all the trees have been felled;
- more uncontrolled bush fires;
- harvest failure;
- the family has to leave the village.

Picture 3:

The Kabyé family has settled in the central region

- dense vegetation;
- fields close to the house;
- good harvest;
- enough water;
- enough wood.

Picture 4:

The same Kabyé village years later

- improved infrastructure
- increased population;
- fields a long way from the house;
- cropping near the house only possible with mineral fertiliser;

G 9

- water shortage;

- young people leave for the towns.

How will life go on?

Will the family have to move away again?

2. Example of picture series: creating an agro-forest system

These pictures show how an agro-forest system should be established. This is a series of technical pictures and therefore proposes solutions to some of the problems in the central region.

Description of picture series

The following is a translation of the text for field advisers that accompanies the pictures.

The series consists of the following pictures:

1. Marking out contour lines
2. Preparing planting holes
3. Distribution of varieties of tree along the row
4. Planting and sowing
5. Protection of trees
6. Phased creation of strips of trees
7. The final agro-forest system

Pictures 1, 4, 6 and 7 are reproduced here.

Aims of the pictures:

After training, every participant should know:

- what a contour line is and how it is marked out;
- that it is essential to cultivate along the contour lines;
- why and how a large planting hole is made;
- how a tree is planted correctly;
- that trees can also be sown;
- that cowpeas should be sown between the trees;
- how trees are protected from fire and animal damage;
- how a strip of trees is created in phases;
- what the advantages of a completed agro-forest system are.

G 9

Pictures 1, 4, 6 and 7:

407

G 9

Points to be explained	Questions put to the farmers:

Picture 1: Marking out contour lines

- What is a contour line?

- when marking out, begin with the lower side of the field

- mark out the other contour lines parallel to the lowest contour line

- the maximum distance between the lines is 38 m (depending on the slope)

- the distance between trees in the row is 2 or 4 m.

- a pole is driven into the ground where the tree is to be planted.

Why cultivate on the contour lines?
Answers:

- to prevent erosion

- to help water to drain away

After the explanation the adviser uses a dumpy level to show how a contour line is marked out.

Picture 2: Preparation of planting holes

- there are three way of planting trees:

  1. Planting trees that have been raised in tree nurseries, e.g.

     - Cassia siamea
     - Neem
     - Kapok
     - Acacia auriciliformis
     - Tamarind
     - Acacia albida
     - Leucaena

G 9

| Points to be explained | Questions put to the farmers |

2. Direct sowing, e.g.

   – Parkia
   – Butyrospermum
   – Cowpea
   – Leucaena
   – Blighia

3. Direct planting (transplanting), e.g.

   – Teak

– The preparation of planting holes is the same whether trees are planted or sown

– The planting hole is made 40 cm x 40 cm one month before planting or sowing.

– It is immediately filled in with good soil and heaped up in a mound 10 cm high. The mound is marked with a stick.

Why must the planting hole be made in this way?
Answers:

– the soft soil allows more rapid root growth

– it is easier for water to soak into the soil

– the soil settles over the month and the mound disappears but without forming a hollow

– a hollow must be avoided to prevent the tree becoming waterlogged in the rainy season

409

G 9

Points to be explained **Questions put to the farmers**

– the soil must be allowed to settle for a month so that the young roots are not damaged.

Picture 3: Distribution of species along the row

– at least three different varieties of tree should be planted in any row of trees

– they should be distributed evenly along the row

– trees with the same characteristics should not be planted side by side (e. g. trees with large crowns or trees that grow slowly, etc.)

Why should trees be mixed when they are planted out?
Answers:

– to avoid big gaps when they are felled

– to prevent too much shade

– to prevent the spread of disease.

Picture 4a: Planting

– remove the stick and make a hole the size of the root bale

– carefully remove the plastic sack by cutting vertically with a razor blade or knife

– do not damage the root bale

– when planted, the top of the roots must be level with the ground

G 9

Points to be explained	Questions put to the farmers
– press the soil round the roots so that it will not sink later – put cut weeds round the tree to form a layer of mulch – finally, the pole is driven into the ground 20 cm from the young tree.	
	Why is it important to plant the tree at the right level in the soil? Answers: – too high would mean that some of the roots are out of the ground. The plant can quickly dry out. – too deep in the soil would mean that the trunk is covered and it would quickly rot. Why is mulching important? Answers: – to retain moisture – to suppress weed growth

Picture 4b: Direct sowing

– The farmer himself collects seed for sowing trees

– The farmer must take the seed of a strong, healthy tree of normal proportions

– Butyrospermum is sown immediately after being harvested because its ability to germinate quickly declines

G 9

Points to be explained: **Questions put to the farmers:**

- The area round the planting hole is cleared of weeds

- 2 – 3 seeds are put into each hole near the stick

- The seeds are set 3 cm below the surface of the soil

- The different species are sown alternately

Picture 4c: Direct sowing of cowpeas

- Cowpeas are sown with 2 – 3 seeds in each hole

- Cowpeas are sown every 80 cm in rows of trees 4 m apart. Thus there are 4 seed holes between every two trees.

- Where the distance between trees is 2 m, a single planting hole is made between every pair of trees.

- If cowpeas are sown in a fallow, a 60 cm strip must be weeded.

Why should cowpeas be sown?
Answers:

- to mark the rows of trees

- as a food and fodder crop.

Picture 5: Protection of trees

- Weeding round the trees is carried out at the same time as crops are weeded.

- The whole row must be protected by a cleared fire strip.

G 9

Points to be explained:	Questions put to the farmers:
– Each tree must be protected from animal damage by a fence (e. g. sorgho stems, branches, palm twigs) or by smearing them with dung.	Are there other ways of protecting trees?

Picture 6: Phased creation of strips of trees

- The farmer can plant with the following distances between the rows:
  - one row
  - two rows with 2 m or 4 m
  - three rows with 2 m or 4 m
  - four rows with 2 m
  - five rows with 2 m

- Every year he can add one or more rows to build up a strip of trees.

- Where there is more than one row, the trees in alternate rows are staggered so that they are opposite the gaps.

- Marking out, preparing the planting holes and protection are the same in all cases.

How many trees can be planted in a 50 m row with intervals between the trees of 2 m (4 m)?

Picture 7: The final agro-forest system

- The strip of trees is 8 m wide

- The distance between strips is 30 m.

- Each strip consists of at least three different species

413

G 9

Points to be explained:	Questions put to the farmers:

- The trees can be pruned or thinned out if they encroach on crops

- The surface roots can be chopped off if they encroach on crops

- A dense strip of trees (2 m intervals, 2 m between the rows) produces firewood, poles and fodder from the fourth year onwards.

- Thinning out and loss of trees means that the final distance between trees is likely to be 4 x 4 m.

What are the advantages of a strip of trees?
Answers:

a) economic
   - firewood
   - fruit
   - building timber
   - wood for tools and equipment
   - fodder

b) ecological
   - raises soil fertility by increasing mineral salts and organic matter

Source:

Ingo BINNEWERG: Landwirtschaftliche Beratung, Strategie, Inhalt, Methode, Mittel. Central Region Togo, Sokodé, 1986.

Photographs:

Ingo BINNEWERG

Compiled by:

Ingo BINNEWERG

G 10

Instructional material for creating awareness and for training from the agricultural extension project Nyabisindu, Rwanda

After the CFSME system (→ A 8) had been declared the national extension system in Rwanda, the GTZ project "Agricultural Extension Project Nyabisindu" also adopted the basic principles of this extension approach. The felt picture method, as most important extension and training aid, was also introduced in Nyabisindu. If we compare the examples from Kibuye given in → D 6 with the pictures produced in Nyabisindu, we notice a number of differences about the Nyabisindu pictures:

- The drawings are bolder and therefore recognisable at a greater distance.

- The order in which the pictures are shown is prescribed, and since they are numbered they are easier to use.

- The text for the Animateur is more rigorously structured. In particular, he is explicitly required to ask many prescribed questions (ask instead of tell!).

- In the last section of the brochure that accompanies the pictures, concrete proposals are made for practical training after initial instruction with pictures.

- At the end of the session the participants are given a leaflet to take home as a reminder. It contains small single-colour reproductions of all the pictures and some keywords in the local language.

As an example of the packs of instructional material, we reproduce the picture series: "Erosion and the creation of erosion control lines".

1. The brochure for advisers/training personnel

Structure

A. Introduction to the topic

B. What is erosion?

C. Erosion control lines as a basic solution

D. Making terraces step by step

G 10

E. Summary of the course

F. Elements of practical training

A. **Introduction to the topic**

Word of welcome:

Thank participants for coming and say how glad you are that they are showing an interest in the topic.

> **?** What are the observable signs of erosion and what effect is it having on our hills?

> **?** What are we doing to overcome the problem?

▶ THE GROUP ANSWERS

> **?** Erosion control is an important job, but for whom?

▶ THE GROUP ANSWERS

The government and the project are making enormous efforts to control erosion. They provide the communities with workers for measuring and staking out the land and a considerable amount of technical equipment for the Umuganda (the weekly half-day "voluntary" community work for everyone). It costs a great deal but is worthwhile if the population takes an effective part in the various erosion control measures.

But, if the active participation of the people is to be achieved, they must be convinced of the need for and the effectiveness of such measures. This is the aim of today's course.

In today's training session, we are going to show you that it is possible to halt erosion and its damaging effects completely on the hills and on your farms.

G 10

> **?** Wouldn't you be pleased if you never had erosion problems again?

1

Degraded and abandoned hill.
CATASTROPHE

> **?** Is your soil threatened by a catastrophe like this?

2

— Hill completely protected against erosion. Obviously a simple ditch on the hillside cannot solve the problem of erosion. So we have to take a variety of steps in the erosion control programme. All these measures can be carried out by the farmers themselves.

Some thoughts on the nature of erosion

B   What is erosion?

— What did some of you say about erosion at the beginning? We will take your ideas and proposals a stage further:

   — What causes erosion?

   — What different kinds of erosion are there?

   — What methods can we use to combat erosion?

— Pause for thought

CAUSES OF EROSION

> **?** What happens when a field is eroded?

417

G 10

▶ THE GROUP ANSWERS

3

The soil on your land is washed away. Every year there is less and less soil left. Water carries the soil and plant nutrients down the hillside. When they get to the bottom they are washed away by streams and lost. The plant stands suffer as a consequence and produce less and less. Ultimately, all that is left is badly degraded fields and rocky terrain.

? Can you explain why the water in the rivers is brown?

▶ ...

? What effect does rain have on the soil?

▶ ...

The top layer of soil is exposed to the rain and, if it is in good condition, it will retain water and provide many nutrients for plant growth. In the case of poor soil, there is no protection and it is therefore more vulnerable.

4

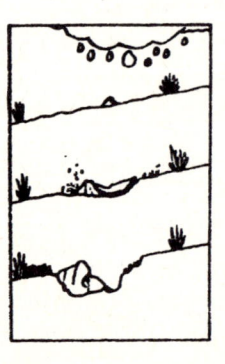

Erosion begins with raindrops. A good soil (fertilised, well-tilled and covered by plants) absorbs large amounts of water. On poor, bare soil heavy raindrops cause the particles of soil to move. This is not a problem on level ground, but on a slope the small particles are moved downwards, leaving small holes behind.

418

G 10

> **?** How do you think rocks get bigger?

▶ ...

5

If we want to avoid these harmful effects of erosion, we should protect the soil with trees, plants and mulching. The leaves of plants and mulch reduce the force of raindrops and disperse them. If there is no erosion control, the surface water collects on the hill until it becomes quite deep and then flows with increasing speed down the hill. At first it takes only fine particles of soil with it, but in the end it causes great damage.

> **?** What measures can we take to cover the soil and therefore to protect it?

▶ ...

Let's look at picture 5 again.
Although there are limits, we can increase the capacity of the soil to retain water if we create thick, permanent soil cover. Because of their roots, plants enable water to penetrate the soil more easily than where it is bare or has not been cultivated.

Water that runs off destroys the soil!

TYPES OF EROSION

> **?** What types of erosion are you familiar with?

419

G 10

▶ ...

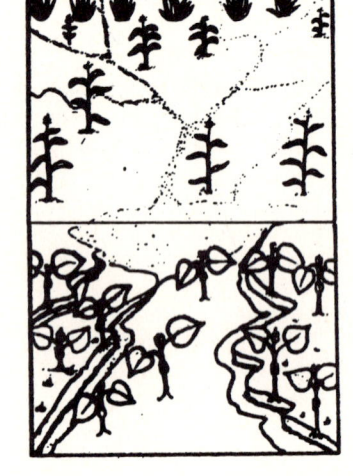

|6|
– **Droplet erosion**
at the beginning erosion is only slight, but it washes away fine particles of soil over a wide area.

|7|
– **Gully erosion**
the water flows freely down the hillside, collects and then flows at high speed. It now washes away large amounts of soil, even large clods. Even small channels can cause heavy soil loss and they quickly turn into deep gullies.

Let's look at picture 3 again:

The small channels are getting deeper and deeper until they finally turn into deep gullies. The state of these gullies gets increasingly serious, especially on broad hillsides. The result is a great loss of soil and therefore of cropping land. Progressive gully erosion can lead to landslides.

C Basic structure: erosion protection lines

? What line protection methods do you know?

▶ ...

– contour lines
setting up contour line protection is not a problem, since surveying and staking out is done by trained teams. It is important not to disturb them in their work, especially when fields are being surveyed. It is advisable to start digging as soon as the stakes are in place, and it is even better if erosion control hedges are planted straightaway.

G 10

▶ ...

— broken lines of ditches

2/8

— Although they are usually dug as part of Umuganda, every farmer should know how to dig them.

? Is everyone familiar with the dimensions?

The soil is piled up above the ditch and immediately planted with deep-rooting grasses, hedges or trees.

— PLANTED LINES AND HEDGES

? What are the main objectives?

▶ ...

— Planted contour lines and hedges are an effective barrier against water trickling down the hillside.
— They stop the fine particles of soil carried by the water.
— They strengthen the embankments and ditches.
— As well as offering erosion protection, they provide a certain amount of fodder, timber and firewood, mulching material, etc.

? Which plants are used?

▶ ...

G 10

The plants used are:
| VETIVERI |
| URUBINGO |
| SETARIYA |
| IGIKARANKA |
| LESENA |

? What are the characteristics of these plants?

▶ ...

It is important to point out that Setariya is planted in double rows, is very useful protection against droplet erosion, but that it ages fairly quickly and has therefore to be renewed regularly. Pennisetum, that is very effective on steep slopes, has to be carefully controlled and pruned because it tends to exhaust the soil at the expense of other crops nearby. Leucaena, planted as hedges on the contour lines, is not only very effective erosion control but is also another source of good fodder for cattle. Finally Vetiva and Themeda provide a constant supply of mulching material for the farm.

? How do we establish protection lines planted with grass?

▶ ...

10

URUBINGO   SETARIYA

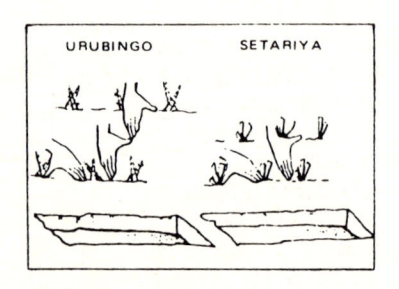

If it is a question of protection lines only or lines in combination with ditches, deep-rooted grasses are planted 20 cm from the edge of the embankment as follows:

Pennisetum:
40 cm between the lines and 20 cm intervals in the line.

Setaria:
20 cm between the lines and 20 cm intervals in the line.

G 10

It goes without saying that weeding is essential and weed control must be continued.

Establishing hedges

Hedges and care of hedges are the subject of a training session that we shall be offering shortly. At this point we would like to make two suggestions:

> **?** Can you remember any plants that are used in hedges? What are they?

▶ ...

| 11 |

Here is a complete hedge!
It is ideal for combating erosion. But there are various alternatives as well:
a) double row of Setaria with ditches
b) ditches protected by rows of Setaria and trees
c) double row of Setaria with trees
d) Leucaena hedges with trees

> **?** Is there any further benefit to the farmer?

▶ ...

| 12 | Example:

Let us recall what we discussed earlier
It is obvious that a hedge takes up a lot of space, but it is also very productive!

- fodder
- timber for building
- mulching material
- fruit
- firewood
- etc.

423

G 10

To reinforce erosion control measures, we will undoubtedly have to plant trees in addition to deep-rooting grasses.

> **?** Have you already planted trees? Which ones? Why?

▶ ...

Bearing in mind the special significance of trees in erosion control, we would like to recommend the topics "Choice of location and varieties for reforestation" and "Integrated Reforestation". On another occasion we shall speak about maintaining erosion protection lines or, put another way, about maintaining the whole erosion control system. Instead of drawing conclusions, we want to draw your attention to future events: during the campaign to combat erosion, a lot of digging will be carried out by the Umuganda, especially on large-scale pastures and on fallow land. But work that has been started in the fields is often not completed or the stakes are destroyed by a few obstinate farmers, ditches are rarely dug, and planting hedges, trees and grass as reinforcement is as good as useless under these circumstances. However, we hope that this course can convince you and get you to take the initiative, so that the major problems of erosion can be solved once and for all.

D   Phased creation of terraces

> **?** Why do we need terraces? Can you remember everything we have discussed so far?

▶ ...

> **?** Can someone tell us how a terrace is made?

▶ ...

G 10

13

The slope is interrupted by ditches and/or lines of planted grasses, hedges or appropriate trees. This stops water run-off.

The small amount of soil washed down the plot is stopped by the hedges and ditches. Gradually the lower part of the plot becomes higher and raises the level of the embankment.

We recommend tilling the soil across the slope. The ditches must be cleared out properly, especially in the early stages.

After a few years the result is:
- no more erosion;
- no steeply sloping land; the land has been levelled;
- work is much easier on horizontal terraces.

Do not forget to protect the edges of the ditches and to reinforce the embankments, that can sometimes be very high, with both deep-rooted grasses and the appropriate trees.

> **?** Anyone getting to this stage has achieved a great deal, hasn't he?
> He deserves a lot of praise, doesn't he?

E Quick revision (5 – 10 minutes)

a) The instructor shows all the pictures again, one after the other. He no longer makes any comment, it is left to the group to pick out what they would like to deal with in more depth. The instructor only corrects farmers if there are serious errors in their contributions.

b) There are many things we could mention in the context of erosion control. We definitely want to talk about other methods in later training sessions, so

G 10

that we can help you in your future efforts to control erosion. For the present, we recommend you to go to your "Moniteur Agricole" or your "Community Agronomist" with all questions concerning the implementation of the various measures.

F Practical training

- After any theoretical training session, all the participants should go with their instructor to a farmer from the cell. At his farm they can continue discussions or demonstrate and apply topics that have been dealt with in training.

- A recommended selection of topics for this practical training:

    - the process of erosion, discussion of the effect of mulching and multi-storey ground cover as soil protection measures;

    - defining different sorts of erosion;

    - deciding on plant species to be used;

    - planting reinforcing grasses and trees;

    - planting a Leucaena hedge with trees.

2. The pictures used on the course

The pictures are 26 x 38 cm or half size. They are drawn in black and white, duplicated on a photocopier and made stiffer by sticking two sheets together. Sawdust is stuck to the reverse side, so that they can be fixed on the felt board, and they are coloured by hand with water colours and then covered with a thin film of clear varnish for protection. The full set of coloured pictures is reproduced on the following pages.

3. The leaflet for participants

When the training session is over, all the participants are given a leaflet folded down the middle to make four pages. It is printed in green, brown or black and reproduces the most important pictures in small format with just a few keywords from the text in the local language. This leaflet is shown on the two previous pages. It should act as a reminder and should also encourage further discussion of the topic in the family or with neighbours.

G 10

Source:

Projet Agro Pastoral de Nyabisindu, Division Vulgarisation-Formation: L'érosion et l'installation des lignes anti-érosives (Traduction du texte de formation en Kinyarwanda), Nyabisindu, Feb. 1984

Photographs:

Volker HOFFMANN

Compiled by:

Volker HOFFMANN

G 10

VETIVERI
URUBINGO
SETARIYA

G 10

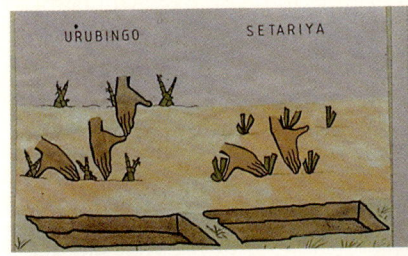

URUBINGO   SETARIYA

IGIKARANKA
LESENA
TIRIBUSAKUMU
DE SIMODIYUMU

G 10

ISULI NO GUTUNGANYA IMILINGOTI

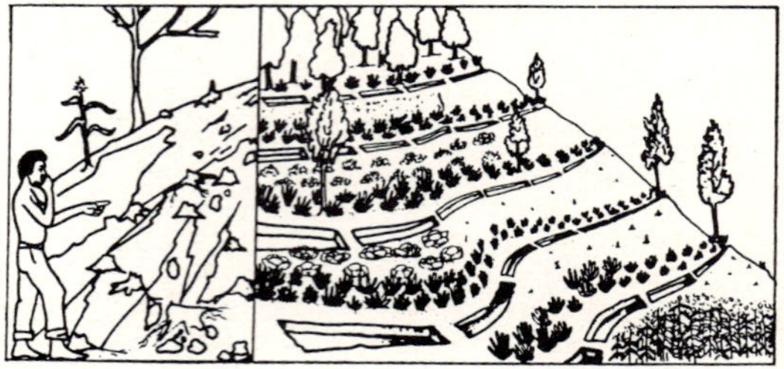

Igice cyo kwigisha no kwamamaza ubuhinzi

Gashyantare 1984

- KURWANYA ISULI MU BISAMBU BYAMEZ IBYATSI BYINSHI LIMWE NA LIMWE NI UGUTA IGIHE KUKO IBYO BYATSI NABYO BIBA BIFASHE UBUTAKA.

  TWIHATE KURUSHAHO IMILIMA IHINGWA KUKO ALIYO ITWARWA N'ISULI CYANE.

- NIDUKORA RERO NEZA UMULIMO WO KURWANYA ISULI TUZAGERA KU MILIMA MWIZA IRAMBITSE.

«AMATERASI»

□ Ahagalika isuli
□ Yongera umusaruro
□ Yoroshya akazi k'umuhinzi

Mugire umwete !

G 10

- **ISULI N'ICYAGO CYAYO**

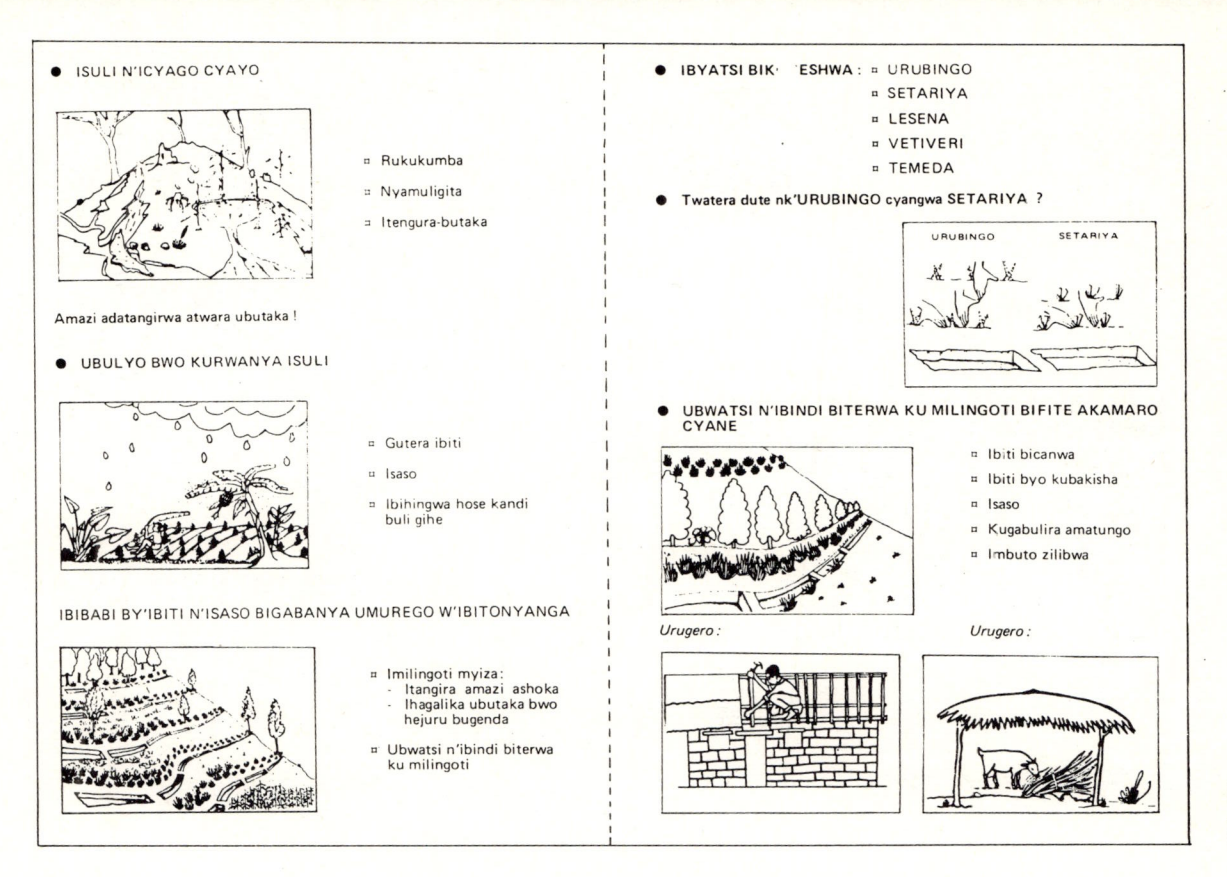

  □ Rukukumba
  □ Nyamuligita
  □ Itengura-butaka

  Amazi adatangirwa atwara ubutaka !

- **UBULYO BWO KURWANYA ISULI**

  □ Gutera ibiti
  □ Isaso
  □ Ibihingwa hose kandi buli gihe

- **IBYATSI BIK'ESHWA** :
  □ URUBINGO
  □ SETARIYA
  □ LESENA
  □ VETIVERI
  □ TEMEDA

- Twatera dute nk'**URUBINGO** cyangwa **SETARIYA** ?

- **UBWATSI N'IBINDI BITERWA KU MILINGOTI BIFITE AKAMARO CYANE**

  □ Ibiti bicanwa
  □ Ibiti byo kubakisha
  □ Isaso
  □ Kugabulira amatungo
  □ Imbuto zilibwa

  Urugero :

  Urugero :

- **IBIBABI BY'IBITI N'ISASO BIGABANYA UMUREGO W'IBITONYANGA**

  □ Imilingoti myiza :
    - Itangira amazi ashoka
    - Ihagalika ubutaka bwo hejuru bugenda
  □ Ubwatsi n'ibindi biterwa ku milingoti

G 11

Instructional material for creating awareness and for training from GRAAP, Burkina Faso

In ➜ D 7 we briefly described the group called GRAAP and the pedagogic concept it recommends (majeutics). Now we present an example of its educational series of felt pictures.

A training pack in several parts was developed by GRAAP at the request of the "Ministry of the environment and tourism" in Ouagadougou, Burkina Faso. The title is "Living in a green environment". We have reproduced the accompanying text of the first analysis for the Animateur, the pictures themselves and the "reminder" poster.

Living in a green environment

First analysis: changes in our environment

The training pack called "Living in a green environment" examines three broad topics:

1. The changes in our environment
2. We need trees to live
3. Being master of our village territory

Investigating each of these topics requires several meetings. If we really want to apply GRAAP's pedagogic approach, we must ensure that as many participants as possible have a chance to speak, i. e. all categories: men, women, young people, old people, immigrants to the area, foreigners, etc.

Thus two, three or four meetings may be necessary to examine each topic. The number depends on the problems addressed and the course of discussions in the groups.

The examination of topics 2 and 3 is followed by other topics that involve basic training in biology and geography (No. 1: The life of trees, No. 3: The circulation of water, No. 4: Life in the soil).

These topics enable the Animateur to define the know-how of the participants, add to it, perhaps to correct it and to develop it further.

Again several meetings are necessary for each of these topics if we are to ensure that the participants express their views on their own know-how and take in and utilise new information.

G 11

Thanks to this basic training, the villagers will have a better understanding of phenomena around them, and they will thus be in a better position to control their lives. The first analysis dealt with in the text for the Animateur is primarily intended **to create awareness**. In keeping with the pedagogic method advocated by GRAAP, it comprises three important steps:

1. Seeing the situation clearly:

   a) questions put to homogeneous groups to make them more aware, announcing and discussing the answers in the plenary meeting;

   b) comparing the environment in the past with today.

2. Thinking about the situation

   a) the consequences for the people, animals and the environment today and tomorrow;

   b) the causes: how this situation comes about. What are we responsible for? What powers do we have as villagers?

3. Acting to change the situation

   a) What can we do ourselves here and now?

      − everyone for himself?

      − all working together?

   b) What can we do at a later stage (start planning now)?

      − everyone for himself?

      − all together?

This first investigation can be the subject of two or three meetings in quick succession (within one week if possible). For example, one meeting on the questions to raise the level of awareness and the comparison of answers and one meeting on thinking about the situation and taking action.

G 11

Questions to create awareness of problems

Since our pedagogic approach puts emphasis on stimulating the subject to respond, this first stage is extremely important.

- The participants are divided into small homogeneous groups of no more than ten people with one person in charge.
- The groups are sufficiently far apart for them not to disturb each other during discussions.
- Each group is asked to nominate one member who will report back to the plenary meeting later.
- Each separate group is given half or three quarters of an hour to think and discuss (more time if required) before they all come together again.

At first, the villagers will certainly not be used to working in this way. The Animateur might encounter difficulties until the idea of several groups to discuss the same theme is accepted. The Animateur should therefore explain the reasoning behind this method very clearly. He should also not feel discouraged if the groups are rather chaotic on the first few occasions or if the groups' answers are not reported back satisfactorily, etc.. Like all new things, this method of working has to be learned, and only then will people be able to discover the advantages and benefit to be derived from this method.

By using this method the villagers can express themselves straight away, and they are therefore directly involved in the investigation of their own lives. As many people as possible are encouraged to speak, because every person in each group is called on to express his opinion and to answer the questions from his personal angle. In this way it is impossible for one or two influential individuals to dominate discussions, for example the village head or the chairman of a cooperative. By creating sub-groups, particular categories (women, men, young people, foreigners) can say what they see and think; they can express their opinions without having to fear reprisals. Finally, the spokesman or spokesmen report back not as individuals but on behalf of the group.

Thus perceptions of situations become truer reflections of reality, more global, and the discussions that follow in the plenary meeting are much richer in ideas, observations and exchanges of experience.

When a person of influence has spoken in a group, we frequently find that no one dares to contradict him, even though they may not agree with what has been said and everyone simply repeats: "What he has just said is precisely what I wanted to say too."

G 11

When the villagers have grown accustomed to discussing the issues in subgroups, we find that exactly the opposite occurs. There is a kind of competition between groups; each one wants to contribute the best, the most interesting answers in the discussion in the plenary meeting.

The people involved are put in a position where they investigate, where they research. So a group dynamic evolves that stimulates them to take an active part, makes them attentive and receptive.

People who would not normally speak in public now do so, different views emerge, explanations are requested. A process of self-development is set in train that will enable the group to deal with its problems and difficulties independently.

First topic to be examined: The changes in our environment
Questions to stimulate awareness:

1. In what ways have the soil, the vegetation and animals changed since our grandparents' days?
2. Are these changes to our advantage or disadvantage? If they are good, in what way? If they are bad, in what way?

Reports to the plenary meeting:

According to the answers from the sub-groups, we now begin to stick the corresponding pictures onto the felt board.

Discussion and use of the pictures:

If they have not identified enough changes, the participants can be encouraged to think more deeply by specific questions:

- How is the soil changing?
- How are the trees changing?
- How are the animals changing?
- How is the village changing?
- How are the villagers changing?
- How is the climate changing?

G 11

- What environmental changes are occurring in the lives of the villagers?
- How is this happening? What are people trying to achieve by acting in this way?
- Did we have certain customs, rites, prohibitions in our community that applied to the soil, plants and animals?
- What were these prohibitions?
- How were these customs kept alive?

Two boards should be used; on the first board (envelope 1a)

– Put the picture depicting **the past** in a line at the top	– Put the pictures depicting **the present** in a line at the bottom
Thick forest	Treeless savanna
Intact monkey bread tree	Half-dead monkey bread tree
Humid valley with rice	Dry, flat terrain
A fine field of millet	A poor field of millet
Wild animals	
Herds of fat animals	Herds of lean animals
Small village	Large village with two quarters
Treeless savanna	
Woman stripping branches from a tree near her house	Woman with a small bundle of wood on her head
Large cloud over the forest	Small cloud over the savanna
	Pile of wood by the roadside
	Bicycle loaded with wood
	Donkey cart with wood
	Lorry with wood

G 11

The soil priest ("chef de terre") is sacrificing an animal. This picture should be placed under the picture of the forest.

Pause for thought

1. The consequences

What are the consequences of these changes for the villagers?

- for the men?
- for the women?
- for young girls?
- for the young men?
- for the children?
- for the old people?

What effects do these changes have on the animals belonging to the village?

What effects do these changes have on the soil and the crops?

What effects do these changes have on the water in the stream, the water in the well?

Are we satisfied with the current situation? Why?

If there are more changes of the same kind, what will happen? What will our village look like tomorrow?

We are proud of what our parents have handed down to us. Will our children be as proud of what we hand down to them?

As the discussion develops, we show the interrelations that are revealed by the pictures already on the felt board.

2. The causes

What actually causes all these changes?

Are we, the villagers, responsible for any of these changes? If so, how?

When people destroy the vegetation, what happens to the water? What happens to the wind?

And animals, are they responsible for any of these things that have happened? If so, how?

Who else is responsible for all these changes, especially changes in habits and customs?

We now want to classify the causes we have established according to their origins.

What is our share of responsibility as villagers for each of the wider categories?

Who is affected most by these changes in the village? Why?

Who can do something here in the village to make sure these changes turn out to our advantage?

We now use the second board (envelope 1b)

- picture of the little cloud

- man setting fire to a rootstock – bush fire – man chopping down a tree – preparing millet beer – ox team – man setting fire to the base of a tree – woman cooking food – sack of charcoal with charcoal burner – group of children

- millet field furrowed by erosion – a tree with its roots laid bare – dust blowing in the wind

- goats stripping the leaves off a young tree – animals stripping hacked-off branches – herd by a well

- forest clearance with a bulldozer – going to school – various religions – money – journeys – administration

What are the consequences of direct action by the villagers?

What do their actions achieve?

What is the connection with animals?

What comes from outside the village?

Action

What causes can we ourselves eliminate? By doing what?

G 11

We want to examine all categories of causes and each related picture to find out what can be done in each individual case. We should begin with those categories that directly affect the villagers and ask: what immediate action can we take?

- Each man for himself? How?

- All together? How?

What action can we take later?

- Each man for himself? How?

- All together? How?

If the cooperative or the village community decides reforestation is a possible solution, the following questions should be asked:

Who does the village land belong to?

Who will the new forest belong to?

- the land?

- the trees?

What should be done now to prevent disputed ownership later?

Who will tend the new trees each year? How?

Who will have the use of the timber resulting from reforestation? How?

As the search for solutions continues, the individual pictures showing causes are presented separately and then put back in their place when that part of the discussion is concluded.

What is the issue? To see better, or to discover?

A) The aim of the questions to create awareness is to get the villagers to identify all the changes that they have become aware of in their environment.

In the past there were lots of trees in the bush, and some of them were big trees as well. Wild animals lived in the bush: lions, hyenas, panthers, etc. Now the big trees have disappeared along with the wild animals. There used to be plenty of monkey-bread trees, Néré and Karité trees; there are fewer and fewer nowadays.

It used to rain much more than it does now, the fields produced more, the soil was more fertile. "We used to have a humid valley where we cropped rice; now the bottom of our valley has become like an arid plain."

We have also got far more domestic animals than in the past.

There are far more people living in the village now, we work more fields as well. The number of people in the towns is increasing too and the demand for firewood is growing all the time. To satisfy the demand, traders come and buy wood in our village.

The sacred forests and bushes of our fathers have disappeared and even certain protected trees like the Karité, Néré and Tamarind have been felled. The soil priests ("chef de terre") and the village heads no longer have their former authority. The social organisation that used to hold the village together as a unit is now a thing of the past.

In the old days bush fires were controlled, but in the last few years everybody thinks he has a right to fire the bush just to hunt a rat.

B) The pause for thought in our investigation gives the villagers a chance to identify the consequences of the changes for people and the environment and then to explore the reasons.

Even if they consider some of the changes to be positive, such as wild animals like lions and hyenas disappearing, many of the changes make life much more difficult for the villagers.

1. The consequences:

The women can no longer find enough firewood for cooking near the village. They are forced to walk for miles through the bush to gather a small bundle of wood that will not last more than two or three days.

It is no longer as easy for them to find flowers, fruits, grains and leaves that they use for making sauces. The few monkey-bread trees that are left in the bush are permanently stripped bare, etc.

It is difficult for the men to find the wooden poles needed for building roofs, barns, sheds, etc. The soils that support fewer and fewer trees become impoverished and dry out, and the millet fields no longer produce the yields of the past.

G 11

Rainfall is lower and much less regular. This fact alone causes catastrophes every year in some regions where the villagers cannot harvest enough crops to feed their families for even one or two months.

Domestic animals are insurance against poor years. But overgrazing makes the soil more susceptible to erosion and stripping leaves for fodder in the dry season only accelerates deforestation.

Bush fires destroy the grass and weeds that protect the soil against erosion and enrich it. These fires also destroy some trees, especially young trees, so that the forest cannot regenerate.

Despite some migration to the towns, the rise in population in the villages means that more and more fields have to be cultivated. The soil no longer has time to recover, and it becomes exhausted and impoverished.

Illegal tree felling and the trade in wood increase by the day. The villagers also cut down more and more trees to sell to cover their cash needs: taxes, medicines, etc.

Although the traditional village organisation is now a thing of the past, nothing has replaced it. Everyone does as he pleases. No one cares about the community. Everyone survives as best he can without bothering about other people. The village unit has disappeared for ever.

2. **The causes**

The examination of causes is intended to make the villagers realise that in many cases they cause the problems themselves. They are directly responsible for a number of changes:

cutting down trees, bush fires, increasing numbers of domestic animals, etc.

Other changes are caused by circumstances and pressures that are imposed on the village from outside, e. g.

the school, religions, the administration, money, etc.

They are all instrumental in the disintegration of village structures.

Having experience of school, travel, new religions, young people no longer adhere to traditional ways. Moreover, the customs that used to govern communal life in the village have not been replaced by anything new. The result is a vacuum in the organisation of the community, and there is no control over individuals, and no one thinks of the common good.

All these developments that are caused by man himself have damaging effects on the environment. Deforestation, firing the bush, etc., mean that nothing is left to combat wind and rain. Thus human destruction is compounded by natural destruction and the soil gets poorer and poorer.

Because man has disrupted the ecological balance that maintains the life of nature, nature is now in the process of destroying itself.

C) The villagers should discover that they are largely responsible for these developments. For the situation to improve, they cannot wait for other people to come and do things for them. It is their job to find out precisely what they must do to eliminate every single cause of the destruction of their environment.

It is the duty of the Animateur to encourage them to look for the many solutions to the whole complex of causes of this degradation and not simply to stop at reforestation.

For example, these solutions could be:

- stop firing the bush! (form proper organisations to achieve this aim);
- avoid overgrazing and excessive tree felling;
- when a new field is cleared, do not destroy all the root systems;
- dig erosion protection ditches;
- protect natural tree and shrub growth (keep animals, especially goats, under control);
- plant trees for wind protection, by the roadside, round fields and houses, round the village, etc.
- make hay for animal feed in the dry season;
- build improved stoves (more economical use of wood);
- organise themselves, create new village laws to control village life;
- tolerate each other and communicate with each other despite different religions; hold meetings to decide jointly what is to be done to improve life

G 11

> in the village. For example, the women agree on a rota for brewing millet beer.

– etc.

The villagers must decide with the help of the list of possible solutions what they are going to undertake straight away, each man for himself with his family, or all together (as a cooperative or the whole village).

They must plan what they can do in the long term, either individually or in groups (as a cooperative or the whole village) and try to predict and organise the training required and the material and financial support.

When reforestation is being discussed, it is important to examine in detail and to come to agreement on all issues that could lead to conflict later, e.g. ownership of land, trees, their maintenance and use of timber, etc.

Before planting is begun, these problems must be discussed in detail with everyone concerned and clearly defined solutions found. The villagers will continue to be committed to whatever work is necessary to carry out reforestation, because they are deeply conscious of the fact that the forest will be there for them and their children in years to come.

The pictures illustrate the pieces provided by GRAAP in two envelopes and the "reminder" poster that the Animateur leaves in the village when he has finished the training sessions.

Source:

GRAAP: Vivre dans un environnement vert. 1èr recherche: Les changements dans notre environnement. Bobo-Dioulasso, Burkina Faso, 2nd edition, 1979

Photographs:

Volker HOFFMANN

Compiled by:

Volker HOFFMANN

G 11

autrefois
formerly
früher

aujourd'hui
today
heute

et demain?
and tomorrow?
und morgen?

G 11

Des causes du changement | Causes of change | Ursachen des Wandels

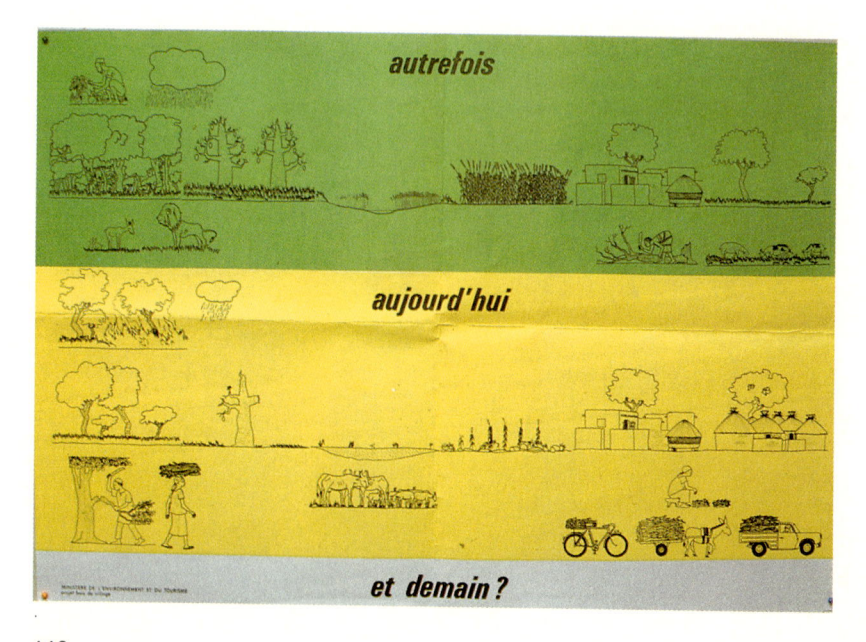

autrefois

aujourd'hui

et demain ?

The Technical Centre for Agricultural and Rural Cooperation (CTA)
Postbus 380 · NL 6700 AJ Wageningen · Telephone (0) 8380 20484 · Telex 30169 CTA NL

The Technical Centre for Agricultural and Rural Cooperation (CTA) was established in 1983 at Ede-Wageningen. It operates under the Lomé Convention between member states of the European Community and the ACP states.

CTA is at the disposal of the ACP states to provide them with better access to information, research, training and innovations in the spheres of agricultural and rural development and extension.

Headquarters: "De Rietkampen", Galvanistraat 9, Ede, The Netherlands
Postal address: Postbus 380, 6700 AJ Wageningen, The Netherlands
Telephone: (0) 8380 20484
Telex: 30169 CTA NL

Deutsche Gesellschaft für Technische Zusammenarbeit (GTZ) GmbH
Dag-Hammarskjöld-Weg 1 + 2 · D 6236 Eschborn 1 · Telefon (0 61 96) 79-0 · Telex 4 07 501-0 gtz d

The government-owned GTZ operates in the field of Technical Cooperation. Some 4,500 German experts are working together with partners from some 100 countries in Africa, Asia and Latin America in projects covering practically every sector of agriculture, forestry, economic development, social services and institutional and physical infrastructure. – The GTZ is commissioned to do this work by the Government of the Federal Republic of Germany and by other national and international organizations.

GTZ activities encompass:

- appraisal, technical planning, control and supervision of technical cooperation projects commissioned by the Government of the Federal Republic of Germany or by other authorities

- advisory services to other agencies implementing development projects

- the recruitment, selection, briefing and assignment of expert personnel and assuring their welfare and technical backstopping during their period of assignment

- provision of materials and equipment for projects, planning work, selection, purchasing and shipment to the developing countries

- management of all financial obligations to the partnercountry.

The series **"Sonderpublikationen der GTZ"** includes more than 230 publications. A list detailing the subjects covered can be obtained from the GTZ-Unit 02: Press and Public Relations, or from the TZ-Verlagsgesellschaft mbH, Postfach 1164, D 6101 Roßdorf 1, Federal Republic of Germany.